# The BEST Book of
# BASEBALL
# FACTS
# & STATS Ever!

REVISED AND UPDATED

This is a Carlton Book

Text and design © Carlton Books Limited 2000, 2001,
2002

Statistics © Stats Inc. 2000, 2001, 2002

ISBN 1 84222 435 2

Commissioning Editor: Martin Corteel
Project Editor: Vanessa Daubney
Production: Sarah Corteel
Design: Exxus Limited

Printed and bound in Great Britain

# The BEST Book of
# BASEBALL
# FACTS
# & STATS Ever!

## LUKE FRIEND & DON ZMINDA

REVISED AND UPDATED

# Contents

## The Players cont.

# Contents

## The Ballparks cont.

## The Key Games 165

## The Stats and Facts 206

## Major League Contacts 300

## Other Useful Websites 302

## Glossary 303

# INTRODUCTION

From Cy Young to Greg Maddux, Babe Ruth to Mark McGwire, the game of baseball has been blessed with many unique and varied talents and its history enriched by the compelling stories and awesome feats that surround these legends. In this book, we take you closer to the men who have impacted the game, changing it forever, from those who pioneered the development of the game in its early years to today's modern superstars. We look closely at the famous ballparks they have graced, the franchises they have represented, the managers who have steered them to their greatest triumphs and their most important, historic performances.

Do you remember when the A's played in Philly? When the Dodgers-Giants rivalry was a New York institution? And when the Red Sox were known as the Pilgrims?

The Franchise Histories chapter that starts this book charts the development of all 30 of today's Major League franchises, from their inception through to their current standing. Each chronology documents the name changes, the new cities and the key moments in each ballclub's history.

Trying to fit baseball's greatest players into one chapter is like trying to get everyone inside Fenway Park for a Game 7 of the World Series. Some people are bound to get left out.

So while the final list in this book cannot be totally comprehensive, it attempts to highlight the careers of those men, who from the dead-ball era to modern day, have elevated the game of baseball to such levels of artistry that their impact on the nation's pastime will be everlasting. And to those truly great players who didn't make the list, sincere apologies.

Just as it is an impossible task to select the game's greatest players without leaving gaps, it is equally difficult to hand-pick the men who have guided them to such distinguished careers. Over the game's history some of its most important contributors and colorful personalities have been found in the dugout. From Casey Stengel to Tommy Lasorda, John McGraw to Joe

Torre, these managers have shaped baseball's tactical development and in doing so have left an indelible mark on the game. The managers chapter seeks to draw attention to these contributions.

Fenway's Green Monster, Wrigley Field's ivy-covered walls, Camden Yards' on-looking warehouse. All are ballpark landmarks as famous and recognizable as those who stroll their outfields and stand atop their mounds, each providing a unique backdrop to the club's travails. In the ballpark chapter we look at both the old and the new, the grand and the not-so grand, of the major league ballparks that have provided the stage for some great theatre. These profiles and the diagrams that accompany them map the progression of baseball stadiums from John Updike's "lyric little bandbox" description of Old Fenway to the retractable roof and swimming pool of the Diamondback's ultra-modern Bank One Ballpark.

Baseball's rich history has been littered with many significant games but there are those rare few that become even more special, due to historic plays, twists of fate and the impossible becoming reality. You may not have been around when Fred Merkle made his infamous gaff, when the Babe launched his called shot or when Bobby Thomsen's pennant-winning home run was heard 'round the world but the chances are these unforgetable moments are fresh in your memory, as if you had been sitting in the bleachers yourself. The Key Games chapter disects baseball's most memorable happenings and lets history live forever in the permanent record of the game's linescore.

The book concludes with a comprenensive Facts and Stats chapter that gives you all the numbers you need. Listed are career statistical leaders, single-game and single-season leaders for both the regular season and the World Series. This chapter also features lists of every final standing and post-season result since 1876 and a complete list of all Hall of Fame inductees, Cy Young, MVP and Rookie award winners.

# A. L. East

**Baltimore Orioles**
**Boston Red Sox**
**New York Yankees**
**Tampa Bay Devil Rays**
**Toronto Blue Jays**

# BALTIMORE ORIOLES

The Baltimore Oriole franchise's roots trace back to 1901, when the original Milwaukee Brewers became a charter member of the American League. A year later, they became the St. Louis Browns. Though they remained in St. Louis for 52 years, the Browns won only one pennant, and that one came against war-weakened competition in 1944. In 1954 the franchise moved to Baltimore and became the Orioles. It also found consistent success beginning in the late 1960s. Hall of Famers Frank Robinson, Brooks Robinson and Jim Palmer, along with manager Earl Weaver, led the club to three straight AL pennants in 1969-71. The club won another pennant in 1979, and the O's won it all in 1983, with shortstop Cal Ripken leading the way. Ripken, who played in a record 2,632 consecutive games from 1982 to 1998, helped popularize the club's beautiful new park, Oriole Park at Camden Yards, which opened in 1992.

**1901** – The Milwaukee Brewers join the American League as a charter member, and set the tone for the first 50 years of the franchise in their first game on April 25. Leading the Detroit Tigers 13–4 entering the bottom of the ninth, the Brewers give up 10 runs and lose, 14–13.

**1902** – The Brewers become the St. Louis Browns and rise from last place to second, five games behind the pennant–winning Philadelphia Athletics. Success is short–lived and the Browns will have only one more first–division – top four – finish between 1903 and 1919.

**1922** – With future Hall of Famer George Sisler hitting .420, the Browns nearly win the AL pennant, finishing only one game behind the Yankees.

**1935** – In the depths of the Great Depression, the seventh–place Browns draw only 80,922 fans all season.

**1944** – The Browns win their only pennant, defeating the Detroit Tigers by one game, but lose the World Series in six games to the crosstown St. Louis Cardinals.

**1951** – Master showman Bill Veeck buys the Browns. His most memorable stunt is to send a midget, Eddie Gaedel, up to pinch–hit.

**1954** – The Browns move to Baltimore and take the name Orioles, but finish in seventh place with 100 losses.

**1966** – Frank Robinson arrives via a trade and wins the Triple Crown to lead the Orioles to their first AL pennant in Baltimore. In the World Series, the O's stun the favored Los Angeles Dodgers with a four–game sweep.

**1970** – After being upended by the Miracle New York Mets in the World Series a year earlier, the O's win 108 games, then lose only one postseason game as they drive to the world title.

**1979** – Eight years after being upset by the Pittsburgh Pirates in the 1971 World Series, the O's return to the Series only to lose again to the Pirates.

**1983** – Earl Weaver retires as O's manager, but his successor, Joe Altobelli, leads the Birds to the world championship, with shortstop Cal Ripken winning the AL Most Valuable Player Award.

**1998** – In the club's final home game of the year, Ripken ends his record consecutive–game streak after playing in 2,632 straight contests.

**2001** – Cal Ripken retires at the close of the regular season, age 41. The Orioles retired his No.8 after 21 seasons in the majors, all with Baltimore.

# BOSTON RED SOX

Loved though possibly "cursed," the Boston Red Sox have been a vital part of New England, not to mention the American League, since their origin as the Boston Somersets in 1901. The early Sox were a league powerhouse, winning six pennants and five World Series between 1903 and 1918. Then, on January 3, 1920, the Sox sold their biggest star, Babe Ruth, to the hated New York Yankees. Whether one believes in the "Curse of the Bambino" or not, the Sox haven't won a World Series since then, though they've come agonizingly close several times. The most painful Red Sox collapse came in Game 6 of the 1986 World Series, when the Sox allowed the Mets to tie, then win in the last inning. Bill Buckner's error to allow the winning run to score is now indelibly etched in the memory of all Boston baseball fans. Win or lose, the Red Sox have provided a century of compelling baseball, from the days of Cy Young to Ted Williams to Carl Yastrzemski to Pedro Martinez.

**1901** – The Boston Somersets begin play in the new American League. In the club's first home game at the Huntington Avenue Grounds on May 8, Cy Young defeats Philadelphia, 12–4.

**1903** – The Pilgrims, as they are known after two AL seasons, win their first pennant with a 91–47 record, then defeat the Pittsburgh Pirates, five games to three, in the first World Series.

**1912** – Renamed the Red Sox five years earlier, the Sox christen their new home, Fenway Park, on April 20, then go on to an American League title and victory over the New York Giants in a tense seven–game World Series.

**1915, 1916, 1918** – With Babe Ruth developing into the best lefthanded pitcher in baseball, the Sox defeat the Philadelphia Phillies in 1915 and the Brooklyn Robins (Dodgers) in 1916 to win two more World Series. By 1918 Ruth is a pitcher–outfielder, leading the American League in home runs with 11 to pace another Boston World Series title.

**1920** – Ruth is sold to the Yankees, effectively ending the Boston dynasty. The Sox quickly become a doormat, finishing last nine times in 11 seasons from 1922 to 1932.

**1933** – Multi–millionaire Tom Yawkey buys the Red Sox to begin a Boston resurgence.

**1941** – Ted Williams, hitting .3995 entering the final day of the season, goes 6–for–8 in a doubleheader against the Athletics to finish the year with a .406 average. He is the last .400 hitter of the century.

**1946** – With Williams earning the Most Valuable Player Award, Boston wins its first pennant since 1918, but bows to the Cardinals in a seven–game World Series.

**1948, 1949** – The Sox go down to the final day each year with a chance to win the pennant, but lose to the Indians in '48 and the Yankees in '49.

**1967** – With Carl Yastrzemski winning the Triple Crown, the Sox win a thrilling four–team pennant race on the last day of the regular season before bowing to the Cardinals in a seven–game World Series.

**1975, 1986** – Two more pennants, two more tough losses in the Series. In one of the most exciting World Series ever, the 1975 Sox lose the Series to the Cincinnati Reds in seven games. Eleven years later, Buckner's error spoils a storybook season in which Roger Clemens won both the MVP and Cy Young Awards.

**1988, 1990, 1995, 1998** – The Red Sox qualify for the playoffs each time, but then are eliminated in the first round.

**1999** – Pedro Martinez' brilliant pitching leads the Sox to a wild–card berth, but the Sox fall to the Yankees in the LCS.

# NEW YORK YANKEES

No American sports franchise has had a more storied history than the New York Yankees, winning 38 American League pennants and 26 World Series titles. The franchise, which began life as the Baltimore Orioles in 1901, before moving to New York two years later, struggled until 1920, when the Yanks purchased Babe Ruth from the Red Sox for a staggering sum of $125,000. With Ruth setting home-run records, the Yanks won their first pennant in 1921 and celebrated the opening of Yankee Stadium in 1923 with their first world championship. From then until the mid-1960s, the Yankees had dominant teams led by dominant superstars: Ruth, Lou Gehrig, Joe DiMaggio and finally Mickey Mantle. A downturn followed, but Reggie Jackson led the club to two more titles in 1977 and 1978; then, after another dry spell, the Yankees returned in glorious fashion with championships in 1996, 1998, 1999 and 2000.

**1903** – With the American and National Leagues making peace, the Baltimore Orioles move to New York and become the New York Highlanders.

**1920, 1921** – Now known as the Yankees, the club purchases Babe Ruth from the Red Sox on January 3, 1920. A year later, the Yanks win their first pennant as Ruth breaks his own record with 59 home runs.

**1923** – Yankee Stadium opens on April 18 before a record crowd of 74,217. With Ruth hitting .393, the Yanks win their third straight pennant, then defeat the Giants to win their first World Series.

**1927** – Ruth breaks his own record with 60 home runs as the Yankees win 110 games, then sweep the Pittsburgh Pirates in the World Series.

**1932** – Ruth's final Yankees championship ends with a four–game sweep of the Cubs in which, according to witnesses, he hits a "called shot" home run off Charlie Root.

**1939** – Sick with the disease that will claim his life two years later, Lou Gehrig ends his consecutive–game streak at 2,130 on May 2, but the Yankees roll to their fourth straight world title.

**1941** – Joe DiMaggio hits safely in a record 56 consecutive games, leading the Yanks to their fifth championship in six years.

**1949** – Casey Stengel is named Yankee manager and leads the Yanks to a pennant with a last–day victory over the Red Sox. The Yanks then beat the Dodgers, four games to one, in the World Series, for the first of a record five straight world championships.

**1956** – Mickey Mantle wins the Triple Crown to spark another Yankee title, but the hero of the World Series is Don Larsen, who throws the first no–hitter in the history of the Series, a perfect game against the Dodgers in Game 5.

**1961** – After a season–long homer duel with Mantle, Yankee right fielder Roger Maris breaks Ruth's record with his 61st homer on the final day of the season. The powerful Yanks win 109 games and rout the Cincinnati Reds, four games to one, in the World Series.

**1977, 1978** – Reggie Jackson earns the nickname "Mr. October" with a record five homers in the Yanks' World Series victory over the Dodgers in 1977. A year later, the Yanks top the Dodgers again for another title.

**1996, 1998** – The Yankees reach the top again in 1996, defeating the Atlanta Braves in the World Series. Two years later, they win a record 114 games in the regular season, then go 11–2 in the postseason to win their second championship in three years.

**1999, 2000** – The Yanks close the century with another title, punctuated by an 11–1 record in the postseason then complete the three-peat defeating the Mets in five games to become the first team since the Oakland A's to win three straight World Championships.

**2001** – In one of the most dramatic World Series in history, the Yankees lose in seven games to the Arizona Diamondbacks. Coming back from a 2-0 deficit—clinching both Game 4 and 5 in extra innings— New York eventually fall just short in Game 7.

# TAMPA BAY DEVIL RAYS

Major league baseball has had a presence in the Tampa Bay area since 1913, when the Chicago Cubs moved their spring training base to Tampa. From that point on, major league teams have trained in the Tampa Bay area every spring except during the period of 1942-45, but the region didn't get serious about landing a major league team until the 1970s. Over the next 20 years, at least a half-dozen teams considered moving to Tampa or St. Petersburg, and the area also stepped up efforts to land an expansion team. Finally, in 1995, the major leagues awarded a franchise to Tampa Bay, with the team to play in the ThunderDome (now known as Tropicana Field) in 1998. Tampa Bay's ownership group, led by Vince Naimoli, hired Chuck LaMar as general manager and Larry Rothschild as manager, and the Devil Rays took the field in 1998 with such established veterans as Fred McGriff, Wade Boggs, Wilson Alvarez and Roberto Hernandez in tow. The Rays won 63 games and drew 2.5 million fans their first year, and improved to 69 victories in 1999, their second season. Determined to build a competitive team that would halt their second-year attendance decline, the Rays spent the 1999 offseason adding sluggers Vinny Castilla and Greg Vaughn but the new 2000 lineup could only manage another 69–win season. In 2001 in dropped to just 62.

**1995** – After pursuing a big league franchise for nearly two decades, Tampa Bay finally gets a team when Major League Baseball awards an expansion franchise to Tampa Bay on March 9, with play to begin in 1998. The league in which the team will play is not yet determined, but the team selects the nickname Devil Rays and announces it will play its home games in the ThunderDome in St. Petersburg (renamed Tropicana Field in 1996). Former Atlanta Braves executive Chuck LaMar is named the club's general manager on July 19.

**1996** – The Devil Rays participate in their first amateur draft on June 4, selecting outfielder–first baseman Paul Wilder as their first pick.

**1997** – Major League Baseball announces on January 16 that the Devil Rays will play their games in the American League. Florida Marlins pitching coach Larry Rothschild is named the club's manager on November 7. Eleven days later, the Devil Rays select Marlins pitcher Tony Saunders as the first pick in the expansion draft. The club deals several of its picks to land veteran players Fred McGriff, Roberto Hernandez, Kevin Stocker and John Flaherty. Before the year ends, the Devil Rays sign veterans Wilson Alvarez, Dave Martinez and Wade Boggs to free–agent contracts.

**1998** – A capacity crowd of 45,369 at Tropicana Field watches the Devil Rays lose their first major league game to the Detroit Tigers, 11–6. After a 10–6 start, the club finishes last in the AL East with a 63–99 record, but draws more than 2.5 million fans. Quinton McCracken is the club's leading hitter with a .292 average, Fred McGriff tops the Rays in home runs (19) and RBI (81), and Rolando Arrojo is the club's top pitcher with a 14–12 record.

**1999** – Strengthened by the addition of free–agent signee Jose Canseco, who leads the club with 34 homers despite missing 49 games with a back injury, the Devil Rays improve to 69 victories. The club still finishes in last place as attendance drops to 1.6 million. McGriff leads the club in batting average (.310) and RBI (104) while Wilson Alvarez (9–9) and Roberto Hernandez (43 saves) top the pitchers. The season highlight is Boggs' 3,000th major league hit on August 7, the first 3,000th hit in history to come on a home run. After the season, the Rays strengthen their club with the addition of sluggers Vinny Castilla and Greg Vaughn.

# TORONTO BLUE JAYS

The Montreal Expos may have been the major leagues' first Canadian franchise, but from the time they first took the field in 1977, the Toronto Blue Jays have truly been Canada's Team. Toronto fans supported the club in its bleak early years, which began with five straight last-place finishes. By the mid-1980s, however, the Jays were a perennial contender, drawing well more than 2 million fans a year, even though they were playing in a park designed for football, Exhibition Stadium. Moving to SkyDome with its retractable roof in midseason 1989, the Jays became the first major league team to draw 4 million fans in a season, doing so three straight years (1991-93). The glory years of the franchise were 1992 and '93, when the Jays made up for years of near-misses with back-to-back world championships. Hurt by the 1994 strike as much as any team, the Jays have declined both at the gate and on the field, but they still drew more than 2 million fans for the 16th straight year in 1999.

**1976** – The American League awards an expansion franchise to Toronto on March 26, with play to begin in 1977. Shortstop Bob Bailor of the Orioles is the Blue Jays' first pick in the November 5 expansion draft.

**1977** – The Blue Jays win their first game in a snowstorm before 44,649 on April 7, defeating the Chicago White Sox, 9–5. The Jays go 10–11 in April but then collapse, finishing last in the AL East with 107 losses.

**1982** – After finishing last in each of their first five seasons, the Jays win 78 games under rookie manager Bobby Cox and tie the Cleveland Indians for sixth place in the AL East.

**1983** – Drawing a club–record 1.9 million fans, the Jays are in first place as late as July 25 before finishing fourth with 89 victories, the first winning season in franchise history.

**1985** – The Jays win their first division title with 99 victories as Cox wins the Manager of the Year Award. In the LCS against the Kansas City Royals, the Jays race to a three–games–to–one lead, but then lose the final three games to drop the series.

**1987** – Leading the East by three–and–a–half games with a week to play, the Jays lose their final seven games, including a season–ending sweep at Detroit, and end up two games behind the Tigers.

**1989** – The Jays celebrate their June 5 move to SkyDome by winning their second AL East title. However, they are eliminated by the Oakland A's in the ALCS, four games to one.

**1990** – The Jays set an all–time major league attendance record, drawing 3.9 million fans, as they finish second, two games behind the division–winning Red Sox.

**1991** – While becoming the first major league franchise to draw 4 million fans in a season, the Jays win another AL East title but once again lose the LCS, this time to the Minnesota Twins in five games.

**1992** – Breaking their own attendance record by once again surpassing the 4 million mark, the Jays end years of frustration by winning their first world championship. After beating the Oakland A's in the ALCS, the Jays defeat the Atlanta Braves in the World Series on Dave Winfield's two–run double in the 11th inning of Game 6.

**1993** – Toronto makes it two titles in a row, winning the World Series on Joe Carter's three–run homer off Mitch Williams of the Phillies in the bottom of the ninth of Game 6.

# A. L. Central

**Chicago White Sox**
**Cleveland Indians**
**Detroit Tigers**
**Kansas City Royals**
**Minnesota Twins**

# CHICAGO WHITE SOX

When Cincinnati sportswriter and magnate Ban Johnson decided to form a new major league in 1901, he convinced his friend and associate Charles Comiskey to become owner of the Chicago franchise. Comiskey's White Sox won the first AL pennant in 1901, and were one of baseball's dominant teams for the next two decades. Then came the news that eight of Comiskey's players had been in on a conspiracy to fix the 1919 World Series. Among those banned for life was Shoeless Joe Jackson, Chicago's greatest player. The sellout was a jolt to the Chicago franchise, and the club didn't revive until the mid-1950s. The speedy, pitching-oriented Sox finally won a pennant in 1959 and contended for most of the 1960s. Since then the team has had its share of success, including division titles in 1983, 1993 and 2000 but the Sox are still looking for their first world title since 1917. "The Curse of Shoeless Joe," perhaps?

**1901** – Playing at the South Side Grounds, the White Sox win the first game in American League history, 8–2, over Cleveland. It's a good omen as the team goes on to win the league's first pennant.
**1906** – The "Hitless Wonder" White Sox, with a .230 team average and only seven home runs all season, win the American League pennant and stun the crosstown Cubs, four games to two, in the only World Series ever contested between the two Chicago teams.
**1910** – Comiskey Park, known as "The Baseball Palace of the World," opens on July 1 before a packed house.
**1917** – With a roster that includes Eddie Collins, Joe Jackson, Buck Weaver and Eddie Cicotte, the Sox roll to the AL pennant, then defeat the New York Giants in six games to win the World Series.
**1919** – With Jackson hitting .351 and Cicotte winning 29 games, the Sox win another pennant, but are stunned by the underdog Reds in the World Series. Though many suspect it, no one knows for sure that the Series was fixed.
**1920** – The Sox are locked in a tight pennant race with the Indians and Yankees on September 28 when the news breaks that eight Chicago players, including Jackson and Cicotte, have been indicted for fixing the 1919 Series. Though a jury will acquit the players, they are banned for life by commissioner Kenesaw Mountain Landis.
**1923** – Future Hall of Famer Ted Lyons makes his Sox debut on July 2. Lyons will pitch for the Sox until 1946, winning 260 games.
**1930** – Another future Hall of Famer, Luke Appling, makes his debut on September 10. Appling will play for the Sox until 1950.
**1933** – Comiskey Park plays host to baseball's first All–Star game, won by the American League, 4–2.
**1951** – After seven straight years in the second division, the Sox rise to fourth with a "Go–Go" club featuring Nellie Fox, Minnie Minoso and star southpaw Billy Pierce.
**1959** – Under new owner Bill Veeck, the Sox finally win their first pennant since 1919, but lose the World Series in six games to the Los Angeles Dodgers.
**1983** – With a club powered by catcher Carlton Fisk, the Sox win the AL West title, but lose in the LCS to the Baltimore Orioles.
**1991** – New Comiskey Park opens to mixed reviews on April 18. The Sox lose their first game in the new park, 16–0 to the Tigers.
**1993** – With Frank Thomas winning the MVP Award, the Sox win the AL West but lose the LCS to the Toronto Blue Jays.
**2000** – Manager Jerry Manuel leads the Sox to the AL Central crown but they are swept by the Seattle Mariners in the divisional playoffs.

# CLEVELAND INDIANS

A charter member of the American League, the Cleveland Indians have had a proud and colorful history, even though the championships have been few and far between. Early Tribe teams included such baseball immortals as Nap Lajoie, Cy Young, Shoeless Joe Jackson and Tris Speaker, who led the Indians to their first world championship in 1920. The 1930s featured the opening of mammoth Municipal Stadium and the debut of teenage strikeout sensation Bob Feller. Colorful showman Bill Veeck bought the club in 1946, and two years later the Tribe won it all before a record 2.6 million fans with a club that featured Hall of Famers Feller, Larry Doby, Bob Lemon and player-manager Lou Boudreau. In 1954 the Tribe won a league-record 111 games, but hard times followed until the opening of beautiful Jacobs Field in 1994. With "The Jake" selling out night after night, the Indians returned to prominence in the late 1990s.

**1901** – The Cleveland Blues play the first game in American League history on April 24, losing to the Chicago White Sox, 8–2.

**1902** – Superstar second baseman Nap Lajoie joins the club, which now is known as the Broncos. A year later the team is renamed the Naps in Lajoie's honor.

**1908** – The Naps miss the pennant by a half–game despite the heroics of pitcher Addie Joss, who wins 24 games and throws a perfect game in the heat of the pennant race on October 2.

**1916** – Now known as the Indians, the club obtains future Hall of Famer Tris Speaker in a trade with the Red Sox. Three years later, Speaker becomes the Tribe's manager.

**1920** – Despite the tragic loss of shortstop Ray Chapman, who dies after being hit by a pitched ball on August 16, the Indians win their first pennant. They then defeat the Brooklyn Dodgers, five games to two, in a World Series that features an unassisted triple play by Cleveland second sacker Bill Wambsganss.

**1932** – The Indians play their first game at Cleveland Municipal Stadium on July 31 before a crowd in excess of 80,000. The Tribe will play all its games at the Stadium in 1933, then use it only for Sunday, holiday and night games until 1947.

**1936** – Seventeen–year–old Bob Feller joins Cleveland and fans 15 batters in his first major league start on August 23.

**1948** – With player–manager Lou Boudreau hitting .355 and winning the MVP Award, the Indians defeat the Boston Red Sox in a one–game playoff for the American League pennant. They go on to defeat the Boston Braves, four games to two, in the World Series.

**1954** – The Indians win a record 111 games to take the AL pennant, but are swept in four straight games by the New York Giants in the World Series.

**1960** – On the eve of the season, Indians general manager Frank Lane stuns the city by trading the team's most popular player, slugger Rocky Colavito, to the Tigers. Indian fans begin boycotting the team and a long down period ensues.

**1994** – A franchise once thought to be on its last legs receives a transfusion when it moves into state–of–the–art Jacobs Field. A year later, the Indians make it to the World Series but lose to the Atlanta Braves in six games.

**1997** – The Indians win the third of five straight Central Division titles, but once again fall short in the World Series, losing to the Florida Marlins in seven games.

**2001** – The Indians win another Central Division title but fall in five games to the Mariners in the Division Series.

# DETROIT TIGERS

For all of the 20th century, the Detroit Tigers played ball at the corner of Michigan and Trumbull - first at Bennett Park, then since 1912 at Tiger Stadium, which also has been known as Navin Field and Briggs Stadium. The Tigers have maintained that same sense of stability in the way they have run their franchise. Ty Cobb and Al Kaline each wore the Detroit uniform for 22 seasons, Charlie Gehringer wore Tiger stripes for 19 campaigns, and Alan Trammell and Lou Whitaker were the club's double-play combo for nearly two decades. The uniforms looked about the same in 1999 as they had in 1939, and the club's broadcaster, Ernie Harwell, has been around since 1960. Now change has come as the Tigers abandoned "The Corner" for a new stadium, Comerica Park. But it's only a mile away from their old haunts, and the proud, stable tradition of the Detroit Tigers figures to continue.

**1901** – The Tigers join the new American League, settling in at 8,500–seat Bennett Park.

**1905** – Eighteen–year–old Ty Cobb makes his Tiger debut on August 30.

**1907–08–09** – With Cobb winning the first three of his record 12 American League batting titles, the Tigers rip off three straight pennants, but lose the World Series each time.

**1912** – Navin Field opens on April 20 at the former site of Bennett Park.

**1934** – With Mickey Cochrane providing a spark as catcher/manager, the Tigers win their first pennant since 1909, but bow to the St. Louis Cardinal Gashouse Gang in a seven–game World Series.

**1935** – The Tigers repeat as AL champs, then top the Chicago Cubs in six games to win their first World Series.

**1938** – Navin Field is expanded and renamed Briggs Stadium after Detroit owner Walter Briggs. Tiger first baseman Hank Greenberg celebrates the redesigned park by belting 58 homers, just two short of Babe Ruth's record.

**1940** – The Tigers win the AL pennant but lose the World Series to the Cincinnati Reds in seven games.

**1945** – After missing four–and–a–half seasons to World War II, Greenberg returns in midyear and sparks another Tiger pennant. The Tigers then defeat the Chicago Cubs, four games to three, to win their second World Series.

**1955** – Twenty–year–old Al Kaline hits .340 to become the youngest batting champion in major league history.

**1968** – After losing the American League pennant on the final day of the 1967 season, the Tigers win 103 games and the AL pennant in '68 behind Denny McLain, the majors' last 30–game winner of the century. With Mickey Lolich winning three games, the Tigers come back from a three–games–to–one deficit to win the World Series.

**1972** – The Tigers win the AL East, but lose the ALCS to the Oakland A's in five games.

**1984** – The Tigers win 35 of their first 40 games, the greatest start in Major League history, and don't stop winning until they've nailed down the World Series.

**1987** – With shortstop Alan Trammell hitting .343, the Tigers win the AL East on the season's final day, but lose the ALCS to the Minnesota Twins in five games.

# KANSAS CITY ROYALS

Though they've only been around since the late 1960s, the Kansas City Royals have a proud tradition. Smartly run by owner Ewing Kauffman, the Royals posted a winning record in only their third season and won their first division title five years later, in 1976. With the farm system producing players like George Brett and Frank White, the front office swinging shrewd deals for the likes of Amos Otis and Hal McRae and the club settled in beautiful Royals Stadium (renamed Kauffman Stadium in 1993), the Royals appeared to be a budding dynasty. Unfortunately, the dynasty never quite developed. The Royals endured agonizing playoff losses to the Yankees in 1976, 1977 and 1978, lost to the Phillies in the 1980 World Series, and lost in the playoffs in 1984 before finally winning it all in 1985. The years since then have been difficult, and the Royals now endure the same struggles as baseball's other small-market teams. The new millennium has begun and the Royals are still looking for that second world championship.

**1968** – A year after the Athletics abandoned the city to move to Oakland, the American League awards an expansion franchise to Kansas City pharmaceutical magnate Ewing Kauffman, with the club to begin play in 1969.
**1969** – Playing in the A's old home, Municipal Stadium, the Royals beat the Minnesota Twins in their first game, 4–3, on April 8. Managed by Joe Gordon, the club finishes a surprising fourth in the six–team AL West with 69 wins.
**1971** – Now managed by Bob Lemon, the Royals post their first winning season with 85 victories as they finish second in their division.
**1973** – Royals Stadium opens on April 10, with the Royals defeating the Minnesota Twins, 12–1. Twenty–year–old George Brett makes his Royals debut on August 2, singling for his first major league hit against Stan Bahnsen of the White Sox.
**1976** – With Brett winning his first batting championship, Whitey Herzog's Royals win the club's first division title with 90 victories. The best–of–five ALCS is tied in the bottom of the ninth of Game 5 when Chris Chambliss of the Yankees homers to win the Series.
**1977** – The Royals win the West again with a franchise–record 102 victories, but once again fall to the Yankees in five games, this time losing the final two contests in Kansas City.
**1978** – Same story: another West title, another playoff loss to the Yankees. This time the Royals lose three games to one.
**1980** – Brett hits .390, the major leagues' highest average since 1941, to lead the Royals to the West title behind rookie manager Jim Frey. The Royals take revenge on the Yankees with a sweep in the ALCS, but lose the World Series to the Philadelphia Phillies, four games to two.
**1984** – Manager Dick Howser leads the Royals to their fifth AL West title in nine years, but the club is swept by the Detroit Tigers in the ALCS.
**1985** – Next year arrives at last as the Royals win the West, then come back from three–games–to–one deficits in both the ALCS (Blue Jays) and World Series (Cardinals) to win the club's first championship.
**1990** – Brett becomes the first player to win batting titles in three decades as he leads the American League with a .329 average.

# MINNESOTA TWINS

"First in war, first in peace and last in the American League" was one comedian's description of the original Washington Senators, who usually could be found in the second division during their 60 years in the Nation's Capital (1901-60). Things have been only slightly better since the club became the Minnesota Twins in 1961, but both the Senators and Twins have had their moments of glory. From 1907–27 the Senators boasted one of the greatest pitchers in major league history in Walter Johnson, who won more than 400 games and led the club to its first two pennants in 1924-25. The Senators won another flag in 1933 with player-manager Joe Cronin, a future Hall of Famer, at the helm. The early Minnesota years were graced by slugger Harmon Killebrew, who helped the Twins win a pennant in 1965 and division titles in 1969 and 1970. Kirby Puckett arrived in 1984 and helped Tom Kelly's small-market Twins win it all in 1987 and 1991.

**1901** – A charter member of the American League, the Senators (also known as the Nationals) finish sixth in their inaugural season, the first of 11 straight years in the second division.

**1907** – Nineteen–year–old Walter Johnson's debut is a 3–2 loss to the AL champion Tigers on August 2, with Ty Cobb getting the first hit.

**1912–13** – Johnson has two of the greatest pitching seasons ever, going 33–12 and 36–7 with ERAs of 1.39 and 1.14 to lift the Senators to a pair of second–place finishes.

**1924** – Still going strong in his 18th season, Johnson wins 23 games to lead the Senators to their first pennant. After losing his first two World Series starts, Johnson comes on in relief in Game 7 and works four shutout innings as the Senators prevail over the New York Giants in 12 innings, 4–3.

**1925** – With Johnson winning 20, the Senators claim another pennant, but blow a three–games–to–one lead in the World Series against the Pittsburgh Pirates.

**1933** – The Senators name 26–year–old shortstop Joe Cronin their manager and watch him lead the club to 99 wins and the AL pennant, but Washington loses the Series to the New York Giants, four games to one.

**1945** – With most of baseball's big stars away at war, the Senators rise from last place to second, losing the League to the Detroit Tigers on the last day of the season.

**1961** – After years of falling attendance, Washington owner Calvin Griffith moves the team to Minnesota and renames it the Twins after the team's new home, the twin cities of Minneapolis–St. Paul.

**1965** – With Harmon Killebrew and AL batting champion Tony Oliva providing the spark, the Twins win the AL pennant, but lose the World Series in seven games to the Dodgers.

**1969–70** – Killebrew wins the 1969 MVP Award as he leads the Twins to the first of two straight AL West titles. But the Twins are swept by the Baltimore Orioles both times in the ALCS.

**1982** – The Twins leave their original Minnesota home, Metropolitan Stadium, for the Hubert H. Humphrey Metrodome.

**1987** – The Twins win the AL West with only 85 wins, but stun both the Detroit Tigers and St. Louis Cardinals to win their first world title under manager Tom Kelly.

**1991** – The Twins win the West again, top the Toronto Blue Jays in the ALCS, and then defeat the Atlanta Braves in one of the most exciting World Series ever, four games to three. Jack Morris is the Series hero with 10 shutout innings in Game 7. They became the first team to go from bottom of the division one season to World Series winners the next.

# A. L. West

**Anaheim Angels**
**Oakland Athletics**
**Seattle Mariners**
**Texas Rangers**

# ANAHEIM ANGELS

Though the Angels franchise has been around for only 40 years, no major league team has had a more star-crossed history. The Angels have never made it to a World Series, but there were agonizing near-misses in 1982, 1986 and 1995. There was the frustration of Angels owner Gene Autry, who died three days after his 91st birthday, still waiting for his team to capture the big prize. And there were the numerous personal tragedies. Pitcher Dick Wantz died of a brain tumor at age 25 in 1965. Shortstop Mike Miley, just 23, was killed in a car crash in 1977. Star outfielder Lyman Bostock, 27, was shot and killed in Gary, Indiana, in 1978. And reliever Donnie Moore, the pitcher who served up the home run that cost the Angels a berth in the 1986 World Series, committed suicide three years later. Despite all their tragedies and misfortunes, the Angels have had many moments of glory, and the club has featured such stars as Nolan Ryan, Reggie Jackson, Jim Fregosi and Don Baylor.

**1960** – Cowboy legend Gene Autry attends the American League expansion meetings hoping to get the broadcasting rights for the new Los Angeles Angels, and winds up as the owner of the team. Fred Haney, the first general manager, selects a number of useful players in the December expansion draft, including Jim Fregosi, Dean Chance, Buck Rodgers, Ken McBride and Albie Pearson.

**1961** – Settling in at tiny Wrigley Field for their first season, the Angels beat the Orioles 7–2 in their first contest and wind up winning 70 games, still a record for a first–year expansion team.

**1962** – The Angels move into Chavez Ravine/Dodger Stadium as tenants of the Los Angeles Dodgers, and then amaze the baseball world by grabbing the American League lead in midseason. The Angels ultimately finish in third place with 86 victories.

**1966** – After changing their name to the California Angels a year earlier, the Angels move into their own park, Anaheim Stadium, in the Orange County city of Anaheim.

**1973** – Nolan Ryan, who had arrived a year earlier in a lopsided trade with the Mets, pitches the first two of his record seven no–hitters and strikes out 383 batters, the highest single–season total in the 20th century.

**1979** – Led by American League MVP Don Baylor, the Angels win their first–ever division title, but lose the LCS to the Orioles in four games.

**1982** – Gene Mauch's Angels win the AL West title, then take a two–games–to–none lead in the best–of–five LCS against the Brewers. Unfortunately the Angels drop the final three games of the Series.

**1986** – After winning another AL West title under Mauch, the Angels take a three–games–to–one lead in the LCS against the Red Sox and are one pitch away from the World Series. But Donnie Moore serves up a home run to Boston's Dave Henderson, and the Angels eventually lose the series in seven games.

**1995** – The Angels take a big lead into the final weeks of the season, but collapse and wind up in a playoff game with the Mariners, which they lose, 9–1.

**1997** – A year after the Walt Disney company takes over as managing general partner of the team, the club is renamed the Anaheim Angels.

**1998** – After being renovated in the 1970s to accommodate the NFL Rams, Anaheim Stadium is reconfigured for baseball and renamed Edison International Field of Anaheim.

# OAKLAND A'S

Someone once wrote that as owner and manager of the Philadelphia A's, Connie Mack served up only two kinds of teams: really great or really lousy. Though Mack, who managed the team for an incredible 50 years (1901-50), died in 1956, that pretty much sums up this franchise. Playing in Philadelphia, Kansas City and Oakland, the A's finished either first (19 times) or last (28) in nearly half of the 100 years of the 20th century. When they've been good, they've been as good as it gets, with no less than four separate dynasties (1910-14, 1929-31, 1971-75 and 1988-92) and a total of nine world titles. Unfortunately the cashed-starved Athletics have continually had to dismantle their great teams for economic reasons, resulting in long stretches at the bottom of the standings, as well as a couple of franchise shifts. But, oh, those great teams: Bender and Plank, Simmons and Foxx, Jackson and Hunter, McGwire and Canseco.

**1901** – Ban Johnson forms the American League and asks Connie Mack to manage the Philadelphia franchise, with an ownership stake thrown in.
**1902** – Colorful lefty Rube Waddell goes 24–7 to pace the A's to their first pennant.
**1905** – Waddell wins 27 games to lead the A's to another pennant, but he misses the World Series with an injury and the A's lose to the Giants, four games to one.
**1909** – Shibe Park, the first steel and concrete park in baseball history, opens on April 12 before a record crowd of 31,160.
**1910–14** – The A's rip off four pennants in five years, with world championships in 1910, 1911 and 1913.
**1915** – Afraid of escalating salaries caused by competition from the new Federal League, Mack sells off most of his best players. The A's plunge to last place in 1915, the first of seven straight years in the cellar.
**1929–31** – A new A's dynasty led by Jimmie Foxx, Mickey Cochrane, Al Simmons and Lefty Grove reaches fruition with three straight pennants and world titles in 1929 and 1930.
**1933** – With the Great Depression at its height, Mack responds to dwindling attendance by once again starting to deal off his best players. Grove, dealt to the Red Sox, is the first big star to go.
**1935** – Their roster all but gutted, the A's begin a stretch in which they finish last or next–to–last 11 times in 12 years.
**1955** – Still struggling both on the field and at the gate, the A's abandon Philadelphia and move to Kansas City.
**1968** – After 13 seasons in Kansas City that were no more successful than the final years in Philadelphia, A's owner Charlie Finley moves the team to Oakland.
**1971–75** – The A's "Mustache Gang," led by Reggie Jackson, Catfish Hunter and Rollie Fingers, win five straight division titles, with World Series victories in 1972, '73 and '74.
**1988–92** – A new A's dynasty begins under Tony La Russa, with Jose Canseco, Mark McGwire and Dennis Eckersley the stars of a team that wins the World Series in 1989, AL titles in 1988 and 1990 and an AL West crown in 1992.
**2000** – The youthful A's clinch the AL West, led by the dynamic Jason Giambi, but go down to the World Champion Yankees in the AL divisional playoffs. Giambi received the AL MVP award for his efforts.
**2001** – The A's season is again ended by the Yankees in the divisional playoffs as they lose in five games after taking a 2-0 lead.

# SEATTLE MARINERS

Seattle got a brief taste of major league baseball when the woefully-underfinanced Pilots played there in 1969, but the club moved to Milwaukee after only one season. After years of legal maneuvering, the American League awarded Seattle an expansion franchise to begin play in 1977, and more than 57,000 baseball-starved fans attended the Mariners' first game at the Kingdome that April. Despite that promising beginning, Seattle's baseball troubles weren't over. The Mariners didn't surpass their first-year attendance of 1.3 million until 1990, their 14th season, and finally had their first winning season a year later. The M's revival coincided with the arrival of Ken Griffey Jr. in 1989, and the 1990s saw the arrival of another superstar, Alex Rodriguez, two division titles and the opening of Safeco Field in 1999. Griffey and Rodriguez may have gone, but Seattle's days as a scuffling franchise finally seem to be over.

**1976** – Seattle and the State of Washington drop their $32.5 million suit against Major League Baseball when the American League awards an expansion franchise to Seattle, with play to begin in 1977. In the expansion draft on November 5, the Mariners choose Royals minor league outfielder Ruppert Jones as their first selection.

**1977** – Opening on April 6 at the Kingdome, the Mariners draw 57,762 fans to their 7–0 loss to the Angels. The M's finish sixth in the seven–team West with 64 wins, and their attendance of 1.3 million is the second best to date for an expansion franchise.

**1981** – California real estate magnate George Argyros purchases the club, but the M's get off to a 6–18 start under manager Maury Wills. Rene Lachemann replaces Wills and briefly gets the Mariners into contention in the second half of the strike year's split season before the club fades to fifth.

**1982** – With Bill Caudill saving 26 games, Gaylord Perry winning his 300th game and Floyd Bannister leading the AL in strikeouts, Lachemann leads the M's to 76 wins and a fourth–place finish, their best yet.

**1989** – Nineteen–year–old Ken Griffey Jr. makes his major league debut on April 3, doubling off Dave Stewart in his first at–bat. Griffey hits .264 with 16 homers as a rookie as the M's finish sixth with 73 wins.

**1991** – The M's finally post their first winning record in their 15th year, going 83–79 under Jim Lefebvre. Griffey leads the way with 22 homers and 100 RBI as the Mariners draw 2 million for the first time.

**1994** – Eighteen–year–old Alex Rodriguez makes his major league debut on July 8 and gets his first major league hit a day later. Rodriguez bats .204 as a rookie as the M's finish third.

**1995** – Edgar Martinez (.356) wins the AL batting title and Randy Johnson (18–2) the Cy Young Award as the M's win their first division title, defeating the California Angels in a one–game playoff. After coming from two games down to beat the Yankees in an epic five–game Division Series, the M's fall to the Indians in six games in the ALCS.

**1997** – Griffey has the first of two straight 56–homer seasons to lead the M's to another division title as the club draws 3 million for the first time. However, the club falls to the Orioles in the Division Series, three games to one.

**1999** – The M's make a midyear move to Safeco Field, opening on July 15 before 44,607 fans. The M's finish third in the West with 79 wins.

**2000** – Despite the loss of Ken Griffey Jr. to the Reds, the Mariners clinch a wildcard berth, and advance to the ALCS, eventually losing to the Yankees, 4-2.

**2001** – Alex Rodriguez leaves for Texas but Seattle remain undetered as they tie the Major League record with 116 wins. However, their stellar play deserts them in the ALCS as they go down 4-1 to the Yankees. Ichiro Suzuki is awarded both Rookie of the Year and MVP honors.

# TEXAS RANGERS

Texas Rangers franchise history can be divided into three parts. In Part I (1961-71), the club played in Washington as the expansion Senators, usually without success. In Part II (1972-93), the club moved to Texas, took the name Rangers and began playing more respectably while continuing to fail to make the playoffs. In Part III (1994-present), the Rangers moved into the beautiful, new Ballpark in Arlington and finally found success on the field. The Rangers were leading the AL West when the strike ended the 1994 season; two years later, they won their first full-season West Division championship but got knocked out in the first round of the playoffs by the Yankees. In both 1998 and 1999, they repeated the same pattern. However, in 2000 and 2001 they finished last in the AL West.

**1960** – With the original Washington Senators scheduled to move to Minnesota in 1961, the American League awards an expansion franchise to Washington, also to be known as the Senators. General Elwood "Pete" Quesada is the club's first president.

**1961** – President John F. Kennedy throws out the first ball as the Senators lose their first game to the Chicago White Sox, 4–3, on April 10 at Griffith Stadium. The club finishes ninth that year with 100 losses. A year later, they will move into new D.C. Stadium (renamed Robert F. Kennedy Stadium in 1969).

**1969** – New Senators owner Bob Short stuns the baseball world by luring Ted Williams out of retirement to serve as the club's manager. Williams' first year is hugely successful as the club wins 86 games for the first winning season in franchise history.

**1971** – With attendance dropping to 655,000 and the club having failed to ever draw a million in a season, Short receives permission to move the Senators to Texas. The franchise's final game in Washington on September 30 is forfeited to the Yankees when fans storm the field in the ninth inning.

**1972** – Renamed the Texas Rangers and playing in Arlington Stadium, the club has a rough first year in Texas, losing 100 games and drawing only 663,000 fans. At the end of the season, Williams resigns as manager.

**1974** – With Billy Martin taking over as manager and outfielder Jeff Burroughs winning the MVP Award, the Rangers win 84 games and finish only five games out of first in the AL West.

**1989** – Nolan Ryan signs with the Rangers and wins 16 games and the AL strikeout crown at age 42. Ryan will win another strikeout crown, toss two no–hitters and win his 300th game in a Rangers uniform before retiring in 1993 as baseball's all–time strikeout king.

**1994** – The Rangers move into The Ballpark in Arlington and are leading the AL West (albeit with a losing record) when a strike ends the season in August.

**1996** – With Juan Gonzalez winning the MVP Award, the Rangers win the AL West for their first division title but are eliminated in the Division Series by the Yankees.

**1998–99** – Two more West titles and two more MVP Awards to Ranger players (one to Gonzalez, another to Pudge Rodriguez) are followed by two more Division Series losses to the Yankees.

**2001** – The Rangers make Alex Rodriguez the highest paid player in history when they sign him to a $252 million, 10-year deal. He posts a .318 average with 135 RBIs and 52 homers in his first season but Texas finish last in the AL West, 43 games behind the red-hot Mariners—the team A-Rod left to join the Rangers.

# N.L. East

Atlanta Braves
Florida Marlins
Montreal Expos
New York Mets
Philadelphia Phillies

# ATLANTA BRAVES

The Braves, along with the Chicago Cubs, are one of only two National League clubs that can trace their origin all the way back to the league's first season, 1876. Beginning in Boston as the Red Stockings and then the Beaneaters, the club won eight pennants between 1877 and 1898. Changing their nickname to Braves in 1912, the Bostonians won a "miracle pennant" in 1914, but their next NL title didn't come until 1948, and the club moved to Milwaukee in 1953. With Hank Aaron, Eddie Mathews and Warren Spahn sparking a pair of pennants, the first few years in Milwaukee were wildly successful. But then attendance slipped, and the Braves headed for Atlanta in 1966. The early Atlanta years were notable mostly for Aaron's successful assault on Babe Ruth's career home-run record, but in the 1990s and into the new millennium the Braves found success on the field as well, with ten division titles and a world championship in 1995.

**1876** – The Boston Red Stockings join the National League as a charter member.
**1877–78** – Manager Harry Wright leads the Red Stockings to back–to–back pennants, with righthander Tommy Bond turning in a pair of 40–win seasons.
**1891–98** – Now known as the Beaneaters, the club wins five pennants in eight seasons behind manager Frank Selee.
**1914** – In last place as late as July 19, manager George Stallings' club – renamed the Braves two years earlier – catches fire and wins the National League pennant. The Braves then stun the heavily favored Philadelphia A's with a World Series sweep.
**1935** – Desperate for a gate attraction, the Braves sign 40–year–old Babe Ruth after the Yankees release him. The Babe has a few memorable moments but bats only .181, as the Braves lose a franchise–record 115 games.
**1948** – "Spahn and Sain and pray for rain" is the chant as the Braves ride their two star pitchers, Warren Spahn and Johnny Sain, to their first pennant in 34 years. However, they lose the World Series to the Cleveland Indians in six games.
**1953** – After attendance drops to 281,000 in 1952, the Braves move to Milwaukee, the majors' first franchise shift since 1903. In their first year in Brewtown, the Braves draw 1.8 million fans.
**1954** – Twenty–year–old Hank Aaron makes his Braves debut on April 13, and hits .280 with 13 homers in his rookie season.
**1957–58** – With Aaron, Spahn and Eddie Mathews leading the way, the Braves win back–to–back pennants, beating the Yankees in the 1957 World Series but losing to the Yanks in '58.
**1966** – Declining attendance prompts the Braves to move to Atlanta, where they draw 1.5 million fans their first year.
**1969** – The Braves win the first NL West title, but lose to the New York Mets in the NLCS.
**1974** – Aaron's long quest ends on April 8 as he blasts career homer No. 715, surpassing Ruth as the all–time home–run king.
**1991–99** – Finishing first in every season except strike–shortened 1994, the Braves enjoy an unprecedented run of success. Unfortunately the club wins only one World Series, topping the Indians in 1995.
**2000** – The Braves continue to be the dominant force in the NL East, winning yet another division title but they are, surprisingly, swept in the divisional playoffs by the red hot St. Louis Cardinals.
**2001** – Again the Braves win the NL East and again they fall just short in the playoffs—this time losing to the eventual World Champion Arizona Diamonbacks in the NLCS.

# FLORIDA MARLINS

Although they've only been around for seven seasons, the Florida Marlins have had more than their share of ups and downs. Beginning play in 1993, the Marlins were a typical expansion team, losing 98 games. Improving slowly but steadily, they finished within two games of .500 in 1996, and that winter Marlins owner Wayne Huizenga decided to go for broke, hiring veteran manager Jim Leyland and signing a number of high-priced free agents. The result was a 92-win season and an NL wild-card berth. In the playoffs, the Marlins rode the clutch pitching of Livan Hernandez and Kevin Brown all the way to the world championship. But the Marlins had little time to celebrate their success. Citing huge financial losses, Huizenga announced that the franchise was for sale and began trading off the club's high-salaried players. In 1998 the Marlins plunged to last place but by 2001 there were signs of improvement as they finished with 76 wins.

**1991** – Major league owners award expansion franchises to Denver and Miami on July 5, with the teams to begin play in 1993. The club takes the name of Florida Marlins and hires former Montreal Expos general manager Dave Dombrowski to run the team on September 19.

**1992** – The Marlins select University of Miami catcher Charles Johnson as their first–ever pick in the June 1 amateur draft. After naming Rene Lachemann as the club's manager on October 23, the club selects outfielder Nigel Wilson as its first choice in the November 17 expansion draft.

**1993** – In their first game on April 5, the Marlins defeat the Los Angeles Dodgers, 6–3, before 42,334 fans at Miami's Joe Robbie (later Pro Player) Stadium. The Marlins draw 3 million fans as they finish sixth in the seven–team NL East with 64 wins.

**1994** – The Marlins finish last in the strike–shortened season, but their .443 winning percentage is nearly a 50–point improvement over 1993. Jeff Conine leads the club with a .319 average.

**1995** – The Marlins improve their winning percentage once again as they move up to fourth in the NL East with 67 wins.

**1996** – Lachemann is replaced by John Boles as the club's manager in midseason as the Marlins finish third with an 80–82 record. Free–agent signee Kevin Brown leads the NL with a 1.89 ERA, and Gary Sheffield leads the club with 42 homers and 120 RBI.

**1997** – Deciding to try to win it all, Marlins owner Wayne Huizenga opens his pocketbook and the club signs high–priced free agents Moises Alou, Alex Fernandez and Bobby Bonilla, as well as former Pittsburgh Pirate manager Jim Leyland. The Marlins win 92 games to qualify as the National League wild card, and the club rolls all the way to the world championship, defeating the San Francisco Giants in the Division Series (3–0), the Atlanta Braves in the NLCS (4–2) and the Cleveland Indians in a seven–game World Series. They come from behind to tie the final game in the bottom of the ninth, and then win it in the 11th on a single by Edgar Renteria.

**1998** – Announcing that the club had suffered massive losses despite the world title, Huizenga puts the team up for sale and begins unloading the club's stars. The Marlins plunge to last place with 108 losses.

**1999** – John Henry becomes the team owner and John Boles the club's manager as the Marlins finish last in the NL East with 64 wins, 10 more than in 1998.

# MONTREAL EXPOS

Baseball has had a long tradition in Canada, but it wasn't until the National League awarded an expansion franchise to Montreal in 1969 that Canadians finally got a chance to see major league ball. Playing at tiny Parc Jarry, the early Montreal Expos were scrappy but overmatched. The club moved to mammoth Olympic Stadium in 1977, right around the time that young players like Gary Carter, Andre Dawson and Steve Rogers were beginning to blossom. After a couple of near-misses, Montreal reached the League Championship Series in 1981, but Rick Monday's ninth-inning home run in the final game ended the Expos' dream. The Expos continued to produce strong clubs through the early '90s, but lost their best chance at a World Series when a strike ended the 1994 season with the club in first place. Since then, a lack of financing has forced the Expos to deal away many of their best players. As the century ended, new ownership took control of the Expos and rekindled discussion concerning a new stadium – their only hope of keeping the franchise in Montreal.

**1968** – The National League awards an expansion franchise to Montreal on May 27, with the club to begin play in 1969.

**1969** – The Expos win a wild first game, defeating the eventual champion New York Mets, 11–10, on April 8. Playing in 28,000–seat Parc Jarry, the club draws 1.2 million fans despite losing 110 games.

**1973** – In their fifth season, the Expos win 79 games under manager Gene Mauch and finish just three–and–a–half games out of the NL East race.

**1977** – The Expos move to Olympic Stadium and draw 1.43 million fans, doubling their 1976 attendance. New manager Dick Williams leads the team to 75 wins, a 20–win improvement over 1976.

**1979** – The Expos lead the NL East much of the year but lose out on the final day as they finish second with a club–record 95 wins, their first winning season. Attendance soars to 2.1 million.

**1980** – The Expos are tied for the East lead with the Phillies entering the final weekend, but lose two of three to the Phils at the Big O to end up a game short.

**1981** – With baseball adopting a split–season format after a midyear players' strike, the Expos reach the playoffs for the first time. They top the Phillies in the Division Series but lose inthe NCLS to the Dodgers, 2–1, on Rick Monday's homer in the ninth inning of Game 5.

**1987** – Though many of the club's early–1980s stars have left via trades and free agency, Buck Rodgers leads the Expos to 91 victories and a third–place finish, only four games behind the division–winning Cardinals.

**1991** – Beset by still more player losses, the Expos finish last with their worst record in 15 years. In September a beam at Olympic Stadium collapses, forcing the team to finish the year on the road.

**1993** – With the farm system producing new talent, Felipe Alou manages the Expos to a second–place finish, only three games behind the division–winning Phillies.

**1994** – Alou's Expos are riding high with baseball's best record when a players' strike ends the season in August.

**1999** – The Expos lose 94 games amid talk that the franchise will move, but the club is purchased after the season by art dealer Jeffrey Loria, who promises to spend money and work for a new stadium in Montreal.

**2001** – Manager Felipe Alou is fired after nine years in charge and a 691–717 record.

# NEW YORK METS

"They're gonna be amazin'," manager Casey Stengel said in talking up his first New York Mets team, and win or lose, the Mets have pretty much lived up to that billing. They've been about as bad as a team can be, losing a modern day-record 120 games in their inaugural season and finishing either ninth or 10th in each of their first seven seasons. They've also been about as good as a team can be, winning 108 games and a world championship in 1986 and roaring down the stretch to win a miracle title in 1969. Tom Seaver and a young Dwight Gooden have worn the Mets' colors; so have Greg Goossen and Marvelous Marv Throneberry. They've played in some of the most exciting games in history, like Game 6 of the 1986 NLCS, Game 6 of the '86 World Series, Games 5 and 6 of the 1999 NLCS and the 2000 Subway Series. They've also had more than their share of bad games and bad teams. . . bad, but seldom dull. All in all, "amazin'" still seems like a pretty good description.

**1960** – Three years after the Dodgers and Giants left New York for the West Coast, the National League announces on October 17 that expansion franchises in New York City and Houston will begin play in 1962.

**1962** – With ex–Yankee general manager George Weiss as president and Casey Stengel as manager, the Mets begin play with an 11–4 loss to the Cardinals on April 11. The club proceeds to lose its first nine games and winds up with 120 losses on the season, a 20th–century record.

**1964** – The Mets open their new park, Shea Stadium, with a 4–3 loss to the Pirates on April 17 and then finish 10th for the third straight year.

**1969** – After never finishing higher than ninth, the "Miracle Mets" win 38 of their last 49 games and come from nine–and–a–half games behind on August 13 to win the NL East title. The miracle continues in the postseason, as the Mets sweep the Atlanta Braves in the NLCS and then stun the heavily favored Baltimore Orioles, four games to one, in the World Series.

**1973** – "It ain't over 'til it's over," proclaims Mets manager Yogi Berra, and the Mets prove him right by coming back from last place on August 30 to win the NL East. Though their 82–79 record is the worst ever for a first–place team, the Mets make it all the way to Game 7 of the World Series before losing to the Oakland Athletics.

**1984** – After seven straight losing seasons, rookie sensation Dwight Gooden helps lift rookie manager Davey Johnson's Mets to second place in the East.

**1985** – The 20–year–old Gooden goes 24–4 with a 1.53 ERA as the Mets finish second again.

**1986**– Led by Gooden, Darryl Strawberry, Gary Carter and Keith Hernandez, the Mets take the NL East, defeat the Houston Astros in a gripping NLCS, and then top the Boston Red Sox, four games to three, in the World Series.

**1988** – The Mets win the NL East with 100 victories but are upset by the underdog Los Angeles Dodgers in the NLCS.

**1993** – Described by one writer as "the worst team money can buy," the high–salaried Mets finish last in the NL East with 103 losses.

**1999** – After nearly falling out of the race in late September, the Mets win the NL wild–card berth in a one–game playoff with the Cincinnati Reds. They advance all the way to the NLCS before losing to the Braves in six games.

**2000** – The Mets go one better, defeating St. Louis in the NLCS to set up a much anticipated Subway World Series with the Yankees. They eventually lose in five after a series of tight match-ups, with no more than two runs deciding any of the games.

# PHILADELPHIA PHILLIES

Of all the 16 major league franchises that have been around since the turn of the century, none has had more struggles than the Philadelphia Phillies. Philadelphia's first National League team in 1883 finished a distant last with a 17-81 record, and that pretty much set the tone for the franchise. The club's first pennant didn't arrive until 1915, and the Phils didn't win their second for another 35 seasons. In most of their other seasons, the Phils usually could be found at the bottom of the standings; during one bleak period (1918-47), the Phillies finished in the second division 29 times in 30 years. The Phils finally got it together in the late 1970s, winning five NL East titles between 1976 and 1983 and their first world championship in 1980. The 1990s brought another World Series appearance in 1993 and the 2001 season saw a young Phillies ballclub push the Braves all the way in the NL East.

**1883** – After a six-year absence, the National League returns to Philadelphia when Al Reach and Colonel John Rogers form the Phillies. In their first season, the Phillies finish last with a 17–81 record.
**1894** – The Phillies bat .349, a major league record to this day, but finish fourth due to a 5.63 team ERA. All three Philadelphia outfielders – Ed Delahanty, Billy Hamilton and Sam Thompson – hit over .400.
**1895** – The Phillies move into a bandbox, Baker Bowl, where the right-field fence is only 272 feet away. It will be their home until 1938.
**1915** – Grover Cleveland Alexander goes 31–10, the first of three straight 30–win seasons, to lead the Phils to their first National League pennant. Alexander beats the Boston Red Sox in the first game of the World Series, but the Phils fall in five games.
**1930** – With Chuck Klein hitting .386 and Lefty O'Doul .383, the Phils bat .315 as a team, but their 6.71 team ERA dooms them to last place.
**1938** – The Phils abandon Baker Bowl and move into Shibe Park (later Connie Mack Stadium), home of the A's. The change doesn't help as they finish last in seven of their first eight seasons at their new home.
**1950** – Led by Robin Roberts, Richie Ashburn and National League MVP Jim Konstanty, the "Whiz Kids" Phillies win the NL pennant on Dick Sisler's 10th–inning homer on the last day of the season. But the Phils are swept by the Yankees in the World Series.
**1964** – The Phils, managed by Gene Mauch, lead the league by six–and–a–half games with 12 to play, but lose 10 straight to blow the pennant.
**1972** – In one of the most remarkable pitching seasons ever, Steve Carlton goes 27–10 with a 1.97 ERA for a last–place Phillie team that wins only 59 games.
**1976–78** – Led by Carlton and slugging third sacker Mike Schmidt, the Phils win three straight NL East titles, but lose in the NLCS each time.
**1980** – After 97 years, the Phils win their first championship by defeating the Kansas City Royals in the World Series. Schmidt hits 48 homers to win the NL MVP Award.
**1983** – The Phillies' aging "Wheeze Kids" make it all the way to the World Series, but lose to the Baltimore Orioles in five games.
**1993** – The Phils return to the World Series, but Toronto's Joe Carter homers off Phillie closer Mitch Williams to end the Series in six games.

# N. L. Central

**Chicago Cubs**
**Cincinnati Reds**
**Houston Astros**
**Milwaukee Brewers**
**Pittsburgh Pirates**
**St. Louis Cardinals**

# CHICAGO CUBS

The Chicago Cubs franchise dates all the way back to 1876, the first year of the National League. Originally called the White Stockings (they finally became known as the Cubs in 1902), the club was one of baseball's most dominant franchises for the next six decades. After winning back-to-back World Series in 1907 and 1908, the Cubs won seven more National League pennants between 1910 and 1945. But there were no more world championships and since World War II there have been no more pennants too. The Cubs came close a few times, winning NL East titles in 1984 and 1989 and a wild-card berth in 1998, but they and their fans always wound up frustrated. Despite the team's postseason futility, the Cubs, one of the Major Leagues' most beloved franchises, provide a storied past that includes beautiful, quaint Wrigley Field and sluggers Ernie Banks and Sammy Sosa. Let's play two today!

**1876** – The Chicago White Stockings join the new National League with Al Spalding the manager as well as the team's pitching star. With Spalding going 47–12, the White Stockings win the first NL pennant.

**1880** – In his first full year as manager, Chicago first baseman Cap Anson leads the White Stockings to the first of three straight NL pennants. Anson will lead the team to two more pennants before ending his career in 1897.

**1906–10** – Built around the Tinker to Evers to Chance double–play combination and a strong pitching staff led by Mordecai "Three Finger" Brown, the Cubs win four pennants in five years. The Cubs vanquish the Tigers in the 1907 and 1908 World Series, but lose to the White Sox in 1906 and fall to the A's in 1910.

**1916** – The Cubs move from the West Side Grounds, their home since 1893, to Weeghman Park, the former home of the Federal League Chicago Whales. The park will be known as Cubs Park until 1927, when it is renamed Wrigley Field in honor of Cubs owner William Wrigley.

**1929** – The Cubs draw a major league record 1.49 million people as they win their first pennant since 1918. The attendance record won't be broken until 1946.

**1935** – Continuing a habit of winning pennants at three–year intervals (they also won in 1929 and 1932), the Cubs win 21 straight games in September to take the NL flag. But as in '29 and '32, they lose the World Series, falling to the Detroit Tigers in six games.

**1938** – The third year's the charm again as the Cubs win another NL pennant, but they lose the World Series in four straight games to the Yankees.

**1945** – With most of the best players serving in World War II, the Cubs take another NL flag. Once again they drop the Series, with the Tigers beating them four games to three.

**1958** – Ernie Banks, the Cubs' first black player (along with second baseman Gene Baker) in 1953, wins the first of two straight NL Most Valuable Player Awards. Banks is the first player to win the MVP while playing for a losing team.

**1984** – The Cubs end a 39–year drought by winning the NL East title. But after winning the first two games of the NLCS, they fall to the San Diego Padres in five games.

**1989** – The Cubs win the NL East again, but once more fall in the LCS, this time to the San Francisco Giants.

**1998** – A year which starts with the February death of beloved announcer Harry Caray end with the Cubs winning the NL wild–card berth with a playoff–game victory over the Giants, but they fall to the Braves in the Division Series.

# CINCINNATI REDS

The first professional team in baseball history was the 1869 Cincinnati Red Stockings, winners of 130 consecutive games under manager Harry Wright. Current Reds history dates back to 1882, when a different group of Reds joined the new American Association. Moving over to the National League in 1890, the Reds didn't win their first NL pennant until 1919, but their World Series victory proved tainted when it was discovered that the Chicago White Sox had sold out to gamblers. Except for pennants in 1939, 1940 and 1961, the next 50 years were rather bleak, but the Reds hit the heights in the 1970s with six division titles, four National League pennants and two world titles. Except for another world championship in 1990, the current Reds have had a difficult time matching the legacy of that '70s Big Red Machine, which featured Johnny Bench, Joe Morgan and Pete Rose.

**1869** – Harry Wright forms the Cincinnati Red Stockings as baseball's first professional team. Touring the country, the Red Stockings go undefeated in 1869 and don't lose until the Brooklyn Atlantics defeat them in June of 1870 after 130 straight Red Stockings win.

**1876–80** – A new group of Red Stockings joins the National League as charter members, finishing last that year with a 9–56 record. The Red Stockings abandon the NL after the 1880 season, in part because the NL won't let them sell beer.

**1882** – Reforming as the Cincinnati Reds, the club joins the new American Association and wins the league's first pennant.

**1890** – The Reds rejoin the NL, finishing fourth their first year.

**1912** – After playing for 10 seasons in the Palace of the Fans, the Reds move into Redland Field, later known as Crosley Field.

**1919** – Manager Pat Moran leads the Reds to a 96–44 record and the National League pennant. They defeat the Chicago White Sox, five games to three, in the World Series. A year later, it is revealed that the Sox had sold out to gamblers.

**1935** – After drawing only 206,000 fans in 1934, Reds general manager Larry MacPhail receives permission to install lights at Crosley Field. The first night game, against the Phillies on May 24, draws more than 20,000 fans, and the Reds more than double their attendance in '35.

**1938** – In the most dominant pair of back-to-back starts in history Johnny Vander Meer throws consecutive no-hitters.

**1939–40** – The Reds win back–to–back pennants behind manager Bill McKechnie. The Reds are swept by the Yankees in the '39 World Series, but defeat the Detroit Tigers in seven games in 1940.

**1961** – Fred Hutchinson's Reds win their first pennant in 21 years, with right fielder Frank Robinson winning the league's MVP Award. However, they are no match for the Yankees, losing the Series in five games.

**1970** – The Reds celebrate a midseason move to Riverfront Stadium by winning the NL East title. After defeating the Pittsburgh Pirates in the LCS, rookie manager Sparky Anderson's club loses the World Series to the Baltimore Orioles in five games.

**1975–76** After losing the World Series in 1972 and falling in the NLCS in '73, the Big Red Machine puts it all together and wins back–to–back world titles. Johnny Bench, Joe Morgan and Pete Rose are the big stars of a club that wins a club–record 108 games in 1975 and 102 in 1976.

**1985** – After returning to the club a year earlier as player–manager, Pete Rose becomes baseball's all–time hit king with a single off San Diego's Eric Show on September 11.

**1990** – Holding first place every day of the season, Lou Piniella's Reds win it all, sweeping the powerful Oakland A's in the World Series.

# HOUSTON ASTROS

Though they're still looking for their first World Series appearance, the Houston Astros have had their share of great moments. Both of the Astros' League Championship Series appearances – against the Phillies in 1980 and the Mets in 1986 – were epic struggles that rank among the greatest postseason series ever, even though Houston lost each time. The club has had more than its share of outstanding pitchers, including Nolan Ryan, who threw his record-breaking fifth no-hitter for the Astros in 1981; 1986 Cy Young Award winner Mike Scott; the great J.R. Richard, whose career was tragically ended by a stroke in 1980; fireballer Don Wilson, who threw two no-hitters for the Astros; and the late 1990s trio of Mike Hampton, Jose Lima and Billy Wagner. The hitters haven't been too shabby, either, with the likes of Joe Morgan, Jose Cruz, Jimmy Wynn, Jeff Bagwell and Craig Biggio. And what other team has played in "The Eighth Wonder of the World" – the Astrodome, Houston's home from 1965 to 1999?

**1960** – Houston and New York City are awarded National League expansion franchises on October 17, to begin play in 1962.

**1962** – Houston's club, the Colt .45s, begins play with an 11–2 victory over the Cubs at their temporary home, Colt Stadium, on April 11. The Colt .45s finish their first season under manager Harry Craft in eighth place in the 10–team National League.

**1965** – Renamed the Astros, the club moves into baseball's first indoor stadium, the Harris County Domed Stadium (aka the Astrodome). Mickey Mantle hits the park's first home run in an exhibition game on April 9. Three days later, the Phillies beat the Astros 2–0 in the first regular–season game.

**1966** – After an unsuccessful attempt to grow grass in their indoor stadium in 1965, the Astros unveil a new artificial surface known as AstroTurf in a 6–3 win over the Phillies on April 18.

**1978** – J.R. Richard strikes out 303 batters to become the first righthander in NL history to fan 300 batters in a season.

**1980** – The Astros win their first division title, topping the Los Angeles Dodgers in a one–game playoff. In an epic LCS in which the final four games go into extra innings, the Astros lose to the Phillies, three games to two.

**1981** – Nolan Ryan throws his record fifth no–hitter on September 26 and leads the NL in ERA with a 1.69 ERA, as the Astros qualify for the playoffs under the strike year's split–season format. Houston wins the first two games of the best–of–five Division Series with the Dodgers, but then drops the final three games of the series.

**1986** – Cy Young Award winner Mike Scott pitches a no–hitter on September 25 to clinch the NL West title. Scott wins twice more in the NLCS against the Mets, but the Astros fall in six games, losing the final contest in 16 innings.

**1997** – The Astros win the NL Central behind Jeff Bagwell, who hits 43 homers and steals 31 bases, but they are swept by the Braves in the Division Series.

**1998** – The Astros win their second straight Central Division title, but fall to the Padres, three games to one, in the Division Series.

**1999** – In the Astrodome's final season, the Astros again win the Central but once more lose the Division Series, with the Braves beating them this time in four games.

**2000** – The Astros play the 2000 season in their new ballpark, Enron Field, but despite its cozy dimensions and their big bats, the team struggles to a fourth place finish.

# MILWAUKEE BREWERS

A small-market team that has had some glory and more than its share of struggles, the Brewers franchise began life as the Seattle Pilots, a 1969 American League expansion franchise. After losing 98 games its first year, the nearly-bankrupt team was sold to Milwaukee car dealer Bud Selig, who moved the franchise to his hometown and renamed it the Brewers. The Brewers posted losing records in their first eight years in Milwaukee, but then a corps of talented young players led by Robin Yount and Paul Molitor turned things around. The Brewers won 93 games in 1978, qualified for the playoffs in 1981 and made it to the World Series in 1982, losing to the St. Louis Cardinals in seven games. Some predicted a Brewer dynasty, but since then the club has finished higher than third place only once. The Brewers shifted to the National League in 1998 and moved into a new stadium, Miller Park, in 2001. Typical of the franchise's misfortunes, the stadium move was delayed a year after a crane mishap killed three construction workers in 1999.

**1968** – The American League awards an expansion franchise to Seattle on January 11, with the club to begin play in 1969.

**1969** – Immortalized in Jim Bouton's book *Ball Four*, the Seattle Pilots lose 98 games in their first season while playing before only 678,000 fans. By the end of the season, the club is near bankruptcy. Boston is traded before the season is out.

**1970** – With the season set to start, a Milwaukee group headed by Bud Selig and Ed Fitzgerald purchases the Pilots for $10.8 million on April 1 and moves it to Milwaukee with the new name of Brewers. Six days later, the club loses its first game to the Angels, 12–0, before 37,237 at County Stadium. With Dave Bristol as manager, the Brewers finish fourth in the AL West with 65 wins.

**1974** – Eighteen–year–old Robin Yount becomes the Brewers' regular shortstop, debuting on April 5. The Brewers win a franchise–record 76 games under manager Del Crandall.

**1975–76** – Returning to Milwaukee for his final two seasons, Hank Aaron hits 22 home runs to finish his career with a record 755.

**1978** – Paul Molitor makes his Brewers debut on April 7 and helps the club win 93 games under rookie manager George Bamberger.

**1981** – Rollie Fingers wins both the Cy Young and MVP Awards as the Brewers qualify for their first postseason in the strike year's split–season format. The Brewers take the best–of–five Division Series to the final game, but lose to the Yankees.

**1982** – With Harvey Kuenn taking over as manager in mid-year, "Harvey's Wallbangers" win the AL East, with Yount capturing the MVP Award. After losing the first two games the Brewers reound to defeat the California Angels in a five-game ALCS. Alas, Milwaukee, after moving to within one game of glory lose the World Series to the St. Louis Cardinals in seven games.

**1987** – Milwaukee make ML history by winning the first 12 games. Paul Molitor hits in 39 straight games, the longest hitting streak in the AL since Joe DiMaggio's 56 straight in 1941, as the Brewers finish third in the East with 91 wins.

**1992** – Yount records his 3,000th career hit on September 9 as the Brewers finish second in the AL East with rookie skipper Phil Garner at the helm.

**1998** – The Brewers switch to the National League, losing their first NL contest to the Braves, 2–1, on March 31. The Brewers finish fifth in the NL Central with 74 wins.

# PITTSBURGH PIRATES

Originally know as the Alleghenys, the Pittsburgh franchise was a founding member of the old American Association when it began play in 1882. Pittsburgh joined the National League five years later and became known as the Pirates in 1891, after "pirating away" second baseman Lou Bierbauer. The club scuffled until 1900, when an influx of players from the NL's defunct Louisville franchise made the Pirates a power. Led by ex-Louisville stars Honus Wagner and player/manager Fred Clarke, the Pirates ripped off pennants in 1901, 1902, 1903 and 1909, and returned to prominence in the mid-1920s. After a downturn, the Pirates arose again in the 1960s inspired by outfielders Roberto Clemente and Willie Stargell, winning world titles in 1960, 1971 and 1979. The early '90s brought three straight division titles under Jim Leyland, but the Pirates' lack of big-market revenue has proven to be an insurmountable problem in recent years.

**1882** – Pittsburgh's Alleghenys club is a founding member of the new American Association, finishing with a .500 record its first year.

**1887** – The Alleghenys move to the more established National League.

**1900** – A seventh–place club in 1899, the team – now known as the Pirates – finishes second after the addition of Honus Wagner, Tommy Leach, Deacon Phillippe and player/manager Fred Clarke from the NL's defunct Louisville team.

**1901–1903** – The Pirates win three straight National League pennants, going 103–36 in 1902. However, the Bucs lose the first World Series, five games to three, to the Boston Pilgrims in 1903.

**1909** – Led by Wagner's league–leading .339 average, the Pirates celebrate the opening of Forbes Field on June 30 by winning 110 games and the National League pennant. In the World Series, rookie Babe Adams wins three games as the Bucs top the Detroit Tigers in seven games.

**1925** – The Pirates win their first NL pennant in 16 years behind manager Bill McKechnie. In the Series, they fall behind three games to one to the Washington Senators, but take three in a row to win the world championship.

**1927** – Led by outfielders Paul and Lloyd Waner, the Pirates win another NL pennant but are swept by Babe Ruth's Yankees in the World Series.

**1946–52** – Pirate outfielder Ralph Kiner wins seven straight NL home–run crowns, but the Pirates stay buried in the second division. From 1946-57, the Pirates finish higher than sixth place only once.

**1960** – With shortstop Dick Groat winning the MVP Award and Vern Law the Cy Young Award, the Pirates win their first pennant in 33 years. In the World Series against the Yankees, Bill Mazeroski's home run in the bottom of the ninth inning of Game 7 gives the Pirates the world title.

**1970–79** – The Pirates survive the tragic loss of Roberto Clemente in a 1972 plane crash to remain a dominant team. Never finishing more than nine games out of first during the decade, the Bucs win six NL East titles and World Series in 1971 and 1979.

**1990–92** – Led by Barry Bonds, Bobby Bonilla and Doug Drabek, Jim Leyland's Pirates win three straight NL titles, but lose the LCS each time.

# ST LOUIS CARDINALS

Baseball and St. Louis have been a perfect marriage since 1882, when the St. Louis Brown Stockings (or Browns) joined the American Association as a charter member. With first baseman Charlie Comiskey serving as manager, the Browns won four straight championships from 1885-88. Moving over to the National League in 1892, the Browns couldn't repeat their early success, but St. Louis fans continued to support them. Finally, in 1916, the team – now known as the Cardinals – hired Branch Rickey to run the organization. The innovative Rickey invented the farm system, keeping the talent he wanted for his Cardinals and selling the surplus players to other teams for a hefty profit. The first championship arrived in 1926, and the Cardinals have been consistently successful ever since then. What memorable players they've had: Rogers, Hornsby and the Dean brothers, Stan Musial and Bob Gibson, Willy McGee and Mark McGwire. This is truly one of baseball's great franchises.

**1882** – The St. Louis Brown Stockings join the new American Association. St. Louis saloonkeeper Chris Von der Ahe is the club's owner.
**1885–88** – Managed by first baseman Charlie Comiskey, the Browns win four straight AA flags.
**1892** – The AA folds and the Browns join the National League.
**1900** – After changing their nickname to the Perfectos for a year, the club permanently adopts the nickname of Cardinals.
**1916** – The Cardinals hire Branch Rickey, who had been serving as business manager of the crosstown Browns, as their new business manager.
**1920** – The Cardinals move from Robinson Field to the American League Browns' home park, Sportsman's Park.
**1924** – Setting a modern–day NL record, Cardinal second baseman Rogers Hornsby bats .424 for the second of his three .400 seasons.
**1926** – With Hornsby serving as player–manager, the Cardinals win the National League pennant. They then top the Yankees in a seven–game World Series, with Grover Cleveland Alexander coming in to save the final game in heroic fashion.
**1928–31** – The Cardinals win NL pennants in 1928, 1930 and 1931, taking the world championship in '31 as Pepper Martin goes wild in the World Series.
**1934** – With Dizzy Dean winning 30 games and his brother Paul 19, the Cardinals' Gashouse Gang wins a thrilling NL pennant race and then tops the Tigers in seven games in the World Series.
**1942–46** – Young Stan Musial sparks the Redbirds to four pennants in his first five major league seasons, clinching world titles in 1942, 1944 and 1946.
**1964–68** – Bob Gibson pitches the Cardinals to three pennants and two world titles in five years. Gibson posts a 1.12 ERA in 1968 and goes 7–2 with a 1.89 in the three World Series.
**1982–87** – With Whitey Herzog at the helm, the Redbirds win NL pennants in 1982, 1985 and 1987, with a world title in '82.
**1998** – Mark McGwire shatters the single–season home–run record by blasting 70 four–baggers.
**1999** – Fernando Tatis becomes the first player ever to smash to grand slams in the same inning. The home run title remains with Mark McGwire with a third-best-ever 65.
**2000** – Mark McGwire's injury plagued year doesn't stop the Redbirds running away with the NL Central crown before finally losing in the NLCS to the New York Mets.

# N. L. West

**Arizona Diamondbacks**
**Colorado Rockies**
**Los Angeles Dodgers**
**San Diego Padres**
**San Francisco Giants**

# ARIZONA DIAMONDBACKS

Spring training has been an Arizona staple since the late 1940s, when the New York Giants (Phoenix) and Cleveland Indians (Tucson) began training there. For years, though, the lack of an adequate stadium facility prevented the area from actively pursuing a permanent Major League team. That changed in 1990, when the Arizona State Legislature approved funding for a baseball-only stadium in Phoenix, on the condition that the city landed a franchise. Jerry Colangelo, owner of the NBA Phoenix Suns, spearheaded the effort to land an expansion team, and he was awarded the Arizona Diamondbacks franchise in March of 1995, with play set to begin in 1998. Working to build a first-class team, Colangelo aggressively spent money on players and facilities. The first year was successful at the gate (3.6 million fans) but not on the field, as the Diamondbacks finished last with 97 losses. Undeterred, Colangelo spent more money and in 2001 the D-backs were crowned World Champions.

**1990** – The Arizona Legislature approves a tax increase to build a baseball–only stadium in Phoenix, on the condition that the area lands a major league franchise.

**1993** – Phoenix Suns owner Jerry Colangelo announces on November 10 that he is putting together an ownership group to apply for a Major League expansion franchise.

**1994** – Mariposa County unveils plans to build a retractable–roof stadium in downtown Phoenix, and Colangelo presents his plan to the Major League expansion committee on November 2.

**1995** – Major League Baseball awards the Arizona Diamondbacks franchise to the Colangelo group on March 9, with play to begin in 1998. The league in which the team will play is not yet determined, but the new park is given the name Bank One Ballpark. Colangelo hires Joe Garagiola Jr. as general manager in March and names former Yankee skipper Buck Showalter the team's field manager in November.

**1996** – The Diamondbacks announce the signing of San Diego State star Travis Lee, who had been declared a free agent by Major League Baseball after his drafting team committed a procedural error, to a record $10 million contract on October 11.

**1997** – Major League Baseball announces on January 16 that the Diamondbacks will be assigned to the National League's West Division. The Diamondbacks select Cleveland Indians pitcher Brian Anderson with their first pick in the November 18 expansion draft, and trade for Indians third baseman Matt Williams two weeks later. They also sign free–agent shortstop Jay Bell to a five–year, $34 million contract.

**1998** – The Diamondbacks draw 47,465 fans to their first regular–season game against the Colorado Rockies on March 31. They lose 9–2, but Travis Lee collects the team's first hit. For the year the Diamondbacks draw 3.6 million fans despite finishing last in the NL West with a 65–97 record. Lee and Devon White tie for the club's home–run lead with 22, and Andy Benes (14–13) is the top pitcher.

**1999** – After signing premium free agents Randy Johnson, Todd Stottlemyre and Steve Finley during the offseason, the Diamondbacks win 100 games and take the NL West title in their second year, the earliest a baseball expansion franchise has ever reached the postseason. In the postseason, the Diamondbacks lose their Division Series to the New York Mets, 3-1.

**2001** – After holding off the Giants to clinch the NL West, the Diamondbacks reach the World Series after just four years in existence – a major league record. The explosive 1-2 punch of Johnson and Curt Schilling gives them a 2-0 lead but the Yankees rally at home to take a 3-2 lead. However, the D-backs win the final two games at the BOB to clinch the series in seven. Schilling and Johnson, who both pitched in a dramatic Game 7, are awarded co-MVP honors.

# COLORADO ROCKIES

There has never been a major league franchise, expansion or otherwise, quite like the Colorado Rockies. Playing their first two seasons in Denver's Mile High Stadium, a massive structure designed for football, the Rockies drew 80,227 fans to their inaugural game in 1993 and an all-time record total of 4,483,350 fans during their first season. Rockies games have been as unique as they have been well-attended. Playing in Denver's mile-high altitude, Rockies contests usually have been wild, high-scoring affairs in which no lead was ever safe. In 1996, for instance, the average score of a game at Coors Field, the Rockies' current home, was Colorado 8, Opponents 7. Colorado's rabid fans have eaten it all up, and it hasn't hurt that the Rockies have generally been successful as well as colorful. The Rockies made the playoffs in 1995, their third season, and until 1999, they had never finished in last place. The only thing they've missed thus far is a championship.

**1991** – Major league owners award expansion franchises to Denver and Miami on July 5, with the teams scheduled to begin play in 1993. The Colorado franchise announces that it has selected the nickname of Rockies.

**1992** – The Rockies name Don Baylor as manager on October 27. In the baseball expansion draft on November 17, the Rockies select Atlanta Braves pitcher David Nied as their first selection. They also sign Andres Galarraga as a free agent, and swing a deal for Dante Bichette.

**1993** – The Rockies begin play on April 5 and are shut out by the Mets' Dwight Gooden at Shea Stadium, 3–0. Four days later, they open at Denver's Mile High Stadium before an all–time Opening Day record crowd of 80,227 as they beat the Montreal Expos, 11–4. For the year they draw an all–time record 4.48 million people, including nine crowds of 70,000 or more, as they finish sixth in the seven–team Western Division with a 67–95 record. Galarraga leads the NL with a .370 batting average.

**1994** – With the season shortened by a players' strike that ends the season in August, the Rockies go 53–64 to finish third in the West, which now consists of only four clubs. The Rockies draw 3.2 million fans in their final campaign at Mile High, despite the abbreviated season.

**1995** – Coors Field opens on April 26 with the Rockies defeating the Mets, 11–9, on Bichette's three–run homer in the bottom of the 14th inning before 50,021 fans. For the year the Rockies go 77–67 and qualify for the playoffs as the National League's wild–card team. Bichette, the club's leading hitter, nearly wins the Triple Crown as he leads the NL in home runs (40) and RBI (128) while finishing third in batting average (.340). In the playoffs the Rockies are defeated by the Atlanta Braves in the Division Series, three games to one.

**1996** – The Rockies finish third in the West with an 83–79 record as Galarraga leads the NL in homers (47) and RBI (150). The Dodgers' Hideo Nomo does the unthinkable on September 17, throwing a no–hitter against the Rockies at Coors Field.

**1997** – The Rockies go 83–79 and finish third again as Larry Walker hits .366 and leads the NL with 49 home runs.

**1998** – The Rockies slide to fourth with a 77–85 record despite Walker's league–leading .363 average. After the season, Baylor is replaced as manager by Jim Leyland.

**1999** – The Rockies finish last (72–90) for the first time in their history despite Walker's league–leading .379 average. Walker becomes the first player since Al Simmons (1929–31) to hit over .360 in three straight seasons.

# LOS ANGELES DODGERS

The Dodgers' glorious history began back in 1884, when a team known as the Brooklyn Bridegrooms joined the old American Association. In 1889 the Bridegrooms won the AA pennant, then switched to the National League and won the NL pennant a year later. Success grew more sporadic as the 20th century dawned and the team later took the nickname Robins. It wasn't until 1941, when Leo Durocher led the team to its first pennant in 21 years, that the Dodgers turned the corner. A year later Branch Rickey took over as general manager, and when Rickey broke baseball's color line by signing Jackie Robinson late in 1945, everything was in place to make the Dodgers the league's dominant team. The club won six NL pennants in Robinson's 10 Dodger seasons, and the move to Los Angeles in 1958 helped them become even more dominant. Since heading West, the Dodgers have won nine NL pennants and five world titles.

**1884** – The Brooklyn Bridegrooms join the three–year–old American Association, playing their games in 2,000–seat Washington Park.

**1889–90** – Behind Parisian Bob Caruthers' 40 wins, the Bridegrooms win the 1889 AA pennant. They switch to the bigger National League prior to the 1890 campaign and finish first again.

**1899–1900** – Now known as the Superbas, Brooklyn picks up several stars from the great Baltimore Oriole squads of the 1890s and wins back–to–back pennants.

**1913–20** – Renamed the Dodgers, the club moves into a new park, Ebbets Field, in 1913 and rewards its fans with pennants in 1916 and 1920. Unfortunately the Dodgers lose both World Series.

**1941** – With Larry MacPhail as general manager and Leo Durocher as manager, the Dodgers win their first pennant since 1920. In the World Series they're about to tie the Yankees at two games apiece when Mickey Owen's dropped third strike costs them victory in Game 4. A day later it's all over.

**1947** – Signed by Dodger general manager Branch Rickey to be the first black major leaguer since the 19th century, Jackie Robinson helps the Dodgers win the NL pennant in his rookie year.

**1949–56** – With Robinson, Roy Campanella, Duke Snider and Pee Weese Reese leading the way, the Dodgers win pennants in 1949, 1952, 1953, 1955 and 1956, with a couple of other near–misses. They play the Yankees each time and finally win their first World Series in 1955. "Next Year" is finally here!

**1957** – Dodger owner Walter O'Malley stuns the city by announcing that the Dodgers will move to Los Angeles in 1958, with the New York Giants joining them in San Francisco.

**1959** – The Dodgers win the NL pennant in their second year in Los Angeles, then beat the Chicago White Sox in the World Series in front of record crowds of 92,000–plus at their temporary home, the Coliseum.

**1963–66** – After moving into Dodger Stadium in 1962, the Dodgers ride the left arm of Sandy Koufax to pennants in 1963, 1965 and 1966, with world titles in '63 and '65.

**1974–81** – The Dodgers win four more pennants in 1974, 1977, 1978 and 1981, the latter three with Tommy Lasorda at the helm. The 1981 club is the only one of these teams to win the World Series, stopping the Yankees in six games.

**1988** – Huge underdogs in both the NLCS and World Series, the Dodgers ride the magic of National League MVP Kirk Gibson and Cy Young Award winner Orel Hershiser all the way to the world championship.

# SAN DIEGO PADRES

Bounded by the Pacific Ocean to the west, Los Angeles to the north, the desert to the east and Mexico to the south, San Diego has never had an easy time supporting major league baseball. Underfinanced in their early years, the Padres finished last in each of their first six seasons and didn't post their a winning record until 1978, their 10th season in the National League. An influx of veterans helped the club win its first pennant in 1984, and the Padres had a near-miss five years later, finishing only three games out of first. The club's greatest success has come in recent years, with a division title in 1996 and a trip to the World Series two years later. Even then, the Padres have had trouble keeping the high-salaried players who got them to the top, and the club still has never had more than two winning seasons in a row. Fortunately one player stuck around through thick and thin: Tony Gwynn, who retired in 2001 after 20 seasons in San Diego.

**1968** – The National League awards an expansion franchise to San Diego on May 27, with the club scheduled to begin play at new San Diego Stadium (later known as Jack Murphy and Qualcomm) the next season. In the expansion draft on October 14, outfielder Ollie Brown is the Padres' first pick.

**1969** – Opening at home before 23,370 fans on April 8, the Padres begin their history with a three-game sweep of the Houston Astros. Success is short-lived as manager Preston Gomez' club winds up last in the NL West with 110 losses.

**1974** – After five straight last-place finishes, McDonald's founder Ray Kroc purchases the Padres, ensuring that the club will stay in San Diego and be financially competitive at last. The Padres finish last again, but Kroc's promise to produce a winner helps the club draw 1 million fans for the first time.

**1976** – Randy Jones goes 22–14 with 25 complete games to win the Cy Young Award as the Padres finish fifth with 73 wins.

**1978** – The Padres go 84-78 for their first winning season, with rookie manager Roger Craig and Cy Young Award winner Gaylord Perry (21–6) leading the way.

**1982** – Tony Gwynn makes his major league debut with two hits against the Phillies on July 19 as the Padres go 81-81 under Dick Williams.

**1984** – Kroc dies on January 14, but Gwynn hits an NL-best .351 to lead the Padres to their first division title. The Padres come back from a two-game deficit to win the best-of-five NLCS over the Cubs, but lose the World Series to the Detroit Tigers in five games.

**1989** – With Gwynn winning his fourth batting crown and reliever Mark Davis taking the Cy Young Award, the Padres close with a 29-10 surge to finish in second place, only three games behind the division-winning Giants.

**1994** – In the much-abbreviated season, Gwynn hits .394, the highest average in the majors since 1941, for his fifth batting title, but the Padres finish last in the West.

**1996** – Ken Caminiti wins the NL MVP Award as the Padres take the NL West title with a season-ending sweep of the Dodgers. In the Division Series, the Padres are swept by the St. Louis Cardinals.

**1998** – The Padres win a club-record 98 games as they win the NL West. The Padres then take the Division Series (Astros) and NLCS (Braves), but are swept by the Yankees in the World Series.

**1999** – Gwynn gets his 3,000th hit on August 6, but the Padres fall to fourth in the West with 74 wins.

**2001** – Gwynn calls it a career at the end of the regular season. He joins his alma mater, San Diego State, as the Aztecs baseball coach in 2002.

# SAN FRANCISCO GIANTS

Looking at his team one day in 1885, New York Gothams manager Jim Mutrie exclaimed, "My big fellows! My Giants!" Thus was born one of the most famous team nicknames in sports history. The New Yorkers were Giants for much of their history, especially during the long managerial tenure of John McGraw. The "Little Napoleon" won his first pennant behind the pitching of Christy Mathewson in 1904, and the Giants would dominate the NL for the next two decades. Three more pennants followed under McGraw's successor, Bill Terry, but the most glorious Giant pennant of all came in 1951, when Bobby Thomson's "Shot Heard 'Round the World" capped the most amazing late-season comeback in baseball history. Three years later, Willie Mays paced the Giants to their last world title in New York. Moving to San Francisco in 1958, the Giants have continued to succeed, with two more pennants (1962 and 1989) and four more division titles (1971, 1987, 1997, 2000).

**1883** – The National League returns to New York for the first time since 1876 when the New York Gothams join the league.

**1888** – Now known as the Giants, the New Yorkers win the first of two straight NL titles under manager Jim Mutrie.

**1902** – John McGraw becomes the Giants' manager in midseason, taking over a club that will finish last.

**1904-05** – Iron Man Joe McGinnity (35–8) and Christy Mathewson (33–12) pace the Giants to McGraw's first flag in 1904. A year later, the Giants win both the pennant and the World Series (McGraw refused to play the AL champions so there was no Series in 1904), topping the Philadelphia Athletics in five games.

**1908** – Rookie Fred Merkle's failure to touch second base after a game-winning hit costs the Giants a crucial late-September game, and they finish in a tie with the Cubs and lose a playoff.

**1911-13** – The Giants win three straight pennants, but lose the World Series each time.

**1921-24** – The Giants become the first 20th-century team to win four straight pennants. They top the Yankees in the 1921 and '22 World Series, but lose to the Yankees in 1923 and to the Washington Senators in '24.

**1933-37** – McGraw retires in the middle of 1932, but first baseman/manager Bill Terry leads the Giants to three pennants in his first five years at the helm. The Giants defeat the Senators for the 1933 world title, but lose to the Yankees in 1936 and 1937.

**1951** – Thirteen-and-a-half games out of first in mid-August, the Giants catch fire, force a best-of-three playoff with the Dodgers and then beat them on a three-run homer by Bobby Thomson in the bottom of the ninth inning of the third game. The Giants lose the Series to the Yankees, but few people care.

**1954** – Willie Mays wins his first MVP Award as the Giants win the NL pennant, then stun the favored Indians with a four-game Series sweep. Mays sets the tone for Series with his catch to deny Vic Wertz a probable game-winning hit in Game One.

**1958** – The Giants abandon New York after 75 seasons and move to San Francisco, with Seals Stadium their first home.

**1962** – As in 1951, the Giants tie the Dodgers for first place; come from behind in the ninth inning to win the third and final playoff game; and then lose the World Series to the Yankees.

**1989** – Roger Craig manages the Giants to their first pennant since '62, but the club is swept by the crosstown A's in the World Series marred by the earthquake which hit Candlestick Parkt just a few minutes before Game Two is due to start.

**2000** – A new era dawns as Pacific Bell Park replaces the notoriously cold and windy field at Candlestick Point, latterly known as 3-Com Park.The Giants respond by winning the NL West and second baseman Jeff Kent wins the MVP award.

**2001** – Barry Bonds compiles a season for the ages, finishing with 73 homers, 177 walks and a .863 slugging percentage – all new major league records – and is awarded the NL MVP.

**45**

# PITCHERS

Grover Alexander
Three Finger Brown
Steve Carlton
Roger Clemens
Dizzy Dean
Dennis Eckersley
Bob Feller
Rollie Fingers
Whitey Ford
Bob Gibson
Lefty Grove
Walter Johnson
Sandy Koufax
Greg Maddux
Juan Marichal
Christy Mathewson
Satchel Paige
Jim Palmer
Nolan Ryan
Warren Spahn
Cy Young

# GROVER CLEVELAND ALEXANDER

**Grover Cleveland Alexander**
**Born:** February 26 1887, Elba, Nebraska
**Died:** November 4 1950, St. Paul, Nebraska
**Throws:** Right
**Bats:** Right
**Height:** 6-1
**Weight:** 185

**"Less than a foot made the difference between a hero and bum."**
**- Grover Alexander on the subtleties of pitching.**

The Cardinals catcher Bob O'Farrell called it "maybe the most famous strikeout in the whole history of baseball." It was the 1926 Fall Classic. St. Louis was edging the Yankees 3-2 in Game 7. With the bases loaded and two out, Tony Lazzeri stepped to the plate. The Cardinals manager Rogers Hornsby, sensing the game and perhaps the World Series slipping away, bought in his trusted, but aging, ace. Legend has it that Pete Alexander was still recovering from a hard night celebrating his Game 6 victory when Hornsby called for him. Nonetheless, the 39-year old fanned Lazzeri in three pitches and the Yankees failed to score in the next two innings. Old Pete had helped the Cardinals to their first World Championship.

Grover Cleveland Alexander etched his place in the game's history with this strikeout but his career was defined by more than one pitch. From 1911 to 1930 he would be one of the era's most dominating pitchers. Playing much of his career in the hitter-friendly Baker Bowl, he pitched 90 shutouts, second only behind Walter Johnson, and won 373 games to equal the National League record held by Christy Mathewson. In 1916 he pitched 16 shutouts, which still stands as a major league record. He had consecutive 30-win seasons from 1915 to 1917. He was renowned for both his durability and his efficiency. Pitching for Philadelphia, he once beat St. Louis in both games of a double-header, the last being a 58-minute shutout enabling the Phillies to catch their train out of St. Louis. As a forty year old in 1927 he won 21 games.

Pete Alexander is also famous for his legendary drinking habits but the story is a sad one. Suffering from both epilepsy and deafness caused by his military service during the War in 1918, he returned to the majors a changed man. Seemingly haunted by the war and the increasingly severe fits he suffered during games, Alexander turned to alcohol and his drinking soon became notorious around the leagues. But he was too great a pitcher for this to be his only legacy.

Playing for the Phillies, the Cubs and the Cardinals he averaged 20 wins a season for his career winning three pennants and the famous 1926 World Series championship.

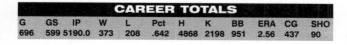

## CAREER TOTALS

| G | GS | IP | W | L | Pct | H | K | BB | ERA | CG | SHO |
|---|----|----|----|----|----|----|----|----|----|----|----|
| 696 | 599 | 5190.0 | 373 | 208 | .642 | 4868 | 2198 | 951 | 2.56 | 437 | 90 |

# MORDECAI THREE-FINGER BROWN

**Mordecai Peter Centennial Brown**
**Born:** October 19 1876, Nyesville, Indiana
**Died:** February 14 1948, Terre Haute, Indiana
**Throws:** Right
**Bats:** Both
**Height:** 5-10
**Weight:** 175

**"Gee, he was one of the wonders of baseball." – Al Bridwell on Three-Finger Brown**

As a seven-year old child, Mordecai Brown lost two of his fingers in an accident with a corn shredder. It could have ended his baseball career before it got going. Instead it sent him to the Hall of Fame.

"That old paw served me pretty well in its time," said Brown of his hand. "It gave me a firmer grip and greater dip." His index finger was amputated at the knuckle, which enabled him to apply more spin than a White House speechwriter. Brown established one of the best curveballs in the game's history as he rivaled Christy Mathewson as the outstanding National League pitcher in the early 1900s.

Tagged "Miner" by his teammates because of his time spent in the coalmines before his break in baseball, Brown made his major league debut in 1903 with the St. Louis Cardinals. The following season with the Cubs he went 15-10 with a 1.86 ERA and by 1906 he was one of the most feared pitchers in the National League. His ERA of 1.04 is the lowest recorded in the National League in the 20th century and he went 26-6 to spark a run of awesome pitching. Beginning with that 1906 campaign he had six consecutive 20-win seasons, with his ERA rising above 1.99 only once. The Cubs won the pennant in 1906 and captured back-to-back World Series in 1907 and 1908. They won the pennant again in 1910.

In 1908 it was Brown who was on the mound in the playoff game against the Giants after Fred Merkle's boner had left the teams tied. After Chicago's Jack Pfiester had walked two and given up three hits, Brown was brought on in relief. He pitched perfectly, shutting out the Giants to win the game and the pennant. It would be the last time he would make it to the World Series. The Cubs, too. After leading the league in wins in 1909 he tore a ligament in his leg and his best days were over. He jumped from team to team, playing with the Reds and Brooklyn, St. Louis and Chicago of the Federal League before returning to the Cubs in 1916 to end his career.

His lifetime ERA of 2.06 is bettered by only Ed Walsh, Addie Joss and Smokey Joe Wood and without his sharp curve, that forced one ground ball after another, "Tinker to Evers to Chance" may never have found its place in baseball vernacular. The poem eulogized the Cubs' infield trio of shortstop Joe Tinker, second base Johnny Evers and first base Frank Chance, and the double plays they turned.

He died in 1948 and was elected into the Hall of Fame at Cooperstown the following year.

**48**

## CAREER TOTALS

| G | GS | IP | W | L | Pct | H | K | BB | ERA | CG | SHO |
|---|----|----|----|----|----|----|----|----|----|----|----|
| 481 | 332 | 3172.1 | 239 | 129 | .649 | 2708 | 1375 | 673 | 2.06 | 271 | 55 |

# STEVE CARLTON

**Steven Norman Carlton**
**Born:** December 22 1944, Miami, Florida.
**Throws:** Left
**Bats:** Left
**Height:** 6-4
**Weight:** 210

**"I've never paced myself. I've always thrown everything as hard as I can for as long as I can." - Steve Carlton**

The pitch was to become his signature. Breaking down and in on right-handers, it was devastatingly effective. "If Carl Hubbell will be known as having the best screwball in the history of the game and Sandy Koufax the best curveball, Steve Carlton will go down as having the best slider," said Tim McCarver. Steve Carlton began developing his hard late-breaking slider in 1969 and a star was born. Alongside a fastball he threw for strikes and a decent curve, Carlton's newest pitch helped him improve with emphatic results. In '69 his ERA dropped by 0.82, his strikeouts rose by 48 and most importantly his wins increased to 17. And things just kept getting better.

Carlton had joined the Cardinals in 1965 and in 1967 won 14 games to help St. Louis to the World Series. He started Game 5 and gave up only two hits and one run in six innings. The Cardinals won the Fall Classic and Carlton had gained some invaluable experience. In 1969 he equaled the since-broken record striking out 19 against the Mets. After a contract dispute soured his 1970 campaign, he bounced back winning 20 games in 1971 and was traded to the Phillies in 1972.

From 1972 to 1986 Carlton won four Cy Young Awards becoming the first pitcher to do so. He had five 20-win seasons and led the league in Ks on six occasions. His finest year was his first in Philadelphia. In 1972 he went 27-10 with a 1.97 ERA and 310 strikeouts to capture his first Cy Young. His record included a 15-game winning streak, 30 complete games and eight shutouts. But despite his awesome performance the Phillies won only 59 games that year. Carlton's luck did improve in 1980 when he captured his third Cy Young Award and the Phillies made it to the World Series. He beat the Royals twice and posted a 2.40 ERA as Philly won the World Series.

Carlton was always something of an enigma. A stoic on and off the mound, he refused to talk with the press for more than a decade. He practiced Kung fu and became fanatical about his training regime, including repeatedly twisting his pitching arm in a barrel of rice to increase its strength.

His career declined rapidly after 1984. Plagued by injuries he went from one franchise to the next, playing in San Francisco, Chicago, Cleveland and Minnesota before finally retiring in 1988, second in career strikeouts. He was elected into the Hall of Fame in 1994, with Tim McCarver's words echoing around Cooperstown.

## CAREER TOTALS

| G | GS | IP | W | L | Pct | H | K | BB | ERA | CG | SHO |
|---|----|----|----|----|----|----|----|----|----|----|----|
| 741 | 709 | 5217.1 | 329 | 244 | .574 | 4672 | 4136 | 1833 | 3.22 | 254 | 55 |

# ROGER CLEMENS

**Roger Clemens**
**Born:** August 4 1962, Dayton, Ohio
**Throws:** Right
**Bats:** Right
**Height:** 6-4
**Weight:** 230

"If you don't come out here with the ambition to be a champion, then you have a real problem. You shouldn't put on a uniform." – **Roger Clemens**

When Roger Clemens took the mound for Game 4 of the 1999 World Series, with New York up 3-0, the air around Yankee Stadium hung thick with expectation, like a sentence waiting to be finished. There was a game to win. A ring to be clinched. And demons to exorcise.

"I think he'd trade all his Cy Youngs for the chance to play in another World Series," said Paul Quantrill, Clemens' teammate in Toronto. He didn't have to. The Yankees had afforded him the opportunity. He gave up just four hits and no runs in his seven innings. New York swept Atlanta. Clemens had his World Series. Sentence completed.

Clemens began his career with the Red Sox in 1983. After impressing in the minors, he went 9-4 in 1984 and bounced back from shoulder surgery with his breakthrough year in 1986. That year Clemens went 24-4, with a 2.48 ERA and 238 Ks. He collected his first Cy Young and won the AL MVP Award. He set a major league record fanning 20 in a 3-1 win against Seattle in April. The Red Sox advanced to the World Series but lost to the Mets. Clemens received two no-decisions. He would have to wait another 13 years before he would return to the game's biggest stage.

In between these two World Series appearances, Clemens has constructed a career and a reputation as impressive as his stuff. He won his second Cy Young in 1987, another in '91 and after leaving Beantown for Toronto, again won consecutive Cy Youngs in 1997 and '98. Elsewhere, in 1992 he equaled Rube Waddell and Walter Johnson's AL record with his 7th consecutive 200-strikeout season. In his last season in Boston he again struck out 20 batters against Detroit. In 1998 he joined Grover Alexander, Lefty Grove and Sandy Koufax as the only men to have won the pitching Triple Crown two straight years.

But in the postseason, the Rocket Man spluttered. In championship series starts he was 1-2 with a 4.10 ERA to go alongside his two no decisions in the World Series. He left Boston without a ring. He fled Toronto to find one. Looks like he chose the right city.

After the joy of '99, Clemens went 13-8 during the 2000 season and won Game 2 of the World Series, behind eight scoreless innings of two-hit ball, helping the Yankees to a three-peat. In 2001 Clemens, at 39, was the Yankees' dominant starter going 20-3—becoming the first player ever to start a season 20-1—with a 3.51 ERA to help New York to another division crown. He also became the first pitcher in history to receive the Cy Young Award six times. The Yanks again made the World Series but were beaten in seven games by the Arizona Diamondbacks in one of the most thrilling Series in history. Clemens won Game 3 and pitched six strong innings in Game 7.

## CAREER TOTALS

| G | GS | IP | W | L | Pct | H | K | BB | ERA | CG | SHO |
|---|---|---|---|---|---|---|---|---|---|---|---|
| 545 | 544 | 3887.0 | 280 | 145 | .659 | 3306 | 3717 | 1258 | 3.10 | 116 | 45 |

# DIZZY DEAN

**Jay Hanna Dean**
**Born:** January 16 1910, Lucas, Arkansas
**Died:** July 17 1974, Reno, Nevada
**Throws:** Right
**Bats:** Right
**Height:** 6-2
**Weight:** 182

**"When ole Diz was out there pitching it was more than just another ballgame. It was a regular three-ring circus and everybody was wide awake and enjoying being alive."**
**– Pepper Martin on Dizzy Dean**

The nickname Dizzy was a no-brainer. Literally.

After being beaned in the 1934 World Series, the Cardinals ace was taken to hospital. "The doctors x-rayed my head and found nothing," said Dizzy after being released. The tag fitted him like a glove.

Jay Hanna Dean was the son of an Arkansas sharecropper and a quintessential country boy. Born in 1911, Dean pitched for his local high school team but preferred to keep this as his only scholarly commitment. Without any formal education, he joined the Army at 16 before joining the Cardinals franchise in 1930. By 1932 Dean was beginning to leave his mark on the majors. He went 18-15 with a 3.30 ERA and a league-leading 191 strikeouts but was receiving just as much publicity for his hilarious braggadocio and homespun sayings.

He was brash, loud and a joy to watch. As a member of the notorious Gashouse Gang he went 30-7 in 1934 and alongside his brother, Paul "Daffy" Dean, took the Cardinals to the World Series. Dizzy went 2-1 with a 1.73 ERA while Daffy won both his starts. St. Louis beat Detroit in seven games and Dizzy won the National League's MVP.

Dean led the National League in complete games from 1933-36 and in strikeouts from 1932-35. He had three 20-win seasons and was even used as a reliever, notching 11 saves in 1936 whilst going 24-13 with a 3.17 ERA.

His career began to falter when, in the 1937 All Star game, his toe was broken by an Earl Averill liner. The injury forced Dean to alter his mechanics and subsequently the change caused a weakening of his right arm. He was traded to the Cubs and continued to pitch until 1941 but he never repeated the numbers of his prime. He then took the natural step for someone who turned "slid" into "slud" and "threw" into "throwed". He became an announcer.

Despite the outrage of the St. Louis Board of Education, Dean was a huge success in the booth. He ambushed the English language from all sides and his malapropisms became renowned. With Stan Musial at the plate, he used to announce, "Moozel looks mighty hitterish up there." In 1947 Dean declared that he could do better than the woeful Browns pitchers. Six years after his last major league start; the St. Louis president gave Dean the opportunity to do so. On September 28, Dean pitched four scoreless innings before leaving the game. He never pitched again and returned to the booth, where he carried on having the last word.

## CAREER TOTALS

| G | GS | IP | W | L | Pct | H | K | BB | ERA | CG | SHO |
|---|----|----|----|----|-----|-----|------|-----|------|-----|-----|
| 317 | 230 | 1967.1 | 150 | 83 | .644 | 1919 | 1163 | 453 | 3.02 | 154 | 26 |

# DENNIS ECKERSLEY

**Dennis Lee Eckersley**
**Born:** October 3 1954, Oakland, California
**Throws:** Right
**Bats:** Right
**Height:** 6-2
**Weight:** 190

**"The ace of all aces" – Oakland A's coach Doug Rader on Dennis Eckersley**

In 1987 Dennis Eckersley's career was in jeopardy. Having made his Major League debut as a member of the Cleveland Indians' starting rotation in 1975, having gone 20-8 with a 2.99 ERA with the Red Sox in 1978, having established himself as one of the game's most promising young hurlers, he was now beset with shoulder injuries that had begun to plague his career as early as 1980.

He had arrived in Oakland searching for rejuvenation. He found it in the bullpen. When the A's closer Jay Howell developed bone chips in his elbow before the 1987 All-Star game, manager Tony La Russa and pitching coach Dave Duncan gave the role to the newly-acquired Eckersley. It turned out to be something of a smart move. He racked up 16 saves that first season and then proceeded to redefine the term closer with 45 saves in 1989. Another 48 in 1990. A further 51 in '92. His control, which had always been his ace card, was awesome. In his new role he walked just 16 batters in three seasons from 1989–91 and never gave up more than 17 in a season during his 12 years in the bullpen.

The Eck was easy to love, with his flowing hair, his excitable manner and his enthusiasm. He talked a great game, too, referring to a weak pitch as "salad" and a big game as a "Bogart." But his career wasn't without its battles. The pitcher who made his name living on the edges of the plate chose the same route away from the mound; Eckersley lost control. He became a hero in Cleveland and then Boston. But with the attention and the adoration came problems. He partied too hard, drank too much. In 1986, Eckersley decided to go into to rehab and came out dry. That he stayed that way is probably his greatest save.

Eckersley retired in 1998, after short spells with the Cardinals and the Red Sox, as probably the greatest closer in baseball history. His 390 saves ranks third all-time to Lee Smith and John Franco. He won the MVP Award in 1992 after posting a 1.91 ERA and 51 saves. In a remarkable four-year period, from 1988 through 1992, he averaged an unbelievable 0.91 walks per 9 innings with a 1.90 ERA and 350 strikeouts. He helped the A's to a World Series championship in 1989, bouncing back from serving up the Kirk Gibson homer during the 1988 Fall Classic. Universally loved by baseball and always remembered as the man who turned both his pitching career and his life around, Eckersley will unquestionably be elected to Cooperstown when he becomes eligible in 2003.

| CAREER TOTALS | | | | | | | | | | | |
|---|---|---|---|---|---|---|---|---|---|---|---|
| G | GS | IP | W | L | Pct | H | K | BB | ERA | CG | SHO |
| 1071 | 361 | 3285.2 | 197 | 171 | .535 | 3076 | 2401 | 738 | 3.50 | 100 | 20 |

# BOB FELLER

**Robert William Feller**
**Born:** November 3 1918, Van Meter, Iowa
**Throws:** Right
**Bats:** Right
**Height:** 6-0
**Weight:** 185

**"I just reared back and let them go." – Bob Feller**

If you want a dictionary definition of the word phenom, look no further than Robert William Feller.

Signed by the Indians while still at high school, he fanned 15 St. Louis Browns in his first ever start in 1936 and followed it up by striking out 17 Athletics to establish a new American League record. He was still only 17-years old.

The Indians were fined for signing Feller while he was still attending high school but they still got their man. As an Iowa farm boy from Van Meter, he gained notoriety for his overpowering fastball while playing American Legion baseball. Once he had made it to The Show things didn't change. It was still his money pitch. Clocked at over 100 mph, Feller's heater helped him to many outstanding outings. In 1938 he set a new major league record by striking out 18 Tigers. He pitched three no-hitters, his first coming on Opening Day 1940, 12 one-hit games and in 1946 set a major league single-season record with 348 Ks. By the time he was 23-years old he had already won 109 games and had been a 20-game winner three times.

In late 1941, after the attack on Pearl Harbor, Feller enlisted. He spent 44 months with the U.S Navy and missed three full seasons. He returned in 1945 and didn't miss a beat. He won five in just nine starts and in 1946, his first full season back, went 26-15 with a 2.18 ERA including a no-hitter against the Yankees. In 1948 Feller played in his only World Series and lost twice to the Braves. But his career wasn't finished. He threw his third no-hitter in 1951 before finally retiring in 1956 with six strikeout titles and six 20-win seasons.

He entered the Hall of Fame with 266 career victories, 2,581 Ks and a 3.25 ERA. His numbers may be reduced by the time he spent serving his country but his reputation isn't. He still remains as one of the fastest pitchers of all time. When Robb Nen's pitch in Game 1 of the 1997 World Series was clocked at 102 mph, Rapid Robert was asked by *Baseball Weekly* if that was the fastest he had ever seen. "That," Feller replied, "was my changeup."

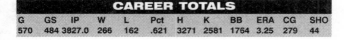

## CAREER TOTALS

| G | GS | IP | W | L | Pct | H | K | BB | ERA | CG | SHO |
|---|---|---|---|---|---|---|---|---|---|---|---|
| 570 | 484 | 3827.0 | 266 | 162 | .621 | 3271 | 2581 | 1764 | 3.25 | 279 | 44 |

# ROLLIE FINGERS

**Roland Glen Fingers**
**Born:** August 25 1946, Steubenville, Ohio
**Throws:** Right
**Bats:** Right
**Height:** 6-4
**Weight:** 195

**"I would plan my pitches days in advance of my start and get so wound up I couldn't sleep." – Rollie Fingers on why he moved to the bullpen**

As an integral part of Charlie Finley's mustachioed gang, Rollie Fingers helped the charismatic Oakland A's to three straight World Series in the 1970s and helped carve himself a niche as one of the game's most dominating closers.

Fingers started his career with the A's in 1968 as a starter but his highly-strung demeanor wasn't ideally suited to that of a rotation, where he had three days to think about his next start. He needed to pitch everyday. Converted into a closer in 1972 he became a classic example of the changing role of the modern-day bullpen, taking to his new relief role like a duck to water.

After racking up 21 saves during the regular season, Fingers continued his dominance in the 1972 World Series. He earned saves in both Games 2 and 7 as Oakland beat Cincinnati in seven games. In 1973 and '74 he was again a critical component in the A's successes. He earned two saves against the Mets in '73, finishing the Series with an astonishing 0.66 ERA. The following October was no different as Fingers again shone under the greatest of pressure winning one and saving two as the A's defeated the Dodgers, 4-1 for their third consecutive World Series crown.

Armed with a lethal sinking fastball, Fingers had established a reputation that made him an extremely valuable commodity. He had three rings and 84 saves from '73 to '76. But unable to reach an agreement with Finley and his A's, Fingers took his rings, his sinker and his reputation and signed as a free agent with the San Diego Padres.

Fingers played in San Diego for four seasons before being traded back to the American League, via St. Louis, with the Brewers. He was an instant hit in Milwaukee winning both the AL MVP and the Cy Young award thanks to a league-leading 28 saves with a 1.04 ERA. In 78 innings pitched he walked 13 and struck out 61.

Fingers hung up his spikes in 1984 after suffering from tendonitis and a herniated disk. Elected into baseball's Hall of Fame in 1992 he ranks sixth all-time in saves and is one of the few players to have had his number retired by three different ballclubs.

## CAREER TOTALS

| G | GS | IP | W | L | Pct | H | K | BB | ERA | CG | SHO |
|---|---|---|---|---|---|---|---|---|---|---|---|
| 944 | 37 | 1701.1 | 114 | 118 | .491 | 1474 | 1299 | 492 | 2.90 | 4 | 2 |

# WHITEY FORD

**Edward Charles Ford**
**Born:** October 21 1928, New York, New York
**Throws:** Left
**Bats:** Left
**Height:** 5-10
**Weight:** 180

**"The way to make coaches think you're in shape in the spring is to get a tan."**
**– Whitey Ford**

"I don't care what the situation was, how high the stakes were – the bases could be loaded and the pennant riding on every pitch, it never bothered him," said Mickey Mantle. "He always pitched his game." It seemed as if New York Yankees lefty Whitey Ford had ice running through his veins. His career record of 236-106 gives him the best winning percentage (.690) of any 20th century pitcher. Quite simply he was the clutch performer of his time. Of any time.

Between 1953 and 1960 he averaged 16 wins but the greater the pressure, the better he seemed to pitch. Because he didn't have overpowering stuff, Ford is often described as crafty and was regularly accused of doctoring the ball but what Ford had in abundance was nerve. He believed in himself and remained cool. The World Series was made for him.

In his 22 starts he pitched 146 innings, won 10 and fanned 94. In the 1960 and '61 Fall Classics, he pitched 32 consecutive scoreless innings. All are World Series records. "If you had one game to win, and your life depended on it, you'd want him to pitch it," said his manager Casey Stengel.

Ford's regular season numbers were also outstanding. In 1961 he won the Cy Young Award going 25-4 with a 3.21 ERA and a career-high 209 strikeouts. He was also awarded the World Series MVP as the Yankees beat the Reds. In 1963 he won 24 games. Ford only twice posted losing records in his 17 years in baseball and Stengel, who changed his rotation so Ford always pitched against the tougher opposition, credited him with slowing down the Yankees' demise. "The Yankees would have fallen a lot sooner if it wasn't for my banty rooster," he once said.

Ford was also legendary for his friendship with Mickey Mantle. Joined at the hip, Casey Stengel dubbed them the "Whiskey Slicks" because of their appetite for the New York nightlife and the carefree attitude both exhibited. Ford and Mantle's careers remained intertwined when both the Mick and Slick were inducted into Cooperstown in 1974. "I couldn't love him more if he was my own brother," Mantle once said.

He retired in 1967 with a 2.75 ERA, 11 pennants and six World Series championship wins.

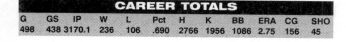

## CAREER TOTALS

| G | GS | IP | W | L | Pct | H | K | BB | ERA | CG | SHO |
|---|---|---|---|---|---|---|---|---|---|---|---|
| 498 | 438 | 3170.1 | 236 | 106 | .690 | 2766 | 1956 | 1086 | 2.75 | 156 | 45 |

# BOB GIBSON

**Robert Gibson**
**Born:** November 9 1935, Omaha, Nebraska
**Throws:** Right
**Bats:** Right
**Height:** 6-1
**Weight:** 195

**"Most of the time when a guy gets hit, it's his fault. You don't usually hit a guy if he's paying attention." – Bob Gibson**

It was 1968. The year of the pitcher. And one hurler stood above the rest.

"You looked at him on the mound," said baseball writer Roger Angell, "and he was dark and forbidding. He never smiled. He was never pleasant." But he led the league in every other category. For the entirety of the season he was practically unhitable. He averaged a meager 1.83 walks per nine innings, 7.92 Ks and held the league to a measly .184 batting average. No smiles. No pleasantries. Just pure chin music. "Bob Gibson was the most formidable and scary pitcher of all time," Angell concluded. Few would argue.

Despite being very ill as a small child Gibson was a standout in many sports. After attending Creighton University on a basketball scholarship, he graduated and spent a year touring with the Harlem Globetrotters before eventually gravitating towards baseball for good. He signed with the St. Louis Cardinals in 1959 and pitched his first complete season in 1961. By 1968 he had already led the Cards to two World Series triumphs thanks to consecutive wins in Games 3 and 5 in 1964 and Games 1, 4 and 7 in 1967. Over this period he had twice been a 20-game winner and had recovered from a broken leg off a Roberto Clemente line drive.

In 1968 he composed his masterpiece. He went 22-9 with a 1.12 ERA, the third lowest all-time and the best mark since 1914. He pitched 13 shutouts and in a 95-inning stretch he gave up just two runs. St. Louis made it to the World Series and in Game 1 Gibson fanned 17 Tigers but they would eventually lose the Series in seven games, despite Gibson's almost perfect showing. He was awarded both the Cy Young and the NL MVP and collected the Cy Young Award again in 1970 after a 23-7 season. He finished his career in 1975 with one no-hitter, eight All Star appearances and the satisfaction of becoming the second man in history to reach 3,000 strikeouts.

Gibson's reputation was built on his ability to intimidate the opposing batters. He was never afraid to pitch inside and always had nasty stuff. It would also be naïve not to recognize the impact of his skin color. "The myth was a lot better than what happened," Gibson said. "I think because I was black I was the big bad bear. I threw inside, but that's the way everybody pitched." But Gibson certainly did "mean" better than anyone.

He currently works in the American League front office and remains one of the game's most respected voices.

## CAREER TOTALS

| G | GS | IP | W | L | Pct | H | K | BB | ERA | CG | SHO |
|---|----|----|---|---|-----|---|---|----|----|----|-----|
| 626 | 500 | 4154.0 | 263 | 192 | .578 | 3520 | 3283 | 1502 | 3.00 | 256 | 57 |

# LEFTY GROVE

**Robert Moses Grove**
**Born:** March 6 1900, Lonaconing, Maryland
**Died:** May 22 1975, Norwalk, Ohio
**Throws:** Left
**Bats:** Left
**Height:** 6-3
**Weight:** 190

"In his windup he looked like an oil rig: His head and hands and torso rose and dipped rhythmically – once, twice, three times-until they rose a final time and he fired." – **Sportswriter William Nack on Lefty Grove.**

It was 1931. The gangling lefthander with the searing fastball and even hotter temper was closing in on a record 17th consecutive win with the A's when rookie outfielder Jim Moore, in for the injured Al Simmons, dropped a simple fly ball. The Browns beat the Athletics 1-0 and the pitcher had lost his shot at surpassing Walter Johnson and Smoky Joe Wood. He hit the clubhouse with the force of a twister, rearranging its contents as his frustrations erupted. It took him years to forgive Simmons – a future Hall of Fame outfielder – for his absence that day. This was typical of Robert "Lefty" Grove, one of the fastest, most dominating pitchers of all time.

Grove, who started life with the Baltimore Orioles of the International League in 1920, went on to become the premier southpaw of his era, perhaps ever. He joined the majors in 1925 as a member of Connie Mack's A's and recorded five 20-win seasons in just eight years. In 1931 he went 31-4 with a 2.05 ERA, 175 strikeouts and 27 complete games. As part of that awesome A's team of Foxx, Simmons and Cochrane, Grove won three pennants and two World Championships. He was sold to the Red Sox in 1935 to help alleviate Mack's debts forced upon him by the Depression. He led the league in ERA four times with Boston and still had his overpowering fastball as his ally. In 1941, aged 41, he beat Cleveland 10-6 to notch up his 300th, and final, career victory.

Grove's fastball was the stuff of legend. Walter Johnson ranked it alongside his own for pure speed and faster than Bob Feller's. Not afraid to pitch inside, Grove became notorious for intimidating hitters with his letter-high heater. And this was just in batting practice!

Because he pitched the majority of his career in the hitter-friendly confines of Shibe and Fenway, Grove's numbers aren't as immediately as impressive as Sandy Koufax's. But he led the American League in strikeouts seven consecutive years from 1925 to 1932 and led in ERA nine times. When park adjusted and normalized for league average, his lifetime ERA of 3.06 is among the very best. His International league record of 121-38 combined with his major league totals of 300-141 gives him a .702 winning percentage, the highest in baseball history.

## CAREER TOTALS

| G | GS | IP | W | L | Pct | H | K | BB | ERA | CG | SHO |
|---|----|----|---|---|-----|---|---|----|-----|----|----|
| 616 | 457 | 3940.2 | 300 | 141 | .680 | 3849 | 2266 | 1187 | 3.06 | 298 | 35 |

# WALTER JOHNSON

**Walter Perry Johnson**
**Born:** November 6 1887 Humboldt, Kansas
**Died:** December 10, 1947 Washington DC
**Threw:** Right
**Batted:** Right
**Height:** 6-1
**Weight:** 200

**"Just speed, raw speed, blinding speed, too much speed." – Ty Cobb on Walter Johnson**

It was merely his debut but Ty Cobb had seen enough of a certain lanky right-hander during his warm-up to realize he was witnessing something very special. "Stand deep in the box today," Cobb warned his Detroit teammates. "This farmer throws out of his hip pocket so fast you can't follow it." Ty Cobb knew then what the whole of baseball was to soon find out. Walter 'Big Train' Johnson might just be the fastest pitcher the game has ever seen.

The country-boy from Idaho spent 21 seasons with the Washington Senators winning 417 games, second all-time behind Cy Young. His side-arm fastball became one of baseball's most dominating pitches, helping him to 3509 career strikeouts, a record 110 shutouts and a reputation that would always precede him. But there was more to Johnson than just his blazing fastball. He was the dead-ball era's iron man. During a four-game road trip against the NY Highlanders in 1908 he pitched three complete-game shutouts in just three days. Between 1910 and 1920 he would win 20 games or more every season and his ERA rose above 2.00 only once.

Arguably his finest year was 1913 when he went 36-7 with a stingy 1.14 ERA. During this campaign Johnson pitched 56 consecutive scoreless innings (a record that stood until it was broken by the Dodgers Don Drysdale in 1968) and 11 shutouts. Naturally he won the AL MVP Award.

When asked about Johnson's fastball, White Sox outfielder Ping Bodie replied, "You can't hit what you can't see."

The Big Train had to wait until 1924 to win his first, and only, World Series. At 36 he was past his best but he still led the league with 23 victories and came on in relief in Game 7 to pitch four scoreless innings and clinch the Championship.

Johnson retired in 1927, his numbers reflecting the overpowering stuff he had throughout his career.

Ping Bodie was right. They couldn't hit what they couldn't see.

## CAREER TOTALS

| G | GS | IP | W | L | Pct | H | K | BB | ERA | CG | SHO |
|---|----|----|----|----|----|----|----|----|----|----|----|
| 802 | 666 | 5914.1 | 417 | 279 | .599 | 4913 | 3509 | 1363 | 2.17 | 531 | 110 |

58

# SANDY KOUFAX

**Sanford Koufax**
**Born:** December 30 1935, Brooklyn, New York
**Throws:** Left
**Bats:** Left
**Height:** 6-2
**Weight:** 210

**"He throws a 'radio ball,' a pitch you hear, but don't see." – Gene Mauch on Sandy Koufax**

Breathtakingly dominant on the mound and fiercely private away from it, the Dodgers Sandy Koufax was armed with a fastball you couldn't see, a knee-buckling curve you couldn't hit and integrity you couldn't touch.

For five seasons Koufax walked on water. Between 1962 and '66 he pitched 1,377 innings, amassed 111 victories, led the league in ERA every year and won three Cy Young awards.

He began his career with his hometown Brooklyn Dodgers but it was when they moved to the West Coast that Koufax truly became a master of his art. He would pitch four no-hitters – including a perfect game – for Los Angeles, as he became perhaps the greatest lefty ever. His 382 Ks in 1965 still stands as a National League record. His 0.95 ERA in 57 World Series innings is ranked fourth all-time. But Koufax will always be remembered for more than just his awesome numbers.

The first game of the 1965 World Series against the Minnesota Twins fell on Yom Kippur. The Dodgers went to the Series. Koufax went to the synagogue. The next day he lost but he came back to win Games 5 and 7, pitching 18 shutout innings, despite pain in his arthritic arm, to finish with a 0.38 ERA, the MVP crown and another World Series. God, team and baseball. Sandy Koufax knew his priorities and was unwavering in his commitment to them.

In 1966 he completed another pitching triple crown, leading the league with 27 wins, 317 strikeouts and a 1.73 ERA. He won his third Cy Young and then on the advice of his doctors, who warned him that he was in danger of losing the use of his arm if he tried to wring any more innings from it, walked away from the game forever.

For those who understood Sandy Koufax it made perfect sense.

The inspirational lefty was elected into baseball's Hall of Fame in 1972 becoming the youngest ever Cooperstown inductee.

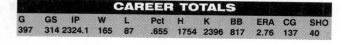

## CAREER TOTALS

| G | GS | IP | W | L | Pct | H | K | BB | ERA | CG | SHO |
|---|---|---|---|---|---|---|---|---|---|---|---|
| 397 | 314 | 2324.1 | 165 | 87 | .655 | 1754 | 2396 | 817 | 2.76 | 137 | 40 |

# GREG MADDUX

**Gregory Alan Maddux**
**Born:** April 14 1966, San Angelo, Texas
**Throws:** Right
**Bats:** Right
**Height:** 6-0
**Weight:** 175

**"Everybody says they'd rather be lucky than good. I'd rather be good than lucky." –**
**Greg Maddux**

"You don't gasp like you did when Gibson and Koufax pitched," says Atlanta Braves announcer Skip Caray in reference to the team's ace. So what made Greg Maddux the best pitcher of the 1990s and one of the premier starters of today?

Well, if Gibson and Koufax overpowered hitters, Maddux outthinks them.

He is widely regarded as the most cerebral of today's pitchers. With a seemingly photographic memory he has constructed a mental encyclopedia of today's hitters and their specific tendencies. "He's almost a savant of baseball," says Caray. "He sees things other people can't." And while Maddux will never be credited with having nasty stuff, his deadly combination of movement and control enables him to keep hitters off-balance, to dominate teams without the aid of one dominating pitch. His fastball has serious movement and he can run it into either corner. And the real rabbit in his hat is a changeup that's as hard to read as Balzac. Maddux has so much belief in this pitch he has been known to deliberately miss the strike zone on a 2-2 count, so he can fool the hitter with a full count changeup. He also locates his pitches better than anyone, making his living nibbling at the outside corner. "Maddux pitches to a bigger strike zone than anyone," says Cards pitching coach Dave Duncan.

The unassuming Maddux owned the '90s. He won his first Cy Young Award in 1992 with the Cubs, the franchise he joined as a rookie in 1987, and then proceeded to become the first pitcher in history to win four straight. He has had 12 consecutive 15-win seasons. In 1994 his 1.56 ERA was 2.65 below the National League average, the biggest differential in modern day history. The following season, with a 1.63 ERA, Maddux became the first hurler since Walter Johnson in 1918-19 to have sub 1.80 back-to-back seasons. He has won twelve straight Gold Gloves and four ERA titles. Between 1993 and 1999, as a member of the Braves, he averaged below 2.00 walks per nine innings and his ERA has risen above 3.00 just once. Maddux has helped Atlanta to eight NL East division titles, four pennants and the 1995 World Series.

Greg Maddux has yet to show signs of slowing down posting a 17-win season in 2001. The winningest pitcher of the '90s, he already has 257 career wins and a 2.84 lifetime ERA.

Enough to make anyone gasp.

| CAREER TOTALS | | | | | | | | | | | |
|---|---|---|---|---|---|---|---|---|---|---|---|
| G | GS | IP | W | L | Pct | H | K | BB | ERA | CG | SHO |
| 505 | 501 | 3551.0 | 257 | 146 | .638 | 3206 | 2523 | 760 | 2.84 | 102 | 34 |

# JUAN MARICHAL

**Juan Antonio Marichal**
**Born:** October 20 1937, Laguna Verde, Dominican Republic
**Throws:** Right
**Bats:** Right
**Height:** 6-0
**Weight:** 185

**"It doesn't matter what he throws. When he's got it, he beats you." – Roberto Clemente on Juan Marichal**

All though Sandy Koufax and Bob Gibson may have been the obvious standouts in the decade of the pitcher, Juan Marichal can stake his claim to being as dominant, as feared and as successful. He was the winningest pitcher of the 1960s, clinching 191 games, and definitely its most recognizable hurler.

It all started with that exaggerated leg kick followed by more delivery options than UPS. Marichal came at the hitter overhand, sidearm and submarine. He threw his fastball, slider and screwball from all these angles, changing the speeds, always pulling the string. Other pitchers kept a hitter off balance. Marichal made them seasick.

Between 1963 and 1969 he was a six time 20-game winner and his ERA never rose above 2.48. He threw a no hitter against Houston in 1963, led the National League in wins in 1963 and 1968 and won the ERA crown in 1969. He still holds San Francisco Giants records for most single-season victories (26), strikeouts (248), shutouts (10) and complete games (30).

Marichal played the majority of his career in San Francisco, joining the Giants in 1960 and playing 14 seasons by the Bay. On his debut he pitched a 2-0 shutout against the Phillies and went on to win six games for the season. In 1961 he went 13-10 and followed it up by winning 18 games in 1962. Then he got hot. From the get-go he had great stuff. But by 1963 he had added confidence and experience to his repertoire.

But other pitchers won the plaudits and the awards. While Marichal had awesome consistency, his best years always seemed to coincide with a truly exceptional performance from another arm. In '65 he went 22-13 with a 2.13 ERA, in '66 he went 25-6 with a 2.23 ERA. Koufax just happened to throw a 26-8, 2.04 ERA season in there followed by 27 wins and 1.73 ERA in '66.

But Marichal was too good to always be the bridesmaid. Against the rival Dodgers he went a career 37-18 before chronic back pain began to plague his pitching. He had his first ever losing season in 1972 and retired in 1975 after short spells with the Red Sox and the Dodgers. He was elected into the Hall of Fame in 1983 with 243 wins – second amongst Latin-American born pitchers – and a 2.89 ERA.

## CAREER TOTALS

| G | GS | IP | W | L | Pct | H | K | BB | ERA | CG | SHO |
|---|----|----|----|----|----|----|----|----|----|----|----|
| 471 | 457 | 3507.1 | 243 | 142 | .631 | 3153 | 2303 | 709 | 2.89 | 244 | 52 |

# CHRISTY MATHEWSON

**Christopher Mathewson**
**Born:** August 12 1880, Factoryville, Pennsylvania
**Died:** October 7 1925, Saranac Lake, New York
**Threw:** Right
**Batted:** Right
**Height:** 6-1
**Weight:** 195

**"I don't remember him as a list of statistics. I think of Matty as one of the great men and competitors sports has had." – Ty Cobb on Christy Mathewson**

Whether they played with him or against him, everybody who came into contact with Christy Mathewson was won over by his charm, intelligence and sheer ability. Baseball's first real hero, he is widely credited with bringing the game to a wider audience as he drew women and children to the ballparks for the first time in the game's history.

A college football star for Bucknell, he was an All-American before joining the Giants in 1900. By 1903 he was the game's premier pitcher and on his retirement in 1916 he had racked up 13 20-win seasons while becoming the quickest to reach 300 victories in just 12 seasons. His 373 wins ranks third all time while his ERA of 2.13 is the fifth best in history.

Mathewson spent his entire career with the Giants apart from a brief spell as the Reds player-manager in 1916. In one of the most spectacular World Series performances ever he threw three shutouts in just six days as New York cruised to victory over Philadelphia in five games. In Ty Cobb's autobiography he describes that 1905 feat as "impossible to equal". In those 27 innings he walked just one man and fanned 18. Mathewson continued to be a clutch performer in the postseason. In 11 World Series games, he pitched 10 complete games with a 1.15 ERA. With his infamous fadeaway pitch, a precursor to the screwball, he exhibited control that would make Greg Maddux look wild. In 1913 he pitched 68 consecutive innings without walking a single batter.

Matthewson died prematurely in 1925 from tuberculosis after he was accidentally exposed to a poisonous gas in 1918 while serving in a Chemical Warfare Unit in France during the War. During his 15-year career he helped McGraw's Giants to five pennants and a World Series. He still leads the Giants in career ERA, wins, strikeouts, shutouts and innings pitched.

The New York Giants catcher Chief Meyers was behind the plate for seven years catching the majority of Mathewson's games. "The greatest that ever lived," Meyers recollected in *The Glory of Their Times*. "There was never a time he couldn't throw that ball over the plate ... we'd break our necks for that guy."

In 1936, eleven years after his untimely death, he was elected to the Hall of Fame in its first ballot.

## CAREER TOTALS

| G | GS | IP | W | L | Pct | H | K | BB | ERA | CG | SHO |
|---|---|---|---|---|---|---|---|---|---|---|---|
| 635 | 551 | 4780.2 | 373 | 188 | .665 | 4218 | 2502 | 844 | 2.13 | 434 | 79 |

# SATCHEL PAIGE

**Leroy Robert Paige**
**Born:** July 7 1906, Mobile, Alabama
**Died:** June 8, 1982, Kansas City, Missouri
**Threw:** Right
**Batted:** Right
**Height:** 6-3
**Weight:** 180

**"Never look back. Something may be gaining on you." – Satchel Paige**

In four decades of baseball, Satchel Paige's exuberance was unrelenting. As a showman he became legendary. And as a pitcher he could bring it like Feller, Johnson and Ryan. Which overshadowed which is open for debate.

Satchel Paige began his career in 1926 with the Chattanooga Black Lookouts and played with the Pittsburgh Crawfords throughout the early 1930s but he gained notoriety through his participation in the barnstorming exhibitions between Negro League teams and major leaguers. In advertising for these games, Paige's name was often the headline as he declared that, first time up; he would retire the team in nine pitches. His heater became known as perhaps the fastest ever.

Paige also loved to entertain the crowds by placing a gum wrapper over home plate and then throwing pitch after pitch over it. He was also known to get his outfielders to sit down in the infield and then, with the tying run on base, strike the side out. Sam Lacy, editor of the *Afro-American* newspaper, was highly critical of Paige, describing his actions as a "combination vaudeville act and pitching performance." Lacy believed that rather than helping the advancement of black ballplayers, Paige only served to confirm stereotypes which detracted from his obvious talents.

The flipside to this argument was that Paige was achieving a level of exposure that no other Negro Leaguer had ever experienced and that he alone could drag the black player from the obscurity of the Jim Crow era. Fortunately, this was the case as Paige's profile and popularity helped ignite the move towards baseball's integration.

After winning five Negro American League pennants and a World Series between 1939-46, Paige left the Kansas City Monarchs for the major leagues. Never one for conformity, the Cleveland Indians' Bill Veeck acquired Paige in 1948 and he made his debut at 42-years old, becoming the oldest rookie to play in the big show. He went 6-1 and the Indians won the World Series. Paige stayed in the majors until 1953 and in 1965 pitched one more game to become, at 59, the oldest hurler in major league history.

Satchel Paige will be remembered for his fastball that turned "from a pumpkin to a pea", his durability and his showmanship. Paige, recognizing his potential as a catalyst for the desegregation of baseball, adhered to his own advice. He never did look back and when Jackie Robinson broke the color barrier in 1947, Paige's exposure had proved invaluable. He'd hit that gum wrapper again.

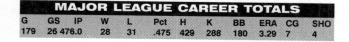

| G | GS | IP | W | L | Pct | H | K | BB | ERA | CG | SHO |
|---|----|----|----|----|-----|---|---|----|-----|----|----|
| 179 | 26 | 476.0 | 28 | 31 | .475 | 429 | 288 | 180 | 3.29 | 7 | 4 |

**MAJOR LEAGUE CAREER TOTALS**

# JIM PALMER

**James Alvin Palmer**
**Born:** October 15 1945, New York, New York
**Throws:** Right
**Bats:** Right
**Height:** 6-3
**Weight:** 196

**"The only thing Earl Weaver knows about big-league pitching is that he couldn't hit it." – Jim Palmer**

In his very first World Series game, just nine days before his 21st birthday, Jim Palmer made the most stunning of entrances. He gave up just four hits. No runs. He beat the Dodgers. Beat Sandy Koufax. And became the youngest ever player to toss a World Series shutout.

The Baltimore Orioles winningest pitcher of all-time made a habit of rising to occasions in his illustrious 20-year career. Constantly at war with his manager Earl Weaver, in the first four pennant-clinching games in the Orioles history (1966, 1969, 1970, 1971), Palmer was the winning pitcher in every one of them. He won eight times in World Series play while posting a 2.61 ERA. And when the O's defeated the Phillies in the 1983 Fall Classic, Palmer became the first pitcher to win World Series games in three decades. "Jim knows exactly what he wants to do with each pitch and he isn't going to change his mind," said Weaver diplomatically. But despite the differences the two men had, it was hard to argue with Palmer's results.

After his heroics in 1966 Palmer experienced such soreness in his pitching arm that he missed all of the 1967 season and much of '68 too. But rather than being another cautionary tale of a young star forced to throw too many pitches, Palmer came back stronger. He led the AL in 1969 with a 2.34 ERA and threw a no-hitter against Oakland on August 13. From 1970 to 1978 he had eight 20-win seasons and collected three Cy Young Awards.

The rest of career was marred by a constant battle with arm injuries. In both 1980 and 1982 he bounced back to record winning seasons and even attended spring training in 1991 with the O's but this time the comeback didn't transpire. He was inducted into Cooperstown in 1990 and embarked on a successful career as broadcaster, businessman and spokesperson.

## CAREER TOTALS

| G | GS | IP | W | L | Pct | H | K | BB | ERA | CG | SHO |
|---|----|----|---|---|-----|---|---|----|-----|----|----|
| 558 | 521 | 3948.0 | 268 | 152 | .638 | 3349 | 2212 | 1311 | 2.86 | 211 | 53 |

# NOLAN RYAN

**Lynn Nolan Ryan**
**Born:** January 31 1947, Refugio, Texas.
**Throws:** Right
**Bats:** Right
**Height:** 6-2
**Weight:** 195

**"It helps if you don't tense up, because you might have to run for your life." – George Brett on facing Nolan Ryan**

It was probably the easiest scouting report Red Murff ever had to compile. After seeing the skinny high-school pitcher throw his first 100 mph fastball, followed by another of equal velocity, the New York Mets scout reached for his notebook and simply wrote, "Best arm I have ever seen in my life."

Lynn Nolan Ryan signed with the Mets in 1965, a raw fireball thrower from Alvin, Texas. He retired in 1993 a legend. In between, he redefined what it meant to be a power pitcher.

He spent six years with the Mets and earned his only World Series ring as a member of the 1969 team. He was wild, he couldn't find the strike zone, had arm troubles and spent as much of his time in the bullpen as in the starting rotation. But there was always that fastball. The Mets finally decided to let him go, unsure if they were making the correct decision. "Whether or if or how he's going to do it, I don't know," said New York manager Gil Hodges after Ryan was traded to the Angels. He soon found out.

In California Ryan found his place in the rotation, giving him the innings he needed to progress. He began to find consistency and control. He also found Tom Morgan. The pitching instructor worked, listened and molded until Ryan found his groove. The groove led him to 138 victories, four no-hitters and six 300-strikeout seasons. In 1973 he set a major league single-season record with 383 Ks. In 1980 free agency beckoned. Ryan became a Houston Astro and baseball's first million-dollar player.

Ryan finished his career in his home state. He played nine seasons with the Astros winning 106 games and pitching his fifth no-hitter in 1981. He then joined Texas in 1989 as a 41-year old but, because of his great conditioning, continued to dominate hitters with his fastball/curve combination. If he had lost anything off his heater, it didn't show. He pitched two more no-hitters in 1990 and '91, won his 300th game and struck out his 5,000th hitter. He retired in 1993 having played in the majors for all or part of 27 different seasons, longer than any other player in history and was inducted into the Hall of Fame at Cooperstown in 1999.

Ryan will be remembered for his fastball, his unparalleled longevity and his ability to intersperse a career of amazing consistency with touches of genius. Today his record book is as thick as *War and Peace*. He holds major league bests for strikeouts (5714), most years with 300-plus strikeouts (6) and most games with 15 or more Ks (27). His record seven no-hitters are three more than Sandy Koufax.

"I feel like God gave me a talent to throw a baseball," said Ryan. "And then it was for me to make the best of it."

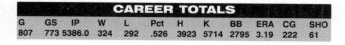

## CAREER TOTALS

| G | GS | IP | W | L | Pct | H | K | BB | ERA | CG | SHO |
|---|----|----|----|----|-----|---|---|----|-----|----|-----|
| 807 | 773 | 5386.0 | 324 | 292 | .526 | 3923 | 5714 | 2795 | 3.19 | 222 | 61 |

# TOM SEAVER

**George Thomas Seaver**
**Born:** November 17 1944, Fresno, California
**Threw:** Right
**Batted:** Right
**Height:** 6-1
**Weight:** 200


**"Blind people come to the park just to listen to him pitch." – Reggie Jackson on Tom Seaver**

Gil Hodges' 1969 New York Mets hold a special place in baseball lore. In performing the game's most unlikely u-turn, going from perennial losers to World Champions, they gave hope to forlorn franchises all over the sports world. But there was really only ever one miracle among those Mets. His name was Tom Seaver.

Seaver joined the majors in 1967 and was sent to the Mets courtesy of a name-from-the-hat draw made necessary by his illegal signing with Atlanta while still at college. Some things are just meant to be.

With his effortless delivery, his ability to blow it past hitters and throw great off-speed stuff, Seaver quickly became the franchise ace. In 1967 he was Rookie of the Year thanks to 16 wins, a 2.76 ERA and 170 strikeouts. The following year he again won 16 games, had 205 Ks and a 2.20 ERA.

The tale of 1969 doesn't need retelling. But Seaver's impact does. It was an incredible run by an improbable team but Seaver was the glue that held the Mets together. Take away his 25 victories and replace them with the same numbers that Jerry Koosman posted (17-9) and the Mets don't even win the NL East. He accounted for one-quarter of their regular season victories and with a 2.21 ERA, 208 strikeouts and 18 complete games was a lock for the Cy Young Award.

Seaver won the Cy Young again in 1973 and 1975 but as the Mets' fortunes dwindled, Seaver was traded to the Reds. He pitched his first, and only, no-hitter in 1978 against the Cardinals but arm injuries began to affect his performances. In 1982 he posted a 5.50 ERA, a career worst, and was traded back to the Mets. But there was to be no miracle this time. He went 9-14, one of only four losing seasons in his 20-year career, and left for the White Sox. Seaver pitched three seasons in Chicago, going 33-28, before joining the Red Sox in 1986.

Seaver retired in 1986 with a 2.86 lifetime ERA and 311 career wins. He had set a handful of records, including career strikeouts by a right-handed pitcher and consecutive strikeouts in a single-game (10). He was a four-time 20-game winner and is seventh all time in career shutouts with 61.

## CAREER TOTALS

| G | GS | IP | W | L | Pct | H | K | BB | ERA | CG | SHO |
|---|---|---|---|---|---|---|---|---|---|---|---|
| 656 | 647 | 4782.2 | 311 | 205 | .603 | 3971 | 3640 | 1390 | 2.86 | 231 | 61 |

# WARREN SPAHN

**Warren Edward Spahn**
**Born:** April 23 1921, Buffalo, New York
**Throws:** Left
**Bats:** Left
**Height:** 6-0
**Weight:** 175

**"I felt like, wow, what a great way to make to a living. If I goof up, there's going to be a relief pitcher coming in there. Nobody's going to shoot me." – Warren Spahn**

Warren Spahn got his first major league start in 1942 with the Boston Braves but had to wait another four years to collect his first victory. In between he went to war.

After playing much of the year with Hartford of the Eastern League, going 17-2, Spahn was drafted and spent three years serving with the Army in Europe. After World War II had ended, Spahn could finally resume his pitching career and picked up his first major league win in 1946. Rather than lamenting the time lost, Spahn actually credits his time spent in the Army as a possible catalyst for his amazing durability that saw him pitch for 21 years. "I matured a lot in three years," Spahn said. "I think I was a lot better equipped to handle major league hitters at 25 than I was at 22."

Spahn won 21 games in 1947 and over the next 17 seasons he would be a 20-game winner a further 12 times. In 1948 the Braves won the pennant and Spahn and Johnny Sain accounted for 39 of Boston's 91 victories. "Spahn and Sain and pray for rain" went the chant but the Indians won the World Series in six games, with Spahn going 1-1 with a 3.00 ERA.

The Braves moved to Milwaukee in 1953 and Spahn continued to rack up the victories. In his 12 seasons in Milwaukee he had nine 20-win seasons and an ERA of less than 3.00 five times. He recorded his 200th win in 1956 against the Phillies and just five years later got win number 300 against the Cubs. In 1963, as a 42-year old, went 23-7 with a 2.60 ERA.

Spahn left the Braves in 1964 and played the final two seasons of his career with the Mets and the Giants. In 1965 he got his 363rd victory making him the winningest lefty in baseball history. Not Koufax. Not Grove. But Warren Spahn. Always credited for his stylish motion and great control, he pitched two no-hitters in consecutive years (1960, '61) and led the NL in wins eight times and in complete games nine times. His 63 career shutouts rank him sixth all-time.

He was elected to the Hall of Fame in 1973.

## CAREER TOTALS

| G | GS | IP | W | L | Pct | H | K | BB | ERA | CG | SHO |
|---|----|----|----|----|-----|----|----|----|-----|----|-----|
| 750 | 665 | 5243.2 | 363 | 245 | .597 | 4830 | 2583 | 1434 | 3.09 | 382 | 63 |

# CY YOUNG

**Denton True Young**
**Born:** March 29 1867, Gilmore, Ohio
**Died:** November 4 1955, Newcomerstown, Ohio
**Threw:** Right
**Batted:** Right
**Height:** 6-2
**Weight:** 210

**"I never had a sore arm and I pitched every third day. Once I pitched every other day for 18 days." – Cy Young**

For Denton True Young baseball was truly a game of firsts.

He was the first, and only, pitcher to throw no-hitters in both the 19th and 20th century. He started the first ever World Series game in 1903. And he remains first all-time in number of wins, starts and complete games. None of the three will probably ever be equaled.

The "Cy" was short for cyclone. Pitching in the Tri-State League for Canton in the 1880s, Young got loose by throwing a few pitches against a fence. His pregame warm-up left the fence obliterated. It was remarked that it appeared as though a cyclone had struck it. Armed with his new nickname, 23-year-old Young was signed by the Cleveland Spiders of the Players League and in his first season he went 9-7 including a three-hitter on his debut. The following year he won 27 games with the Spiders. He went onto record eight consecutive 20-win seasons including going 36-12 in 1892. He moved to Boston in 1901 and the newly formed American League proved to be the perfect arena for Young's talents.

From 1901–11 Young won 221 games and led the AL in wins in 1901, '02 and '03. The Pilgrims won baseball's first World Series in 1903 as Young went 2-1 with 1.59 ERA for the series. He returned to Cleveland in 1909 before finishing his career with the Boston Braves.

When he retired in 1911 at age 44, Young had set records that were written in stone. His 511 wins are 94 more than Walter Johnson. He pitched 7,356 innings, over one thousand more than Pud Galvin. He had 16 300-inning seasons and, in 1904, pitched the first perfect game of the 20th century. He is ranked number one all time in 20-win seasons with 16 and second all time in 30-win seasons with five. These numbers are testimony to his incomparable durability and while he may not be remembered as baseball's best hurler, he set a precedent for others to follow and ushered in a new era for the national pastime with grace and skill.

After Young's death in 1955, Commissioner Ford Frick decided it was appropriate to name an award after him, to be presented to the year's outstanding pitcher in the Majors. Fortunately, the idea stuck and in 1956 the first Cy Young Memorial Award was presented to Don Newcombe of the Brooklyn Dodgers. For the first 11 years, there was only one Cy Young Award-winner, but from 1967, there has been an Award in both the National League and the American League.

## CAREER TOTALS

| G | GS | IP | W | L | Pct | H | K | BB | ERA | CG | SHO |
|---|----|----|---|---|-----|---|---|----|----|----|----|
| 906 | 815 | 7356.0 | 510 | 316 | .617 | 7092 | 2803 | 1217 | 2.63 | 749 | 76 |

# CATCHERS

**Johnny Bench**
**Yogi Berra**
**Roy Campanella**
**Carlton Fisk**
**Josh Gibson**

# JOHNNY BENCH

**Johnny Lee Bench**
**Born:** December 7 1947, Oklahoma City, Oklahoma
**Bats:** Right
**Throws:** Right
**Height:** 6-1
**Weight:** 195

"Every time Bench throws, everybody in baseball drools." – **Harry Dalton on Johnny Bench**

He once proclaimed that he could "throw out any runner alive" and at times it appeared true. From his rookie season in 1967 to his retirement in 1983, Johnny Bench was quite simply the best catcher in the game. And after he had put away his tools of ignorance, his career complete, his value began to rise. The greatest catcher in National League history? The greatest ever?

What made Bench so good was his ability to perform at the highest level on both sides of the plate. Defensively, he had no peer. He had a rocket launcher of an arm and was fearless when it came to blocking home plate. He was also very adept at calling the game and handling his pitchers. Growing up in Oklahoma, Bench's father taught him how to build up his arm, constantly throwing from a crouched position until he could fire the ball 254 feet, exactly twice the distance from home plate to second base. Bench is also credited with redefining some of the basic fundamentals of catching, including keeping his throwing hand behind his back to guard it from fouls tips and catching with one hand.

Bench joined the Cincinnati Reds in 1967 and in his rookie season of 1968 made an immediate impact. He hit .275 with 15 dingers and 82 RBIs.

He was elected to the All-Star game and was voted National League Rookie of the Year. He caught 154 games that season, a rookie record, and claimed the first of his ten consecutive Gold Glove Awards.

As an integral member of the Big Red Machine, Bench had a chance to shine on baseball's grandest stage. In the 1975 World Series against Boston, Bench drove in four with one home run and the following season he had the opportunity to improve on his post-season numbers. He took it. Against the Yankees, Bench hit .533 with two homers and six RBIs including going yard twice in Game 4 to clinch the Championship. His performance behind the plate was just as emphatic. In Game One he caught Mickey Rivers stealing. The Yankees didn't attempt a steal the rest of the series.

Bench retired in 1983 due to aching knees after a brief stint at third base. He was elected into the Hall of Fame in 1989 as a two-time MVP in 1970 and '72. He finished his 17 years in the majors with six 100-RBI seasons and eight 20-home run seasons.

## CAREER TOTALS

| G | AB | R | H | 2B | 3B | HR | RBI | BB | K | SB | Avg | Slg | OBP |
|------|------|------|------|-----|-----|-----|------|-----|------|-----|------|------|------|
| 2158 | 7658 | 1091 | 2048 | 381 | 24 | 389 | 1376 | 891 | 1278 | 68 | .267 | .476 | .342 |

70

# YOGI BERRA

**Lawrence Peter Berra**
**Born:** May 12 1925, St. Louis, Missouri
**Bats:** Left
**Throws:** Right
**Height:** 5-7
**Weight:** 185

"Nobody goes there anymore; it's too crowded." – **Yogi Berra on a popular New York restaurant.**

Immortalized for his "Yogisims", it is sometimes easy to forget that, as the Yankees' catcher, Yogi Berra was part of more World Series winners than any player in history. With Yogi it really wasn't over until it was over, as he captured 14 pennants and 10 World Series in a 19-year career full of hilarious observations, clutch hits and one ring after another.

Berra signed with the Yankees and made his big league debut in 1946, playing in seven games. Sharing the catching duties Berra quickly improved under the watchful gaze of future Hall of Famer Bill Dickey. Playing some leftfield when not behind the plate, Berra had problems with the early evening shadows cast across Yankee Stadium, prompting the classic Yogisim "It gets late early out here." But by 1948 he was New York's everyday catcher and he had his first big year at the plate, hitting .305 with 98 RBIs.

Over the next 15 seasons, Berra would develop into one of baseball's greatest ever catchers. Defensively, he led the American League in putouts eight times and in fielding and assists three times. He won the AL MVP three times in 1951, '54 and '55 and played in 15 consecutive All-Star games. As a hitter, Berra was consistent rather than spectacular, racking up 11 20-plus home run seasons and reaching the 100-RBI mark four years on the spin. Always regarded as a bad ball hitter, Yogi was more than happy to take a cut at pitches outside the strike zone. "The pitchers were afraid of him because he'd hit anything, so they didn't know what to throw," said Hector Lopez. "Yogi had them psyched out and he wasn't even trying."

Berra also gained the reputation as an outstanding clutch performer and had many opportunities to prove it. He holds the World Series record for at bats (259), hits (71), doubles (10) and games by a catcher (63). His 39 RBIs and 41 runs are second only to Mickey Mantle and just the Babe and the Mick have more Fall Classic homers.

After retirement in 1963, Berra went onto manage and coach both the Yankees and the Mets, guiding each team to a pennant in 1964 and 1973 respectively. Berra returned to Yankee Stadium in 1999 after a 14-year hiatus caused by his feud with George Steinbrenner after the owner fired Berra as manager in 1985. The reconciliation was marked with a Yogi Berra Day at Yankee Stadium made all the more special by David Cone's perfect game 43 years after Berra caught Don Larsen's moment of perfection in the 1956 World Series.

It was like déjà vu all over again.

## CAREER TOTALS

| G | AB | R | H | 2B | 3B | HR | RBI | BB | K | SB | Avg | Slg | OBP |
|------|------|------|------|-----|----|-----|------|-----|-----|----|------|------|------|
| 2120 | 7555 | 1175 | 2150 | 321 | 49 | 358 | 1430 | 704 | 414 | 30 | .285 | .482 | .348 |

71

# ROY CAMPANELLA

**Roy Campanella**
**Born:** November 19 1921, Philadelphia, Pennsylvania
**Died:** June 26 1993, Woodland Hills, California
**Bats:** Right
**Throws:** Right
**Height:** 5-9
**Weight:** 200

**"My father had a zen approach to life." – Roy Campanella Jr. on Roy Campanella**

If courage were something you could learn, Roy Campanella would have been its most persuasive of teachers. Instead, he just showed you what it meant. A patch of ice, a telephone pole and a tragedy ended his baseball career. He refused to let them end his life.

When the Brooklyn Dodgers' catcher was paralyzed in an automobile accident in 1958, the most exciting of players and the most decent of men was taken from behind the plate and placed in a wheelchair. But rather than disappear, Campanella chose to look adversity right in the eyes. He coached for his beloved Dodgers, continued to act as an ambassador for the game, and refused to accept defeat. "To me, this is Campy-Campy of the fighting heart," said Howard A. Rusk, the director of NYU's institute of Rehabilitation Medicine. "His neck was broken, but never his spirit."

Campanella began his career with the Baltimore Elite Giants of the National Negro League, was named to the All-Star teams in 1941, '44 and '45, and finally made it to the majors in 1948 with the Dodgers. He had a cannon of an arm, called a great game, and led the league in putouts six times and fielding twice. As a power hitter, he was just as impressive. While his batting average fluctuated from the great (.325 in 1951) to the not so great (.207 in 1954), his power numbers were always consistent. In 1951 he hit 33 homers, drove in 108 runs and had a .590 slugging percentage to win the NL MVP Award. He won the Award again in 1953 with a .312 average, 41 home runs and 142 RBIs and after an injury plagued 1954, rebounded to win his third MVP crown in 1955, hitting .318 with 32 homers and a .583 slugging percentage. In his short Major League career, the stocky Campanella saw much postseason action. He was part of the losing Brooklyn teams in 1952 and 1953 but in the 1955 World Series he hit two home runs as the Dodgers beat the Yankees in seven games.

In only 10 major league seasons, Campanella made himself into one of the game's greatest catchers. Only Stan Musial and Mike Schmidt can equal his three National League MVP Awards. He hit 20 or more homers seven times, was elected to the All-Star game four times and on average threw out two of every three runners who attempted to steal on him.

He was elected into the Hall of Fame in 1969, 10 years after he was honored by 93,103 Dodgers fans at the Coliseum, setting a record for baseball's largest ever attendance. He died in 1993.

## CAREER TOTALS

| G | AB | R | H | 2B | 3B | HR | RBI | BB | K | SB | Avg | Slg | OBP |
|------|------|-----|------|-----|----|-----|-----|-----|-----|----|------|------|------|
| 1215 | 4205 | 627 | 1161 | 178 | 18 | 242 | 856 | 533 | 501 | 25 | .276 | .500 | .360 |

72

# CARLTON FISK

**Carlton Ernest Fisk**
**Born:** December 26 1947, Bellows Falls, Vermont
**Bats:** Right
**Throws:** Right
**Height:** 6-2
**Weight:** 220

"This was always my favorite hat!" – **Carlton Fisk on his announcement that he will wear a Red Sox cap into Cooperstown.**

He was a rookie by name only.

When Carlton Ernest Fisk arrived at Boston's Fenway Park in 1969 he already had a nickname, a body built for the punishing rigors of catching and an acute understanding of the Red Sox Nation's urgency for some postseason success.

Tagged Pudge as a kid because of his stocky build, Fisk was a Vermont native who followed the Sox and dreamed of playing at Old Fenway. He had shared in the franchise's disappointments. He knew all about the Curse. He was perfect. And in time he became as quintessentially Boston as the Citgo sign and Sam Malone.

Fisk's rookie year was 1972 and it proved an unforgettable start. He hit .293 with 22 homers, won a Gold Glove and became the first unanimous American League Rookie of the Year. He belted another 26 homers the following year but in 1974 broke his collarbone and missed the majority of the season. He returned in 1975; hit .331 in just 79 games and the Red Sox made it to the World Series.

Game 6 of the 1975 season is ingrained in the mind of every Red Sox fan the world over. Fisk's dramatic extra-innings homer is one of the game's most indelible images. The more Fisk willed the ball fair, the more it seemed to listen. Standing at home plate, waving like he was directing traffic, Fisk urged his 12th inning blast off Pat Darcy against the leftfield foul pole for a game-winning home run and an unforgettable celebration. The Red Sox lost Game 7 against the Reds but Fisk had entered baseball folklore and defined his place among Boston's true greats.

Fisk left Boston in 1980 after the Red Sox front office had failed to secure his new contract in time. He became a free agent and joined the Chicago White Sox, playing there until his retirement in 1993.

Remembered for his tenacity, his heroics and his spirit, Fisk was a seven time All-Star with eight 20- home run seasons and 14 seasons with 100 or more hits. He is second only to Johnny Bench in career home runs for a catcher and remains the all-time major league leader in games played at this position.

He was elected into the Hall of Fame in 2000.

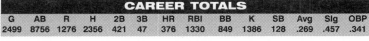

## CAREER TOTALS

| G | AB | R | H | 2B | 3B | HR | RBI | BB | K | SB | Avg | Slg | OBP |
|------|------|------|------|-----|----|-----|------|-----|------|-----|------|------|------|
| 2499 | 8756 | 1276 | 2356 | 421 | 47 | 376 | 1330 | 849 | 1386 | 128 | .269 | .457 | .341 |

73

# JOSH GIBSON

**Josh Gibson**
**Born:** December 21 1911, Buena Vista, Georgia
**Died:** January 20 1947, Pittsburgh, Pennsylvania
**Batted:** Right
**Threw:** Right
**Height:** 6-1
**Weight:** 210

"Josh was a natural hitter. He just ate fastballs up!" – **Jimmy Crutchfield on Josh Gibson**

He was often described as the black Babe Ruth. It was meant as a compliment, a testimony to his legendary power. But he shouldn't be rendered to memory as a replica of another player, even if he is being compared to the greatest. Josh Gibson could stand on his own two feet.

"When I broke in with the Baltimore Elite Giants in 1937 there were already a thousand legends about him," said fellow Hall of Fame catcher Roy Campanella. "And once you saw him play you knew they were all true." Because of the notoriously unreliable Negro League statistics Gibson's exact records remain in doubt. His talents don't. He has been credited with as many as 962 homers and a .391 lifetime batting average. It is said that he once hit 84 dingers in a single-season. In the 1930s his slugging percentage is said to have reached 1.000. But listen to the respect he was afforded and the awe he induced and the ambiguity of his numbers fades.

Bill Veeck described him as "two Yogi Berras" while Walter Johnson stated that he hit the ball "a mile." Satchel Paige went one better. "He was the greatest hitter who ever lived," Paige said.

Gibson began his professional career with the Homestead Grays in 1930. He was in the stands watching the game when the Grays catcher Buck Ewing injured his thumb. Homestead manager Judy Johnson knew of Gibson's semi-pro success and climbed into the bleachers to look for him. Gibson played that day and was signed. He stayed with the Grays until 1931 when he signed for the Pittsburgh Crawfords. With Pittsburgh he won the home run title in 1932, '34 and '36 before rejoining the Grays in 1938 when he reportedly hit .440 and again won the home run crown.

His moon shots are among baseball's most famous. In a 1934 Negro League game at Yankee Stadium, Gibson hit a home run that struck two feet from the top of the stadium wall above the center field bleachers. It measured approximately 580 feet. In the same game the Chicago American Giants infielder Jack Marshall said that Gibson hit a ball clean out of the stadium, over the left field bullpen. Fact or fiction, there can be no better metaphor for the injustice of baseball's color barrier than Gibson sending a ball flying out of the House that Ruth Built.

Josh Gibson died suddenly in 1947 from a stroke, just three months before Jackie Robinson made his major league debut.

# FIRST BASE

**Jimmie Foxx**
**Lou Gehrig**
**Hank Greenberg**
**Harmon Killebrew**
**Willie McCovey**
**Mark McGwire**
**Eddie Murray**
**George Sisler**

# JIMMIE FOXX

**James Emory Foxx**
**Born:** October 22 1907, Sudlersville, Maryland
**Died:** July 21 1967, Miami, Florida
**Bats:** Right
**Throws:** Right
**Height:** 6-0
**Weight:** 195

**"With all those muscles, he hit drives that sounded like gunfire." – Ted Williams on Jimmie Foxx**

Jimmie Foxx had all the attributes necessary to be remembered as the greatest first baseman in history. He had power to burn, he clinched pennants and won honors and earned the respect of the game. He also had the misfortune to play the same position as Lou Gehrig.

Foxx was the embodiment of a real slugger. He had arms as thick as a Pacific Bell directory and hit one towering home run after another. Though impossible to eclipse the impact that Gehrig had made on their position, Foxx still had enough highlight reels to fill a U-Haul.

Many of his homers became legendary. He hit a ball clear out of Comiskey Park, smashed a seat in the left field upper deck at Yankee Stadium in 1937 and won Game 5 of the 1930 World Series when he parked one over left center field in Sportsman's Park. When Yankees pitcher Lefty Gomez was watching Neil Armstrong's moon landing, his wife asked him what the white sphere was that the astronaut had just picked up. "That's the ball Foxx hit off me in New York in 1937," Gomez said.

Double X's rookie year was 1925 but it was three seasons before he began to make an impact with the A's. After time spent keeping the bench warm, Connie Mack platooned Foxx both behind the plate and at third and in 1928 he hit .328 with 79 RBIs in 118 games. The following year Mack moved him to first base and the Beast was born. He batted .354 and hit 33 homers in the regular season and helped the A's beat the Cubs in five games to clinch the World Series with 7 hits, 5 RBIs and 2 home runs in 21 at bats. In 1932 Foxx had probably his finest year. He hit 58 home runs, 169 RBIs and had issued the first real challenge to the Babe's supremacy as the game's dominant slugger. He was named the MVP. He won the Triple Crown in 1933 and again captured the MVP crown. He was sold to the Red Sox in 1935.

The Red Sox have always had a love affair with right-handed sluggers and Foxx ate up Fenway's short porch in left field. In 1938 he won his third MVP award, hitting .349 with 50 dingers and 175 RBIs. He was the perfect complement to Ted Williams when the Kid came to Boston from the Millers. Williams said of Foxx, "Next to DiMaggio, Jimmie Foxx was the greatest hitter I ever saw." He left Fenway with a .320 average and 222 home runs.

Foxx retired in 1945 with the Phillies after a brief stint with Chicago. He had 12 30-homer seasons and his 534 career home runs rank him 11th all time.

## CAREER TOTALS

| G | AB | R | H | 2B | 3B | HR | RBI | BB | K | SB | Avg | Slg | OBP |
|------|------|------|------|-----|-----|-----|------|------|------|-----|------|------|------|
| 2317 | 8134 | 1751 | 2646 | 458 | 125 | 534 | 1922 | 1452 | 1311 | 87 | .325 | .609 | .428 |

# LOU GEHRIG

**Henry Louis Gehrig**
**Born:** June 19 1903, New York, New York
**Died:** June 2 1941, Riverdale, New York
**Batted:** Left
**Threw:** Left
**Height:** 6-0
**Weight:** 200

**"He just went out and did his job every day." – Bill Dickey on Lou Gehrig**

It all began with just a simple headache.

On June 2 1925, the Yankees regular first baseman Wally Pipp felt unwell and sat out the game. He was replaced at first by a 22-year old rookie who the Yankees had signed in 1923 out of Columbia University. Pipp would never play first base in pinstripes again. The rookie was one Henry Louis Gehrig.

Gehrig's 2,130 consecutive game streak is perhaps how he is best remembered. But he was so much more than just New York's iron man. As an integral part of the Yankees overpowering offense, Gehrig drove in 100 runs 13 seasons in a row and had seven 150-RBI seasons. In a career spanning from 1923–39, Gehrig helped the Yankees to seven pennants and six World Championships.

But much of Gehrig's was a career spent in the shadow of Babe Ruth. He was the antithesis of the Babe. Gehrig quietly went about his work, while Ruth raised the roof of every ballpark he played in. Away from the diamond, Ruth continued to treat life like one big vaudeville show while unassuming, family man Gehrig was virtually anonymous. It suited him. "I'm not a headline guy," he liked to say. But while he didn't make great copy, he lit up box scores.

In 1931 he set an American League record of 184 RBIs that still stands today. He is the game's all time grand slam leader with 23. He won two AL MVP awards and won the Triple Crown in 1934 with a .363 average, 49 homers and 165 RBIs. On seven occasions he finished the year with 200 hits and 100 walks. And in 1932 he became the first AL player to hit four homers in a single game. He really could do it all.

As a player he seemed indestructible. And as a gentleman batted 1.000. So, when he learned that he had an incurable disease called amyotrophic lateral sclerosis, it somehow seemed all the more tragic. It was 1939. He was just 36 years old. The Iron Horse suddenly was dented.

But Lou Gehrig was never to be remembered as a forlorn figure. He was too strong for that. On July 4 1939 at Yankee Stadium on Lou Gehrig Appreciation Day, he spoke to the players, to the crowd, to the game. "Today I consider myself the luckiest man on the face of the earth," he said in a speech that forever lingers in baseball's memory.

He died on June 2 1941 from the disease that would later bear his name, eternally the Pride of the Yankees.

| CAREER TOTALS | | | | | | | | | | | | | |
|---|---|---|---|---|---|---|---|---|---|---|---|---|---|
| G | AB | R | H | 2B | 3B | HR | RBI | BB | K | SB | Avg | Slg | OBP |
| 2164 | 8001 | 1888 | 2721 | 534 | 163 | 493 | 1995 | 1508 | 790 | 102 | .340 | .632 | .447 |

# HANK GREENBERG

**Henry Benjamin Greenberg**
**Born:** January 1 1911, New York, New York
**Died:** September 4 1986, Beverly Hills, California
**Bats:** Right
**Throws:** Right
**Height:** 6-4
**Weight:** 210

"Hank Greenberg has class. It stands out all over him." – **Jackie Robinson on Hank Greenberg**

In 1934 Detroit's slugging first baseman Hank Greenberg had a decision to make. His Tigers were in the middle of a pennant race and Yom Kippur was approaching. Greenberg chose not to play and instead spent the Jewish Day of Atonement in prayer at the Shaarey Zedek synagogue in Detroit. "I don't think anybody can imagine the terrific importance of Hank Greenberg to the Jewish community," said a dedicated Tigers Fan. "He made baseball acceptable to our parents."

Greenberg joined the Tigers in 1930 and by 1933 had begun to establish himself as a genuine power threat. In 1934 he hit .339 with 26 homers and 139 RBIs. Detroit lost the World Series to the St. Louis Cardinals but Greenberg performed well hitting a home run and driving in seven runs. In 1935 he led the American League with 36 homers and 170 RBIs and again the Tigers made an appearance in the Fall Classic, beating out the Cubs in six games. Greenberg was awarded the AL MVP. In 1937 he had 183 RBIs to go alongside a .337 average and 41 homers followed by a run at the Babe's home run record in 1938. He eventually finished with 58, two shy of Ruth's mark. Greenberg joined the Army early in the 1941 season, having collected his second MVP award in 1940 thanks to a .340 average, 41 dingers and 150 RBIs. He had moved to left field that season, so Greenberg became the first man to receive the MVP award in two different positions.

After the war Greenberg returned to Detroit and helped them to a World Series Championship in 1945 before ending his career with the Pirates in 1947. Like many players of his era, while the war may have shortened his career and cut down his numbers, his impact was felt nonetheless.

"Jewish women on my block would point me out as a loafer, a bum who always wanted to play baseball," Greenberg once said. He changed that. He became a role model for Jewish kids the county over, deflecting the anti-semitism of the time with a quiet dignity. At 6-4 and over 200 pounds he was also a symbolic figure for Jewish pride in America. "He eliminated all those jokes that started with 'Did you hear the one about the little Jewish gentleman," said actor and baseball fan Walter Matthau.

He was elected into the Hall of Fame in 1956 having hit .300 eight times, driven in 100 runs seven times and had six 30-homer seasons in 13 Major League seasons.

## CAREER TOTALS

| G | AB | R | H | 2B | 3B | HR | RBI | BB | K | SB | Avg | Slg | OBP |
|------|------|------|------|-----|-----|-----|------|-----|-----|-----|------|------|------|
| 1394 | 5193 | 1051 | 1628 | 379 | 71 | 331 | 1276 | 852 | 844 | 58 | .313 | .605 | .412 |

# HARMON KILLEBREW

**Harmon Clayton Killebrew**
**Born:** June 29 1936, Payette, Idaho
**Bats:** Right
**Throws:** Right
**Height:** 6-0
**Weight:** 195

"Every time he comes to the plate, he is dangerous. I have more respect for him than anyone." – **Boog Powell on Harmon Killebrew**

The 1969 American League MVP winner Harmon Killebrew got his start in baseball thanks to a local politician with a Washington connection and a passion for the game.

In 1954 Senator Herman Welker of Idaho urged the Washington Senators owner Clark Griffith to scout a young player who he had likened to Mickey Mantle. Welker was fond of talking up the exploits of ballplayers from his home state and had previously recommended Vernon Law to Griffith. He didn't sign Law but when he saw Killebrew the Senators owner made sure he didn't make the same mistake again.

In his 22 years in the majors, Harmon Killebrew became one of the most potent sluggers in baseball history. He didn't hit for average and was only an ordinary defensive player. What Killebrew did was hit home runs. And he retired swatting them at a rate only bettered by the Babe and Ralph Kiner. Among players active in 2001 only Mark McGwire, Barry Bonds and Juan Gonzalez can improve on Killebrew's average of a homer every 14.22 at bats. His 573 career dingers rank him sixth all-time.

Killebrew played in Washington until 1960 and remained with the team when it relocated and became the Minnesota Twins in 1961. In his first season in the Twin Cities, he hit 46 home runs followed by 48, 45 and 49 the following three years, leading the American League 1962–64.

In 1965 the Twins won the pennant, eventually losing to the Dodgers in the World Series. Killebrew played much of the season injured and only had one extra base hit during the Fall Classic. Not surprisingly it was a home run. He rebounded in 1967 to win his fifth home run title and repeated again in 1969 as the Twins captured the AL West title. He finished his career with Kansas City in 1975 having had eight 40-homer seasons and having driven in 100 runs or more nine times.

The Killer was elected to Cooperstown in 1984.

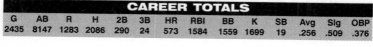

| CAREER TOTALS | | | | | | | | | | | | | |
|---|---|---|---|---|---|---|---|---|---|---|---|---|---|
| G | AB | R | H | 2B | 3B | HR | RBI | BB | K | SB | Avg | Slg | OBP |
| 2435 | 8147 | 1283 | 2086 | 290 | 24 | 573 | 1584 | 1559 | 1699 | 19 | .256 | .509 | .376 |

# WILLIE McCOVEY

**Willie Lee McCovey**
**Born:** January 10 1938, Mobile, Alabama
**Bats:** Left
**Throws:** Left
**Height:** 6-4
**Weight:** 210

**"He is clearly one of the finest players ever to have worn a San Francisco Giants uniform."**
**– Giants executive vice-president Larry Baer on Willie McCovey**

As a hitter he couldn't have had a better mentor. And as a major leaguer he couldn't have wished for a better start.

In the minors Willie McCovey's tutor was one Ted Williams. It was like having Sinatra teach you scales. Soaking up his idol's advice, McCovey was soon called up from Phoenix in 1959 and on his debut with the San Francisco Giants went 4-4 including two triples. He finished the season with a .354 batting average and won the NL Rookie of the Year award.

By 1963 he had developed into one of the league's most potent hitters. With his towering home runs and blistering line drives, the sweet-swinging lefty could do it all. As well as hitting for power and average McCovey was christened Stretch for his great range at first base. He led the league in homers in 1963, '68 and '69 and RBIs in 1968 and '69 becoming only the fifth player in the game's history to win consecutive home run and RBI crowns. In 1969 he lost out on the Triple Crown, batting .320 to Pete Rose's .348, but won the MVP award.

McCovey was traded to the Padres in 1973 after a series of injuries had seemingly slowed him down. He played two seasons in San Diego before returning to the Bay Area in 1976. He played out that season with the A's and was back in a Giants uniform ready for the 1977 campaign. Met with a standing ovation that made the tears flow, McCovey, at aged 39, silenced his doubters by remaining injury free and with his 28 dingers and 86 RBIs was awarded the NL Comeback Player of the Year.

Calling it quits in 1980, McCovey's career spanned 22 years and four decades. The six-time All-Star was elected into the Hall of Fame in 1986 with 521 home runs, a total that ties him 12th with Ted Williams on the career list. To honor his commitment to the Giants, the franchise created the Willie Mac Award in 1980, given annually to the San Francisco player who captures the same enthusiasm and spirit that defined McCovey's career with the Giants.

## CAREER TOTALS

| G | AB | R | H | 2B | 3B | HR | RBI | BB | K | SB | Avg | Slg | OBP |
|------|------|------|------|-----|----|-----|------|------|------|----|------|------|------|
| 2588 | 8197 | 1229 | 2211 | 353 | 46 | 521 | 1555 | 1345 | 1550 | 26 | .270 | .515 | .374 |

# MARK McGWIRE

**Mark David McGwire**
**Born:** October 1 1963, Pomona, California
**Bats:** Right
**Throws:** Right
**Height:** 6-5
**Weight:** 250

**"He's a freak. There are power hitters and then there is Mark McGwire." – Cardinals catcher Tom Pagnozzi on Mark McGwire**

The bat resembled a toothpick in his massive hands, as he swatted one helpless ball after another towards the upper deck, head-first into history. When St. Louis Cardinals slugger Mark McGwire shattered the single-season home run record in 1998 with his 70 dingers, and hit another 65 in 1999, he cemented his place as one of the game's greatest ever home run hitters. Barry Bonds broke the record again in 2001 with 73 homers but McGwire's status remains.

The historic '98 season was a culmination of previous years when McGwire hinted at what he could do as he began to launch baseballs further and with greater frequency than any other slugger. In his first full season with the A's in 1987 he hit 49 homers in 151 games. He then reeled off five 20-homer seasons including 39 in '90 and 42 in '92. After injury plagued years in 1993 and '94 he returned to belt another 39 in 1995. Since 1996 McGwire, who joined the Cardinals in 1997, has hit 284 homers in a five-year purple patch. The comparisons to the Babe are obvious. And McGwire more than holds his own. In Ruth's most productive five-year period from 1927 to 1931 he hit 255 dingers. McGwire also became the fastest player to reach both the 400 and 500 home run mark. His 65 homers in 1999 made him the first player in baseball history to record four consecutive 50-homer seasons.

The 2001 season was one of dissapointment for McGwire. After an injury plagued 2000, the ailments continued, limiting him to just 97 games and in the off-season he announced his retirement from the game. In 16 seasons he won a World Series ring with the '89 A's and reached at least 100 RBIs seven times. He has a .589 career slugging percentage and moved to fifth, ahead of Harmon Killebrew, in the all-time home run list with 583.

But there is also a man behind these awesome numbers and this made the McGwire story all the more compelling. In '98 he was involved in the most famous chase since OJ jumped in his Ford Bronco but he handled himself with dignity and his reluctance to embrace the fame made him all the more appealing. Seemingly genuinely in awe of his accomplishments, he may have been 250 pounds of inevitability at the plate but his philosophy was typically modest. "See the ball, hit the ball," said McGwire. And away from the game he was, and is, just as impressive, donating large sums of money annually to the foundation he set up to help abused and neglected kids. And while it is easy to say that he should be prepared to help the community that supports him, when so many don't, all that matters is he does.

In life, as in baseball, Mark McGwire sees the ball and hits it.

## CAREER TOTALS

| G | AB | R | H | 2B | 3B | HR | RBI | BB | K | SB | Avg | Slg | OBP |
|------|------|------|------|-----|----|-----|------|------|------|----|------|------|------|
| 1777 | 5888 | 1119 | 1570 | 248 | 6 | 554 | 1350 | 1261 | 1478 | 12 | .267 | .593 | .398 |

81

# EDDIE MURRAY

**Eddie Clarence Murray**
**Born:** February 24 1956, Los Angeles, California
**Bats:** Both
**Throws:** Right
**Height:** 6-2
**Weight:** 220

**"When I came up through the Baltimore farm system, they wanted me to be a power hitter. I just wanted to be a good hitter." – Eddie Murray**

When the Baltimore Orioles retired Eddie Murray's number in 1998, they managed the impossible. To get their former first baseman and future Hall of Famer to show some emotion. The usually stoic Murray, who icy relationship with the press had been well documented, even surprised himself. "I didn't think it could be done," said Murray in reference to the tears in his eyes, "but it's been done."

For 21 years Eddie Murray quietly worked on securing his place in the baseball record books. He did it by producing day in, day out, retaining a consistency that allowed him to creep up on the game's hallowed numbers and ambush them from behind. Because Murray was largely uncooperative with the media he developed a reputation as just another ornery ball player, but to those who knew him Murray was a real professional, perhaps misunderstood, definitely underrated. "He was quiet," said former manager Earl Weaver. "He came to the park and did his job."

Drafted by Baltimore, Murray was called up to the Majors in 1977 and became an instant success. He hit .282 with 27 homers and 88 RBIs to win the AL Rookie of the Year award. The following year Murray became the O's everyday first baseman and replicated his rookie numbers, hitting .285 with 27 home runs and 95 RBIs. A trend had begun. For the next 17 seasons he would post similar numbers. He had seven .300 seasons, six 100-RBI seasons and hit 25 or more homers 12 times. He also only hit less than 20 home runs eight times in his 20-year career and finished with a .287 batting average.

Murray helped the Orioles to win the World Series in 1983 before leaving Baltimore for Los Angeles in 1988. He played three seasons with the Dodgers, hitting a career-high .330 in 1990, before joining the Mets and the Indians, where he reached the 3,000-hit plateau. Murray was back with the Birds in 1996, played one season in Anaheim and, before retiring in 1997, returned to the Dodgers.

Because of both his consistency and his longevity, Murray ranks alongside some of baseball's biggest stars. He joins Hank Aaron and Willie Mays as the only players with 3,000 hits and 500 home runs. His 1,917 RBIs is the eighth best all-time – tops among all switch-hitters – and he ranks tied for fifth all-time in games played and sixth outright in at-bats. Before moving to DH, Murray also won three Gold Gloves at first and was selected to play in the All-Star game seven times.

He is a lock for the Hall of Fame when he becomes eligible in 2003.

## CAREER TOTALS

| G | AB | R | H | 2B | 3B | HR | RBI | BB | K | SB | Avg | Slg | OBP |
|---|---|---|---|---|---|---|---|---|---|---|---|---|---|
| 3026 | 11336 | 1627 | 3255 | 560 | 35 | 504 | 1917 | 1333 | 1516 | 110 | .287 | .476 | .359 |

# GEORGE SISLER

**George Harold Sisler**
**Born:** March 24 1893, Manchester, Ohio
**Died:** March 26 1973, Richmond Heights, Missouri
**Bats:** Left
**Throws:** Left
**Height:** 5-11
**Weight:** 170

**"A stylist, a tremendous hitter and as crafty as they come." – Ty Cobb on George Sisler**

Ty Cobb called him "the finest first baseman of them all" while Paul Waner described him as "the best I ever saw." Whatever the superlative, George Sisler was one of the most complete players baseball has ever witnessed.

His strength was that he had no weakness. He tore up the base paths, had astounding agility on defense and hit for both average and power. He was a five-tool player before it ever entered baseball's phraseology.

Branch Rickey first recognized Sisler's talents while he attended the University of Michigan. When Rickey left Ann Arbor to become a scout for the St. Louis Browns he kept an eye on him. Sisler, who at the time was recognized primarily as a pitcher, graduated with an engineering degree in 1915 and was signed to the Browns by Rickey, who had since become the manager. Sisler, who had been strong enough to beat Walter Johnson early in his career, moved to first for good in 1916. He finished with a .305 batting average that year, followed by .353, .341 and .352. And then he really started to hit.

In 1920 Sisler batted .407 to lead the league and his 257 hits still stands as the all-time single-season record. To illustrate his versatility he also had 122 RBIs and 42 stolen bases. In 1922 Sisler had his best year. He hit .420 and also led the league in runs, hits, stolen bases and triples as well as putting together a 42-game hitting streak and collecting the inaugural AL MVP Award. Throughout his 16-year career, Sisler's average dropped below .300 just three times. In his rookie season with the Browns and twice after 1923 when he missed the entire season after contracting sinusitis that permanently affected his eyesight. He continued to hit for average but his numbers dropped off and he left St. Louis in 1928.

Sisler eventually retired in 1930 after spending short periods with the Senators and the Braves. His hitting prowess and thoughtful nature made him a successful coach but he struggled as the Browns manager, finishing with a 218-240 record.

He entered the Hall of Fame in 1939 with a .340 lifetime average, now the 12th best in baseball history.

## CAREER TOTALS

| G | AB | R | H | 2B | 3B | HR | RBI | BB | K | SB | Avg | Slg | OBP |
|------|------|------|------|-----|-----|-----|------|-----|-----|-----|------|------|------|
| 2055 | 8267 | 1284 | 2812 | 425 | 164 | 102 | 1175 | 472 | 327 | 375 | .340 | .468 | .379 |

# SECOND BASE

**Rod Carew**
**Charlie Gehringer**
**Rogers Hornsby**
**Nap Lajoie**
**Joe Morgan**
**Jackie Robinson**

# ROD CAREW

**Rodney Cline Carew**
**Born:** October 1 1945, Gatun, Panama
**Bats:** Left
**Throws:** Right
**Height:** 6-0
**Weight:** 180

"He's the only player in baseball who consistently hits my grease. He sees the ball so well, I guess he can pick out the dry side." – **Gaylord Perry on Rod Carew**

His consistency, control and versatility at the plate made him one of the most feared hitters of his era. It appeared there wasn't anything Rod Carew couldn't do with a bat. He made his living finding the gaps, laying down bunts, hitting for average. "He's the only guy I know who can go four-for-three," said Chicago's Alan Bannister.

Carew was born in Panama in 1945 but moved to New York City when he was 16 to escape the poverty of his youth. He was signed by the Twins after being noticed on the sandlots of New York and made it the majors in 1967. He hit .292 and won the AL Rookie of the Year Award and by 1969 had already displayed the talents that would eventually make him a household name. He won the batting crown, hitting .332 for the season, as well as stealing home seven times. In 1970 he tore a knee ligament and was on the DL for three months but still batted at a .300 clip. It was where he would spend the majority of his career.

From 1969–83, Carew put together 15 consecutive .300-seasons to join Ty Cobb, Honus Wagner, Stan Musial, Cap Anson, Tony Gwynn and Ted Williams as the only other players to accomplish this feat. During this run of sublime contact hitting, Carew also won seven batting crowns, a number bettered only by Cobb, Wagner and Gwynn. In 1977 he hit .388, the best number posted since Ted Williams in 1957, led the league with 239 hits and was voted the American League MVP.

Unhappy with the Twins' owner Calvin Griffith, Carew demanded a trade and in 1979 he became an Angel. He continued to hit for average and reached the 3,000 hit mark on August 4 1985. Never a great defensive player, Carew was moved from second base to first to try to prolong his career but retired in 1985 when his contract with the California Angels expired.

Elected into the Hall of Fame in 1991, Carew's numbers place him alongside some of baseball's greatest hitters. When asked about his career, Carew replied, "I wasn't a flashy power hitter but a guy who hit to spots, who bunted and stole bases." And a guy who did it better than most.

## CAREER TOTALS

| G | AB | R | H | 2B | 3B | HR | RBI | BB | K | SB | Avg | Slg | OBP |
|---|----|----|----|----|----|----|-----|----|----|----|-----|-----|-----|
| 2469 | 9315 | 1424 | 3053 | 445 | 112 | 92 | 1015 | 1018 | 1028 | 353 | .328 | .429 | .393 |

# CHARLIE GEHRINGER

**Charles Leonard Gehringer**
**Born:** May 11 1903, Fowlerville, Michigan
**Died:** January 21 1993, Bloomfield Hills, Michigan
**Bats:** Left
**Throws:** Right
**Height:** 5-11
**Weight:** 180

**"You just wind him up on opening day and forget about him." – Doc Cramer on Charlie Gehringer**

Detroit Tigers second baseman Charlie Gehringer was so reserved that when he was honored by his fans with a "Charlie Gehringer Day" and presented with a set of regular golf clubs, the lefty, rather than make a fuss, learned to play the game right-handed. This too was how he approached baseball. No fuss. "He says 'hello' on opening day and 'goodbye' on closing day," said Detroit catcher Mickey Cochrane, "and in between he hits .350."

Gehringer grew up in Fowlerville, Michigan and learned the game on the family farm. He attended the University of Michigan and was soon scouted by the Tigers. Bobby Veach recommended him to manager Ty Cobb and, like most players who received the Veach seal of approval, was signed. Gehringer spent the majority of 1924 and '25 with Toronto of the International League. Signed because of his methodical stroke and smooth defense, Gehringer didn't disappoint, leading the league in both RBIs and fielding percentage. In 1926 he became Detroit's everyday second baseman.

Gehringer stayed with the Tigers until his retirement in 1942. He had 13 seasons hitting .300 or better and seven 100-RBI seasons. He regularly led the American League in fielding, assists and putouts. During the 1929 season he hit .339 while leading the league in eight statistical categories. In 1937 he was named the AL MVP, hitting .371 with 209 hits and 96 RBIs.

Perhaps because of his systematic approach and relaxed temperament, Gehringer always seemed to excel in the postseason. As one third of Detroit's "G-Men" offense, Gehringer, alongside Hank Greenberg and Goose Goslin, led the Tigers to back-to-back pennants in 1934 and '35 and after losing in seven games to the Cardinals in '34, they rebounded to win the 1935 World Series against the Cubs. In the 1934 Series, Gehringer batted .379 with 11 hits; a year later his average was .375.

Gehringer became the Tigers GM in 1951 and he remained as a vice president of the franchise until 1959. Dubbed the "Mechanical Man", Gehringer's effortless play at second base resulted in none other than Joe DiMaggio describing him as "No.1 in my book" while his teammates always greatly appreciated his silent efficiency.

He was elected to the Hall of Fame in 1949.

## CAREER TOTALS

| G | AB | R | H | 2B | 3B | HR | RBI | BB | K | SB | Avg | Slg | OBP |
|---|---|---|---|---|---|---|---|---|---|---|---|---|---|
| 2323 | 8860 | 1774 | 2839 | 574 | 146 | 184 | 1427 | 1186 | 372 | 181 | .320 | .480 | .404 |

# ROGERS HORNSBY

**Rogers Hornsby**
**Born:** April 27 1896, Winters, Texas
**Died:** January 5 1963, Chicago, Illinois
**Bats:** Right
**Throws:** Right
**Height:** 5-11
**Weight:** 175

**"Everytime I stepped up to the plate, I couldn't help but feel sorry for the pitcher."**
**- Rogers Hornsby**

He was possibly baseball's greatest ever right-handed hitter. Dedicated. Assiduous. Disciplined. "Baseball is my life. It's the only thing I know and care about," the "Rajah" once said. And many of Rogers Hornsby's teammates, managers and owners would agree. His approach to the game didn't leave any room for pleasantries and friendships. Only an unrelenting assault on the National League record-books.

Hornsby hit the major leagues as 19-year old with the Cardinals in 1915. At first he struggled, hitting just .246, and was plagued by the same defensive problems that had led to him commit 58 errors in the Texas League. But Hornsby came back in 1916, bigger, stronger and with added pop in his bat. He hit .313 to lead the Redbirds but it wasn't until 1920, when manager Branch Rickey switched him to second base, that he fully realized his talents. He hit .370 that year and won the batting title for the next five seasons. He led the league in five offensive categories in 1921 and in 1922 he had one of the game's most dominant seasons, leading the National League in 10 offensive categories. He hit .401 with 42 homers and 152 RBIs to easily win the Triple Crown. He also led in hits, runs and doubles, total bases, extra-base hit, slugging percentage and on-base percentage.

Hornsby was something of an anomaly. He didn't drink or smoke, stay up late, read books or visit the movies. He didn't want to damage his health, eyesight or curtail his career in any way. In fact his only visible vice was the horses. This regimented lifestyle gave him the reputation of being distant and coupled with his hot-temper and healthy ego, Hornsby often found himself in direct conflict with his managers and owners. He was traded to the Giants in 1927 after holding out for a new three-year deal. He didn't fare any better with the Giants who traded him to the Boston Braves in 1928. Same story, different team; he was fired and joined the Cubs in '29, becoming their player-manager in 1930. Hornsby helped Chicago to the pennant in 1929 with another MVP season. He played until 1937 before managing the Browns and the Reds.

Hornsby's .424 batting average in 1924 is a modern-era record and his career .358 average – second only to Ty Cobb – still stands as the best in the National League. He led the Cardinals to the 1926 World Series, beating the Yankees in seven games. It was the franchise's first championship.

## CAREER TOTALS

| G | AB | R | H | 2B | 3B | HR | RBI | BB | K | SB | Avg | Slg | OBP |
|---|----|----|----|----|----|----|-----|----|----|----|-----|-----|-----|
| 2259 | 8173 | 1579 | 2930 | 541 | 169 | 301 | 1584 | 1038 | 679 | 135 | .358 | .577 | .434 |

# NAP LAJOIE

**Napoleon Lajoie**
**Born:** September 5 1874, Woonsocket, Rhode Island
**Died:** February 7 1959, Daytona Beach, Florida
**Bats:** Right
**Throws:** Right
**Height:** 6-1
**Weight:** 195

**"He was always laughing and joking. Even when the son of a gun was blocking you off the base, he was smiling and kidding with you. You just had to like the guy." – Tommy Leach on Nap Lajoie**

How many major league ballplayers have been so respected that they had their ballclub named after them?

Napoleon "Larry" Lajoie was such a draw at the turn of the century he had this very honor bestowed on him when the Cleveland Broncos became the Naps in 1905. Lajoie was the game's obvious star. As both a second baseman and a hitter he had few rivals. Defensively he was as polished as they come. "Every play he made was executed so gracefully that it looked like it was the easiest thing in the world," said Tommy Leach. And offensively he created havoc wherever he went.

In 21 major league seasons, from 1896–1916, he had 17 .300 seasons and on 10 of those occasions he batted over .350. He won the Triple Crown in 1901 with a .422 batting average, 14 homers and 125 RBIs. He took the batting title four times in total and his lifetime .338 batting average ranks him 16th all time.

Lajoie joined the Phillies in 1896 and was an immediate success. In 1897 he hit .361 and had a league leading 310 total bases and in 1901 he joined the fledgling American League when Connie Mack offered him $4000 to join his A's. However after his Triple Crown season with the Athletics, the Phillies sued Mack for instigating the contract jumping and Lajoie was ordered by the Pennsylvania Supreme Court to return to the Phillies. AL president Ban Johnson intervened and Lajoie eventually signed with Cleveland.

He won batting titles in 1903 and 1904 and he was made player-manager the following year. His numbers began to suffer, however, and in 1909 he stepped down as manager to concentrate solely on playing. In 1910 he was embroiled in a battle with Ty Cobb for the batting crown and on the last day of the season against the Browns Lajoie got seven bunt singles to clinch the title with a .384 average to Cobb's .383. The Browns manager Jack O'Connor hated Cobb with such passion he presented the title to Lajoie with his tactic of playing the third baseman very deep to make a bunt possible. But a Cobb error was changed to a single some days later and the Georgia Peach seemingly had it won. It took 70 years to clear up the debate as it was found that Cobb had been given a double entry during the season. Lajoie was the 1910 American League batting champion.

It was Lajoie's fourth and last batting title. He retired in 1916.

## CAREER TOTALS

| G | AB | R | H | 2B | 3B | HR | RBI | BB | K | SB | Avg | Slg | OBP |
|---|----|----|----|----|----|----|-----|----|----|----|-----|-----|-----|
| 2480 | 9589 | 1504 | 3242 | 657 | 163 | 82 | 1599 | 516 | 85 | 380 | .338 | .466 | .380 |

# JOE MORGAN

**Joseph Leonard Morgan**
**Born:** September 19 1943, Bonham, Texas
**Bats:** Left
**Throws:** Right
**Height:** 5-7
**Weight:** 160

**"I was one of those guys that did all they could do to win." – Joe Morgan**

You will often hear him described as "the spark plug" of the Big Red Machine's offense. Many who watched him play would say Joe Morgan was the whole engine.

In 1975 he hit .327 with 163 hits and 67 stolen bases. He was named the NL MVP and in the World Series came up with clutch singles to win both Games 3 and 7, helping Cincinnati beat Boston 4-3. The following season the Reds were dominant again and it was still Morgan who was at the heart of the team's success. He was again awarded the MVP, hitting .320 with 27 homers and 60 stolen bases. In the Reds' sweep of the Yankees in the World Series, Morgan had a .333 average. In a lineup that included Pete Rose, Tony Perez and Johnny Bench, Morgan managed to more than find his niche. He had great speed, surprising power and serious baseball savvy.

Morgan began his career with his home state Astros and quickly developed into a solid second baseman, winning the 1965 Rookie of the Year Award. He was traded to the Reds in 1972 and spent eight seasons in Cincinnati before returning to Houston where he helped the Astros win their first ever division title. He then spent short periods with the Giants, the Phillies and the A's before retiring in 1984.

Morgan seemingly excelled in every facet of the game. He retired with the most homers by a second baseman (since broken by Ryne Sandberg) and still holds the career record for second baseman in games played (2,527). He had nine 40-stolen base seasons and eight 100-walk seasons and retired with an awesome .981 fielding average. During his 22-year career he helped his teams to seven divisional titles, four pennants and two World Series. Unsurprisingly he was elected into baseball's Hall of Fame in 1990.

Morgan currently works as an ESPN analyst and has developed a successful partnership with Jon Miller on Sunday Night Baseball. Widely regarded as the best in the business, Morgan brings the same intelligence and enthusiasm into the booth that defined his play in the majors.

## CAREER TOTALS

| G | AB | R | H | 2B | 3B | HR | RBI | BB | K | SB | Avg | Slg | OBP |
|------|------|------|------|-----|----|-----|------|------|------|-----|------|------|------|
| 2737 | 9464 | 1665 | 2553 | 454 | 99 | 270 | 1143 | 1883 | 1046 | 689 | .270 | .424 | .390 |

89

# JACKIE ROBINSON

**Jack Roosevelt Robinson**
**Born:** January 31 1919, Cairo, Georgia
**Died:** October 24 1972, Stamford, Connecticut
**Bats:** Right
**Throws:** Right
**Height:** 5-11
**Weight:** 200

**"If one can be certain of anything in baseball, it is that we shall not look upon his like again." – Author Roger Kahn on Jackie Robinson**

"We have to get behind Jackie," said Dodgers pitcher Ralph Branca. "He's gonna be here. He's here to stay. And he's gonna help us win the pennant." It was a simple statement but one that spoke volumes. Two months into the 1947 season and Branca had realized what many soon would. Jackie Robinson was there for good. It was time to embrace his talents and acknowledge his bravery.

But it was never quite as simple as that. Robinson had to endure the taunts and threats of players, managers and fans and the cold-shoulder of some teammates. Being a pioneer came with a huge price but his talents as a ballplayer couldn't be ignored. For years some questioned whether black players could hold their own in the major leagues. Robinson has answered the question emphatically. Baseball had been integrated, the color barrier smashed and sports in America would, thankfully, never be the same again.

While Robinson's social impact was vast, its importance immeasurable, it is easy to forget what a great athlete he was. As UCLA's first ever four-letter man in baseball, football, basketball and track, his talent was obvious. After playing with the Kansas City Monarchs, Branch Rickey chose Robinson as the perfect person to integrate baseball. He signed a contract in 1946 and Rickey sent him to the Dodgers' minor league affiliate in Montreal. Robinson had an outstanding season with Montreal, but the acid test would come in 1947, when Robinson would play in the Majors. That Robinson was talented enough, Rickey had no doubt, but would he be mentally tough enough to endure the hatred he was certain to encounter? Rickey thought Robinson would be able to handle it all, and his instinct was proved right.

Not only did Robinson always play with his head held high he also became an integral part of the Dodgers success. In his 10 major league seasons he hit .300 or better six times, failed to reach double-digits in homers just once and tore up the bath paths with his speed, intelligence and instinct. In 1949 he stole 37 bases and 197 for his career. He won the Rookie of the Year award in '47, testimony to his ability to perform when the abuse was at its most fervent and just two seasons later he would clinch the NL MVP award, hitting .342 with 203 hits and 124 RBIs.

Robinson died too young in 1972 from a heart attack but will never be forgotten as a real American pioneer, symbolic of a changing nation and the hope of a brighter future. Baseball universally retired his number 42 on the 50th anniversary of his Major League debut and he became the first black player inducted into Hall of Fame at Cooperstown.

## CAREER TOTALS

| G | AB | R | H | 2B | 3B | HR | RBI | BB | K | SB | Avg | Slg | OBP |
|---|----|----|----|----|----|----|-----|----|----|----|-----|-----|-----|
| 1382 | 4877 | 947 | 1518 | 273 | 54 | 137 | 734 | 740 | 291 | 197 | .311 | .474 | .409 |

# SHORTSTOP

**Ernie Banks**
**Derek Jeter**
**Cal Ripken Jr.**
**Ozzie Smith**
**Honus Wagner**
**Robin Yount**

# ERNIE BANKS

**Ernest Banks**
**Born:** January 31 1931, Dallas, Texas
**Bats:** Right
**Throws:** Right
**Height:** 6-1
**Weight:** 180

**"It's a great day for a ball game; let's play two!" - Ernie Banks**

Ask who hit the most homers from 1955 to 1960, and no doubt the names; Mays, Mantle and Aaron would be at the top of everybody's list. And those lists would be wrong. In fact, it was Mr. Cub himself, Ernie Banks.

Banks didn't look like your archetypal slugger. He didn't look particularly strong and he certainly didn't look aggressive. But in that six-year period, armed with his quick wrists, a buggy whip swing and a bat that weighed less than a good steak, he belted 248 homers.

Voted the Greatest Cub of All Time, Banks spent 19 years in Chicago where he developed into one of the most dominant power hitters of the '50s and '60s. Despite never getting within a bloop single of the postseason, Banks won both the 1958 and 1959 National League MVP Awards and became popular throughout baseball for playing the game with an infectious enthusiasm. His "Let's play two!" attitude perfectly captured the optimistic resilience of a franchise that hadn't won a World Series since 1908.

Banks got his start in the Negro Leagues with the Kansas City Monarchs and was signed by the Cubs in 1953 becoming one of the franchise's first black players when he teamed up with Gene Baker in their '53 debut. Installed at shortstop by 1954, Banks immediately went on a tear and in 1955 hit 44 home runs and 117 RBIs. He won the MVP in 1958 hitting .313 for the season with 47 dingers and 129 RBIs. He repeated the next year with a .303 average, 45 home runs and a career-best 143 RBIs. He won his first Gold Glove in 1960 and another the following year. Banks was moved to first base in 1962 and continued his solid work with the leather winning the fielding title in 1969 and leading NL first baseman in assists five times. In 1970 he belted his 500th homer and his immortality was assured.

Elected to the All-Star game 11 times, Banks retired in 1971 having had five 40-homer seasons and. Both his 512 career home runs and his 47 roundtrippers in '58 are records for a shortstop and he was elected to the Hall of Fame in 1977. Today, Ernie Banks remains a Chicago institution, as recognizable and popular as ever. The Sears Tower in spikes. And eternally Mr. Cub.

## CAREER TOTALS

| G | AB | R | H | 2B | 3B | HR | RBI | BB | K | SB | Avg | Slg | OBP |
|---|---|---|---|---|---|---|---|---|---|---|---|---|---|
| 2528 | 9421 | 1305 | 2583 | 407 | 90 | 512 | 1636 | 763 | 1236 | 50 | .274 | .500 | .330 |

# DEREK JETER

**Derek Sanderson Jeter**
**Born:** June 26 1974, Pequannock, New Jersey
**Bats:** Right
**Throws:** Right
**Height:** 6-3
**Weight:** 195

**"He hasn't paused a bit to look in the mirror and say, 'How good I am.' He just concentrates on getting better." – Yankees manager Joe Torre on Derek Jeter**

Four World Series rings makes for a heavy hand and a stellar career in anyone's book. But for New York Yankees shortstop Derek Jeter it is seemingly only the beginning.

After just six full seasons in the majors, Jeter has established himself as the heartbeat of another Yankees dynasty, winning four titles in five years, including the three-peat in 2000. While most players pray for just one shot at a World Championship, the 27-year-old has spent the majority of his short career enjoying one successful playoff run after another. "He's played his whole career in the World Series," said Chili Davis, a former teammate. "To him this is just how major league baseball should be."

Jeter was selected by the Yankees out of Kalamazoo Central High in 1992 and in 1995 was called up to the majors. The following year he played his first full season in New York and as one of a trifecta of new stars at short–alongside Alex Rodriguez and Nomar Garciaparra–was an immediate hit finishing with a .314 average. His asent to team captain and arguably the game's biggest star has been swift. In 1998 he compiled a .324 average with 203 hits and 84 RBIs and improved in 1999, batting .349 with 219 hits and 102 ribbies. In 2000 he solidified his glowing reputation with a .339 average, 201 hits and 15 homers. The 2001 season saw Jeter finish with a .311 average and 21 home runs all while playing water-tight defense in the most demanding of positions.

But it is in the playoffs that Jeter's true colors really show through, proving an integral member of the Yankees World Series triumphs in 1996 and 1998-2000. During a pennant race he is reliable and unrelenting in his effort but in a Series match-up he is clutch, routinely providing the Yankees with the inspiration they need during close games on baseball's biggest stage. He has reached safely in 55 of his 60 career postseason games and has a .342 World Series batting average. For added proof, look no further than the Yanks' 2000 Subway Series win over the Mets. Named Series MVP–to go alongside his All-Star MVP, becoming the first player in history to receive both awards in the same season–Jeter hit a first-pitch dinger in Game 4 to spark a 3-2 win, putting the pinstripes up 3-1 in the series. He followed it up with a game-tying solo shot in Game 5. In fact, during the entire postseason, every time Jeter went deep, the Yankees won. In the 2001 Series, despite the Yankees going down in seven games to Arizona, he still made his mark hitting only the 12th walk-off homer in World Series history in a dramatic Game 4 at Yankee Stadium.

Elevated to a Gotham icon and already the undisputed leader of the Yankees, Jeter's potential appears limitless, his future beyond bright. Running out of fingers seems a very real possibility, indeed.

## CAREER TOTALS

| G | AB | R | H | 2B | 3B | HR | RBI | BB | K | SB | Avg | Slg | OBP |
|---|----|----|----|----|----|----|-----|-----|----|----|------|------|------|
| 936 | 3744 | 715 | 1199 | 188 | 38 | 99 | 488 | 397 | 671 | 135 | .320 | .470 | .392 |

# CAL RIPKEN JR.

**Calvin Edwin Ripken, Jr.**
**Born:** August 24 1960, Havre De Grace, Maryland
**Bats:** Right
**Throws:** Right
**Height:** 6-4
**Weight:** 220

**"One question I've been repeatedly asked these last few weeks is how do I want to be remembered. My answer is simple: To be remembered at all is pretty special." – Cal Ripken Jr.**

It was the indelible record of the ending of an indelible record. Where the Baltimore Orioles had for so long written one man's name now sat a black ink mark. It was the line-up card that will sit in Cooperstown. September 20 1998. The day Cal Ripken Jr. decided not to play ball.

For 2,632 consecutive games he had pulled on a uniform and gone to work, surpassing Gehrig's record in 1995, providing an on-going lesson in class, loyalty and work-ethic that began on May 29 1982 and will last forever.

While Ripken was creating the Streak he was also changing the mold for future shortstops. He played 23 games in 1981 with the O's before becoming their everyday shortstop in 1982. It was bold move by Earl Weaver. At 6-4 Ripken wasn't your normal shortstop but as he progressed he began to alter people's perceptions. He hit .264 his first year, belted 28 homers and showed promise with the leather. He was rewarded with the AL Rookie of the Year award.

Over the next 19 seasons in Baltimore, Ripken would become the best all-round shortstop in baseball. He compiled 12 seasons with at least 20 home runs and 15 with at least 75 RBIs. In 1983 he won the AL MVP award hitting .318 with 27 dingers and 102 RBIs while leading his position in assists. During the '83 postseason Ripken continued his outstanding defense as he commited zero errors as the Birds beat the Phillies in the World Series. Ripken was awarded his second MVP crown in 1991 thanks to a .323 batting average, 34 homers, 114 RBIs and a Gold Glove at short. In July 1996 Ripken moved to third base before ending the Streak in '98 but when many thought his career would follow he showed up in 1999 and hit .340 with 18 homers in just 86 games. The 2000 season saw Ripken reach another milestone as he became just the 23rd major leaguer in history to reach the 3,000 hit plateau when he singled off Twins reliever Hector Carrasco on April 15 at the Metrodome.

In 2001, Ripken decided to call it a career. The numbers he leaves behind are impressive—including the most homers in history by a shortstop (345), 19 consecutive All-Star appearances, a World Series ring, two MVP awards, 3,184 hits—but it was his work ethic, his sportsmanship, his passion and his class that made him so important to the game. "Cal Ripken is one of the greatest players of our generation," said commissioner Bud Selig. "He has become a symbol for the American working man. He also became a symbol of everything that is great about the game of baseball."

## CAREER TOTALS

| G | AB | R | H | 2B | 3B | HR | RBI | BB | K | SB | Avg | Slg | OBP |
|---|---|---|---|---|---|---|---|---|---|---|---|---|---|
| 3001 | 11551 | 1647 | 3184 | 603 | 44 | 431 | 1695 | 1129 | 1305 | 36 | .276 | .447 | .340 |

# OZZIE SMITH

**Osborne Earl Smith**
**Born:** December 26 1954, Mobile, Alabama
**Bats:** Both
**Throws:** Right
**Height:** 5-11
**Weight:** 170

**"Instead of his '1' his number should be an '8' turned sideways because the possibilities he brings to his position are almost infinite." – Writer Thomas Boswell on Ozzie Smith**

He was the original human highlight reel. A blur of color, twisting, throwing, never meeting a sharp one-hopper he didn't like.

Ozzie Smith made it to the Show with the San Diego Padres in 1978 and was a walking, taking version of his scouting report. No power, exceptional glove. He hit .258 with 46 RBIs his rookie year and hovered just above the Mendoza line the rest of his time in San Diego. But what he lacked at the plate he more than made up for with his defensive talent. He won his first Gold Glove in 1980 and another in '81 before being traded to the St. Louis Cardinals in 1983.

In 1985 the "Wizard of Oz" helped St. Louis advance to the World Series. He again led the league in fielding for shortstops and won his annual Gold Glove and in the NLCS hit a crucial game-winning homer in Game 5. The Cardinals overcame the Dodgers in six games as Smith finished with a .435 average, 10 hits and three RBIs. Joy turned to misery in the Fall Classic as the cross-state Kansas City Royals won a controversial World Series in seven games.

Smith continued to improve as a hitter but only reached the .300 mark once in his career. In 1987 he hit .303 as the Cardinals again made it the World Series losing to the Minnesota Twins in seven games. He became more patient at the plate, increased his number of walks and when on base had enough speed to finish his career with 16 consecutive 20-steal seasons.

But what Ozzie Smith did with a bat was just a bonus. He was born to play shortstop with his outstanding agility, great range and lightning-quick reflexes. The baseball record books are testament to these skills. He holds numerous shortstop records including highest single-season fielding percentage (.987), least errors in a single-season (8) and years leading the league in fielding percentage (7). He also holds major league records for most 500-assist seasons (8) and in 1980 broke Glenn Wright's 56-year-old mark for most assists in a season with a staggering 621. Smith also won an unprecedented 13 consecutive NL Gold Gloves at short and is the second all-time in games played in this position.

Smith retired in 1996 and will undoubtedly be elected into Cooperstown in 2002, as one of the best defensive shortstops baseball has ever known.

## CAREER TOTALS

| G | AB | R | H | 2B | 3B | HR | RBI | BB | K | SB | Avg | Slg | OBP |
|---|----|----|----|----|----|----|-----|-----|----|----|-----|-----|-----|
| 2573 | 9396 | 1257 | 2460 | 402 | 69 | 28 | 793 | 1072 | 589 | 580 | .262 | .328 | .337 |

# HONUS WAGNER

**John Peter Wagner**
**Born:** February 24 1874, Chartiers, Pennsylvania
**Died:** December 6 1955, Carnegie, Pennsylvania
**Bats:** Right
**Throws:** Right
**Height:** 5-11
**Weight:** 200

**"There is something Lincolnesque about him, his rugged homeliness, his simplicity, his integrity and his true nobility of character." – Writer Arthur Daley on Honus Wagner**

His appearance often belied his easy-going demeanor. Ty Cobb likened his long arms and colossal hands to those of a gorilla. "He had those huge shoulders and those bowed legs," said Pirates third baseman Tommy Leach. But nothing could disguise Honus Wagner's skills.

He was the National League's MVP before it ever existed. His defensive skills were so sublime that is it is generally believed he could have played every position and still have been the league's best. He finally settled at shortstop. But Wagner was perhaps even more dominant at the plate.

In his first season in the majors in 1897, he hit .344 with Louisville. The team folded in 1899 and Wagner joined the Pittsburgh Pirates where he would become a legend. In a career spanning 21 years he had 17 consecutive .300 seasons, seven of them above .350. He won eight National League batting crowns and had nine 100-RBI seasons. Despite his appearance, the stocky Wagner was also dominating on the base paths. The "Flying Dutchman" led the league in stolen bases six times and finished with a career total of 720.

Wagner was part of an ascendant Pittsburgh franchise at the beginning of the 20th century that won four pennants and a World Series in 1909. Wagner batted .333 for the series and outshone Detroit's Ty Cobb. Wagner finally retired in 1917 at age 43. He tried his luck at managing but his kind-hearted nature didn't lend itself to the rigors of the job. He resigned after just four games in charge. He remained in Pittsburgh as an instructor from '33 to '51 and was among the first group of players elected into Cooperstown in 1936.

Honus Wagner was emblematic of baseball's lost past. The son of Bavarian immigrants, he had no formal education and played baseball during his lunch break from the coalmines of Pennsylvania. He loved the game for what it was and never negotiated his contract when he became a professional, happy to accept what the Pirates offered him. He remains today one of the greatest players to don a Pittsburgh uniform and a statue stood outside Three Rivers Stadium in his honor as the most fitting of accolades for a Steeltown legend.

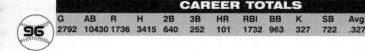

## CAREER TOTALS

| G | AB | R | H | 2B | 3B | HR | RBI | BB | K | SB | Avg | Slg | OBP |
|---|----|----|-----|-----|-----|-----|------|-----|-----|-----|------|------|------|
| 2792 | 10430 | 1736 | 3415 | 640 | 252 | 101 | 1732 | 963 | 327 | 722 | .327 | .466 | .391 |

# ROBIN YOUNT

**Robin R Yount**
**Born:** September 16 1955, Danville, Illinois
**Bats:** Right
**Throws:** Right
**Height:** 6-0
**Weight:** 170

**"He can beat you four ways. With his glove. With his arm. With his bat. With his legs. Those are the four things you look for in a ballplayer, and he can do all of them." – Brewers GM Harry Dalton on Robin Yount**

At first glance, Robin Yount's career numbers don't exactly jump off the page. Sure, there's the 3,142 hits which guaranteed his place in Cooperstown in 1999 but to really appreciate the skills of the three-time All-Star, you have to dig deeper to find a player who optimized consistency in two of the game's most demanding positions.

Selected by the Brewers as their number one pick in the 1973 draft, Yount became Milwaukee's starting shortstop at just 18 years of age. He played 11 years, from 1974 to 1984, in this most important of positions and excelled. In 1982 he put together one of the best years ever by a shortstop, hitting .331 with 29 home runs, 114 RBIs and 210 hits. He became the first shortstop ever to lead the American League in slugging percentage with a .578 mark and despite playing in a small-market city was awarded the AL MVP.

After shoulder surgery during the 1984 off-season, Yount switched to play centerfield. His intelligence and great athleticism made him a quick study in his new position. He continued to hit for average with some power and in 1989 joined Stan Musial and Hank Greenberg as the only players in major league history to win MVP Awards at two different positions. He hit .318 in 1989 with 101 runs, 103 RBIs and 21 homers and led the league with a .997 fielding percentage becoming the only player to lead this category as both an infielder and an outfielder.

Yount retired in 1994 as one of the game's most durable performers. Always reliable and the epitome of a team leader, Yount graced Brewers baseball with his silent determination for 20 years becoming the club's leader in virtually every offensive category. The company he keeps highlights his versatility. Only George Brett and Willie Mays can equal Yount's 3,000 hits, 250 home runs, 200 stolen bases and 100 triples and no other player in baseball history has played 1,000 games at both short and centerfield. But numbers only tell so much of the story. "He has never known what his batting average was," said Jim Gantner. "He just cared about the W."

## CAREER TOTALS

| G | AB | R | H | 2B | 3B | HR | RBI | BB | K | SB | Avg | Slg | OBP |
|------|-------|------|------|-----|-----|-----|------|-----|------|-----|------|------|------|
| 2856 | 11008 | 1632 | 3142 | 583 | 126 | 251 | 1406 | 966 | 1350 | 271 | .285 | .430 | .342 |

# THIRD BASE

**Wade Boggs**
**George Brett**
**Eddie Mathews**
**Paul Molitor**
**Brooks Robinson**
**Mike Schmidt**

# WADE BOGGS

**Wade Boggs**
**Born:** June 15 1958, Omaha, Nebraska
**Bats:** Left
**Throws:** Right
**Height:** 6-2
**Weight:** 197

**"Boggsy is the best hitter I've seen, day in and day out." – Don Mattingly on Wade Boggs**

The swing was honed at an early age. With his father looking on, the young boy repeated the instructed move again and again under the Floridian sun, waiting until the last second to hit the ball, spraying line drives to an imaginary left field. Eventually, the imaginary became the real, but the ingrained swing hadn't changed. Nor the results. As a rookie Red Sox in 1982, Wade Boggs slapped hit number one through the hole at short to leftfield. Eighteen seasons and three teams later, Boggs, in a Tampa Bay Devil Rays uniform, grabbed hit number 3,000 in 1999. In between those two hits, he carved a niche as one of the game's premier contact hitters, each bloop, every liner, one hit nearer Cooperstown. His 3,000th hit was, unusually a home run and he became the first man ever to have a homer as his 3000th hit.

Having retired after the completion of the '99 season, Boggs' Hall of Fame credentials are now being scrutinized by fans and writers alike. They make for impressive reading. 3,000 hits alone should guarantee a plaque but Boggs also won five batting titles and hit below .300 only three times in his 18-year Major League career.

Boggs made it to the majors with the Boston Red Sox and soon found that his swing was made for Fenway. Launching one line drive after another against the Green Monster, Boggs averaged .369 in his 11 seasons of home games in Beantown. Fenway's cozy dimensions were right up his alley as he compiled seven consecutive 200-hit seasons from 1983–89. In 1985 Boggs batted at a .368 clip with a career-high 240 hits, 42 doubles and 78 RBIs.

Despite becoming a legend with the Red Sox fans, Boggs developed an adversarial relationship with the Boston press corps, occupying the front and back pages of the local papers with seemingly similar frequency. He left the Red Sox in 1992 for the Yankees becoming perhaps the only sports star ever to move to the Big Apple in search of anonymity. Somehow he managed to find it. He didn't need to find his swing. Making some minor adjustments to his mechanics, Boggs was soon hitting low to leftfield and high to right to accommodate the differences between Fenway and Yankee stadium. In his five seasons with New York he made ink for all the right reasons. He continued to hit for average, the only aberration being 1992 when he hit .292. Boggs joined the expansion Devil Rays in 1998, his home town, and reached achieved hit number 3,000 against the Cleveland Indians. At his retirement Boggs' seven 200-hit seasons was fourth all-time, his .328 lifetime average ninth amongst the 3,000 hit group.

## CAREER TOTALS

| G | AB | R | H | 2B | 3B | HR | RBI | BB | K | SB | Avg | Slg | OBP |
|---|----|----|----|----|----|----|-----|-----|-----|----|------|------|------|
| 2440 | 9180 | 1513 | 3010 | 578 | 61 | 118 | 1014 | 1412 | 745 | 24 | .328 | .443 | .415 |

# GEORGE BRETT

**George Howard Brett**
**Born:** May 15 1953, Glen Dale, West Virginia
**Bats:** Left
**Throws:** Right
**Height:** 6-0
**Weight:** 200

**"I don't see how you could manage anybody better than George Brett." – Whitey Herzog on George Brett**

Perhaps no player ever meant more to his franchise than George Brett. Playing his entire career with the one team, he put Kansas City on the map and the Royals on the road to success. He epitomized the Midwestern values of hard-work and honesty and though he wasn't a native son he soon became as much. "George Brett was the Kansas City Royals," said General Manager Herk Robinson.

Brett made his big league debut in 1973 as a gutsy 20-year old who had developed a reputation in the minors for his intensity, his hustle and the ability to hit to all areas of the ballpark. Brett won his first batting crown in 1976, hitting .333 for the season. He won another in 1980 when his .390 mark became the highest season total since Ted Williams' .406 in 1941. He also hit 24 homers and drove in 118 runs but 1980 was mostly the year that baseball discovered Brett's propensity for the dramatic. In Game 3 of the ALCS against the Yankees he launched a three-run shot into the upper deck of Yankee Stadium to clinch the pennant and send Kansas City to its first ever World Series.

Something of a throwback, Brett continued to play out his career as if he was on a permanent adrenaline rush, always playing the game with a passion that captured the heart of baseball, both fans and players alike. "If there was ever a player I would have wanted to be, it would have been George Brett," said fellow Hall of Famer Robin Yount.

Probably the clutch player of his era, Brett was again the hero during the 1985 season. He hit .335 with 30 homers and 112 RBIs to lead the Royals to the AL West title. They clinched the pennant, beating the Toronto Blue Jays in seven games. Brett again led by example with a .348 average, three home runs and five RBIs and in the all-Missouri World Series, hit .370 to help Kansas City defeat the St. Louis Cardinals in seven games.

Having retired in 1993, Brett was elected into the Hall of Fame in 1999. He still remains the only player to win batting titles in three different decades and joins the select group of Hank Aaron and Willie Mays as the only players with 3,000 hits, 300 home runs and 200 stolen bases. His lifetime average of .305 is surpassed by his postseason mark of .337 and is the Royals career leader in every offensive category except stolen bases.

## CAREER TOTALS

| G | AB | R | H | 2B | 3B | HR | RBI | BB | K | SB | Avg | Slg | OBP |
|------|-------|------|------|-----|-----|-----|------|------|-----|-----|------|------|------|
| 2707 | 10349 | 1583 | 3154 | 665 | 137 | 317 | 1595 | 1096 | 908 | 201 | .305 | .487 | .369 |

# EDDIE MATHEWS

**Edwin Lee Mathews**
**Born:** October 13 1931, Texarkana, Texas
**Died:** February 18 2001, San Diego, California
**Bats:** Left
**Throws:** Right
**Height:** 6-1
**Weight:** 200

**"Eddie was all anger and in your face. Every game was like a street fight to him." – the Mets' Ron Swoboda on Eddie Mathews**

Labeled a "can't miss" prospect, Eddie Mathews was scouted heavily in high school and was signed literally at the earliest possible moment. In 1949, at one minute past midnight on the day of Mathews' graduation dance in Santa Barbara, Braves' scout Johnny Moore got the John Hancock he had fought so hard to get. He had beaten out Branch Rickey and the Dodgers. Mathews was on his way to Boston.

Mathews would remain a Brave for the majority of his career, becoming the only man to play for the Braves in Boston, Milwaukee and Atlanta. He quickly established a reputation in Boston as a sweet swinger with serious power. Ty Cobb described Mathews' stroke as one of the "three or four perfect swings" that he had seen. In 1952 he hit 25 homers and when the Braves moved to Milwaukee, Mathews went with them. He slugged 47 home runs his first year, narrowly losing the MVP Award to Roy Campanella and was integral part of the Braves' 1957 season that culminated in a World Series triumph over the Yankees.

Mathews clinched Game 4 with a tenth-inning homer, scored the only run in Game 5 started by his infield single and in Game 7 snared Moose Skowron's hard-hit liner, stepping on third base to end the game and win the Championship. The fiery Mathews recalls that diving stop as one of his career highlights. "I'd made better plays," he said, "but that big one in the spotlight stamped me the way I wanted to be remembered."

He was traded to the Astros in 1967 and hit his 500th home run with Houston off Juan Marichal, becoming only the seventh player in history to reach this mark. Mathews retired the following year after playing just 31 games for the World Champion Detroit Tigers. He was reunited with the Braves franchise when he was appointed manager in 1972, eventually calling it day in 1974.

Elected to Cooperstown in 1978, Mathews had nine 30-homer seasons, four 40-homer seasons and only failed to hit at least 20 dingers three times in his 17-year career. As a Brave he became synonymous with Hank Aaron as the two combined to become the greatest home-run hitting teammates ever. Their combined career total of 863 gives them 60 more homers than Babe Ruth and Lou Gehrig.

## CAREER TOTALS

| G | AB | R | H | 2B | 3B | HR | RBI | BB | K | SB | Avg | Slg | OBP |
|---|----|----|----|----|----|----|-----|-----|-----|----|-----|-----|-----|
| 2391 | 8537 | 1509 | 2315 | 354 | 72 | 512 | 1453 | 1444 | 1487 | 68 | .271 | .509 | .376 |

# PAUL MOLITOR

**Paul Lee Molitor**
**Born:** August 22 1956, St. Paul, Minnesota
**Bats:** Right
**Throws:** Right
**Height:** 6-0
**Weight:** 195

"That's the 'Molly,' that's what I call his swing. I don't know how he does it, but it's beautiful." – **Kirby Puckett on Paul Molitor**

He was the classic contact hitter. With his short, quick jab of a swing, he looked the part. Spraying line drives to all fields, Paul Molitor played the part, too.

After attending the University of Minnesota on a baseball scholarship, Molitor was selected in the first round of the 1977 draft by the Milwaukee Brewers. He worked hard with the team's hitting instructors, changing his long, flowing collegiate swing into a sharp, compact stroke designed to survive the rigors of major league pitching. Armed with his new move, Molitor hit .273 in his rookie season, stole 30 bases and had 142 hits. He played the majority of the season at second, but also saw some time at short and as the team's DH.

In 1979 Molitor's numbers began to improve. He raised his batting average to .322, stole 33 bases and drove in 62 runs. But for the next eight seasons Molitor played with injuries and was constantly sidelined. In his first 10 years as professional he only played more than 125 games on four occasions. But when he was healthy, he performed. In 1982 he hit .302 and scored 136 runs and in 1987 he had a .353 average with 114 runs, 41 doubles and 16 homers. He continued his form in the World Series, where the Brewers lost in seven games to the St. Louis Cardinals. "The Ignitor" did his bit, however, recording the only five-hit game in Series history. Molitor worked hard to maintain his fitness and soon began to reap the rewards, playing less than 125 games just twice after 1988.

A free agent in 1993, Molitor joined the Toronto Blue Jays as their DH and had 211 hits, a .322 average as well as stealing 22 bases and hitting a career-high 22 dingers. He also got to fulfill a dream, winning his first World Series. The Jays defeated the Phillies in six games and Molitor was on fire. He led the team with a .500 average, 10 runs and 12 hits. In the strike shortened season of 1994, Molitor batted .341 in 115 games before leaving to join his hometown Twins. He played three seasons in Minnesota, leading the league in hits in '96, before retiring in 1998.

One of baseball's most astute players, Molitor was not just a great contact hitter but also one of the game's best baserunners using his baseball savvy and what he describes as "instinct and alertness" to finish his career with 504 thefts. His 3319 hits ranks him ninth all-time while his 1782 runs is the 16th best total. "You see some of the names you're passing up," Molitor said, "and you almost wonder how you got to be in the company of these players." With Cooperstown beckoning, come 2004, Molitor will be in their company again. Forever.

## CAREER TOTALS

| G | AB | R | H | 2B | 3B | HR | RBI | BB | K | SB | Avg | Slg | OBP |
|---|---|---|---|---|---|---|---|---|---|---|---|---|---|
| 2683 | 10835 | 1782 | 3319 | 605 | 114 | 234 | 1307 | 1094 | 1244 | 504 | .306 | .448 | .369 |

# BROOKS ROBINSON

**Brooks Calbert Robinson**
**Born:** May 18 1937, Little Rock, Arkansas
**Bats:** Right
**Throws:** Right
**Height:** 6-1
**Weight:** 190

**"To me, baseball was a passion to the point of obsession." – Brooks Robinson**

When it came to playing the hot corner, few were cooler than Brooks Robinson. He was so spectacular with the glove that Johnny Bench said, "I will become a lefthander hitter to keep the ball away from that guy." He was nicknamed "Hoover" because he literally sucked up everything that was hit near him. He won 15 consecutive Gold Gloves from 1960 to 1975 and set major league records for putouts, assists, double plays and fielding percentage.

Robinson's first season was in 1955. He played in only six games, hit well below the Mendoza line and was sent down. After several cups of coffee in the majors, Robinson made it into the Orioles line-up for good in 1958. In all, he would play in all or part of 23 seasons in the Major Leagues.

He showed no power his first year and only hit .238 but his defensive skills were already apparent. His power numbers began to increase and he was developing into a solid contact hitter, too. In 1964 he was awarded the American League MVP, posting a .317 average with 194 hits, 28 homers and a league leading 118 RBIs. But like many legends Robinson seemed to have the innate ability to raise his performance at the most important times.

When the playoffs began, Robinson shifted a gear. In the 1969 American League Championship Series he hit .500 as the O's beat the Twins and the following season, when the two teams met again in the ALCS, Robinson again performed at the plate, batting .583 with seven hits in 12 at bats. But he saved his best for last. In the World Series Robinson did it with both the leather and the lumber. He drove in six runs, hit two homers to finish with a .429 average for the series. In Game 3 he robbed one Cincinnati hitter after another, as he denied Tony Perez and Johnny Bench base hits with his outstanding play at third. The O's crushed the Reds, 4-1 and Robinson was named the World Series MVP.

Robinson retired in 1977 and was elected into the Hall of Fame in 1983 as one of the game's all-time defensive third baseman.

## CAREER TOTALS

| G | AB | R | H | 2B | 3B | HR | RBI | BB | K | SB | Avg | Slg | OBP |
|------|-------|------|------|-----|-----|-----|------|-----|-----|-----|------|------|------|
| 2896 | 10654 | 1232 | 2848 | 482 | 68 | 268 | 1357 | 860 | 990 | 28 | .267 | .401 | .322 |

103

# MIKE SCHMIDT

**Michael Jack Schmidt**
**Born:** September 27 1949, Dayton, Ohio
**Bats:** Right
**Throws:** Right
**Height:** 6-2
**Weight:** 200

**"I don't think I can get into my deep inner thoughts about hitting. It's like talking about religion." – Mike Schmidt**

If you're looking for a turning point in the career of Phillies legend Mike Schmidt, then the off-season of 1973 might just be it. Playing winter ball in Puerto Rico after a disappointing rookie campaign left him with a .196 average, Schmidt worked hard, tweaking his swing until something clicked. "I was standing at the plate nice and relaxed and that sucker went off my bat a mile," he told *Sport* magazine.

Schmidt would never toy with the Mendoza line again. The next season he hit 36 homers to lead the NL and drove in 116 runs, while also leading the league with a .546 slugging percentage. He had raised his average to .282 and was elected to his first All-Star game. It's safe to say he had turned the corner. Over the next 15 years Schmidt developed into one of the great all-round players and power hitters. He led the National League in homers eight times and in RBIs four times. In 1976 against the Cubs at Wrigley Field he hit four home runs in four at bats and became the fourth fastest player in history to reach 500 homers. His final total of 534 is the most ever by a third baseman. Schmidt also did it with the glove. Never scalded by the hot corner, he was the dominant third baseman of his time winning ten Gold Gloves and leading the league in assists on seven occasions, a record he jointly holds with Ron Santo.

After shouldering much of the blame for the Phillies' post-season defeats in 1976, '77 and '78, Schmidt silenced his critics in the 1980 Fall Classic with a performance for the ages. Having changed his approach at the plate in 1978, Schmidt began to hit to all fields, and in the World Series against the Royals it all began to fall into place. In Game 1 he scored two runs and his double in the eighth ignited the game-winning rally. In Game 2 he drove in the winning run and in Game 5 he hit a two-run shot followed by a single in the ninth to spark another come-from-behind victory. Finally, in Game 6 he had two base hits as the Phillies closed out the Royals. He finished the series with a .381 average, two homers and seven RBIs to win the MVP.

He retired in 1989 as the only Phillie in history with 1,000 RBIs, walks and runs. He is a three-time National League MVP, joining Stan Musial and Roy Campanella as the only players to achieve this honor—Barry Bonds has four. Elected to the Hall of Fame in 1995, Schmidt is generally regarded as the greatest third baseman of all time.

## CAREER TOTALS

| G | AB | R | H | 2B | 3B | HR | RBI | BB | K | SB | Avg | Slg | OBP |
|------|------|------|------|-----|-----|-----|------|------|------|-----|------|------|------|
| 2404 | 8352 | 1506 | 2234 | 408 | 59 | 548 | 1595 | 1507 | 1883 | 174 | .267 | .527 | .380 |

# *The* **Players**

## OUTFIELD

**Hank Aaron**
**Cool Papa Bell**
**Barry Bonds**
**Oscar Charleston**
**Ty Cobb**
**Joe DiMaggio**
**Ken Griffey Jr.**
**Tony Gwynn**
**Roberto Clemente**
**Rickey Henderson**
**Shoeless Joe Jackson**
**Reggie Jackson**
**Al Kaline**
**Mickey Mantle**
**Willie Mays**
**Stan Musial**
**Mel Ott**
**Frank Robinson**
**Pete Rose**
**Babe Ruth**
**Duke Snider**
**Sammy Sosa**
**Tris Speaker**
**Willie Stargell**
**Ted Williams**
**Carl Yastrzemski**

# HANK AARON

**Henry Louis Aaron**
**Born:** February 5 1934, Mobile, Alabama
**Bats:** Right
**Throws:** Right
**Height:** 6-0
**Weight:** 180

**"I don't want them to forget Ruth. I just want them to remember me." – Hank Aaron**

As a player Hank Aaron always preferred the making of history over histrionics. He quietly approached becoming the game's home run king, its all-time RBI leader, with little fuss and in return received none of the adulation usually reserved for players of his ability. Slowly but surely he posted his numbers, year in year out. And he caught them all by surprise.

Aaron hit the headlines only when he closed in on Babe Ruth's career home run record. His qualities were only appreciated years later when he spoke of the racial hatred he endured when he attempted and succeeded in stepping out of the Bambino's shadow. But Aaron's talents had been on show all along. America just hadn't looked hard enough. On April 8 1974 with one crisp swing, he became a legend, but for the previous 20 years before he hit his 715th dinger, Aaron had been carving a career of outstanding consistency. Naturally unassuming and without the obvious flair of a Mantle or Mays, he went largely unnoticed as one of baseball's true greats.

After playing with the Indianapolis Clowns of the Negro League, Aaron made his big league debut in 1954 with the Milwaukee Braves and moved with them to Atlanta in '66. It quickly became apparent to his peers, if not the public, that he was something special. "Aaron was to my time what DiMaggio was to his," said Mickey Mantle. His accomplishments are vast. He was a 24-time All-Star with the Braves and Brewers; he averaged .305 for his 23 seasons in the majors and won the 1957 NL MVP award. Both his career home run and RBI records are testimony to his continued high level of performance. He never had a monster year, his highs being 46 homers and 132 RBIs, but he hit less than 20 home runs only three times and failed to drive in at least 75 runs just four times. Defensively Aaron was no slouch either, winning three Gold Gloves in the outfield.

In 1999, 25 years after his historic blast, Major League Baseball celebrated both the man and his record and finally, to some degree, Hammerin' Hank got his dues. New fans learned of the pain and pride he experienced in becoming the game's all-time home run leader. But they also learned that one swing of the bat doesn't make a career. Henry Aaron was and is so much more than just the holder of baseball's most treasured number. He was a real team player who in retirement has been a constant, eloquent voice in such important issues as minority hiring in baseball. "He speaks with his heart and conscience," said NL President Len Coleman. "He contributed when he played and he continues to do so now."

## CAREER TOTALS

| G | AB | R | H | 2B | 3B | HR | RBI | BB | K | SB | Avg | Slg | OBP |
|---|----|----|----|----|----|----|-----|----|----|----|-----|-----|-----|
| 3298 | 12364 | 2174 | 3771 | 624 | 98 | 755 | 2297 | 1402 | 1383 | 240 | .305 | .555 | .374 |

# COOL PAPA BELL

**James Thomas Bell**
**Born:** May 17 1903, Starkville, Mississippi
**Died:** March 7 1991, St. Louis, Missouri
**Bats:** Both
**Throws:** Left
**Height:** 5-11
**Weight:** 140

**"They used to say 'If we find a good black player, we'll sign him.' They were lying." – Cool Papa Bell**

In terms of pure speed, Cool Papa Bell and the wind ran just about neck and neck.

He was once timed circling the bases in 12 seconds. He routinely stole two bases on one pitch, scored from second on a sacrifice fly and beat out weakly hit ground balls for fun. Negro League stars loved to add to Bell's mythology as the fastest man in baseball. "When we were playing with the Crawfords against the Birmingham team," said team mate Jimmy Crutchfield, "he hit a ground ball right past the pitcher and that ball hit Cool Papa as he slid into second base!" And of course, as the great pitcher Satchel Paige loved to recount, "He could switch out the light and be in bed before it got dark!"

James Bell joined the St. Louis Stars in 1922 and his speed was an immediate asset. As an outfielder he had great range and on the basepaths he was untouchable. Despite the unreliability of Negro League statistics, it is widely believed that he stole 175 bases in less than 200 games. A switch hitter, Bell had a .341 lifetime batting average and raised it to .391 in exhibition games against major leaguers.

In 1932 he joined the Pittsburgh Crawfords and was given the tag "Cool Papa" because of his ability to perform in the clutch. During his 21 years in baseball he also played for the Homestead Grays, Kansas City Monarchs, Chicago American Giants, Detroit Senators and the Memphis Red Sox. He also routinely played winter ball in Cuba and Mexico.

Bell's preeminent years were during the 1930s and though he officially retired in 1950 he never really had the opportunity to benefit from baseball's integration. However, as a coach with the Monarchs he worked closely with Jackie Robinson before he broke the game's color barrier in 1947. In 1972 his achievements were recognized when he was elected into the baseball Hall of Fame.

# BARRY BONDS

**Barry Lamar Bonds**
**Born:** July 24 1964, Riverside, California
**Bats:** Left
**Throws:** Left
**Height:** 6-2
**Weight:** 210

"Everybody was telling me just be patient, be patient. I'm glad its over. My wife gets to sleep now" – **Barry Bonds after hitting home run No. 70**

With Bobby Bonds as his father and Willie Mays as his godfather, Barry Bonds can stake his claim to the best family tree in baseball. With that kind of lineage it's no surprise that the Giants' leftfielder can also lay claim to the title of most complete player of his era. And after 2001, the best season, too.

At 37, Bonds compiled a season to challenge the very best in baseball history, as he chased one offensive record after another. He started on a tear, hitting 11 homers in 10 games in May, and by June 4 he had reached 30 home runs—the fastest ever to that mark. Suddenly the race for baseball's favorite number was on again.

Bonds eventually reached and passed Mark McGwire's single-season record of 70 home runs, finishing the year with an incredible 73 dingers. In compiling this otherworldly number, he also became a member of the 500-career homer club on April 17. But Bonds' record breaking didn't stop there. He smashed Babe Ruth's .847 slugging percentage record set in 1920 and broke his 1923 walk record of 170 by seven. He homered every 6.52 at-bats to pass McGwire's 1998 pace of every 7.27 at-bats while his .515 on-base percentage was the best in the majors since 1957. He received an unprecedented fourth MVP award in recognition. "It's the greatest year I've seen from a single player," said Giants skipper Dusty Baker.

Bonds first joined the majors in 1986. He won his first MVP Award in 1990 with the Pirates, hitting .301 with 33 home runs, 114 RBIs and 52 stolen bases. He was again the National League's MVP in 1992 thanks to a .311 average, 34 homers and 39 stolen bases. On both occasions Pittsburgh won the NL East division title.

Bonds left for San Francisco in 1993 and after hitting .336 with 46 dingers and 123 RBIs became the first player in National League history to win three MVP crowns in four years. Bonds has continued to be a force with the Giants using his enviable combination of speed, power and intelligence to find his way into the record books. In 1998 he became the first player in over fifty years to receive an intentional walk with the bases loaded. Bonds again proved his worth in 2000, leading the Giants to the NL West crown and his awesome numbers in 2001, including 137 RBIs, kept his team in the heat of the battle into the final week of the season. He is also the only player in history with 400 home runs and 400 stolen bases and needs only 16 more SB's to reach 500-500, illustrating the versatility that makes him one of the most feared players in the game.

"I think he is the best player in the National League by far," said Tony Gwynn. "It's not even close. He's the one guy who can beat you by himself, and he knows it," adds Gwynn. "Heck, we all know it."

## CAREER TOTALS

| G | AB | R | H | 2B | 3B | HR | RBI | BB | K | SB | Avg | Slg | OBP |
|---|-----|------|------|-----|----|-----|------|------|------|-----|------|------|------|
| 2296 | 7932 | 1713 | 2313 | 483 | 71 | 567 | 1542 | 1724 | 1282 | 484 | .292 | .585 | .419 |

# OSCAR CHARLESTON

**Oscar McKinley Charleston**
**Born:** October 14 1896, Indianapolis, Indiana
**Died:** October 5 1954, Philadelphia, Pennsylvania
**Batted:** Left
**Threw:** Left
**Height:** 6-0
**Weight:** 190

"The great Negro League player of his time." – **Umpire Jocko Conlon on Oscar Charleston**

Oscar Charleston was probably the Negro Leagues first real star. In a career lasting four decades he played and managed in the majority of leagues established for black baseball. He was charismatic, aggressive and supremely talented, described by teammate Ben Taylor as the "greatest outfielder that ever lived."

Joining the Indianapolis ABCs in 1915, the Hoosier Comet was instantly a standout. In 1920 Rube Foster's Negro National League was born and the ABCs were among the first of its teams. And Charleston was its premier attraction. In 1921 he hit .446, led the league in homers and was a standout in centerfield. However, what seemed to separate Charleston from many of his counterparts was his innate ability to read situations and adapt accordingly. He joined the Eastern Colored League in 1922 as the Harrisburg Giants player-manager.

After winning back-to-back batting titles with the Giants, the league disbanded and Charleston took over as the skipper of the American Negro League's Philadelphia Hilldales before managing the Homestead Grays in 1931-32. During this period he twice hit over .400 and established his reputation as not only a fearsome player but also a dynamic manager.

From 1932–36, Charleston was the player-manager with the Pittsburgh Crawfords and teamed up with fellow slugger Josh Gibson to form the Negro League's most potent one-two punch. He retired in 1941 with a .376 lifetime average and the respect of all those who had played with and for him. He continued to manage, with Branch Rickey's Brooklyn Brown Dodgers and his hometown Indianapolis Clowns, until his death in 1954.

In his prime he was, somewhat ironically, compared to Ty Cobb because of his volcanic temper and refuse-to-lose approach but unlike Cobb, Charleston was a respected figure, credited with the development of many young players who played under him. Upon his death he had played and managed for 17 Negro League teams and was inducted into the Hall of Fame in 1976.

# ROBERTO CLEMENTE

**Roberto Clemente Walker**
**Born:** August 18 1934 in Carolina, Puerto Rico
**Died:** December 31 1972 off San Juan, Puerto Rico
**Batted:** Switch
**Threw:** Right
**Height:** 5-11
**Weight:** 175

**"He had about him a touch of royalty." – Commissioner Bowie Kuhn.**

It took patience, dominating performances on the game's biggest stages and, ultimately, a tragedy for Roberto Clemente to become fully appreciated on a national level. But he got there.

Originally signed by the Dodgers, but eventually drafted by the Pirates in 1955, Clemente began his career quietly. As a 20-year old from Puerto Rico he was still learning English and absorbing a new culture while he tried to contend with the rigors of Major League baseball. He persevered. The Pittsburgh Pirates improved. Clemente, too.

In 1960 he had a breakout year. Clemente hit .314, drove in 94 runs and was selected for his first All-Star game. His Pirates won the World Series beating the New York Yankees in seven games. But Clemente remained relatively unheralded, particularly by baseball's media.

Clemente was as potent a right fielder as baseball has ever known; winning 12 consecutive Gold Gloves, thanks largely to a hugely powerful arm that was feared throughout the National League. He was equally as dominant at the plate. In his 17 seasons he batted .300 or better 13 times while becoming the 11th player in baseball history to reach 3,000 hits. Between 1961 and 1967 he won four batting crowns and a National League MVP award. And in the 1971 World Series he exploded.

In a performance for the ages Clemente seemingly beat the Orioles single-handedly as he batted .414 for the Series enabling Pittsburgh to edge Baltimore 4-3. He was awarded the World Series MVP and finally achieved the universal acclaim his talents deserved.

On December 23 1972, an earthquake struck the city of Managua, Nicaragua and Clemente, who organized humanitarian projects in Puerto Rico, began to help arrange support for the thousands who had been made homeless. On New Years Eve a plane carrying relief supplies to Managua crashed shortly after take-off. There were no survivors. And Roberto Clemente was on board.

Upon his death he became the first Hispanic player to be elected into the Hall of Fame and the world of baseball finally realized what it once had and now lost. A great ballplayer. An even greater man.

## CAREER TOTALS

| G | AB | R | H | 2B | 3B | HR | RBI | BB | K | SB | Avg | Slg | OBP |
|---|----|---|---|----|----|----|----|----|----|----|----|----|----|
| 2433 | 9454 | 1416 | 3000 | 440 | 166 | 240 | 1305 | 621 | 1230 | 83 | .317 | .475 | .359 |

# TY COBB

**Tyrus Raymond Cobb**
**Born:** December 18 1886, Narrows, Georgia
**Died:** July 17 1961, Atlanta, Georgia
**Batted:** Left
**Threw:** Left
**Height:** 6-1
**Weight:** 175

"When I came to Detroit I was just a mild-mannered Sunday-school boy." – **Ty Cobb**

His nickname was "the Georgia Peach," but there was nothing remotely soft – or sweet – about Ty Cobb. His violent temper and far-reaching prejudices are as much a part of his legend as his astonishing numbers.

Born in 1886 and raised in Royston, Georgia, Cobb made the big leagues as an 18-year old with the Detroit Tigers. He had a batter's eye, a prizefighter's aggression and a chip on his shoulder the depth of the Grand Canyon. "He was still fighting the Civil War and as far as he was concerned we were all damn Yankees," said team mate Sam Crawford. "But who knows, if he hadn't had that terrible persecution complex, he never would have been about the best ballplayer who ever lived."

He was loathed by opposing players and disliked by many of his Detroit team-mates, but Cobb played the game with an intensity that has perhaps never been matched. He was rampant on the base paths where he showed no fear. He was often accused of sharpening his spikes to slice the infielder blocking the base and Cobb seemed to enjoy this reputation. But Ty Cobb needed little fabrication to enhance his standing in baseball.

In his 24 seasons in the major leagues, he won 12 batting titles and nine consecutive from 1907–16. He finished with a career batting average of .366, which still ranks number one all-time. He stole 892 bases and became the first player ever to have back-to-back .400 seasons. His 2,245 runs scored was only surpassed in 2001. During this time he also jumped into the stands at New York's Hilltop Park and beat a heckler into submission, pistol-whipped a man who attempted to rob him and his wife and fought long and hard with establishment, players and teammates alike. On and off the field Cobb was both unforgiving and unrelenting.

Cobb left the Tigers in 1926 after a short spell as player-manager. He joined the Philadelphia Athletics where he reached another career milestone, the first player to 4,000 hits. On his retirement in 1929 he held the lifetime records for many offensive categories, including hits, runs, and RBIs. While time has seen many of Cobb's records eclipsed his fearsome reputation and awesome skill are forever preserved.

## CAREER TOTALS

| G | AB | R | H | 2B | 3B | HR | RBI | BB | K | SB | Avg | Slg | OBP |
|------|-------|------|------|-----|-----|-----|------|------|-----|-----|------|------|------|
| 3034 | 11434 | 2245 | 4190 | 725 | 295 | 117 | 1937 | 1249 | 357 | 892 | .366 | .512 | .433 |

# JOE DiMAGGIO

**Joseph Paul DiMaggio**
**Born:** November 25 1914 in Martinez, California
**Died:** March 8 1999 in Hollywood, Florida
**Bats:** Right
**Throws:** Right
**Height:** 6-2
**Weight:** 190

**"You saw him standing out there and you knew you had a pretty darn good chance to win the baseball game." - Red Ruffing.**

It was always about more than his understated style in centerfield or his graceful swing that seemed to belie the force generated. He wasn't just the complete ballplayer, the Yankee icon or the man who married Marilyn Monroe. Joe DiMaggio was, and is, the game personified. In the sepia tones of his youth, in the graying dignity of his retirement and ultimately in his death, Joltin' Joe is baseball as we would always like to remember it.

Much of DiMaggio's mystique however is born from his greatness on the diamond. "He remains a living symbol of excellence, elegance, power," said *New York Times* writer Ira Berkow. And these are the very attributes that made him the finest all-around player of his time. DiMaggio started his baseball career with the San Francisco Seals. In 1933 he had a 61-game hit-streak. Inevitably he didn't stay there long. He was going to be a Yankee.

DiMaggio's career with the New York Yankees, which began as a rookie in 1936 and ended in 1951, was filled with personal achievements and unparalleled team success. His Yankee teams won 10 American League Pennants and nine World Series while he captured three MVP awards. In eight of his 13 seasons he drove in 100-runs and he dropped below .300 only twice in his career. He was a beautiful centerfielder but never flashy and was seemingly uncomfortable with the attention his talents bought. But DiMaggio was also fiercely competitive. In 1941, his finest year, he finished with a .357 average, 125 RBI, 30 homers and a 56-game hitting streak that may never be beaten. He won the MVP and the Yankees the World Series.

He retired in 1951 because of a nagging ankle injury but despite being intensely private Joe DiMaggio as an icon remained. He found his way into Simon and Garfunkel's hit record "Mrs. Robinson" – released 16 years after he retired – and Ernest Hemingway's novella "The Old Man and the Sea".

He died on March 8 1999, still the only player in baseball history to have more than 300 home runs and fewer than 400 strikeouts. It is a record that mirrors the man. Perfectly disciplined, standing alone. This is the Joe DiMaggio preserved in song, prose and forever in America's memory.

## CAREER TOTALS

| G | AB | R | H | 2B | 3B | HR | RBI | BB | K | SB | Avg | Slg | OBP |
|---|-----|------|------|-----|-----|-----|------|-----|-----|-----|------|------|------|
| 1736 | 6821 | 1390 | 2214 | 389 | 131 | 361 | 1537 | 790 | 369 | 30 | .325 | .579 | .398 |

# KEN GRIFFEY JR.

**George Kenneth Griffey, Jr.**
**Born:** November 21 1969, Donora, Pennsylvania
**Bats:** Left
**Throws:** Left
**Height:** 6-3
**Weight:** 205

**"We love Griffey because he is everything we would like to be. He's young, good-looking and he's a heroic athlete. There hasn't been anyone like that since … Reggie Jackson." –**
## Reggie Jackson on Ken Griffey Jr.

Whether chasing down a fly ball, one effortless stride after another, or hitting a towering home run with his syrupy swing, Ken Griffey Jr. appears to have been born in spikes.

About the same time he was learning to walk, Griffey was learning the difference between a splitter and a slider. His father was a major leaguer with the Reds and Junior was a regular fixture in the clubhouse. His father taught him the subtleties of the game and a batting stroke that would stand the test of time. He quickly developed as a player and in 1987 was chosen by the Seattle Mariners as the number one draft pick. In his very first Major League at bat in the Kingdome on April 10 1989 he hit a line drive over the right field wall for a home run. He has yet to slow down.

Since 1990 Griffey has had seven .300 seasons but power remains his forte. He became the youngest player ever in baseball history to hit 350 homers at just 28 years, 308 days. He finished an injury-shortened 2001 season with 22 dingers giving him 460 for his career. Inevitably talk of Griffey surpassing Hank Aaron's all-time record is now commonplace and he appears to have been blessed with the consistency to truly challenge 755. Since 1993 he has failed to hit 40 or more home runs on only two occasions when he missed the majority of the '95 season with a wrist injury and played only 111 games in 2001. But the relaxed Griffey refuses to be drawn on the Aaron issue, stating, "records don't drive me," before adding, "The most important numbers are in the won-lost column." It is a salient point.

In 1999 he finished with 123 runs, 173 hits, 48 home runs and 134 RBIs but the Mariners still ended up with a losing record. It is his ambition to fill the only notable blank on his otherwise glowing resume. By the entry for World Series appearances, there is nothing. So, in 2000, Griffey came home. After much speculation he joined the Cincinnati Reds, where his father played and now coaches. But despite his 40 home runs and 118 RBIs, the Reds couldn't advance to the playoffs and 2001 provided more disappointment as the Reds finished 27 games out of first in the NL Central. Griffey will have to wait at least another year for his championship ring.

The most enigmatic player to patrol center field since Willie Mays, Griffey is often favorably compared to the Say-Hey Kid. Not only does he put up equally impressive power numbers he is also a 10-time Gold Glove winner in centerfield, making highlight-reel catches seem effortless, just as Mays once did. Still only 32, Griffey has racked up eight 100-RBI seasons, with a career best 147 in '98, and 1995 aside, has reached triple-digits for hits in each of his 13 Major League seasons.

## CAREER TOTALS

| G | AB | R | H | 2B | 3B | HR | RBI | BB | K | SB | Avg | Slg | OBP |
|---|---|---|---|---|---|---|---|---|---|---|---|---|---|
| 1791 | 6716 | 1220 | 1987 | 362 | 35 | 460 | 1335 | 885 | 1173 | 175 | .296 | .566 | .379 |

113

# TONY GWYNN

**Anthony Keith Gwynn**
**Born:** May 9 1960, Los Angeles, California
**Bats:** Left
**Throws:** Left
**Height:** 5-11
**Weight:** 220

**"I think my place in history is already set with these eight batting titles, but 3,000 hits kind of says, 'He was very good at what he did.'" – Tony Gwynn**

He had done it, literally, thousands of times before. On August 8 1999 he reached down low on a 1-2 pitch and lofted a line drive over second base for another single. But this was no ordinary base hit. 2,284 games after his major league debut Tony Gwynn had reached hit number 3,000.

Gwynn made it to the show with the San Diego Padres in 1982 as a good, but not outstanding, prospect. But he quickly became the latter. In his first full season in 1984 he batted .351 with 213 hits, displaying the very attributes that would become the hallmark of his career. When it comes to getting good wood on the ball, Gwynn has had few peers. A classic contact hitter, his swing stays so level through the hitting zone you could balance a glass of water on the barrel and none would be spilt. The result has been a career of remarkable consistency and longevity. One line drive after another. Base hit following base hit.

After his impressive start in the majors, Gwynn went on to capture four batting crowns during the 1980s; his highest mark a .370 average in 1987. He won his first batting title of the new decade, hitting a career high .394 in the strike-shortened season of 1994. He then proceeded to win three more on the trot, hitting .368, .353 and .372, to join Rod Carew, Ty Cobb, Wade Boggs and Rogers Hornsby as the only players in major league history to win four consecutive batting titles. He closed out the 20th century hitting .338 for the Padres, his 17th .300 season on the spin.

When he reached number 3,000 against the Expos, he did so with the fourth highest average of those 21 players in this elite category. Only Cobb, Tris Speaker, Nap Lajoie and Cap Anson bettered his career .338 mark when they reached 3,000 and only the Georgia Peach has won more batting crowns than Gwynn's eight. However, after a 2000 season that ended prematurely thanks to knee surgery on June 27, Gwynn called it a career in 2001. One of baseball's real gentlemen and as an intelligent player as you could wish to find, *Sports Illustrated* described Gwynn as "the best hitter since Ted Williams." It's easy to see why.

The first exclusively National Leaguer since Lou Brock to reach 3,000 hits, Gwynn also compiled five 200-hit seasons and his career .338 batting average is the best in the majors since Williams. In his 21 seasons with the Padres he recorded just one three-strikeout game and hit .300 his final 19 seasons to break Honus Wagner's record of 17 straight. Gwynn played in two World Series with San Diego and was a 15-time All-Star.

"It's been wonderful," Gwynn said after his final game on October 7 2001. For baseball fans lucky enough to have followed his career, the feeling was mutual.

## CAREER TOTALS

| G | AB | R | H | 2B | 3B | HR | RBI | BB | K | SB | Avg | Slg | OBP |
|---|----|----|---|----|----|----|-----|----|---|----|-----|-----|-----|
| 2440 | 9288 | 1383 | 3141 | 543 | 85 | 135 | 1138 | 790 | 434 | 319 | .338 | .459 | .388 |

# RICKEY HENDERSON

**Rickey Henley Henderson**
**Born:** December 25 1958, Chicago, Illinois
**Bats:** Right
**Throws:** Left
**Height:** 5-10
**Weight:** 190

**"He has this aura about him unlike any player I've ever been around." – Padres GM Kevin Towers on Rickey Henderson**

Rickey Henderson may have played for nine different ballclubs in four decades but the one constant in his career has been his level of intensity and commitment. And at 43 years' old he is still going strong.

Unquestionably baseball's greatest ever leadoff man and base stealer, Henderson began his career with the Oakland A's in 1979, having impressed in the minors where his speed on the base paths had helped him win the California League's MVP in 1977. He stole 100 bases with the A's in 1980 after swiping 33 in just 89 games his rookie year. A star was born.

In 1982 he broke Lou Brock's single-season stolen base record of 118 when he compiled an otherworldly 130 steals. Tagged the "Man of Steal", Henderson was also developing into a solid contact hitter with some power and combined with his consistently high on-base percentage became an ignitor in the leadoff spot.

Henderson was traded to the Yankees in 1985 where he played for almost five seasons before landing back in Oakland for the remainder of the 1989 season. His return sparked the A's to a World Series triumph over their Bay Area neighbors, the Giants, hitting .474 for the Series. He won the MVP award in 1990, hitting .325 with 65 stolen bases. In 1991 Henderson caught Brock again and became the undisputed stolen base king when he surpassed Brock's all-time mark of 938.

After leaving the A's in 1993, Henderson played for the Blue Jays, the Padres, the Angels, as well as third spell with Oakland. He added his priceless experience to the Mets' line-up in 1999 and the Mariners in 2000. He helped New York into the postseason where they eventually lost in the NLCS to the Braves, while the Mariners advanced to the ALCS, losing to the Yankees in six. In 2001 he joined the San Diego Padres.

During his 23 seasons in the majors, Henderson has managed to maintain an awesome level of consistency. He has achieved 13 100-run seasons and has stolen at least 50 bases 13 times. His OBP has never been lower than .338, the mark he set his first year out. In 2001 he passed Ty Cobb to become the game's all-time runs leader and passed Babe Ruth as the career walks leader. A certain first-ballot Hall of Famer, Henderson shows no obvious signs of slowing down, ending a memorable 2001 season by joining the 3,000-hit club. "You have to be hungry and you have to love it," said Henderson regarding his ability to stay motivated and play hard despite his age. "And I still love it."

## CAREER TOTALS

| G | AB | R | H | 2B | 3B | HR | RBI | BB | K | SB | Avg | Slg | OBP |
|---|----|----|----|----|----|----|----|----|----|----|----|----|----|
| 2979 | 10710 | 2248 | 3000 | 503 | 65 | 290 | 1094 | 2141 | 1631 | 1395 | .280 | .420 | .402 |

# SHOELESS JOE JACKSON

**Joseph Jefferson Jackson**
**Born:** July 16 1889, Pickins County, South Carolina
**Died:** December 5 1951, Greenville, South Carolina
**Bats:** Left
**Throws:** Left
**Height:** 6-1
**Weight:** 200

**"The greatest natural hitter I ever saw." – Ty Cobb on Joe Jackson**

"Say it ain't so, Joe!"

It is the immortal line, allegedly uttered by a young White Sox fan but mouthed by an entire nation, which would define Shoeless Joe Jackson's tumultuous career in baseball.

The story hardly needs retelling. When the heavily favored White Sox lost the 1919 World Series to the Reds, the rumors of a fix were already floating around. Had the Chicago players been bribed by gamblers? By 1920, these rumors had wings. Facts surfaced. Eight players had accepted $5000 each to throw the World Series. Shoeless Joe was one of them and the Commissioner was determined to unearth the truth. The finer details remain shrouded in mystery but after the grand jury transcripts disappeared and the accused Sox players were acquitted, Jackson, and the other players, were still banned for life by Commissioner Landis and would never play another major league game again. What is clear is that Jackson had no intention of throwing the Series once he set foot on the diamond. He hit .375 for the Series, with 12 hits and 6 RBIs.

Joe Jackson does deserve to be remembered for more than just his participation in the Black Sox scandal. As a pure hitter the illiterate Jackson was as good as it gets. So much so that Babe Ruth used him as his model when he entered the big leagues. In 1911 Jackson hit .408 for Cleveland, followed by .395 in 1912. With his smooth, effortless swing he didn't just hit for average, he generated power too, recording at least 20 doubles nine times and 15-plus triples six times during the dead-ball era. And he could always hit them where they ain't, compiling eight 150-hit seasons and four 200-hit seasons. In his last year of major league ball, he hit .382 with 218 hits, 42 two-baggers and 121 RBIs. It was pretty clear that Jackson would have been in his element as the new lively-ball era took shape.

Nicknamed "Shoeless" because he once played a game in his socks after his new spikes had induced blisters, Jackson continued to play outlaw baseball and according to lore was spotted playing for a mill team during the 1940s when he was more than fifty years old.

As time passed and the Black Sox fix became woven into America's cultural fabric, Jackson developed into the sympathetic character of the piece and the fight continues to clear his name so he can take his place amongst the greats of Cooperstown, where his outstanding numbers belong.

## CAREER TOTALS

| G | AB | R | H | 2B | 3B | HR | RBI | BB | K | SB | Avg | Slg | OBP |
|------|------|-----|------|-----|-----|-----|-----|-----|-----|-----|------|------|------|
| 1330 | 4981 | 873 | 1772 | 307 | 168 | 54 | 785 | 519 | 158 | 202 | .356 | .517 | .423 |

# REGGIE JACKSON

**Reginald Martinez Jackson**
**Born:** May 18 1946, Wyncote, Pennsylvania
**Bats:** Left
**Throws:** Left
**Height:** 6-0
**Weight:** 200

**"The only reason I don't like playing in the World Series is I can't watch myself play." – Reggie Jackson**

When fall came around, slugger Reggie Jackson was in his element.

The pressure mounted, the World Series was in the balance, but Jackson seemed impervious to the unique demands that were placed upon players in the heat of the postseason. His broad shoulders left plenty room for the weight of his teammates, a franchise and a city. Through it all, Jackson just swung hard. All or nothing. No wonder they called him Mr. October.

Jackson made it the majors in 1967 with the Kansas City Athletics and moved with the A's to Oakland the following season. He got a taste for October early in his career. He won the 1973 AL MVP award hitting 32 homers, 117 RBIs and leading Oakland into the World Series. His debut was an awesome prelude of things to come. He hit .310 with six RBIs, three doubles and a home run in Game 7 as the A's closed out the Mets.

In total Jackson won 10 division titles, six pennants and five World Series with three different clubs, the A's, the Yankees and the Angels. He ranks number one all-time in World Series slugging percentage with .755. In 1977 with the Yankees he hit homers off three consecutive pitches in Game Six as New York defeated the Dodgers. He finished that Series with five home runs and 10 runs scored, both World Series records. As a clutch hitter, Jackson was able to raise the quality of his performance to meet the severity of the challenge, illustrated by his lifetime World Series average of .357, considerably higher than his career average of .262.

As a player, Jackson was a statue in the outfield and didn't hit well for average, reaching the .300 mark just once in his 20-year career. But when it came to power, he was among baseball's best. He won four home run crowns and his 563 home runs ranks eighth all-time. A self-confessed hot-dog, he always followed a towering home run by nonchalantly dropping his bat and watching the ball intently as it headed out, before sauntering around the bases. Always swinging for the fences, Jackson is also the game's strikeout leader. His 2,597 career strikeouts leave him with a whiff every 3.8 at bats.

After his great success in New York, Jackson headed back West. He played five seasons with the Angels before finishing his career in 1987 with one last season in Oakland. Jackson was elected into Cooperstown in 1993 with 16 20-home run seasons and six times with 100 or more RBIs.

## CAREER TOTALS

| G | AB | R | H | 2B | 3B | HR | RBI | BB | K | SB | Avg | Slg | OBP |
|---|----|----|----|----|----|----|-----|-----|------|----|-----|-----|-----|
| 2820 | 9864 | 1551 | 2584 | 463 | 49 | 563 | 1702 | 1375 | 2597 | 228 | .262 | .490 | .356 |

117

# AL KALINE

**Albert William Kaline**
**Born:** December 19 1934, Baltimore, Maryland
**Bats:** Right
**Throws:** Left
**Height:** 6-2
**Weight:** 180

**"I don't know where I'd would have been without baseball. I guess I'd be working with my dad in that Broom factory." – Al Kaline**

"All I've heard since I've been in baseball is that I make the game look easy," said the Detroit outfielder in a 1963 interview with *Baseball Digest*. "People say 'Look at that Kaline – he's got the perfect swing, the perfect stride, the perfect everything.'"

Guess they all forgot where perfection comes from.

Al Kaline hit the big leagues at 18 and after his first at bat – a pop-up off hard-throwing Harry Byrd – he soon realized what it would take to succeed. Hard work. Practice. And then some.

After his inauspicious debut in 1953, Kaline began to change his swing, learned to deal with pitches high and inside, and by 1955 was the owner of a picture-perfect swing. At just 20, he hit .340 with 102 RBIs and 27 homers and became the youngest player ever to win a batting title. He was also developing a reputation as a great right fielder. For the next 13 seasons Kaline continued to hit for average with some power. Between 1956 and 1968 he had six .300-seasons and seven 20-homer seasons.

In 1968 the Tigers made it to the World Series and in a season dominated by pitching beat the Cardinals and Bob Gibson in seven games. In Game 5 Kaline produced two clutch RBIs, singling in both the tying and go-ahead runs. He finished hitting .379 for the series, driving in eight with two homers.

Kaline retired in 1974 with a lifetime .297 average, 3007 hits and 399 home runs. Widely appreciated as among the best defensive right fielders ever, he won 10 Gold Gloves and during the 1971 and '72 seasons he went 242 games without committing an error. Elected to 18 All Star games in his 21 seasons, Kaline was a Tigers favorite thanks to his solid leadership skills, exemplary work ethic and remarkable consistency both at the plate and in the field.

He was inducted into the Hall of Fame in 1980.

## CAREER TOTALS

| G | AB | R | H | 2B | 3B | HR | RBI | BB | K | SB | Avg | Slg | OBP |
|------|-------|------|------|-----|----|-----|------|------|------|-----|------|------|------|
| 2834 | 10116 | 1622 | 3007 | 498 | 75 | 399 | 1583 | 1277 | 1020 | 137 | .297 | .480 | .376 |

# MICKEY MANTLE

**Mickey Charles Mantle**
**Born:** October 20 1931, Spavinaw, Oklahoma
**Died:** August 13 1995, Dallas, Texas
**BatS:** Both
**Throws:** Right
**Height:** 5-11
**Weight:** 195

**"You guys got to see this kid we have in camp. Out of Class C ball, hits 'em both ways - 500 feet both ways! You've got to see him." – *Bill Dickey* on Mickey Mantle**

He was a fractured hero. Perfect. Imperfect. But definitely a hero.

With a body carved from granite, he looked, at times, invincible. At his best, he seemed to run faster, swing harder, and hit it further than anyone. He was a country boy in the biggest of cities, with the biggest of teams, playing out the fantasies of every kid and living the American dream. But he also played in pain. Lived in it, too.

Mickey Mantle was raised in Commerce, Oklahoma and joined the New York Yankees after just two years in the minors. In an 18-year career, cut short due to injuries and illness, Mantle still managed to soar to great heights. From his rookie season in 1951 to his retirement in 1968 at just 36 years old, Mantle won 12 pennants and seven World Series crowns with the Yankees. For ten seasons he batted over .300 and captured back-to-back MVP awards in 1956 and '57. And he invented the tape measure home run.

But Mantle's career was characterized by his battles. He had to replace an icon in centerfield and the knee injury he received during the 1951 World Series would forever plague him. But Mantle overcame it all. He won the respect of the fans during the 1956 season when he hit .353 with 52 home runs and 130 RBIs to take the Triple Crown. And he won their hearts during the 1961 home run race with Roger Maris. Of course, DiMaggio was never to be forgotten, but the Commerce Comet, whose 54 dingers that season remains a record for switch-hitters, had found his place.

But for all heroics, his record 18 World Series home runs, it was his last at bat that proved to be his most memorable, his most important.

For many years Mantle had drunk heavily. He took a cut at life like it was a high heater and he paid the price. Just before his death from liver cancer in 1995, he took stock. He began to raise awareness for organ donation. Immediately, donations increased all over the country. He warned of replicating his life, he urged everyone to learn from his mistakes. This time the tape was needed to measure his bravery, his heart and his honesty. Mickey Mantle was back being the hero again.

In his eulogy at Mantle's funeral, Bob Costas said, "He was the most compelling baseball hero of our lifetime … exuding dynamism and excitement but at the same time touching your heart – flawed, wounded. We knew there was something poignant about Mickey Mantle before we knew what poignant meant."

## CAREER TOTALS

| G | AB | R | H | 2B | 3B | HR | RBI | BB | K | SB | Avg | Slg | OBP |
|------|------|------|------|-----|----|-----|------|------|------|-----|------|------|------|
| 2401 | 8102 | 1677 | 2415 | 344 | 72 | 536 | 1509 | 1733 | 1710 | 153 | .298 | .557 | .421 |

# WILLIE MAYS

**Willie Howard Mays**
**Born:** May 6 1931, Westfield, Alabama
**Bats:** Right
**Throws:** Right
**Height:** 5-10
**Weight:** 170

**"He is the only ballplayer I ever saw who could help a team just by riding on the bus with it." – Braves manager Charley Grimm on Willie Mays**

If you were looking to create the perfect all-around ballplayer, a man who could hit for both average and power, with intelligence, speed and great defensive ability, it's a safe bet he'd end up looking a lot like Willie Mays.

The "Say Hey Kid" had all the above attributes, coming as close to perfection as one can get, but he also had character. Whether hitting a towering home run or making a spectacular play in centerfield, Mays always did it with an exuberance that made him impossible not to love. He added a dramatic flair to his five-tool game that meant when Willie Mays set foot in his office, baseball shone just that little bit brighter.

His 22 seasons in the major leagues were both statistically outstanding and visually stunning. After playing for his father's Negro League club, the Birmingham Barons, Mays joined the Giants in New York as a 20-year old. He would go on to hit .300 or better 10 times, have 11 30-home run seasons and 10 100-RBI seasons. He stole at least 20 bases on six occasions, had 12 consecutive 100-run campaigns and reached the 150-hit mark 13 times. And then there were the Mays moments.

The Catch off Vic Wertz in the 1954 World Series, the incredible 330-foot throw to home plate to halt the Dodgers' Billy Cox in 1951 and the four home runs against Milwaukee in 1961 to set a Giants franchise record. Whether he was playing in New York or San Francisco, Mays always bought his unique style to the table, deliberately wearing his cap too small so it fell off when he flew about the outfield, becoming the most electric of all Giants' legends.

Mays left the Giants franchise in 1972 and finished his final two seasons as a Met. His numbers had dramatically dropped off and his career had become almost ceremonial but nothing could erase the memories and the contributions the 24-time All-Star had given to the game.

When Joe DiMaggio passed away in March 1999, talk immediately turned to who would replace the Yankee Clipper as owner of the soubriquet, "the game's greatest living player." Mays was the hands-down winner, the obvious choice, but for some he had owned the title all along. When former St. Louis Cardinals ace Bob Gibson was questioned on the handing over of DiMaggio's crown, he spoke for many who had witnessed the Mays in his prime. "You're assuming DiMaggio was the greatest living ballplayer," Gibson replied.

## CAREER TOTALS

| G | AB | R | H | 2B | 3B | HR | RBI | BB | K | SB | Avg | Slg | OBP |
|---|---|---|---|---|---|---|---|---|---|---|---|---|---|
| 2992 | 10881 | 2062 | 3283 | 523 | 140 | 660 | 1903 | 1464 | 1526 | 338 | .302 | .557 | 384 |

# STAN MUSIAL

**Stanley Frank Musial**
**Born:** November 21 1920, Donora, Pennsylvania
**Batted:** Left
**Threw:** Left
**Height:** 6-0
**Weight:** 175

**"He could hit .300 with a fountain pen." - Joe Garagiola on Stan Musial**

On the bronze statue outside Busch Stadium, below the frozen slugger, is inscribed a short quotation. It reads, "Here stands baseball's perfect warrior. Here stands baseball's perfect knight." The statue is of Stan Musial. The words are Ford Frick's. The sentiment is perfect.

Stan "The Man" Musial was the game's dignified assassin. He was genial when playing but armed with some of the keenest eyes in the game and a corkscrew stance that unleashed scorching line drives. Musial took aim at National League pitchers for 22 seasons with awesome success. Playing his entire career in St. Louis from 1941–63 – he missed the 1945 season on wartime duty – Musial had 18 .300 seasons, six 200-hit seasons and was elected to 24 All-Star games while being named National League MVP in 1943, '46 and '48.

Musial remarkably started his baseball journey as a pitcher but in 1940 after going 18-5 in the Florida State League, he injured his shoulder while playing in the outfield for Class D Daytona Beach, and his days on the mound were over. He had already illustrated his batting prowess for Daytona Beach when he wasn't starting and quickly moved up the ranks of the Cardinals' organization. At just 21 years of age he reached the Big Show and in 1942, his first full season, he hit .315 as the Redbirds won the World Series.

He would go on to win two more World Series with the Cardinals in 1944 and '46. He also captured seven NL batting titles and led the league in runs on five occasions, sharing the record with another St. Louis legend, Rogers Hornsby. In 1954 he entered the record books again, becoming the first player to hit five homers in a double header against the Giants.

Musial credits his amazing achievements to his memory. "I consciously memorized the speed at which every pitcher in the league threw his fastball, his curve and slider," he said. "I'd pick up the speed of the ball in the first thirty feet of its flight and knew how it would move once it had crossed the plate." This approach was typical of the diligent Musial.

Musial received his nickname "The Man" after another breathtaking performance at Ebbets Field. As he stood in the on-deck circle, a Dodgers fan was heard to say, "Oh no, here comes the man again!"

It was a cry that could have been uttered at every National League park, by every opposing fan on any day Stan Musial came to play ball.

## CAREER TOTALS

| G | AB | R | H | 2B | 3B | HR | RBI | BB | K | SB | Avg | Slg | OBP |
|---|----|----|----|----|----|----|----|----|----|----|----|----|----|
| 3026 | 10972 | 1949 | 3630 | 725 | 177 | 475 | 1951 | 1599 | 696 | 78 | .331 | .559 | .417 |

# MEL OTT

**Melvin Thomas Ott**
**Born:** March 2 1909, Gretna, Louisiana
**Died:** November 21 1958, New Orleans, Louisiana
**Batted:** Left
**Threw:** Right
**Height:** 5-9
**Weight:** 170

"Excuse me. Somebody important just came in." - **Toots Shor to Mr. Penicillin, Alexander Fleming, when Mel Ott walked into his restaurant**

It was impossible not to notice Mel Ott.

At 5-9 he was much smaller than the prototypical home run hitter and his batting stance was as unique as a fingerprint. He began by lifting his right foot off the ground and, as the ball approached the plate, he would step toward the mound. His bat reached a horizontal position before he whipped the barrel through the strike zone on a perfectly level plane. He didn't look like a slugger. He didn't swing like a slugger too. And he finished his 22-season major league career with 511 homers, 1860 RBIs and 1780 walks.

Ott joined the Giants in 1925 as a 16-year old under John McGraw. Concerned that a minor league hitting instructor would be inclined to tamper with his swing, McGraw preferred to keep Ott on the bench. He broke through the following year hitting .383 in 35 games and by 1928 he had began to show the power that would come to define his career.

Ott remained a Giant for life and took great advantage of the Polo Grounds' short porch in right field. Only 257 feet from home plate, he hit 323 of his dingers in this area and the right field bleachers came to be known as "Ottville." He was a model of consistency, both offensively and defensively, throughout his career. He hit 25 or more homers on 13 occasions and had 11 .300 seasons. His great eye and patience at the plate led to 10 100-walk seasons and his lifetime total of 1708 ranks him eighth all time. Throughout his career he averaged 17 assists per season in the outfield.

He helped the Giants to win the 1933 World Series, contributing a .389 average, seven hits, four RBIs and two home runs including a tenth-inning shot that clinched the title, and consecutive pennants in 1936 and '37. He became New York's player manager in 1942. After trying to emulate McGraw's intense managerial style, Ott reverted to the placid nature that had made him so popular as a player. He was replaced by Leo Durocher in 1948 and managed Oakland of the Pacific Coast League until 1952.

Mel Ott died tragically in a car accident in 1958, just seven years after his induction into Cooperstown. He is still the holder of several Giants records, including career leader in RBIs and walks and ranks second only to Willie Mays in games, runs, hits and homers.

## CAREER TOTALS

| G | AB | R | H | 2B | 3B | HR | RBI | BB | K | SB | Avg | Slg | OBP |
|---|----|----|----|----|----|----|-----|-----|-----|----|-----|-----|-----|
| 2730 | 9456 | 1859 | 2876 | 488 | 72 | 511 | 1860 | 1708 | 896 | 89 | .304 | .533 | .414 |

# FRANK ROBINSON

**Frank Robinson**
**Born:** October 31 1935, Beaumont, Texas
**Bats:** Right
**Throws:** Right
**Height:** 6-1
**Weight:** 195

**"I don't see why you reporters keep confusing Brooks and me. Can't you see that we wear different numbers?" - Frank Robinson**

It was probably the most ill advised deal since Manhattan Island went for a buck. In 1965, the Reds General Manager Bill DeWitt, doing his best impersonation of Harry Frazee, traded his MVP third baseman Frank Robinson to Baltimore for Milt Pappas, Jack Baldschun and Dick Simpson. Pappas, Baldschun and Simpson flopped. Robinson hit .316 with 49 homers and 122 RBIs in his first season to become the only player to win MVP crowns in both leagues.

Robinson made his big league debut with the Reds in 1956 and was an immediate star. He was voted Rookie of the Year, hitting .290 with 38 home runs, tying Wally Berger's rookie record. He continued to hit for both average and power and in 1961 received the MVP Award with a .323 average, 37 homers, 124 RBIs and 22 stolen bases. The following year he had a career high .342 average before finding himself traded to the Orioles in 1965, supposedly washed-up after just ten seasons in the Show. The rest is history.

Robinson's finest moment with the Orioles came in the 1966 World Series. Having already proved DeWitt wrong with his awesome regular season display, Robinson batted at .286 clip for the series and in the bottom of the fourth in Game 4 he hit a home run off Don Drysdale to secure the sweep of the Dodgers. He was awarded the World Series MVP.

Beginning in 1972, Robinson played three seasons in California with both the Dodgers and the Angels before finishing his career in Cleveland in 1976. Always noted for his on-field leadership, Robinson became baseball's first black manager when he took over the Indians in 1975 as a player-manager. Just like Jackie Robinson some 29 years earlier, Frank Robinson became a symbol of courage and hope as he broke another of the game's archaic barriers. Once he had hung up his spikes, Robinson stayed in management and went onto take the helm in both San Francisco and Baltimore before becoming the Orioles assistant GM in 1991.

## CAREER TOTALS

| G | AB | R | H | 2B | 3B | HR | RBI | BB | K | SB | Avg | Slg | OBP |
|---|----|----|----|----|----|----|-----|-----|------|-----|------|------|------|
| 2808 | 10006 | 1829 | 2943 | 528 | 72 | 586 | 1812 | 1420 | 1532 | 204 | .294 | .537 | .389 |

# PETE ROSE

**Peter Edward Rose**
**Born:** April 14 1941, Cincinnati, Ohio
**Bats:** Both
**Throws:** Right
**Height:** 5-11
**Weight:** 200

**"Somebody's got to win and somebody's got to lose. And I believe in letting the other guy lose." - Pete Rose**

No wonder they named him "Charlie Hustle".

During his 26 years in the majors, Rose scrapped and slid his way to six pennants, three World Series and a place in the record books. He became baseball's official Hit King on September 11 1985, when he passed Ty Cobb's record of 4,191. He was 44 years' old.

He was never pretty to watch but his passion for the game, and for winning, made him a huge draw. Part of the dominating Big Red Machine of the mid-1970s, Rose ignited the Reds with his enthusiasm. He would run to first base on a walk, talk up his achievements at every opportunity, and play the game with a reckless abandon. If Rose were to have a statue made in his honor you could forget any stately pose. No, he would be a dipped in-bronze whirlwind, skidding head first for home.

But it is unlikely Rose will ever be sculpted for posterity.

In 1989, Commissioner Bart Giamatti suspended Rose for "conduct not in the best interests of baseball." Rose had been suspected of gambling on the game while still managing the Reds and an investigation headed by lawyer John Dowd resulted in a damning report that saw Rose suspended from baseball. And in 1990 Rose served a jail sentence for federal tax evasion. He had finally been forced to give up the hustle.

Rose is still subject to an indefinite ban from the game and joins Shoeless Joe Jackson as the most glaring omission from Cooperstown. But while his absence from the Hall of Fame remains one of the game's hottest debates, his numbers cannot be disputed.

Alongside his hits record, Rose amassed three batting crowns (1968, '69, '73) and a 44-game hit streak in 1978 that equaled the National League record. In 1975 he led Cincinnati to another World Series victory thanks to a .370 batting average, .469 on-base percentage and 10 hits. After leaving the Reds for Philly and then Montreal, Rose finished his career back with the Reds as a player before managing the team to a 412-373 record. Both his 3562 games played and his 10 200-hit seasons remain as all-time records.

Pete Rose still protests his innocence and hopes one day to be elected into the Hall of Fame. He made headlines at the 1999 World Series when the All-Century team was announced with Rose elected, although still ineligible for Cooperstown. He remains excluded to this day, and will probably remain so until he comes to some sort of agreement with the Commissioner over an admission of culpability. Without Rose – and Jackson – the Hall lacks two of baseball's all-time greats.

## CAREER TOTALS

| G | AB | R | H | 2B | 3B | HR | RBI | BB | K | SB | Avg | Slg | OBP |
|------|-------|------|------|-----|-----|-----|------|------|------|-----|------|------|------|
| 3562 | 14053 | 2165 | 4256 | 746 | 135 | 160 | 1314 | 1566 | 1143 | 198 | .303 | .409 | .375 |

# BABE RUTH

**George Herman Ruth**
**Born:** February 6 1895, Baltimore, Maryland
**Died:** August 16 1948, New York, New York
**Bats:** Left
**Throws:** Left
**Height:** 6-2
**Weight:** 215

"I swing big with everything I've got. I hit big and I miss big. I love to live as big I can." -
**Babe Ruth**

It is almost impossible to do justice to Babe Ruth.

To just describe him as the greatest ballplayer is like describing Mount Everest as just the tallest mountain. He was a great, great ballplayer, the best, but his impact on the game he played and in turn the nation who followed it so passionately, is immeasurable. More than fifty years after his death, Babe Ruth still means everything to baseball, everything to America. It's hard to imagine it ever being any other way.

Ruth certainly transcended baseball and sports. He was too large a character, too representative of a changing America, to be confined merely to the sports pages. But it is amongst these pages where he made most sense. "Everything he did in those days, from smoking cigars to smoking fastballs, smacked of hyperbole," wrote William Nack. "He ate too much. He drank too much. He womanized to a fare-thee-well." But the smoked fastballs, like most everything he did on the diamond, didn't need the hyperbole. The reality was more than enough.

He could have been one of the game's best pitchers, he finished 94-46 with a 2.28 ERA, but his power at the plate was impossible to ignore. The Red Sox bought Ruth's contract from the minor league Baltimore Orioles and gave him his big league debut in 1914. Boston began to use him more and more as an outfielder to exploit his potential as a hitter. And as a hitter he would change the game, forever.

Joining the Yankees in 1920 he waved goodbye to the dead ball era by launching it further, and with greater frequency, than ever imagined. His first year with the Yankees Ruth became the first major leaguer to hit 30 homers in a season with 54. It was a trend he would continue, with 59 in 1921 and 60 in 1927, totals that were first beaten by Roger Maris in 1961. Each new mark echoed his growing status within the country. The home run was firmly on the map as baseball's most grandiose of statements and Ruth was its finest exponent.

His life ended prematurely in 1948 after a battle with throat cancer but he packed enough into his 53 years to last several lifetimes. He had a stadium named after him. A curse, as well. He could promise you a home run and hit three. He won ten pennants, seven World Series and a million hearts. But Ruth was not just power; he hit .300 17 times – his .342 average is ninth best all-time – and he led the league in homers a record 12 times. He could beat you with the bellyache, break 80 from the back tees and still make you glad you went along for the ride.

Babe Ruth's remarkable life is a timeline for America, the Dream, with its incomparable highs and pitfalls of success, laid bare for all to see. He was an original. The original.

## CAREER TOTALS

| G | AB | R | H | 2B | 3B | HR | RBI | BB | K | SB | Avg | Slg | OBP |
|------|------|------|------|-----|-----|-----|------|------|------|-----|------|------|------|
| 2503 | 8399 | 2174 | 2873 | 506 | 136 | 714 | 2213 | 2062 | 1330 | 123 | .342 | .690 | .474 |

# DUKE SNIDER

**Edwin Donald Snider**
**Born:** September 19 1926, Los Angeles, California
**Bats:** Left
**Throws:** Left
**Height:** 6-0
**Weight:** 190

"Win and Loss are the important things. You always knew where you were in the standings
... your numbers you had to look in the Sunday papers to find out what you were batting."
**- Duke Snider**

One of the original Boys of Summer, Duke Snider was a picture perfect ballplayer; equal parts power and style, with the sweetest swing this side of Count Basie. In the era for center fielders, Snider spent the 1950s dueling with Mantle and Mays for New York's attention and while his illustrious peers often overshadowed him, Snider was always the Duke of Flatbush.

Snider got his big league call-up in 1947 and by 1949 was the Dodgers' starting centerfielder. He hit 23 homers that year as Brooklyn won the pennant but hit just .143 in 21 at bats during the World Series as the Dodgers lost to the Yankees in five games. Snider continued to improve, hitting .321 with 31 homers in 1950 and in 1952 hit four homers during the World Series as Brooklyn again lost out to the Yankees. Despite the disappointment of the World Series, Snider came back with his best year in 1953, hitting .336 with 42 home runs and 126 RBIs. Again the Dodgers made it to the Fall Classic. Again the Yankees were waiting for them. And again the Bronx edged Brooklyn.

Snider and the Dodgers got to lay to rest the ghosts of World Series past in 1955. After another dominant regular season, they beat the Yankees in seven to win Brooklyn's only World Series. Snider batted at a .320 clip and again went yard four times to become the only player in history to hit four home runs in two different World Series. Snider wasn't just a power hitter, though. As a centerfielder he was as smooth as they came and though not as spectacular as Mays, he played the position with a controlled efficiency that looked effortless. Ralph Kiner even went as far as to compare Snider with another New York legend. "I'd say Duke covers more ground and is more consistent than anyone since DiMaggio," said Kiner.

The Dodgers moved to Los Angeles in 1958 and Snider helped them to a World Series in 1959 over the White Sox. The Coliseum was a far cry from the cozy Ebbets Field and Snider's power numbers began to fade, as he often played hurt. He finally retired in 1964.

Elected into Cooperstown in 1980, Snider remains an iconic figure, immortalized in Roger Kahn's classic *Boys of Summer*. In his 18 seasons Snider had five consecutive 40-homer seasons to tie Ralph Kiner, six 100-RBI seasons and his 11 World Series homers still remains a NL record.

## CAREER TOTALS

| G | AB | R | H | 2B | 3B | HR | RBI | BB | K | SB | Avg | Slg | OBP |
|---|-----|------|------|-----|----|-----|------|-----|------|----|------|------|------|
| 2143 | 7161 | 1259 | 2116 | 358 | 85 | 407 | 1333 | 971 | 1237 | 99 | .295 | .540 | .380 |

# SAMMY SOSA

**Sammy Sosa**
**Born:** November 12 1968, San Pedro de Macoris, Dominican Republic
**Bats:** Right
**Throws:** Right
**Height:** 6-0
**Weight:** 215

**"Good hitters make you pay for every mistake. That's what Sammy does." - Mark Parent on Sammy Sosa**

Before the 1998 season, the Cubs' outfielder Sammy Sosa was just another talented major leaguer. He had put up some big numbers, 40 homers in '96, 119 RBIs in both '95 and '97 and had combined his slugging prowess with speed in 1993 becoming the Cubbies' first ever 30-30 man. But there were obvious chinks in the armor.

Sosa was undisciplined at the plate with a career batting average below .300 and when he struck out, which was often, he did so swinging, never looking. But the incredible year of 1998 changed all that. And much, much more.

The home run race with Mark McGwire that captivated baseball made Sosa a very visible hero in both America and his native Dominican Republic. The much-talked about camaraderie between the players was refreshing, as was Sosa's unbridled joy at being a part of history. But underneath the shiny veneer of baseball's summer of love, of Sosa's 66 glorious home runs, was a player who had finally come of age.

Sosa made it to the majors in 1989 with the Texas Rangers, escaping the poverty, the shoe shining and the struggles of San Pedro de Marcoris, before joining the White Sox the following season. He played at Comiskey until 1991 before jumping across town to the Cubs. His lack of discipline at the plate was well documented as he racked up the strikeouts in pursuit of personal goals and gaudy numbers. And meanwhile the Cubs suffered. But '98 saw a change born of maturity. He had more hits than strikeouts, something he had failed to do the previous years, he batted at a .300 clip finishing the season at .308, over 40 points higher than his career average. His walks shot up from 45 in '97 to 73. And Chicago made it to the postseason.

His 66 home runs were 10 better than former Cub Hack Wilson's old NL record – if four behind McGwire's final total. However, Sosa earned the MVP award over McGwire with his ability to carry his team in the heat of a pennant race tipping the balance in his favor.

His 1999 performance was almost as impressive as he silenced those who assumed that '98 was just an anomaly, hitting 63 homers with 180 hits, 141 RBIs, 114 runs and 78 walks. In 2000 he became the first ever Cub to drive in 100 runs in six consecutive seasons, while finishing with a .320 average and a league leading 50 homers. His numbers in 2001 solidified his position as one of the game's greatest offensive talents as he batted .328 with 146 runs, a league-leading 160 RBIs and 64 homers, joining McGwire as the only men in major league history to record four consecutive 50-homer seasons.

## CAREER TOTALS

| G | AB | R | H | 2B | 3B | HR | RBI | BB | K | SB | Avg | Slg | OBP |
|---|----|----|----|----|----|----|-----|----|----|----|-----|-----|-----|
| 1725 | 6470 | 1093 | 1795 | 278 | 41 | 450 | 1239 | 635 | 1690 | 231 | .277 | .542 | .343 |

# TRIS SPEAKER

**Tristram E. Speaker**
**Born:** April 4 1888, Hubbard, Texas
**Died:** December 8 1958, Lake Whitney, Texas
**Bats:** Left
**Throws:** Left
**Height:** 5-11
**Weight:** 193

"In my Red Sox pitching days, I would hear the crack of the bat and say 'There goes the game.' But Tris would turn his back to the plate and make a diving catch. Not once, but a thousand times." - **Babe Ruth on Tris Speaker**

His lifetime batting average is identical to Ted Williams'. He had more hits than Honus Wagner, more runs than Frank Robinson and matches Joe DiMaggio in RBIs. But Tris Speaker is still better remembered at the player who redefined his position.

Signed by the Red Sox in 1907, Speaker began to change the way center field was played. By playing extremely shallow he doubled up as an extra infielder and with his great range he could get to balls that would have otherwise dropped for easy singles, cover second and still track down deep fly balls. He was the Albert Einstein of center fielders, working out a methodology based on what he saw at the plate. "I figured that 98 percent of all safe hits to the outfield drop in front of outfielders. That's why I played close in," Speaker said. "I also studied the batters so when he started to swing, I knew if he would hit to my left or right and I was on my way."

The Red Sox won the World Series in 1912 and Spoke was at the very heart of their success. They beat the Giants in seven games and Speaker hit a game-tying single in the 10th inning to kick-start a Boston rally. The Red Sox eventually won the game 3-2 and clinched the Series. Speaker stayed in Beantown until 1915 when he was traded to Cleveland for refusing to accept a 50 percent reduction in his salary. He hit .386 his first year to win the batting crown and followed it by hitting .352 and .318 the following years.

In 1919 he was named manager of the Indians. In his first full season, Speaker guided Cleveland to the AL pennant and the World Series. He resigned in 1926 after allegations arose that he, Ty Cobb and Joe Wood had conspired to fix a Tigers-Indians game on September 25 1919. After an investigation took place both Speaker and Cobb were exonerated in 1927 and allowed back into the game, with Spoke playing for the Washington Senators. Speaker joined Connie Mack's A's in 1928 before retiring the same year. He continued to manage with Newark of the International League before becoming a broadcaster.

Elected into the Hall of Fame in 1937 Tris Speaker is first all-time in doubles, fifth in hits and seventh in batting average. In his 22-year career he had 18 .300-seasons and his record 448 lifetime assists remain as a testament to his awesome ability with the leather.

## CAREER TOTALS

| G | AB | R | H | 2B | 3B | HR | RBI | BB | K | SB | Avg | Slg | OBP |
|---|----|----|----|----|----|----|-----|----|----|----|-----|-----|-----|
| 2789 | 10195 | 1882 | 3514 | 792 | 222 | 117 | 1529 | 1381 | 220 | 432 | .345 | .500 | .428 |

# WILLIE STARGELL

**Wilver Dornel Stargell**
**Born:** March 6 1940, Earlsboro, Oklahoma
**Died:** April 9, 2001, Wilmington, North Carolina
**Bats:** Left
**Throws:** Left
**Height:** 6-2
**Weight:** 225

**"I never saw anything like it. He doesn't just hit pitchers, he takes away their dignity."** -
**Don Sutton on Willie Stargell**

For many of Willie Stargell's colossal home runs a tape measure wasn't the right tool
for the job. A Rand McNally was often more appropriate.

In his 20 years in the majors, the Pittsburgh Pirates slugger really knew how to take
them deep. With his aggressive uppercut swing and his powerful body, a search party
was needed to locate some of Stargell's most memorable moon shots. Of the 18 balls
hit out of Forbes Field, he crushed seven of them. Pops hit two balls completely out of
Dodger Stadium.

Stargell made his big league debut in 1962 with the Pirates and by 1964 had
already begun to post good power numbers. He hit 21 homers that season and
continued to hit at least 20 a season for the rest of the 1960s. During the 70s Stargell
hit more home runs than any other player. He hit 48 in '71 to lead the league, 33 the
following year and in 1973 lead the league in homers (44), RBIs (119) and slugging
percentage (.646). In total he had nine 20-home runs seasons for the decade.

After several injuries had threatened to end his career in 1977, Stargell bounced
back in 1979 with his best year ever. He hit 32 dingers during the regular season as the
Pirates won their division and entered the postseason. Pittsburgh swept the Reds in the
NLCS as Stargell hit .455 with two home runs, including a game winning shot in the 11th
inning of Game 1. In the World Series, Stargell again led by example with three homers
and seven RBIs. The Pirates beat the Orioles in seven games. Stargell's seven extra-
base hits established a new Fall Classic record. He also went on to set a new record
for most MVP Awards in a season as he won both the NLCS and World Series MVPs
while sharing the NL MVP Award and *Sports Illustrated's* Sportsman of the Year with
Keith Hernandez and the Steelers' star quarterback Terry Bradshaw respectively.

Stargell was elected to Cooperstown in 1988 and died in 2001. He will always be
remembered for his awesome power and his invaluable leadership qualities. Loved by
his teammates for his humor and his enthusiasm, Stargell awarded "Stargell Stars" to
Pirates who came up with clutch hits and heads-up plays. It was typical of a man who
preferred to deflect attention onto others and who understood better than most that
there is no "I" in team.

## CAREER TOTALS

| G | AB | R | H | 2B | 3B | HR | RBI | BB | K | SB | Avg | Slg | OBP |
|------|------|------|------|-----|----|-----|------|-----|------|----|------|------|------|
| 2360 | 7927 | 1195 | 2232 | 423 | 55 | 475 | 1540 | 937 | 1936 | 17 | .282 | .529 | .360 |

# TED WILLIAMS

**Theodore Samuel Williams · OF**
**Born:** August 30 1918, San Diego, California
**Throws:** Right
**Bats:** Left
**Height:** 6-3
**Weight:** 205

**"A man has to have goals – for a day, for a lifetime – and that was mine, to have people say, 'There goes Ted Williams, the greatest hitter who ever lived.'" - Ted Williams**

They said he could read the label on a record as it went round on the turntable. That he could decipher a car license plate number from hundreds of yards away. With such acute eyesight recognizing a slider from sixty feet six inches must have seemed a breeze for Teddy Ballgame.

"They used to write a lot of bull about my sight," Williams said. But myth and hyperbole aside, Theodore Samuel Williams could flat out hit a baseball.

He began his career with his hometown San Diego Padres of the Pacific Coast League but was quickly snapped up by the Boston Red Sox as a 20-year old in '38. In 1939, his first year in the majors, Williams hit .327 with 31 home runs. The Red Sox had struck gold and Boston had a new hero. They dubbed him "The Kid" and Williams responded by tipping his cap after every homer. But the following year he was less successful at the plate and the fans grew tired of his below average play in leftfield. Williams began to hear boos. He stopped tipping his cap. And a love-hate relationship was born.

Williams seemed to thrive among the adversity. In 1941 he hit .406 becoming the last player to hit over .400. His 521 career home runs rank him tied for 12th all-time. He has the second highest slugging percentage (.634) in baseball history. And he achieved all this despite serving in World War II from 1942-45 and in the Korean War between 1952-53.

Ted Williams elevated hitting to a science. It was his obsession. His ability to know the strike zone and get the pitch he wanted to hit was second to none. In 7,706 at bats Williams struck out just 709 times. Only the Babe and Rickey Henderson walked more. This disciplined approach led him to two triple crowns in 1942 and '47, six American League batting titles and 18 All-Star appearances. And while his frosty relationship with the media remained, the Splendid Splinter became the Olde Town Team's greatest ever player and a Fenway legend thanks to his exploits on the field and his tireless work with the New England children's cancer charity, The Jimmy Fund, away from it.

In his final major league game the 42-year old Williams responded to the outpouring of the fans by hitting a home run in his very last at bat. It was hugely symbolic moment in a wonderful career full of them.

## CAREER TOTALS

| G | AB | R | H | 2B | 3B | HR | RBI | BB | K | SB | Avg | Slg | OBP |
|------|------|------|------|-----|----|-----|------|------|-----|----|------|------|------|
| 2292 | 7706 | 1798 | 2654 | 525 | 71 | 521 | 1839 | 2019 | 709 | 24 | .344 | .634 | .482 |

# CARL YASTRZEMSKI

**Carl Michael Yastrzemski**
**Born:** August 22 1939, Southampton, New York
**Bats:** Left
**Throws:** Left
**Height:** 5-11
**Weight:** 180

"I think about baseball when I wake up in the morning. I think about it all day and I dream about it at night. The only time I don't think about it is when I'm playing it." - **Carl Yastrzemski**

Just as Mickey Mantle had had to deal with the pressures of replacing Joe DiMaggio in centerfield, in 1961 a rookie came to Fenway Park also faced with the enormity of figuring just how you substitute for a legend.

When Carl Yastrzemski arrived in Boston to replace Ted Williams in leftfield his first reaction was to panic. It was like trying to follow the Three Tenors in a Karaoke contest. "I was a scared rookie," Yaz said, "hitting .220 after the first three months of my baseball season, doubting my ability." So what do you do if you are trying to replicate the numbers of probably the greatest hitter ever? You go seek his advice. Williams aborted a fishing trip in New Brunswick to return to Boston to work with his replacement. "Don't let anybody monkey with your swing," said Teddy Ballgame. Yaz raised his average to .266 but what his numbers didn't reveal was the confidence that Williams had installed into Yastrzemski.

Yaz played 23 seasons in Boston, ending his career in 1983 as the all-time Red Sox leader in several offensive categories including runs, hits, total bases and RBIs as well as games and at bats. He became the only American League player with 3,000 hits and 400 home runs and won three batting titles in 1963, '67 and '68. The 18-time All-Star also won seven gold gloves handling the subtleties of the Green Monster with great skill.

Although his career is full with highlights, Yastrzemski remains intrinsically linked with 1967. It was the year of Boston's "Impossible Dream", when the Red Sox, led by Yaz, went from ninth – out of ten – in the American League in 1966 to a World Series appearance. The Sox began badly but when Yastrzemski's bat got hot, so did the team. He finished the season with a .326 average, 44 home runs and 121 RBIs to clinch the Triple Crown and the pennant. Yastrzemski batted .400 for the Series but the Red Sox lost to the Cardinals in seven games. Yaz was awarded the AL MVP in recognition of his awesome season in which, at times, he appeared to carry the whole of Boston on his shoulders as he chased down Minnesota and Detroit and finally made it to the World Series.

He continued to play until 1983 and was elected to the Hall of Fame at Cooperstown in 1988. "I was lucky enough to have the talent to play baseball," said Yaz. "I didn't think I was anybody special."

What goes around comes around. He arrived in Boston to fill a void. He departed leaving one.

## CAREER TOTALS

| G | AB | R | H | 2B | 3B | HR | RBI | BB | K | SB | Avg | Slg | OBP |
|---|----|---|---|----|----|----|-----|----|----|----|-----|-----|-----|
| 3308 | 11988 | 1816 | 3419 | 646 | 59 | 452 | 1844 | 1845 | 1393 | 168 | .285 | .462 | .379 |

# The Managers

Walt Altson
Sparky Anderson
Bobby Cox
Leo Durocher
Ralph Houk
Miller Huggins
Tony La Russa
Tommy Lasorda
Connie Mack
Joe McCarthy
John McGraw
Bill McKechnie
Joe Torre
Earl Weaver

# WALTER ALSTON

**Walter Emmons Alston**
**Born:** December 1 1911 in Venice, Ohio
**Died:** October 1 1984 in Oxford, Ohio
**Teams Managed:** Brooklyn Dodgers, Los Angeles Dodgers
**23 yrs     2040 wins**
*Pennants:* 1955, 1956, 1959, 1963, 1965, 1966, 1974
*World Series:* 1955, 1959, 1963, 1965

**"Do your best and forget the consequences" - Walter Alston**

It all started with an innocuous one-year contract, and it was 23 Major League seasons, seven National League pennants and five World Series rings later that Walter Alston retired a true Dodgers legend.

Alston began managing in 1947 after only one major league at bat and an unsuccessful period as a player-manager in the bush leagues. Branch Rickey appointed him to manage one of the Dodgers farm teams and he was an instant success. His reserved nature made him popular with his players and he was an integral part of Rickey's plan to break baseball's color barrier. Alston was assigned to Nashua of the New England League where he provided support for both Roy Campanella and Don Newcombe.

Alston took over the Brooklyn Dodgers in 1954 and in '55 brought them the ultimate prize, capturing the World Series in seven games from the Yankees. In December 1957 the Dodgers announced they were moving West, to Los Angeles. Alston, still only renewing his one-year contact on an annual basis, went with them. In L.A he won five pennants and three World Series, in 1959, '63 and '65. He won 2,040 games and received the Manager of the Year accolade 14 times by various sports publications.

Because of his stoicism with the media and his low-key approach to managing, Alston failed to fire the public's imagination. He neither provoked a reaction like Leo Durocher nor demanded your attention like Casey Stengel. But he won. And a certain hard-throwing lefty reaped the benefits of his patient approach. Under Alston, Sandy Koufax was allowed the space to grow as a player and despite his lack of control in his early years, Alston saw the potential. He was rewarded when Koufax led the Dodgers to World Series wins in 1963 and 1965. It was the perfect the example of a manager who treated his players with respect.

# SPARKY ANDERSON

**George Lee Anderson**
**Born:** February 22 1934 in Bridgewater, South Dakota
**Teams Managed:** Cincinnati Reds, Detroit Tigers
**26 yrs**          **2185 wins**
**Pennants:** 1970, 1972, 1975, 1976, 1984
**World Series:** 1975, 1976, 1984

"The great thing about baseball is when you're done, you'll only tell your grandchildren the good things. If they ask me about 1989, I'll tell them I had amnesia." - **Sparky Anderson**

It was just another Class AA ballgame in Fort Worth, Texas but the radio announcer was paying particular attention to the second baseman with the good glove and the fiery temperament. "The sparks are really flying tonight," said the announcer as the player went at it with the umpire. It was that simple. George Anderson had himself a nickname. And it stuck.

Sparky Anderson managed in the majors for 26 seasons, between 1970 and 1995, becoming the third winningest manager in baseball history. With the Reds and then the Tigers he would achieve unparalleled success for these two proud franchises. He led Cincinnati to five NL West titles, four pennants and two World Series. When he took over at Detroit he won the World Series again in 1984 and a division title in 1987. He is the all-time leader in wins for both ballclubs, the only manager to lead two franchises in victories.

Sparky's name fits him to perfection. As a manager he displayed the same quick temper that gave him his tag, but despite his intensity Anderson became a player's manager, forging deep relationships with many of the players he worked with. His enthusiasm for the game was infectious. Sparky loved to talk baseball, make outlandish predictions and wrestle with the English language.

Anderson's finest years were those spent in control of Cincinnati's Big Red Machine. Blessed with the juggernaut offense of Johnny Bench, Joe Morgan, Pete Rose and Tony Perez, Anderson won back-to-back World Series titles in 1975 and '76. He became the Detroit manager in 1979 and in 1984 led the team to its first World Series title since '68. Again Anderson had a nucleus of outstanding players and the team of Alan Trammell, Lance Parrish, Kirk Gibson and Jack Morris, who had won 104 regular season games, beat the Padres in five. Anderson always liked to downplay his achievements. "The players make the manager, it's never the other way around," he once said.

Anderson retired in 1995 after several lean years with a weak Detroit team, including 103 defeats in 1989. He still remains the only manager in the game's history to win a World Series title in both the American League and the National League.

He was elected into the Hall of Fame in 2000.

# BOBBY COX

**Robert Joe Cox**
**Born:** May 21 1941, Tulsa, Oklahoma.
**Teams Managed:** Atlanta Braves, Toronto Blue Jays, Atlanta Braves.
**20 yrs      1704 wins**
**Pennants:** 1991, 1992, 1995, 1996, 1999
**World Series:** 1995

**"This team is not the Atlanta Braves without Bobby Cox." - Chipper Jones on Bobby Cox**

Underrated is not the first word that springs to mind when discussing Atlanta's manager Bobby Cox. After all this is the same guy who has steered his Braves to ten consecutive division titles, four pennants and one World Series since joining the organization in 1990. But that's exactly how Buck Showalter describes the most dominant manager of the '90s. "He's the guy who keeps that team together," says Showalter.

It seems that Showalter isn't alone. "Bobby, to me, doesn't get anywhere near the credit he deserves," says Braves pitcher Tom Glavine.

This is what happens when you dominate the National League for a decade and have a starting rotation that thinks the Cy Young Award is only presented to those who pitch their home games in Georgia. You get called a pushbutton manager. But Bobby Cox has heard it all before. "People ask me if I'm concerned about a lack of recognition," Cox says. "That doesn't bother me. I'm not the show. The players are. I'll just stay in the background."

Cox began his career in the shadows when he retired as a player in 1970 with bad knees. He managed for six years in the minors before taking over the Braves in 1978. He struggled for three seasons before being fired. He wound up in Toronto and led the Blue Jays to their first ever division title in 1985. He was soon back in Atlanta.

From 1986 to 1990 Cox was Atlanta's GM. He acquired, among others, Chipper Jones, Javy Lopez John Smoltz and Tom Glavine before returning to the dugout in 1991. His personnel skills paid off. The Braves went from worst to first. And stayed there. In 1999 Cox took the Braves to the World Series for the fifth time in the '90s. He has managed four All-Star games during this time (1992, '93, '96 and '97) and became the Braves' winningest manager in 1998.

Cox is widely regarded by many as one of the best managers in the game. He is a something of a throwback, making his players wear sports coats on team flights and not allowing any music in the clubhouse. But all his players respect him. And play hard for him. "He's the ultimate," says Braves ace Greg Maddux. "When you lose a big game, you feel worse for Bobby than you do yourself."

Cox has compiled a 1704-1345 record in the majors, second only to Tony La Russa among active managers. He has led the Braves to four 100-win seasons and despite losing more World Series than he has won, Bobby Cox continues to push all the right buttons, and so much more.

# LEO DUROCHER

**Leo Ernest Durocher**
**Born:** July 27 1905 in Springfield, Massachusetts
**Died:** October 7 1991 in Palm Springs, California
**Teams Managed:** Brooklyn Dodgers, New York Giants, Chicago Cubs, Houston Astros
**24 yrs      2008 wins**
*Pennants:* 1941, 1951, 1954
*World Series:* 1954

**"I never questioned the integrity of an umpire. Their eyesight, yes." - Leo Durocher**

Leo "The Lip" Durocher loved to drink, bet on the horses and chase women. And somewhere in between he found time for baseball.

Durocher was a short, scrappy infielder and the hub of the notorious "Gas House Gang", the wild Cardinals team of the 1930s. He learned to hustle in his teens and he took his gambler's instincts onto the diamond as both a player and a manager. He could be obnoxious, aggressive and confrontational. But he had the ability to motivate teammates and later his players as well as any manager in the game's history.

After 17 years as a player with the Yankees, Dodgers, Reds and Cardinals, Durocher was put in charge of the Brooklyn Dodgers in 1939. He went on to win 2,008 games over 24 seasons with the Dodgers, Giants, Cubs and Astros. He won three pennants and led the Giants to their surprise victory over the Cleveland Indians in the 1954 World Series.

His baseball savvy was legendary. He pioneered the aggressive use of the bullpen as he sort the match-ups he wanted while managing to squeeze every drop of effort from his players, humiliating them into trying harder and harder. A Leo Durocher ballclub would win at all costs, intimidating opposing players and umpires. "Give me some hungry ballplayers who want to kill you," was how he once described his selection process.

Durocher was blessed with many ups and downs in his managerial career. He managed the 1951 Giants and was instrumental in New York's 16-game win-streak that enabled them to haul in the Dodgers and eventually win the pennant with Bobby Thomson's "Shot heard 'round the World." In 1954 his Giants swept the Indians in the World Series. But it was also Durocher who was at the helm when the Cubs were caught and passed by the 1969 Miracle Mets.

His reputation as a hell-raiser always proceeded him and he was often under investigation, most notably in 1947 when he was suspended from baseball for a year and in 1971 when commissioner Bowie Kuhn began proceedings against him. But Durocher was thick-skinned. He had fought and scraped all his life and unfazed by the public's opinion of him he carried on managing until 1973, inadvertently changing the blueprint for baseball managers forever.

# RALPH HOUK

**Ralph George Houk**
**Born:** August 9 1919, Lawrence, Kansas
**Teams Managed:** New York Yankees, Detroit Tigers, Boston Red Sox
**20 yrs      1619 wins**
*Pennants:* 1961, 1962, 1963
*World Series:* 1961, 1962

**"Did I consider taking him out? No. There wasn't any blood showing, was there?" - Ralph Houk after pitcher Bill Stafford was hit by a liner during the 1962 World Series.**

Ralph Houk managed some 3,150 major league games in a 20-year, three-team career, but it was his 11-year tenure with the New York Yankees that helped secure him his place in baseball history.

Houk became the Yankee manager in 1961 after three years leading their Triple A ballclub in Denver and serving one season as their first base coach. He was immediately faced with the pressures of replacing the seemingly irreplaceable Casey Stengel and while it was too much to ask for him, or perhaps anyone, to emulate the incredible success of Stengel, Houk certainly ensured that the Yankee winning tradition, that had brought them 18 World Series, continued.

Armed with the dynamic offensive tag-team of Mickey Mantle and Roger Maris and the irrepressible Whitey Ford as his ace, Houk led the Yankees to the American League pennant his first season out, beating the Detroit Tigers by eight games. And while Maris received much of the attention for his record-breaking 61 dingers, Houk quietly prepared his ballclub for a World Series match-up with the Reds. Described as "blunt and decisive" by his players, Houk commanded respect and always got it. In the '61 Series his Yankees comfortably defeated Cincinnati 4-1.

Houk followed his dream start in management by repeating the feat the following season, winning the pennant by five from the Minnesota Twins before beating the San Francisco Giants in seven games.Houk again won the pennant in 1963 for three straight but the Yanks were swept in the Fall Classic by the Los Angeles Dodgers and an electrifying performance by ace Sandy Koufax who won Game 1, fanning 15 Yankees, and closed it out with another victory in Game 4. Houk was moved upstairs.

After three years as the Yankees GM, Houk again took the helm in 1966 and stayed in the Big Apple until 1973. But the club failed to win a pennant during this time and Houk left for Detroit at the end of the '73 campaign. After four seasons with the Tigers, Houk finished his managerial career in Boston with the Red Sox, eventually retiring in 1984.

Despite his 1619 career wins, his three consecutive AL pennants and his back-to-back World Championships, Houk has yet to be inducted into the Hall of Fame, perhaps lost among the greatness of the Yankee managers who proceeded and followed him.

# MILLER HUGGINS

**Miller James Huggins**
**Born:** March 27 1879, Cincinnati, Ohio
**Died:** September 25, 1929, New York, New York
**Teams Managed:** St. Louis Cardinals, New York Yankees
**17 yrs**          **1413 wins**
**Pennants:** 1921, 1922, 1923, 1926, 1927, 1928
**World Series:** 1923, 1927, 1928

"A manager has his cards dealt to him and he must play them." - **Miller Huggins**

Miller Huggins may have been only 5-6 and 140 pounds but during his time as manager of the Yankees he was willing to go toe to toe with his team's biggest egos. And he usually won.

Huggins was a light-hitting but sure-handed second baseman for the Reds and the Cardinals. He became the player-manager of St.Louis in 1913 and his intelligence and baseball savvy immediately shone through. He became the full-time manager in 1917 when Rogers Hornsby became the Cards everyday second baseman. Huggins had invested wisely in the stock market and pieced together investors to buy the team. The owners rejected his offer. Huggins resigned. And a dynasty was born.

Huggins became manager of the Yankees in 1918 and he quickly began assembling a roster he felt could bring a much-needed pennant to New York. The owners Ruppert and Huston had essentially given their manager a blank checkbook. He signed Carl Mays from Boston in 1919 and then landed the biggest fish of all. George Herman Ruth.

Huggins paid $100,000 for the Babe and so began a tumultuous relationship that would span the remainder of Huggins tenure. Huggins, who was extremely volatile by nature, despised Ruth's lack of discipline while Ruth didn't enjoy being told what to do. But by 1922 the Yankees were firmly Miller Huggins' team.

However, they lost the World Series in both 1921 and 1922. The Yankees finally won the World Series in 1923, the year they moved into their own, eponymous, stadium, aka "The House that Ruth Built". By 1925 Ruth had become a permanent headache for Huggins. Ruth's hard living had him hospitalized and batting only .245. Manager and superstar were at war on a daily basis but Huggins dug his heels in and refused to be pushed around. With Ruppert's backing Huggins fined Ruth $5,000, the largest fine of it's kind, and the war was effectively won.

Huggins would go onto win six pennants and three World Series. His 1927 team, dubbed the "Murderers' Row," was probably the finest group of ballplayers ever to be assembled. The team led by Ruth, Lou Gehrig, Tony Lazzeri and Bob Meusel went 110-44 and swept Pittsburgh in the World Series. During his 17 years Huggins won 1,413 games for a .555 winning percentage.

Huggins' health declined rapidly in 1929 and he left the Yankees with 11 games remaining in the season and his team in second place, behind the Philadelphia A's. He died from blood poisoning after spending just three days in hospital.

# TONY LA RUSSA

**Anthony La Russa**
**Born:** October 4 1944, Tampa, Florida
**Teams Managed:** Chicago White Sox, Oakland A's, St. Louis Cardinals
**23 yrs     1827 wins**
*Pennants:* 1988, 1989, 1990
*World Series:* 1989

**"If I ever do a book, Tony La Russa would be a whole chapter. He's one intense, complicated guy, who changed my life." - Dennis Eckersley on Tony La Russa**

When asked their thoughts on Tony La Russa, most of his players, past and present, will tell you the same thing. Tough to get along with. But one of the very best teachers in the game. It is a paradox that many players seem happy to live with. "The man treated me like a dog," said Tony Phillips who played under La Russa at Oakland. "But I never learned more about baseball than when I played for him."

La Russa played for the A's, the Braves and the Cubs in 6-year career that promised much but never delivered. His analytical mind seemed better suited to other pursuits. After games La Russa would attend Florida State and eventually graduated with a law degree 1978. But he didn't hit the courtrooms. The dugout seemed altogether more appealing.

He was appointed manager of the Chicago White Sox in 1979 and in 1983 they won the AL West, with La Russa earning the Manager of the Year award. But after a 26-38 start in 1986 La Russa was fired. He took over the reins at Oakland in 1987 and in 1988 it all began to click for La Russa. His A's won 104 regular season games but lost surprisingly to the Dodgers in the World Series. But La Russa had put his stamp on the game. He had converted starter Dennis Eckersley into Oakland's closer in what became one of the managerial decisions of the era. Eck led the league in saves from 1988 to '92 and La Russa had shown that he had one of the finest minds in baseball. *Sports Illustrated* tagged him "Mastermind' in an infamous cover story that La Russa has always strived to play down.

He would go onto even greater success with Oakland, aided by the lethal combination of the "Bash Brothers," Jose Canseco and Mark McGwire. He steered them to the World Series in 1989 and he was named Manager of the Year twice.

In 1996 he became manager of the Cardinals and guided them to the postseason immediately, losing to the Braves in the NL Championship Series. La Russa then watched McGwire make history while his team failed to make the postseason in both 1998 and '99. Heading into 2000 his win-loss record with the Cardinals was 319-328, but behind the the bats of Jim Edmonds and Will Clark, aquired on July 31 to replace the injured McGwire, and 20-game winner Darryl Kile, they won 95 games and the NL Central. In 2001 the Cards again made it into the playoffs, helping to solidify La Russa's position as one of the most respected managers in baseball.

With 1,827 career wins La Russa is the leader among active managers and he still remains as focused and as meticulous as ever. His statistical charts are his bible, with McGwire calling him "the most well prepared manager in the game."

# TOMMY LASORDA

**Thomas Charles Lasorda**
**Born:** September 22 1927, Norristown, Pennsylvania
**Teams Managed:** Los Angeles Dodgers
**21 yrs       1599 wins**
*Teams:* LA 1976-96
*Pennants:* 1977, 1978, 1981, 1988
*World Series:* 1981, 1988

**"Wait until Tommy meets the Lord and finds out that He's wearing pinstripes."** -
**Gaylord Perry on Tommy Lasorda.**

"I want to die working for the Dodgers," Tommy Lasorda once said. "Then, on my tombstone, I want the Dodger schedule so people can drop by old Lasorda's grave to see if the team is in town or on the road." And some people have dared called him obsessive.

When Lasorda said that he bled Dodger blue he wasn't over emphasizing his commitment to the team he managed for 20 years. Between 1977 and 1996 he led the Dodgers to eight National League West titles, four National League pennants and two World Series. But Lasorda didn't just win. He became synonymous with the team that has consumed him for so much of his life.

As a pitcher with Brooklyn and Kansas City, Lasorda didn't have great stuff but brimmed with enthusiasm, bravado and aggression. And as a manager these attributes would define him. He was a rah-rah guy who loved to wax lyrical about his beloved Dodgers. He was overtly friendly with his players but could also be extremely volatile. "Put a TV camera in a room and Lasorda would light up," said John Feinstein in his book *Play Ball*. "But ask him a question he didn't like and you'd better duck."

Undoubtedly his finest moment as a Dodger was his team's surprise victory over the powerful Oakland Athletics in the 1988 World Series. The team's indomitable spirit, instilled into them by the hyperactive Lasorda, was typified by Kirk Gibson's dramatic home run in Game 1.

Only Connie Mack, John McGraw and the man he replaced, Walt Alston, have managed one team for longer than Lasorda. Only Casey Stengel betters his record of 61 postseason games. His 1,599 career victories rank him thirteenth all-time. And remarkably Lasorda managed nine of the Dodgers' 16 Rookies of the Year winners. "He knows how to read people and knows what they need to get them going," said Dodgers catcher Mike Scioscia. "That's what made him a great manager."

While his public and private personas may have differed, Lasorda has undoubtedly been one of the game's true ambassadors. "I love baseball as much as anyone ever has," he said. He was elected to the Hall of Fame in 1997 and as LA's Vice-President still remains as passionate about the Dodgers and baseball as ever. If proof were needed, Lasorda managed Team USA to gold at the Sydney 2000 Olympics, defeating Cuba in the final. "I managed in four World Series," said the 73-year-old Lasorda. "This is bigger. When the Dodgers won, Cincinnati fans weren't happy or San Francisco fans weren't happy. Today, all United States fans are happy."

# CONNIE MACK

**Cornelius Alexander McGillicuddy**
**Born:** December 22 1862 in East Brookfield, Massachusetts
**Died:** February 8 1956 in Germantown, Pennsylvania
**Teams Managed:** Philadelphia Athletics
**53 yrs       3731 wins**
*Pennants:* 1902, 1905, 1910, 1911, 1913, 1914, 1929, 1930, 1931
*World Series:* 1910, 1911, 1913, 1929, 1930

"Humanity is the keystone that holds nations and men together. When that collapses, the whole structure crumbles. This is as true of baseball teams as any other pursuit in life."
**- Connie Mack**

The Philadelphia Athletics pitcher Eddie Rommel passed his manager, who was talking to his players, in the hotel lobby after another disappointing performance on the mound. "Good night, boys," he called. It was well before the team's curfew. "Excuse me," the manager said to his players. "I'll be right back." The manager walked to the back of the hotel and waited at the bottom of the fire escape. Within seconds Rommel began to descend the stairs. "Good night, Eddie," said the manager. Rommel went back up the fire escape to bed, his plans for a night on the town ended. This is Ty Cobb's favorite story of his favorite manager. Connie Mack.

Mack was a master tactician, an outstanding scout, and above all a gentleman. Always immaculate in a suit he would stand in the dugout, looking pensive, directing his runners with the wave of his ever-present scorecard. It remains one of baseball's most enduring images.

He managed and part-owned the Philadelphia Athletics for 50 years leading them to nine pennants and five World Series victories. He single-handily built the A's from the ground up to create a baseball dynasty and when, in 1915, financial instability and the cash-rich Federal League threatened the very foundation of his team, Mack sold the majority of his players and began to again concentrate on the building of another championship winning team.

During his managerial career, which began in 1894 and would span seven decades, Mack lost more games than he won but this is purely a reflection of his longevity rather than his skill as a manager. Mack won the World Series in 1910, 1911 and 1913 but it was for his World Series winning teams of 1929 and 1930 that he shall be best remembered. The nucleus of that team reads like a Who's Who of baseball: Al Simmons, Jimmy Foxx, Mickey Cochrane and Lefty Grove. Every one of them a Hall of Famer. And every one of them handpicked by Mack, scouted in the minors, and acquired with one purpose: to win the World Series. Between 1929-31 the A's won 313 games, 3 pennants and two World Series. For this period they were simply the best, as dominant as the '27 Yankees whose reign they ended.

Mack would never be able to assemble this kind of talent again. In 1935 he was again forced to sell players and until he retired in 1950, Mack's A's would struggle. He stepped down aged 85 having managed for 53 seasons.

# JOE McCARTHY

**Joseph Vincent McCarthy**
**Born:** April 21 1887, Philadelphia, Pennsylvania
**Died:** January 13 1978, Buffalo, New York
**Teams Managed:** Chicago Cubs, New York Yankees, Boston Red Sox
**24 yrs      2125 wins**
*Pennants:* 1929, 1932, 1936, 1937, 1938, 1939, 1941, 1942, 1943
*World Series:* 1932, 1936, 1937, 1938, 1939, 1941, 1943


**"So I eat, drink and sleep baseball 24 hours a day, What's wrong with that?"**
**- Joe McCarthy**


Joe McCarthy grew up in Pennsylvania as an ardent A's fan and a huge admirer of Connie Mack. As a manager he would strive to emulate Mack's demeanor. He would have no such problems emulating his success.

Viewed by many as the game's greatest manager, McCarthy won nine pennants and seven World Series in his 24 seasons. His .615 winning percentage is baseball's best and his 2,125 wins ranks fifth all-time. With the Yankees he won four World Championships in a row from 1936–39 and became the first manager to clinch pennants in both leagues.

As a player, McCarthy never made it to the big show, and his early managerial days were dogged by his time as a bush leaguer. His first triumph came in 1921 when he led Louisville of the American Association to the pennant in 1921. He repeated this feat in 1925 and was hired as the Cubs' manager in 1926. His first act was to send staff ace Grover Cleveland Alexander to St.Louis and to acquire Hack Wilson from Toledo. He had quickly shown that he was not afraid to manage despite the criticism that he lacked the playing experience required to manage at major league level. McCarthy steered Chicago to a pennant in 1929 but lost the World Series. However, with four games remaining in 1930, McCarthy was replaced as manager by Rogers Hornsby, The third-place-finishing Yankees hired him to replace Bob Shawkey for the 1931 season. The rest is history.

His Yankee teams won the World Series first in 1932 and then, in an incredible purple patch, from 1936–43, they won seven pennants and six World Series. These teams featured Lou Gehrig and Joe DiMaggio, Lefty Gomez and Spud Chandler – the latter had the best winning percentage and ERA in the 1940s. Only World War II could halt McCarthy's progress.

After the War had ended McCarthy returned to the Yankees but clashed frequently with the new owner Larry MacPhail. McCarthy quit and took over the Red Sox in 1948. Boston lost the 1948 pennant in a playoff and the '49 pennant on the last day of the season. In 1950 McCarthy called it a day.

Naturally reserved, McCarthy remained detached from his players as he sought to achieve the gentlemanly aura of Connie Mack. However he was greatly respected by them and his strength as a manager came from his ability to communicate strongly without saying too much. He was a disciplinarian but never a dictator and his players all had a purpose and knew it. The first to separate his pitching staff into starters and relievers, Joe McCarthy died in 1978 with the highest winning percentage – .615 – in baseball history.

# JOHN McGRAW

**John Joseph McGraw**
**Born:** April 7 1873 Truxton, New York
**Died:** February 25 1934, New Rochelle, New York
**Teams Managed:** Baltimore Orioles, New York Giants
**33 yrs      2763 wins**
**Pennants:** 1904, 1905, 1911, 1912, 1913, 1917, 1921, 1922, 1923, 1924
**World Series:** 1905, 1921, 1922

**"There is but one game and that game is baseball" - John McGraw**

Little Napoleon. It was as apt a nickname as the game has ever known.

From 1902–32 John McGraw's tenure as the New York Giants manager was characterized by his attention to detail, his acute baseball mind and his intense personality. McGraw began his life in baseball as a scrappy third baseman for the Baltimore Orioles where he first displayed the temper that would make him such a volatile manager. It was also where he developed the tactical genius that would make him legendary.

Between 1899, when he became player-manager of the Orioles, and 1932 when he resigned, McGraw compiled a record of 2,763-1,948, second only behind Connie Mack in career wins. He won 10 National League pennants and three World Series with the Giants. But more than just the victories, John McGraw defined what it meant to be a baseball manager. He was the first to hire a coach and one of the first to employ relief pitchers and professional bench players. He brought tactics to the forefront and left no stone unturned in his pursuit of victory. During the dead-ball era he built his teams with speed as a prerequisite and is widely recognized as the inventor of the hit and run. However, McGraw was also very adaptable and when the game changed in 1920, McGraw's teams changed with it.

Much of his legend, however, is born from the autocratic style with which he managed the Giants. He would often call the game from the dugout and loved to boast how he "signaled for every ball" when the Giants pitched to Babe Ruth in the 1923 World Series. His players knew who was boss and those who questioned his authority would quickly learn to regret it. McGraw once ordered his outfielder Red Murray to lay down a sacrifice bunt. Murray stepped into the batter's box, turned on a high fastball, and hit a game-winning home run. McGraw fined him $100 dollars for ignoring the signal.

But above all John McGraw was a true fan of baseball. He lived to teach the game and had a huge impact on the careers of hundreds of young men, including Hall of Famers Christy Mathewson and Mel Ott.

Connie Mack paid him the ultimate tribute when he said, "There has been only one manager, and his name is John McGraw."

# BILL McKECHNIE

**William Boyd McKechnie**
**Born:** August 7 1887, Wilkinsburg, Pennsylvania
**Died:** October 29 1965, Bradenton, Florida
**Teams Managed:** Pittsburgh Pirates, St. Louis Cardinals, Boston Braves, Cincinnati Reds
**25 yrs      1896 wins**
***Pennants:*** 1925, 1928, 1939, 1940
***World Series:*** 1925, 1940

**"He had a remarkable ability for evoking respect." - Johnny Vander Meer on Bill McKechnie**

Like Connie Mack, Bill McKechnie was a perfect gentleman. His players respected him and in response played hard. He was the antidote to the in-your-face teachings of John McGraw and Leo Durocher. Johnny Vander Meer, who pitched back-to-back no-hitters with McKenchie's Reds, described his manager as "one of the greatest individuals I have met in my life, either on the field or off." This was a typical response from players who had played under the guidance of McKechnie.

McKechnie's first began managing in 1915 with Newark of the Federal League. This third league – which began play in 1914 – survived only until the end of the 1915 so McKechnie returned to National League for 1916, playing for both the New York Giants and Cincinnati Reds. He joined the Pittsburgh Pirates in 1918 and played for three years before becoming manager in 1922 after one season out of the Majors. He inherited a weak team, but part of McKechnie's managerial strength was his ability to devise a strategy and to stick to it. Using his fundamentals of sound defensive players and a line-up that hit for average and got on base, Pittsburgh won the pennant in 1925 and beat the Washington Senators to win their World Series since 1909.

However, the Pirates struggled in 1926 and McKenchie was fired. He was immediately hired by St.Louis as a member of their coaching staff and was appointed manager in '28. McKechnie won the pennant but again lost in the World Series to the mighty bats of the Yankees. And again he lost his job.

Despite suffering at the hands of over zealous owners McKenchie stayed in management and from 1930–37 helped the hapless Boston Braves achieve some degree of respectability. Nobody appeared to get more from their players than Bill McKenchie.

In 1938 his legendary patience was rewarded. He became the manager of the Cincinnati Reds, who had finished last in 1937, and in true McKenchie fashion turned their fortunes around. They won the pennant in 1939 and beat the Tigers in seven to capture the 1940 World Series. He stayed in Cincinnati until 1946 and officially retired from baseball in 1953 after spending time as coach with Cleveland and Boston.

Perhaps his greatest asset as a manger was his ability to communicate with players of all dispositions. Rabbit Maranville was McKechnie's favorite player despite having a voracious appetite for the high life. The deeply religious McKechnie decided to room with Maranville and they became baseball's answer to Oscar and Felix, the "Odd Couple." Maranville would be a fixture on McKechine's teams for ten years.

McKenchie died in 1965 with a 1,896-1723 record. He ranks tenth all-time in victories and is the sixth longest serving manger in baseball history.

# CASEY STENGEL

**Charles Dillon Stengel**
**Born:** July 30 1889, Kansas City, Missouri
**Died:** September 29 1975, Glendale, California
**Teams Managed:** Brooklyn Dodgers, Boston Braves, New York Yankees, New York Mets
**25 yrs        1905 wins**
*Pennants:* 1949, 1950, 1951, 1952, 1953, 1955, 1956, 1957, 1958, 1960
*World Series:* 1949, 1950, 1951, 1952, 1953, 1956, 1958

"Casey knew his baseball. He only made it look like he was fooling around."
## - Sparky Anderson on Casey Stengel

He had a language all his own and a style to match. He was loved by the media for his ability to play the clown, make great copy and still win ballgames. He was both intuitive and impulsive in his decision-making. Casey Stengel was truly one of a kind.

He finished his career in 1965 having managed 3,766 games for four different ball clubs. He equaled Joe McCarthy for most World Series wins (7) and had his number retired by both the Yankees and the Mets. But perhaps more than his records Casey Stengel is remembered for his use of the English language. His twisted phrases, mispronounced names and meandering sentences became known as Stengelese and he never failed to disappoint. Asked to testify to the Senate in 1958 regarding baseball's anti-trust exemption Stengel put on a vintage performance often leaving the Senators bewildered yet in hysterics.

Stengel played for 14 seasons in the majors and helped the Giants win the 1923 World Series with game-winning homers in games 1 and 3. It was also during his time with the Giants that he met the man who would have the greatest impact on his managerial career: John McGraw.

Many of Stengel's managerial nuances were derived from watching and absorbing McGraw at work. On the surface the two men couldn't appear more different but Stengel's love of platooning and his ability to motivate players were both seemingly picked-up from his time with McGraw's Giants.

Stengel managed the Dodgers and the Braves between 1934 and 1943 but it was with the Yankees that he really made his name. In 12 seasons, 1949–60, he guided New York to an unprecedented 10 pennants and seven World Series. Using all his players, platooning at will, and relying heavily on his bullpen, Stengel made his distinctive approach work.

Stengel's Yankees lost the 1960 World Series to the Pirates and he was fired. But rather than opting for retirement the 70-year old Stengel became manager of the expansion Mets in 1962. The Mets stunk but were a huge draw largely due to their lovable-losers image and of course, Stengel. He retired just three years later and died in 1975 aged 86.

Casey Stengel's 54 years in baseball were rich with success and always accompanied by neither a dull moment nor a dry eye. "There comes a time in every man's life, and I've had plenty of them," he once acknowledged.

He always did know how to say it best.

# JOE TORRE

**Joseph Paul Torre**
**Born:** July 18 1940, Brooklyn, New York
**Teams Managed:** New York Mets, Atlanta Braves,
St. Louis Cardinals, New York Yankees
**20 yrs    1455 wins**
*Pennants:* 1996, 1998, 1999, 2000, 2001
*World Series:* 1996, 1998, 1999, 2000

**"When you're sending quality players up there, it's not hard to look smart."**
**- Joe Torre**

Ask ex-Yankees pitcher David Cone what makes Joe Torre so special and he won't talk about his manager's strategical brilliance or his insatiable desire to win. For Cone, Torre's greatness comes from that intangible that separates the best from the rest. "Joe just commands respect," says Cone. "From Day One he just came in and took over. He has a presence about him."

Torre has guided the Yankees to four World Series wins in just six seasons since joining the franchise in 1996. He has compiled an awesome 56-22 postseason record with New York thanks largely to a clubhouse stacked with talented players and his ability to unite them as a team. But it hasn't always been a smooth ride for Torre.

He had completed a stellar 18-year playing career with the Atlanta Braves, St. Louis Cardinals and New York Mets and won the 1971 MVP but he never played in the World Series. As a manager he seemed destined for more of the same.

He managed the Mets, Braves and Cardinals and despite leading Atlanta to their first divisional title since 1969, he joined the Yankees in 1996 with an 894-1003 record and the indignity of having been fired by every club he had managed. But pinstripes have proved to be the perfect fit.

He led the Yankees to a World Series in his first season, beating the Braves in six, and in 1998 New York won 114 regular season games to establish a new AL record. They swept the San Diego Padres in the World Series to finish with 125 wins to better the 1906 Cubs major league record of 118. Torre had become only the third Yankee manager to reach the postseason in his first three seasons, joining Casey Stengel and Ralph Houk. In 1999 he went one better.

After being diagnosed with prostate cancer, Torre made a rapid recovery and rejoined his team in May. Again he led his team to the AL East title, the pennant and completed another victory over the Braves in the World Series.

In 2000 Torre guided the Yankees to their third straight World championship, beating the Mets on the way to an incredible 26th title, making them the most successful franchise in pro sports history. Four straight proved just too much in 2001 as Torre and his Yankees lost to the Diamondbacks in seven. His illness, his successes and failures, means that Torre always maintains a healthy perspective despite managing in the cauldron of New York City. Worshiped by his players, he has the ability to touch them all, getting something from everyone. Whether they beat you with a barrage of homers of by playing little ball, Torre's Yankees do it as a team. "You play the game for the guy next to you," says Torre.

Named AL Manager of the Year in 1996 and '98, Torre still remains modest to a fault. "It's the players who get the job done, not me," he says.

# EARL WEAVER

**Earl Sidney Weaver**
**Born:** August 14 1930, St. Louis, Missouri
**Teams Managed:** Baltimore Orioles
**17 yrs       1480 wins**
*Pennants:* 1969, 1970, 1971, 1979
*World Series:* 1970


**"I don't think anybody could kick dirt like Earl." - Davey Johnson on Earl Weaver**

On the golf course, Earl Weaver always found a way to win. "He made you give him enough strokes so that if he played bad, he'd still beat you," said Dodgers manager Davey Johnson who played under Weaver at Baltimore. "He didn't give you a chance." It is a sentiment that is no doubt shared by those who faced Weaver at his day job, too.

As passionate as they come, kicking dirt on home plate to show his frustrations, Weaver managed the Orioles for 17 seasons compiling a .583 winning percentage that ranks him fifth among 20th century managers with at least 10 years' service.

Weaver is perhaps best known for his advocacy of the big inning and what came to be known as the "Baltimore Way." Both provide windows to Weaver's baseball soul. He loved the big inning, and had a disdain for the bunt and the stolen base, despite the 1970s being the era for speed. More than anything his tactics illustrated his enormous self-belief and an innovative streak that would spread throughout his managerial style.

As a minor league manager in the Orioles organization Weaver devised a series of practice techniques based on sound baseball fundamentals. These were installed throughout the organization, to help aid a player's transition from one level to the next. Weaver firmly believed in strategy and discipline. Both were the cornerstones of the Baltimore Way.

Every player in Weaver's line-ups was there for a reason. He found out what a player's strengths were and gave them a clearly defined role based on these strengths. Not every one of Weaver's men was an Eddie Murray or a Cal Ripken Jr. "They're not all great players, but they can all do something," he liked to say.

His intensity and intelligence were unparalleled in his era. He scanned his elaborate situational charts, platooned like it was going out of style and went toe-to-toe with umpires on a regular basis, leading to 91 ejections and six suspensions. Between 1968 and 1986, Weaver won 1480 games, six AL East titles, four pennants and the 1970 World Series. His thorough approach and will to win helped his O's compile five 100-win seasons, a record only bettered by Joe McCarthy and his Yankees and equaled by Connie Mack's A's.

After retiring in 1982 Weaver was persuaded to once again manage the struggling Orioles in 1986. They finished a disappointing 73-89 and he again retired, this time for good. It was his first and last losing season.

# The Ballparks

Oriole Park
"Old" Comiskey Park
Wrigley Field
Fenway Park
Jacobs Field
Tiger Stadium
The Astrodome
Dodger Stadium
Ebbets Field
Polo Grounds
Yankee Stadium
Shibe Park
Bank One Ballpark
Forbes Field
Sportsman's Park
Griffith Stadium

# Oriole Park at Camden Yards, Baltimore

The St. Louis Browns moved to Baltimore for the 1954 season and were renamed the Baltimore Orioles. They played in Memorial Stadium until Oriole Park at Camden Yards, the first of a new generation of ballparks, opened in 1992. Its design incorporated elements of the classic ballparks, but with all of today's modern amenities, including a system for hearing impaired fans to link to for audio coverage of the game at their seats.

It is 318 feet down the right-field line and there is a 25-foot wall in right field, an inviting target for lefthanded hitters. The most striking feature of the ballpark actually lies outside its walls. The Baltimore & Ohio Warehouse, which is used as the Orioles' business office, dominates the view in right field and is only 432 feet from home plate. Babe Ruth was born two blocks from the ballpark and his father owned a bar that was located in what is currently center field.

Oriole legend Cal Ripken Jr. broke the immortal Lou Gehrig's consecutive-game streak on September 6, 1995, when he played in his 2,131st straight game. Ripken voluntarily ended his streak at 2,633 games late in the 1998 season.

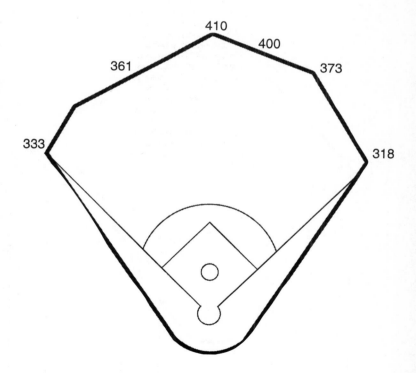

# Fenway Park, Boston

Fenway Park, the oldest ballpark (1912) in the major leagues, contains an array of unique nooks and crannies that have added to its personality. From the stands down the left-field foul line that jut out close to the playing field, to the diminutive five-foot wall at the right-field foul pole, the park's many idiosyncrasies have created improbable bounces and a distinct home-field advantage for the Old Towne team. The dominant feature of this ballpark is the 37-foot-high wall in left field, named the Green Monster.

One of baseball's most memorable home runs involved the Green Monster. Boston's Carlton Fisk hit the climatic home run to win Game 6 of the 1975 World Series, just off the left-field foul pole. That dramatic homer was the conclusion to what many baseball historians consider the greatest World Series game ever played. Just three seasons later, another memorable home run was hit over the Green Monster, this time by Yankee shortstop Bucky Dent. That homer came in a one-game playoff between Boston and New York at season's end, completing one of the greatest come-from-behind finishes in baseball history by the Yankees.

This storied ballpark has been the home for many baseball notables, including Babe Ruth, Ted Williams, Carl Yastrzemski and the current star in Boston, Nomar Garciaparra.

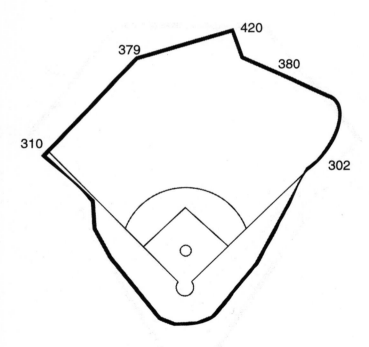

# "Old" Comiskey Park, Chicago

The original Comiskey Park opened in 1901 and was the home of the Chicago White Sox until 1990, when the team moved across the street to the new Comiskey Park. The original ballpark was symmetrical in design and featured the first exploding scoreboard in deep center field, starting in the 1960 season. The ground crews were known to give the hometown team an advantage, such as watering down the infield in front of home plate when White Sox sinkerball pitchers were to pitch. They also lowered the visitor's bullpen pitching mound to mess up the rhythm of opposing hurlers.

The first All-Star Game was played here on July 6, 1933. The longest game in American League history was played over the period of two days, May 8-9, 1984, and went 25 innings before Chicago's Harold Baines stroked a home run to win the game. Hoyt Wilhelm set the all-time record for pitching appearances in his 907th game here on July 24, 1968. Chicago outfielder Al Smith was showered with beer after the Dodgers' Charlie Neal hit a home run into the left-field stands in Game 2 of the 1959 World Series. The White Sox were forced to forfeit the second game of a doubleheader on July 12, 1979. Fans stormed the field during an album-burning promotion called "Disco Demolition Night," and the umpires declared the field unplayable.

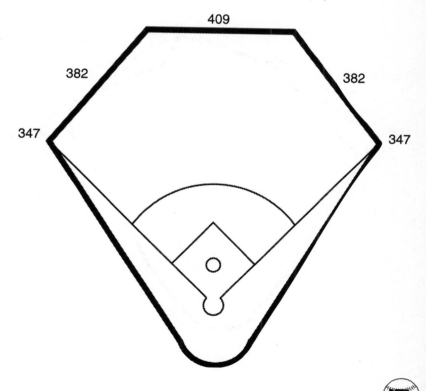

# Wrigley Field, Chicago

The oldest ballpark in current use in the National League, and arguably the most popular, Wrigley Field is known as much for its ivy-covered walls as it is for the team's forgiving fans. The Chicago Cubs, who have played here since 1914, have not won a World Series in Wrigley Field. Their last appearance in the Series was 1945, when they lost four games to three to Detroit. Despite the failings of the Cubs, their fans are some of the most loyal in baseball and continue to fill the park. The highest-scoring game in major league baseball was played here, when the Phillies beat the Cubs 26-23 on August 25, 1922.

Even without winning a World Series, Wrigley Field has had its share of personalities pass through its gates. Ernie Banks, known widely as "Mr. Cub," is equally known for the famous saying, "Let's play two," a phase that displayed his passion for the game. Baseball lore was recorded here when Babe Ruth allegedly pointed to the right-field bleachers, then hit a home run there during the 1932 World Series. In 1988, Wrigley Field became the last ballpark to install lights and host night baseball. Two Hall of Fame announcers, Jack Brickhouse and Harry Caray, have covered the Cubs.

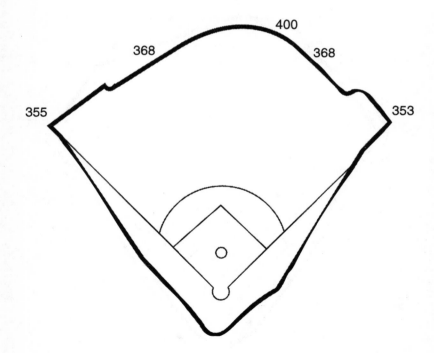

# Jacobs Field, Cleveland

The Cleveland Indians moved from the cavernous, old and dreary Cleveland Stadium into Jacobs Field in 1994. Like the Orioles' Camden Yards, the Jake (as it is affectionately called by Indian fans) is modeled after the classic ballparks of the past. Because of the poor weather early and late in the season, the plan was to build a domed stadium. That idea was rejected by voters, and they "settled" for an open-air ballpark. The Jake's birth in 1994 has contributed to a renaissance in downtown Cleveland. The layout is almost symmetrical in terms of distances, but the varying heights of the park's walls add personality to the Jake. A shorter version of the Green Monster was built at a height of 19 feet in left field. While it hurts some righthanded hitters by turning home runs into doubles, Jacobs Field still is a hitter-friendly ballpark.

The Cleveland franchise wallowed in mediocrity in the decades prior to the opening of Jacobs Field. In only the second season in its new ballpark, the Tribe became annual American League contenders by winning 100 games and taking the Atlanta Braves to Game 6 before losing the 1995 World Series. It was Cleveland's first appearance in the Fall Classic since 1954.

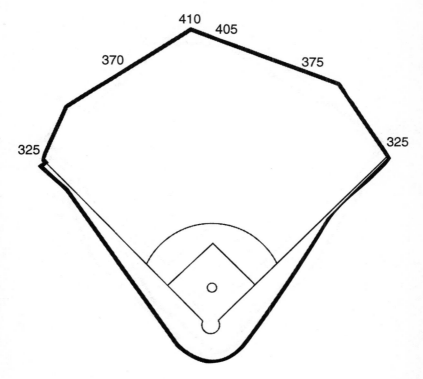

# Tiger Stadium, Detroit

Tiger Stadium opened as Bennett Park in 1912. The name was changed to Navin Field, then to Briggs Field, and finally it became Tiger Stadium in 1960. The American League Detroit Tigers played there from 1912 through the 1999 season. The team moved into a new ballpark near downtown Detroit for the 2000 campaign. In its early days, Tiger Stadium was the only ballpark with double-deck bleachers in the outfield. The second deck in right field hung over the field in fair territory by ten feet, turning some routine flyballs into home runs. Tiger Stadium was one of the last ballparks in the majors to install lights.

Hall of Famer Ty Cobb, who played 22 of his 24 seasons in Detroit, won 12 batting titles and three American League pennants, but never enjoyed a World Series. Ted Williams won the 1941 All-Star Game with a ninth-inning, three-run homer into the upper deck in right-center field. One of the game's more colorful characters, Mark "The Bird" Fidrych, won over Tiger fans with his antics on the mound, which included talking to the baseball. Lou Gehrig's "Iron Man" streak ended at Tiger Stadium in 1939.

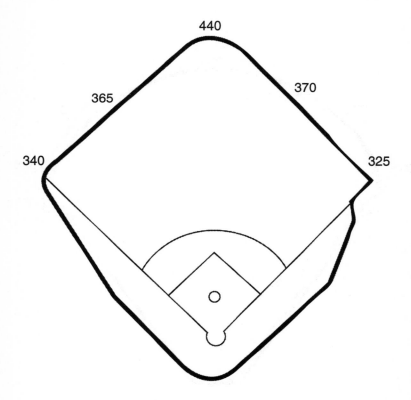

# The Astrodome, Houston

The Astrodome was the second covered stadium in baseball. The first was the field under the Queensboro Bridge in New York, which was used by the Negro Leagues in the 1930s. The Astrodome, of course, was the first fully-enclosed indoor stadium. The highest point inside the dome was 208 feet, just behind second base. When the Astrodome opened it had clear glass in the ceiling, but that caused problems with the fielders, so the glass was painted white. While that helped fielders see the ball, shutting out the light killed the grass inside. So, the Houston Astros installed a new product called AstroTurf, an artificial grass made of plastic. Only one game ever was rained out here, and that was due to flooding in the streets, which prevented fans from getting to the stadium.

Hall of Famer Mickey Mantle hit the first home run at the Astrodome, during an exhibition game before the start of the Astros' (known then as the Colt 45s) inaugural season in 1965. Nolan Ryan became the first pitcher to strike out 4,000 batters here on July 11, 1985. Ryan also threw his record fifth no-hitter here. Astros pitcher Mike Scott hurled a no-hitter on September 25, 1986, to clinch Houston's first division title in the dome.

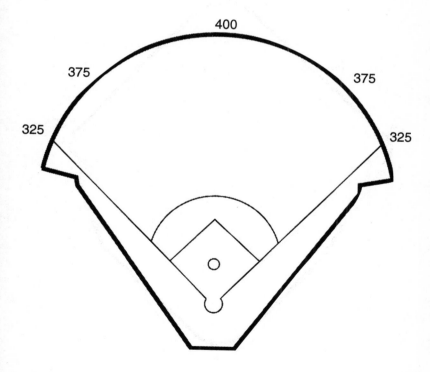

# Dodger Stadium, Los Angeles

The Brooklyn Dodgers moved from Brooklyn's Ebbets Field to Los Angeles in 1958, and the Los Angeles club opened its current park, Dodger Stadium, in 1962. Dodger Stadium also is known as Chavez Ravine, for the location on which the ballpark was built. The Los Angeles (now Anaheim) Angels also played here from 1962-1965, and this American League expansion club preferred the latter name, so as not to promote the National League Dodgers. By either name, it's the only major league ballpark that has not changed its seating capacity (56,000) since its inception. Even though the ballpark is less than 40 years old, it has been the scene of some of baseball's great accomplishments.

In Game 1 of the 1988 World Series, the Dodgers were trailing the Oakland Athletics 4-3 entering the bottom of the ninth. Oakland's Dennis Eckersley, one of the most dominant closers of all time, walked the leadoff hitter. Kirk Gibson, hobbled by knee problems, was not expected to play in the Series. But manager Tommy Lasorda decided to pinch-hit Gibson and he responded with a dramatic home run into the right-field stands for the win. Orioles reliever Moe Drabowsky struck out 11 Dodgers in Game 1 of the 1966 World Series, still a Series record. Reliever Mike Marshall pitched in a record 106 games in 1974. Manny Mota set the career pinch-hit record (150) at Dodger Stadium on October 5, 1980. Sandy Koufax set the National League mark for most strikeouts in a season with 382 during the 1965 season.

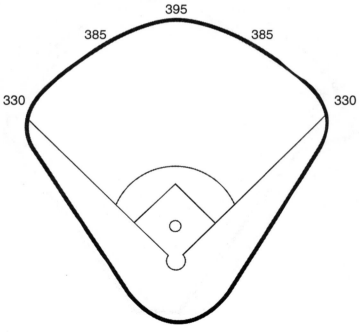

# Ebbets Field, New York

The beloved Brooklyn Dodgers played here from 1913 until 1957, when the franchise was moved to Los Angeles and renamed the Los Angeles Dodgers. The Brooklyn Dodgers won nine National League pennants and one World Series title. Brooklyn lost five World Series to the hated cross-town Yankees before finally winning its only championship (vs. the Yankees) in 1955.

Ebbets Field had its share of odd angles and walls. The distance down the right-field line was a mere 296 feet, but right field featured a 38-foot wall that was similar in size and concept to Fenway Park's Green Monster. The scoreboard was located in right field, which provided at least 289 different angles for the ball to carom. In Ebbets Field's first decade, the Dodgers' George Cutshaw hit a groundball home run when the ball bounced up a concave wall and over the fence.

Johnny Vander Meer hurled his second no-hitter here in 1938 to complete the only back-to-back no-hitters by the same pitcher in baseball history. A home run in 1946 by Bama Rowell of the Boston Braves broke the right-field scoreboard clock. This was the inspiration for the home run hit in the movie "The Natural."

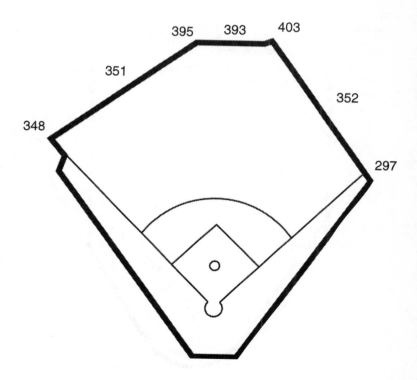

# Polo Grounds, New York

The name of this ballpark is misleading because polo was never played here. The name came from the owner and a field adjacent to the ballpark. The New York Giants of the National League called the Polo Grounds home from 1911 through the 1957 season. The Giants moved to San Francisco, California, and the team's name was changed to the San Francisco Giants at the start of the 1958 season. This fabled park had one more tenant, the New York Mets, during the expansion franchise's inaugural season in 1962.

The Polo Grounds always will be remembered for two great events in baseball. The first was the pennant-winning home run by Giants outfielder Bobby Thomson on October 3, 1951, in a game that was dubbed the "Greatest Game Ever Played." The second was a remarkable catch by Hall of Famer Willie Mays (off Vic Wertz), who hauled in a 440-ft drive with an over-the-shoulder catch while on the run, preserving a win during the '54 World Series.

The ballpark had a unique design: the shape of a horseshoe. Quirks of the Polo Grounds included the upper deck in left field, which hung over the field slightly and was in play, an outfield that was sunken below the level of the infield, and bullpens that were located in fair territory in right and left-center fields.

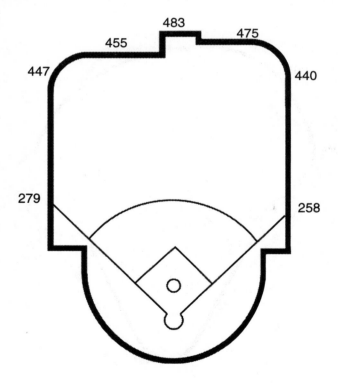

# Yankee Stadium, New York

No ballpark in baseball has been the scene of more baseball history than Yankee Stadium. Babe Ruth hit his record-setting 60th homer here in 1927, and 34 years later Roger Maris hit his 61st on the last day of the 1961 season to establish the new mark. Lou Gehrig's consecutive-games streak began here, as did Joe DiMaggio's 56-game hitting streak. In 1956, Don Larsen threw the only no-hitter and perfect game in postseason action at the Stadium. The individual feats are endless. The Yankees franchise now has played more than 100 postseason games here, capturing 26 World Series championships.

The Yankees began playing here in 1923, and the Stadium has undergone several renovations, including a major makeover in 1974-1975. Still, the personality of the ballpark has remained the same. Lefthanded pull hitters still have a short porch down the right-field line. Left-center field has been reduced from the cavernous 500 feet in 1923 to a more modest 399 feet in its current form. The distance down the left-field line has grown from the short 280 feet of 1923 to its current distance of 318.

In left-center field, beyond the outfield wall, is an area that contains monuments and plaques, celebrating Yankee greats Lou Gehrig, Babe Ruth, Mickey Mantle, Roger Maris, Whitey Ford and Thurman Munson-and several Roman Catholic popes as well.

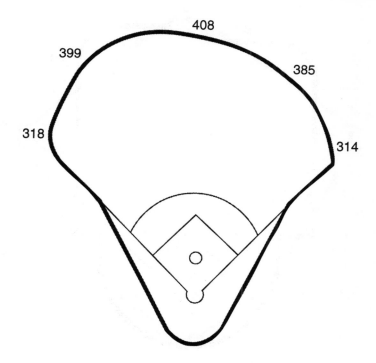

# Shibe Park, Philadelphia

Shibe Park was the home of the American League Philadelphia Athletics from 1909 to 1954, as well as the National League Philadelphia Phillies from 1927 to 1970. It was the first major league ballpark to be built with concrete and steel, and it featured an outside facade that resembled a church.

The first American League night game was played at Shibe Park on May 16, 1939, with the A's losing 8-3 to Cleveland. This ballpark was the stage for many great individual performances. The most notable may have been by Ted Williams during the 1941 season. He entered the last day of the campaign with a .39955 batting average. Williams went 4-for-5 in the first of two contests, and was 2-for-3 in the second game to finish the season at .406. Williams became the last player to hit .400. Jimmie Foxx hit his 500th home run to dead center field in 1940, and Lou Gehrig belted four straight homers there in 1932.

Connie Mack, nicknamed the Grand Old Man, graced the ballpark as the Athletics manager from 1901 through 1950. The National League franchise will always be remembered for a 10-game losing streak late in the 1964 season, which cost the Phillies the pennant.

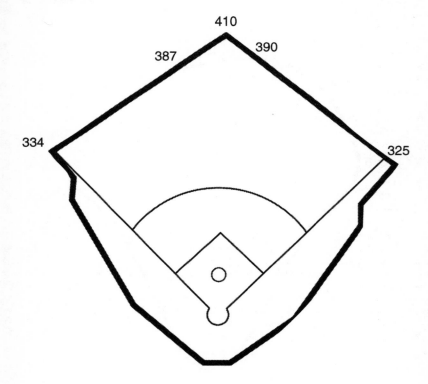

# Bank One Ballpark, Phoenix

The expansion Arizona Diamondbacks opened up Bank One Ballpark in April 1998. The BOB, as it is nicknamed, is designed with the old-fashion ballparks in mind but not to the degree that Camden Yards and Jacobs Filed were. It was built at an elevation of 1,100 feet, second highest only to the Colorado Rockies' Coors Field. The dimensions are almost equal down the lines, with the distance between home and the outfield wall a mere four feet longer down the right-field line.

To combat the intense heat of Arizona, this ballpark was built with a retractable roof. The roof can be opened or closed in less than six minutes. The air conditioning system needs almost three hours to lower the temperature from 100 degrees to a comfortable 75 degrees. Eighty percent of the seats are between the foul poles and there is no upper deck around the outfield. Located in right-center field is the unique Sun Pool Party Pavilion. This area, which consists of a swimming pool, hot tub, fountains, catering service and other amenities, can hold 35 people. The BOB is the only ballpark in the major leagues that has a pool. The Diamondbacks made the National League playoffs in their second season and won the World Series in just their forth, both records for an expansion team.

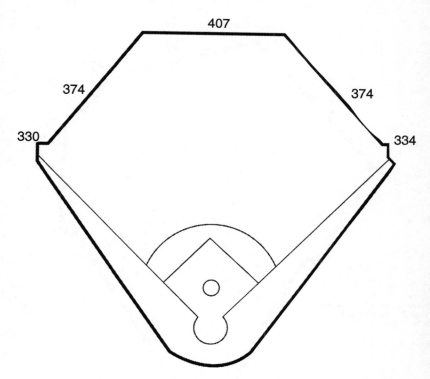

407

374            374

330            334

# Forbes Field, Pittsburgh

The home of the Pittsburgh Pirates from 1909 until 1970, Forbes Field also housed the Negro League Grays from 1939 to 1948. It was the locale for Babe Ruth's last home run, which also was the first to be hit completely out of the ballpark. Five days later Ruth played his last major league game here. While Forbes Field enjoyed a reputation as a pitcher's ballpark, there never was a no-hitter thrown on this spacious field. The ballpark also had a reputation for its rugged infield, considered the hardest in the majors. Yankee shortstop Tony Kubek was knocked unconscious from a bad-hop grounder during the 1960 World Series. Fans who sat in the far upper-left corner of the left-field bleacher had their home-plate view partially blocked by the stands near third base. The major league's last tripleheader was played here in 1920. Forbes also was the first ballpark to place protective foam padding along the outfield wall to protect outfielders in the 1950s.

Bill Mazeroski, a Pirate second baseman, connected on the most memorable home run ever hit in the bottom of the ninth inning, clinching the 1960 World Series over the Yankees in Game 7. Another memorable postseason hit at Forbes was a bases-loaded double by Pirate Kiki Cuyler to lead Pittsburgh to the 1925 World Series title.

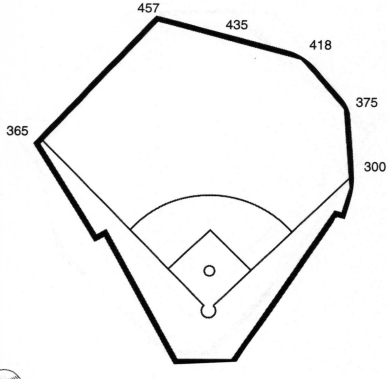

# Sportsman's Park, St. Louis

The American League St. Louis Browns (1909-1953) and the National League St. Louis Cardinals (1920-May 8, 1966) shared Sportsman's Park. The ballpark's most memorable moment occurred when owner Bill Veeck pulled a marketing stunt for publicity. He brought in a 65-pound, three-foot-seven inch midget by the name of Eddie Gaedel who was used as a pinch hitter once on August 19, 1951. Gaedel walked in his only appearance in the majors.

The St. Louis Cardinals won 10 National League pennants as residents of Sportsman's Park, while the St. Louis Browns secured only one. Ironically, they won their respective pennants in 1944 and faced each other in the World Series, which was dubbed the "Streetcar Series." The Cardinals won in six games and were the champions of St. Louis and all of baseball.

The most notable player to call Sportsman's Park his ballyard home was Stan "The Man" Musial, whose sweet lefthanded swing produced seven batting championships. As a Cardinal, he won two World Series titles and election into the Hall of Fame. Brothers Dizzy and Paul Dean combined to win 49 games for the Cardinals in 1934. Pete Gray, a one-armed outfielder, made his debut here in 1945 for the Browns.

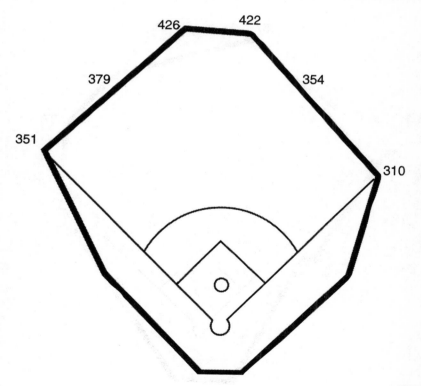

# Griffith Stadium, Washington D.C

Located in the nation's Capitol, Griffith Stadium was home to the Washington Senators from 1911 through 1961, as well as to several Negro League teams between 1924 and 1938. The ballpark was known for being built around a group of five duplex homes in center field, which produced a 31-foot-high wall in center and a unique right-center field. President William Taft, a huge baseball fan, was credited with creating the seventh-inning stretch, when fans stand up to stretch between the top and bottom of the seventh inning. When Taft stood up, everyone else around him did so out of respect to him-and an ongoing tradition was born in 1910.

Griffith Stadium was considered a pitcher's ballpark, and one of the most difficult to homer in. Only Josh Gibson (twice) and Mickey Mantle ever hit balls completely out of the park in left. Mantle's home run was one of the longest ever estimated at 565 feet. Pitcher Walter Johnson was the most notable player to perform here. Johnson played for the Senators from 1907 through 1927, winning 417 games and leading the American League in strikeouts 12 times. Only three pennants were won by the Washington franchise in this ballpark.

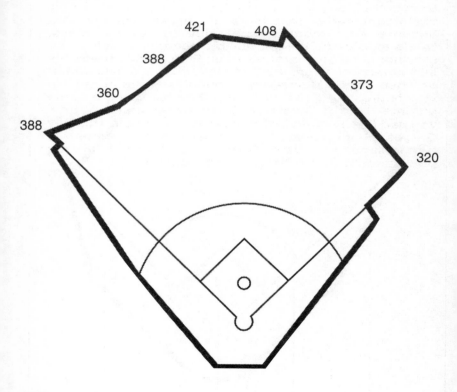

**Key Games**

Baseball's rich history has been littered with many significant games but there are those rare few that become even more special, due to historic plays, twists of fate and the impossible becoming reality. You may not have been around when Fred Merkle made his infamous gaff, when the Babe launched his called shot or when Bobby Thomsen's pennant-winning home run was heard 'round the world but the chances are these unforgettable moments are fresh in your memory, as if you had been sitting in the bleachers yourself. This Key Games chapter disects baseball's most memorable happenings and lets history live forever in the permanent record of the game's linescore.

# October 13 1903

**Boston Pilgrims**     3
**Pittsburgh Pirates**     0

**October 13 1903, Huntington Avenue Grounds, Boston**

The Boston Pilgrims had gone 91-47 to clinch the American League Pennant thanks largely to the pitching of Cy Young and Bill Dinneen. Both had been 20-game winners as Boston cruised to the AL title, finishing 14½ games ahead of the Philadelphia A's.

In baseball's first modern World Series it would be no different. Dinneen won Games 2 and 6 for the Sox and again took the mound for Game 8. Up against the Pirates ace Deacon Phillippe, Dinneen gave up just four hits in nine innings. He managed to silence the bats of Honus Wagner, who had led the National League with a .355 average, Tommy Leach and Ginger Beaumont to pitch a shutout, giving Boston baseball's inaugural World Championship.

A two-run fourth inning, plus an insurance run in the sixth was all that Boston needed to shock the favored Pireates., In baseball's first-ever postseason, Dinneen had finished an impressive 3-1 with a 2.06 ERA.

| | 1 | 2 | 3 | 4 | 5 | 6 | 7 | 8 | 9 | R | H | E |
|---|---|---|---|---|---|---|---|---|---|---|---|---|
| Pittsburgh Pirates | 0 | 0 | 0 | 0 | 0 | 0 | 0 | 0 | 0 | 0 | 4 | 3 |
| Boston Pilgrims | 0 | 0 | 0 | 2 | 0 | 1 | 0 | 0 | x | 3 | 8 | 0 |

E--Phelps, Bransfield, Wagner. LOB--Pirates 4, Pilgrims 7.
Scoring Position--Pirates 0-for-1, Pilgrims 3-for-6.
3B--Sebring, Freeman, LaChance.
S--LaChance. SB--Wagner. CS--Leach.

| Pittsburgh Pirates | IP | H | R | ER | BB | K |
|---|---|---|---|---|---|---|
| Deacon Phillippe (L) | 8.0 | 8 | 3 | 2 | 0 | 2 |

| Boston Pilgrims | IP | H | R | ER | BB | K |
|---|---|---|---|---|---|---|
| Bill Dinneen (W) | 9.0 | 4 | 0 | 0 | 2 | 7 |

Time--1:35. Attendance--7,455.
Umpires--HP, O'Day. Bases, Connolly.

# September 23 1908

**Chicago Cubs**      1
**New York Giants**     1

**September 23 1908, Polo Grounds, New York**

When it comes to boneheaded plays, none is more infamous than the one made by Fred Merkle on the basepaths.

On September 23 1908 the New York Giants met the Chicago Cubs at the Polo Grounds. The two teams were tied for first in the National League and with only a week left of the season. In the bottom of the ninth with the score tied at 1-1, Giants shortstop Al Bridwell stepped to the plate. There were runners on first – Merkle – and third – Moose McCormick – with two outs. Bridwell hit a sharp single to centerfield off Jack Pfiester. McCormick scored with ease from third and Merkle cruised towards second base. The crowds flocked onto the field and the players exited towards the clubhouses. Everyone at the Polo Grounds presumed the game was over. Merkle was no exception and made for the safety of the Giants clubhouse.

Cubs' second baseman Johnny Evers noticed Merkle's had not touched second base and shouted to center fielder Artie Hoffman to find the ball. Remarkably Hoffman found the ball out at right center and threw it towards Evers. Eyewitness accounts vary, but it seems that Giants third base coach Joe McGinnity grew wise to what was happening, intercepted the ball, and threw it away. Somehow Johnny Evers ended up with the ball. Did Cubs pitcher Rube Kroh punch a fan who retrieved the ball and then hand it to Evers? Was the right ball ever found?

Despite the ensuing chaos, the indisputable facts are that Merkle did not touch second base and Evers was holding a ball touching that bag. Merkle was out and the inning was over. The score was still 1-1, but because of the huge numbers of people on the field Chicago's manager Frank Chance appealed to the umpires that the Giants should forfeit the game. Unable to resume, it was called a tie and would be replayed as a playoff game if necessary. Naturally, they did end the 1908 season tied, the Cubs won the playoff game 4-2, and Fred Merkle became the game's original goat.

| | 1 | 2 | 3 | 4 | 5 | 6 | 7 | 8 | 9 | | R | H | E |
|---|---|---|---|---|---|---|---|---|---|---|---|---|---|
| Chicago Cubs | 0 | 0 | 0 | 1 | 0 | 0 | 0 | 0 | 0 | | 1 | 5 | 3 |
| NewYork Giants | 0 | 0 | 0 | 0 | 1 | 0 | 0 | 0 | 0 | | 1 | 6 | 0 |

E--Tinker 2, Steinfeldt. DP--Chicago 3, New York 1.
LOB--Chicago 3, New York 7. HR--Tinker. SF--Bresnahan.

| Chicago Cubs | IP | H | R | ER | BB | SO |
|---|---|---|---|---|---|---|
| Jack Pfiester | 9.0 | 6 | 1 | 0 | 2 | 0 |

| New York Giants | IP | H | R | ER | BB | SO |
|---|---|---|---|---|---|---|
| Christy Mathewson | 9.0 | 5 | 1 | 1 | 0 | 9 |

HBP--McCormick by Pfiester. Time--1:30. Attendance--20,000.
Umpires--HP, O'Day. Bases, Emslie.

# July 19 1910

**Cleveland Naps**      5
**Washington Nationals**      2

**July 19 1910, Griffith Stadium, Washington D.C**

By 1910 Cy Young was no longer the great pitcher he once was, having to succumb to the unavoidable limitations of an ageing arm and a game now dominated by young hurlers such as Walter Johnson, Christy Matthewson and Mordecai "Three Finger" Brown.

But there was one landmark left for the legendary Young to reach. Win number 500. On July 19, Young, now playing for Cleveland, faced the Washington Nationals. The still durable Young showed the heart that had exemplified his career by going 11 strong innings, determined to earn his 500th lifetime victory, which he sealed with a 5-2 win. He finished the season 7-10 with a 2.54 ERA and would retire the following season with 511 career wins, a record that will surely never be broken.

| | 1 | 2 | 3 | 4 | 5 | 6 | 7 | 8 | 9 | 10 | 11 | R | H | E |
|---|---|---|---|---|---|---|---|---|---|---|---|---|---|---|
| Cleveland Naps | 0 | 0 | 0 | 0 | 0 | 0 | 0 | 0 | 2 | 0 | 3 | 5 | 7 | 2 |
| Washington Nationals | 1 | 0 | 0 | 0 | 0 | 0 | 0 | 0 | 1 | 0 | 0 | 2 | 4 | 2 |

E--Turner, Young, Street, Reisling. DP--Washington 1.
LOB--Washington 5, Cleveland 6. SH--Turner, Birmingham, Reisling.
SF--Easterly, Stovall. SB--Lajole.

| Cleveland Naps | IP | H | R | ER | BB | SO |
|---|---|---|---|---|---|---|
| Cy Young (W) | 11.0 | 4 | 2 | - | 3 | 3 |

| Washington Nationals | IP | H | R | ER | BB | SO |
|---|---|---|---|---|---|---|
| Doc Reisling | 9.0 | 5 | 2 | - | 2 | 3 |
| Bob Groom (L) | 2.0 | 2 | 3 | - | 3 | 0 |

HBP--Birmingham. Time--2:10. Umpire--Perrine.

# May 2 1917

**Cincinnati Reds** 1
**Chicago Cubs** 0

**May 2 1917, Weeghman Park, Chicago**

A no-hitter is such a baseball rarity, the thought of a double nine-inning no-hitter seems almost ridiculous, but in 1917 at Chicago's Weeghman Park – it would be renamed Wrigley Field a year later – that's exactly what happened.

For nine innings, the Cubs' James "Hippo" Vaughn and Cincinnati's Fred Toney, both lefties, went toe-to-toe, matching each other out by out, to pitch the game's only double no-hit game.

The game was finally decided in the 10th inning when Vaughn gave up a couple of hits to Gus Getz and Jim Thorpe, with Getz scoring the winning run. While Toney celebrated the most unusual of victories, the Cubbies' Vaughn was left to contemplate the fact that he had just tossed a pitching masterpiece. And still lost.

|  | 1 | 2 | 3 | 4 | 5 | 6 | 7 | 8 | 9 | 10 | R | H | E |
|---|---|---|---|---|---|---|---|---|---|----|---|---|---|
| Cincinnati Reds | 0 | 0 | 0 | 0 | 0 | 0 | 0 | 0 | 0 | 1 | 1 | 2 | 0 |
| Chicago Cubs | 0 | 0 | 0 | 0 | 0 | 0 | 0 | 0 | 0 | 0 | 0 | 0 | 1 |

E--Zeider, Williams. DP--Chicago 2. \
LOB--Cincinnati 1, Chicago 2. SB--Chase. CS--Neale.

| Cincinnati Reds | IP | H | R | ER | BB | SO |
|---|---|---|---|---|---|---|
| Fred Toney (W) | 10.0 | 0 | 0 | 0 | 2 | 3 |

| Chicago Cubs | IP | H | R | ER | BB | SO |
|---|---|---|---|---|---|---|
| Hippo Vaughn (L) | 10.0 | 2 | 1 | 0 | 2 | 10 |

Time--1:45. Attendance--2,500.
Umpires--HP, Orth. Bases, Rigler.

169

# May 1 1920

**Brooklyn Robins**       1
**Boston Braves**       1

**May 1 1920, Braves Field, Boston**


A pitching duel that turned into a marathon also became a unique slice of hardball history when, in 1920, the Brooklyn Robins' Leon Cadore and the Boston Braves' Joe Oeschger pitched the longest game ever played in the Major Leagues, a 26-inning effort that saw Cadore give up 15 hits and Oeschger just nine.

Brooklyn scored their solo run in the top of the 5th inning. At the bottom of the 6th inning, Boston tied it up when Tony Boeckel drove in Walt Cruise. Cadore and Oeschger would then show unparalleled pitching stamina, throwing 20 scoreless innings and the only thing that could stop them was the ensuing dark.

Still tied at 1-1, the game was eventually called because of bad light.

| | 1 | 2 | 3 | 4 | 5 | 6 | 7 | 8 | 9 | 10 | 11 | 12 | 13 | 14 | 15 |
|---|---|---|---|---|---|---|---|---|---|---|---|---|---|---|---|
| Brooklyn Robins | 0 | 0 | 0 | 0 | 1 | 0 | 0 | 0 | 0 | 0 | 0 | 0 | 0 | 0 | 0 |
| Boston Braves | 0 | 0 | 0 | 0 | 0 | 1 | 0 | 0 | 0 | 0 | 0 | 0 | 0 | 0 | 0 |

| | 16 | 17 | 18 | 19 | 20 | 21 | 22 | 23 | 24 | 25 | 26 | | R | H | E |
|---|---|---|---|---|---|---|---|---|---|---|---|---|---|---|---|
| Brooklyn Robins | 0 | 0 | 0 | 0 | 0 | 0 | 0 | 0 | 0 | 0 | 0 | | 1 | 9 | 2 |
| Boston Braves | 0 | 0 | 0 | 0 | 0 | 0 | 0 | 0 | 0 | 0 | 0 | | 1 | 15 | 2 |

E--Pick 2, Olson, Ward. DP--Brooklyn 1, Boston 1.
LOB--Brooklyn 11, Boston 17. 2B--Maranville, Oeschger.
3B--Cruise. SH--Hood, Powell, Holke, O'Neil, Cruise, Oeschger.
SB--Myers, Hood. CS--Myers, Boeckel.

| Brooklyn Robins | IP | H | R | ER | BB | SO |
|---|---|---|---|---|---|---|
| Leon Cadore | 26.0 | 15 | 1 | 1 | 5 | 7 |

| Boston Braves | IP | H | R | ER | BB | SO |
|---|---|---|---|---|---|---|
| Joe Oeschger | 26.0 | 9 | 1 | 1 | 4 | 7 |

WP--Oeschger. Time--3:50. Attendance--4,500.
Umpires--HP, McCormick. Bases, Hart.

# September 30 1927

**New York Yankees**      4
**Washington Nationals**      2

**September 30 1927, Yankee Stadium, New York**

Babe Ruth and his 1927 season have become synonymous with baseball greatness. The best at his best. William Nack described Ruth's '27 season as "the enduring symbol of the man and his myth." In 1921, the Babe had changed the game, leaving the dead-ball era far behind as he belted 59 home runs. The homer had become his calling card and in 1927 he elevated his game, and the whole of baseball, by going on a tear that lasted the whole season.

Having tied his old mark the day before, Ruth now had just two games left to set a new home run record. facing the Nationals' Tom Zachary with the game tied at 2-2 in the 8th, Ruth launched Zachary's 1-1 screwball deep into the rightfield bleachers. The noise around the stadium grew louder and louder and when the game was over he was mobbed by the fans, eager the show their appreciation for the game's greatest slugger.

When Ruth finally made it into the Yankees clubhouse, he hollered, "Sixty, count 'em, 60!", and challenged someone, anyone, to beat his record. It would be some 34 years before anyone could.

| | 1 | 2 | 3 | 4 | 5 | 6 | 7 | 8 | 9 | | R | H | E |
|---|---|---|---|---|---|---|---|---|---|---|---|---|---|
| **Washington Nationals** | 0 | 0 | 0 | 2 | 0 | 0 | 0 | 0 | 0 | | 2 | 5 | 0 |
| **New York Yankees** | 0 | 0 | 0 | 1 | 0 | 1 | 0 | 2 | x | | 4 | 9 | 1 |

E--Gehrig. DP--Washington 2. LOB--Washington 7, New York 4.
2B--Rice. 3B--Koenig. HR--Ruth. SF--Meusel. SB--Rice, Ruel, Bluege.

| **Washington Nationals** | IP | H | R | ER | BB | SO |
|---|---|---|---|---|---|---|
| **Tom Zachary (L)** | 8.0 | 9 | 4 | 4 | 1 | 1 |

| **New York Yankees** | IP | H | R | ER | BB | SO |
|---|---|---|---|---|---|---|
| **George Pipgras** | 6.0 | 4 | 2 | 2 | 4 | 0 |
| **Herb Pennock (W)** | 3.0 | 1 | 0 | 0 | 1 | 0 |

HBP--Rice by Pipgras. Attendance--8,000.
Umpires--HP, Dinneen. 1B, Connolly. 2B, Owens.

# October 1 1932

New York Yankees     7
Chicago Cubs     5

**October 1 1932, Wrigley Field, Chicago**

It was classic Babe Ruth. A larger than life story, full of bravado. A legendary tale from the game's most legendary player. The date was October 1 1932 and the Yankees were at Wrigley Field for Game 3 of the '32 World Series.

New York had won the first two games with some ease and a feeling of animosity grew between the two teams with the Bambino becoming the primary target of the Cubs' dugout. As the heckling grew worse, Ruth decided to take action the best way he knew. Facing Chicago's right-hander Charlie Root, the Babe gestured towards the centerfield bleachers with his bat, as if to call the shot, to predict the home run. He looked at two strikes, one of which certainly seemed borderline, then, on a 0-2 count, he proceeded to send the ball in the direction he had pointed. The ball sailed over the centerfield fence for his second dinger of he game.

The Yanks would go onto sweep the Cubs, Charlie Root would deny that Ruth did call the shot and the Sultan of Swat's legend grew ever larger. No one knows for sure whether Ruth did indeed mean the gesture but audacity was his middle name and it was entirely fitting of his character. When asked about the called shot, the Babe replied, "Aw, everybody knows that game, the day I hit the homer off ole Charlie Root there in Wrigley Field, the day October first, the third game of that thirty-two World Series. But right now I want to settle all arguments. I didn't exactly point to any spot, like the flagpole. Anyway, I didn't mean to, I just sorta waved at the whole fence, but that was foolish enough. All I wanted to do was give that thing a ride... outta the park... anywhere."

|                  | 1 | 2 | 3 | 4 | 5 | 6 | 7 | 8 | 9 | R | H | E |
|------------------|---|---|---|---|---|---|---|---|---|---|---|---|
| New York Yankees | 3 | 0 | 1 | 0 | 2 | 0 | 0 | 0 | 1 | 7 | 8 | 1 |
| Chicago Cubs     | 1 | 0 | 2 | 1 | 0 | 0 | 0 | 0 | 1 | 5 | 9 | 4 |

E--Herman, Jurges 2, Lazzeri, Hartnett. DP--Yankees 1 (Sewell to Lazzeri to Gehrig),
Cubs 1 (Herman to Jurges to Grimm). LOB--Yankees 11, Cubs 6.
Scoring Position--Yankees 2-for-8, Cubs 0-for-8.
2B--Chapman, Cuyler, Grimm, Jurges. HR--Ruth 2, Gehrig 2, Cuyler, Hartnett.
GDP--Ruth, Stephenson. SB--Jurges 2. CS--Chapman, English.

| New York Yankees | IP | H | R | ER | BB | K |
|------------------|-----|---|---|----|----|---|
| George Pipgras (W) | 8.0 | 9 | 5 | 4 | 3 | 1 |
| Herb Pennock (S) | 1.0 | 0 | 0 | 0 | 0 | 1 |

| Chicago Cubs | IP | H | R | ER | BB | K |
|--------------|-----|---|---|----|----|---|
| Charlie Root (L) | 4.1 | 6 | 6 | 5 | 3 | 4 |
| Pat Malone | 2.2 | 1 | 0 | 0 | 4 | 4 |
| Jakie May | 1.1 | 1 | 1 | 0 | 0 | 1 |
| Bud Tinning | 0.2 | 0 | 0 | 0 | 0 | 1 |

Pipgras pitched to two batters in the 9th.
HBP--Sewell by May. Time--2:11. Attendance--49,986.
Umpires--HP, Van Graflan. 1B, Magerkurth. 2B, Dinneen. 3B, Klem.

# June 15 1938

**Cincinnati Reds**     6
**Brooklyn Dodgers**     0

**June 15 1938, Ebbets Field, New York**

Cincinnati Reds' lefty Johnny Vander Meer had a rookie season for the ages in 1938, when after tossing a no-hitter against the Boston Bees on June 10th, he did the unthinkable his next start, shutting down the Dodgers to pitch his second consecutive no-hit game.

In Ebbets Field's first ever night game, Vander Meer struck out seven and walked eight as he pitched his way onto baseball history. The final out saw Vander Meer facing the Dodgers' Leo Durocher with the bases loaded, but he got Durocher out on a flyball to preserve the historic win. Vander Meer finished his rookie year 15-10 with a 3.12 ERA.

| | 1 | 2 | 3 | 4 | 5 | 6 | 7 | 8 | 9 | | R | H | E |
|---|---|---|---|---|---|---|---|---|---|---|---|---|---|
| Cincinnati Reds | 0 | 0 | 4 | 0 | 0 | 0 | 1 | 1 | 0 | | 6 | 11 | 0 |
| Brooklyn Dodgers | 0 | 0 | 0 | 0 | 0 | 0 | 0 | 0 | 0 | | 0 | 0 | 2 |

E--Lavagetto 2. LOB--Cincinnati 9, Brooklyn 8.
2B--Berger. 3B--Berger. HR--McCormick. SB--Goodman.

| Cincinnati Reds | IP | H | R | ER | BB | SO |
|---|---|---|---|---|---|---|
| Johnny Vander Meer (W) | 9.0 | 0 | 0 | 0 | 8 | 7 |

| Brooklyn Dodgers | IP | H | R | ER | BB | SO |
|---|---|---|---|---|---|---|
| Max Butcher (L) | 2.2 | 5 | 4 | 4 | 3 | 1 |
| Tot Pressnell | 3.2 | 4 | 1 | 1 | 0 | 3 |
| Luke Hamlin | 1.2 | 2 | 1 | 1 | 1 | 3 |
| Vito Tamulis | 1.0 | 0 | 0 | 0 | 0 | 0 |

Time--2:22. Attendance--38,748.
Umpires--HP, Stewart. 1B, Stark. 2B, Barr.

# October 2 1938

**Detroit Tigers** 4
**Cleveland Indians** 1

**October 2 1938, Cleveland, Stadium, Cleveland**

As soon as pitching phenom Bob Feller arrived in the majors, it was clear that he could live up to the hype and more. In his rookie year he went 5-3, fanning 76 in just eight starts and the following year again exhibited the kind of power that would earn him the name Rapid Robert, racking up 150 K's in 149 innings in 1937.

But in 1938 Feller, still only 19-years old, fully realized his potential as he showcased his nasty stuff that would become the hallmark of his career. On October 2, using his outstanding fastball as his money pitch, Feller fanned 18 Detroit Tigers in nine innings to set a new major league record. Strangely, as with Tom Seaver's 19-strikeout performance of the 1960s, it was in a losing cause, as the Tigers won 4–1.

Feller's is still widely recognized as having one of the baseball's finest fastballs.

| | 1 | 2 | 3 | 4 | 5 | 6 | 7 | 8 | 9 | R | H | E |
|---|---|---|---|---|---|---|---|---|---|---|---|---|
| **Detroit Tigers** | 0 | 0 | 0 | 0 | 0 | 2 | 0 | 2 | 0 | 4 | 7 | 1 |
| **Cleveland Indians** | 0 | 0 | 0 | 0 | 0 | 0 | 0 | 0 | 1 | 1 | 4 | 0 |

E--McCoy. DP--Detroit 1. 2B--Greenberg, Tebbets.
SB--Cullenbine, Piet.

| Detroit Tigers | IP | H | R | BB | SO |
|---|---|---|---|---|---|
| **Harry Eisenstat (W)** | 9.0 | 4 | 1 | 3 | 3 |

| Cleveland Indians | IP | H | R | BB | SO |
|---|---|---|---|---|---|
| **Bob Felller (L)** | 9.0 | 7 | 4 | 7 | 18 |

HB--Feller. Umpires--Hubbard, Grieve, and Moriarty

# July 17 1941

**New York Yankees**      4
**Cleveland Indians**      3

**July 17 1941, Municipal Stadium, Cleveland**

The 1941 season will always be remembered as one of baseball's finest, with two outstanding performances from two of the game's legends stealing the show. Having already passed Wee Willie Keeler's record of hitting safely in 44 consecutive games, New York's Joe DiMaggio continued to captivate America as he added, game by game, to his amazing streak.

The Streak finally came to an end in Cleveland after DiMaggio had brought the record to 56 consecutive games with at least one base hit. In the 8th inning, the Indians' shortstop Lou Boudreau turned a double-play that saw DiMaggio out at first and the streak finally over.

Pitchers Al Smith and Jim Bagby Jr. had already retired the Yankee Clipper twice and walked him earlier in the game. When it came to MVP voting it was DiMaggio's 56-game hit streak that won through, just over-shadowing Boston's Ted Williams and his .406 batting average, the first time a player had hit over .400 since Bill Terry in 1930.

| | 1 | 2 | 3 | 4 | 5 | 6 | 7 | 8 | 9 | | R | H | E |
|---|---|---|---|---|---|---|---|---|---|---|---|---|---|
| New York Yankees, | 1 | 0 | 0 | 0 | 0 | 0 | 1 | 2 | 0 | | 4 | 8 | 0 |
| Cleveland Indians | 0 | 0 | 0 | 1 | 0 | 0 | 0 | 0 | 2 | | 3 | 7 | 0 |

DP--Cleveland 1. LOB--New York 5, Cleveland 7.
2B--Rolfe, Henrich. 3B--Keller, Rosenthal. HR--Gordon, Walker. SH--Boudreau.

| New York Yankees | IP | H | R | ER | BB | SO |
|---|---|---|---|---|---|---|
| Lefty Gomez (W) | 8.0 | 6 | 3 | 3 | 3 | 5 |
| Johnny Murphy (S) | 1.0 | 1 | 0 | 0 | 0 | 0 |

| Cleveland Indians | IP | H | R | ER | BB | SO |
|---|---|---|---|---|---|---|
| Al Smith (L) | 7.1 | 7 | 4 | 4 | 2 | 4 |
| Jim Bagby Jr. | 1.2 | 1 | 0 | 0 | 1 | 1 |

Gomez pitched to two batters in the 9th.
Time--2:03. Attendance--67,468.
Umpires--HP, Summers. 1B, Rue. 2B, Stewart.

# April 15 1947

**Brooklyn Dodgers**     5
**Boston Braves**     3

**April 15 1947, Ebbets Field, New York**

Throughout baseball's illustrious history no game has ever had such lasting impact and far-reaching significance as the Brooklyn Dodgers' season opener against the Braves in 1947.

The Dodgers won the game 5-3 but for once the score was almost irrelevant. When Jackie Robinson donned the Brooklyn uniform that day, breaking the game's color barrier, baseball and America took a giant leap forward. Becoming the game's first black player was fraught with trouble and it would take some time before the slurs and the chin music were no longer thrown so frequently in Robinson's direction, but that day in 1947, thanks to one man's bravery, baseball truly became America's pastime and a game for all.

Robinson's went hitless for the game, but he did get on base and scored the winning run. He would go on to win the inaugural Rookie of the Year Award, helping the Dodgers to win the National League pennant..

| | 1 | 2 | 3 | 4 | 5 | 6 | 7 | 8 | 9 | | R | H | E |
|---|---|---|---|---|---|---|---|---|---|---|---|---|---|
| Boston Braves | 0 | 0 | 0 | 0 | 1 | 2 | 0 | 0 | 0 | | 3 | 8 | 1 |
| Brooklyn Dodgers | 0 | 0 | 0 | 1 | 0 | 1 | 3 | 0 | x | | 5 | 6 | 1 |

E--Torgeson, Edwards. DP--Boston 1, Brooklyn 1.
LOB--Boston 12, Brooklyn 7. 2B--Reiser, Reese.
SH--Sain 2, Culler, Masi, Robinson.

| Boston Braves | IP | H | R | ER | BB | SO |
|---|---|---|---|---|---|---|
| Johnny Sain (L) | 6.0 | 6 | 5 | 4 | 5 | 1 |
| Mort Cooper | 1.0 | 0 | 0 | 0 | 0 | 0 |
| Walt Lanfranconi | 1.0 | 0 | 0 | 0 | 0 | 2 |

| Brooklyn Dodgers | IP | H | R | ER | BB | SO |
|---|---|---|---|---|---|---|
| Joe Hatten | 6.0 | 6 | 3 | 2 | 3 | 2 |
| Hal Gregg (W) | 2.1 | 2 | 0 | 0 | 2 | 2 |
| Hugh Casey (S) | 0.2 | 0 | 0 | 0 | 0 | 0 |

Sain pitched to three batters in the 7th.
HBP--Litwhiler by Hatten, Edwards by Sain, Neill by Gregg.
WP--Hatten. Time--2:26. Attendance--25,623.
Umpires--HP, Pinelli. 1B, Barlick. 2B, Gore.

# October 3 1951

**New York Giants**     5
**Brooklyn Dodgers**     4

**October 3 1951, Polo Grounds, New York**

If you're looking for the most dramatic moment, the most famous swing, the most memorable call in baseball history, October 3 1951 at the Giants' Polo Grounds is a pretty good place to start your search.

After finishing tied at the end of the regular season, the Giants and the Dodgers met for a three-game playoff series to decide who would meet the Yankees in the World Series. The first two games were split and the third was just as tight. The game was tied after 8 innings, but the Dodgers scored three in the top of the 9th. Don Newcombe was taken out of the game in the bottom of the 9th with Bobby Thomson coming up to bat and one Giant run already in. Runners were on second and third for Brooklyn's Ralph Branca. Thomson hit a 0-1 fastball hard towards left field. Put simply, if it was long enough to clear the wall for a home run, the Giants would win 5-4, defeat their bitter rivals and advance to the World Series.

Russ Hodges take it away!

"Branca throws...there's a long drive. It's going to be, I believe...The Giants win the pennant! The Giants win the pennant! The Giants win the pennant..."

| | 1 | 2 | 3 | 4 | 5 | 6 | 7 | 8 | 9 | R | H | E |
|---|---|---|---|---|---|---|---|---|---|---|---|---|
| Brooklyn Dodgers | 1 | 0 | 0 | 0 | 0 | 0 | 0 | 3 | 0 | 4 | 8 | 0 |
| New York Giants | 0 | 0 | 0 | 0 | 0 | 0 | 1 | 0 | 4 | 5 | 8 | 0 |

One out when winning run scored.
DP--Brooklyn 2. LOB--Brooklyn 7, New York 3.
2B--Irvin, Lockman, Thomson. HR--Thomson. SH--Lockman.

| Brooklyn Dodgers | IP | H | R | ER | BB | SO |
|---|---|---|---|---|---|---|
| Don Newcombe | 8.1 | 7 | 4 | 4 | 2 | 2 |
| Ralph Branca (L) | 0.0 | 1 | 1 | 1 | 0 | 0 |

| New York Giants | IP | H | R | ER | BB | SO |
|---|---|---|---|---|---|---|
| Sal Maglie | 8.0 | 8 | 4 | 4 | 4 | 6 |
| Larry Jansen (W) | 1.0 | 0 | 0 | 0 | 0 | 0 |

Branca pitched to one batter in the 9th.
WP--Maglie. Time--2:28. Attendance--34,320.
Umpires--HP, Jorda. 1B, Conlan. 2B, Stewart. 3B, Goetz.

# September 29 1954

**New York Giants**       5
**Cleveland Indians**       2

**September 29 1954, Polo Grounds, New York**

When baseball fans, players and writers talk about "The Catch" they are referring to a little piece of Willie Mays magic that lit up the 1954 World Series.

It was in the 8th inning of Game 1 and the Giants and the Indians were tied at 2-2. Cleveland had two men on base with nobody out, and they had chased Sal "the Barber" Maglie out of the game. Any base hit would have given the Indians a two-run lead for their ace Bob Lemon, who was looking very strong.

Vic Wertz was at the plate for Cleveland, having already doubled and tripled, and he launched a moon shot off Don Liddle. It would have been home run in most other ballparks, but this was the Polo Grounds. Playing in the vast expanse of centerfield, Willie Mays took off early, heading for the wall, never looking back. Just as the ball began to drop some 450 feet from home plate, Mays caught up, extended his glove outward and grabbed the ball. But that wasn't all. Mays stopped, wheeled and threw the ball back to the infield. The two runners, thinking it was a base hit had not tagged up and were sprinting back to their previous bases to avoid being doubled off. They made it back, but could not score as Marv Grissom came in and put out the fire.

The Giants won the game and went onto win the series in four. The Catch was typical Mays, showing off his outstanding speed, his incredible agility and his penchant for the spectacular. "My most famous catch was the one off Vic Wertz in the '54 World Series," Mays said years later. "But I made a lot of catches like that."

| | 1 | 2 | 3 | 4 | 5 | 6 | 7 | 8 | 9 | 10 | R | H | E |
|---|---|---|---|---|---|---|---|---|---|---|---|---|---|
| Cleveland Indians | 2 | 0 | 0 | 0 | 0 | 0 | 0 | 0 | 0 | 0 | 2 | 8 | 0 |
| New York Giants | 0 | 0 | 2 | 0 | 0 | 0 | 0 | 0 | 0 | 3 | 5 | 9 | 3 |

E--Irvin, Mueller 2. LOB--Indians 13, Giants 9.
Scoring Position--Indians 1-for-16, Giants 3-for-11.
2B--Wertz. 3B--Wertz. HR--Rhodes. S--Irvin, Dente. SB--Mays.

| Cleveland Indians | IP | H | R | ER | BB | K |
|---|---|---|---|---|---|---|
| Bob Lemon (L) | 9.1 | 9 | 5 | 5 | 5 | 6 |

| New York Giants | IP | H | R | ER | BB | K |
|---|---|---|---|---|---|---|
| Sal Maglie | 7.0 | 7 | 2 | 2 | 2 | 2 |
| Don Liddle | 0.1 | 0 | 0 | 0 | 0 | 0 |
| Marv Grissom (W) | 2.2 | 1 | 0 | 0 | 3 | 2 |

Maglie pitched to two batters in the 8th.
WP--Lemon. HBP--Smith by Maglie. Time--3:11. Attendance--52,751.
Umpires--HP, Barlick. 1B, Berry. 2B, Conlan. 3B, Stevens.

# October 15 1956

**New York Yankees**     2
**Brooklyn Dodgers**     0

October 15 1956, Yankee Stadium, New York

To achieve perfection on the diamond at any time is special. To do it during the World Series is, well, extra-special. And just about every other superlative you can think of.

In Game 5 of the '56 World Series, with the New York Yankees and Brooklyn Dodgers tied at two games apiece, Don Larsen did achieve perfection. 27 Dodgers came up, 27 sat down. The game ended when pinch hitter Dale Mitchell struck out looking, and with the no-hitter preserved for all-time.

Yankees catcher Yogi Berra ran to the mound and jumped into the waiting arms of Larsen. It was truly magical. Incredibly, Larsen threw only 97 pitchers on the way to his perfect game but it wasn't without some drama.

In the 5th inning, Brooklyn's Gil Hodges hit a ball hard to center field. Fortunately for Larsen this was Yankee Stadium. Which meant 408 feet to clear the wall. And Mickey Mantle. The Mick chased down the ball and made the catch.

Larsen is the only pitcher in baseball history to toss a perfect game in the World Series and, to the end of the 2000 season, no other pitcher has even thrown even a no-hitter in the postseason.

| | 1 | 2 | 3 | 4 | 5 | 6 | 7 | 8 | 9 | | R | H | E |
|---|---|---|---|---|---|---|---|---|---|---|---|---|---|
| **Los Angeles Dodgers** | 0 | 0 | 0 | 0 | 0 | 0 | 0 | 0 | 0 | | 0 | 0 | 0 |
| **New York Yankees** | 0 | 0 | 0 | 1 | 0 | 1 | 0 | 0 | x | | 2 | 5 | 0 |

DP--Dodgers 2 (Reese to Hodges; Hodges to Campanella to Robinson).
LOB--Dodgers 0, Yankees 3.
Scoring Position--Dodgers 0-for-0, Yankees 1-for-3. HR--Mantle (3). S--Larsen.

| Dodgers | IP | H | R | ER | BB | K | ERA |
|---|---|---|---|---|---|---|---|
| Sal Maglie (L) | 8.0 | 5 | 2 | 2 | 2 | 5 | 2.65 |

| New York Yankees | IP | H | R | ER | BB | K | ERA |
|---|---|---|---|---|---|---|---|
| Don Larsen (W) | 9.0 | 0 | 0 | 0 | 0 | 7 | 0.00 |

Time--2:06. Attendance--64,519.
Umpires--HP, Pinelli. 1B, Soar. 2B, Boggess. 3B, Napp.

# September 28 1960

**Boston Red Sox**     5
**Baltimore Orioles**     4

**September 28 1960, Fenway Park, Boston**

For a player who prided himself on being the greatest hitter there ever was, it was the picture-perfect ending to a glorious career. At home in Fenway Park where he had developed into a legend, Ted Williams had the opportunity to end his career in style and in front of the adoring Red Sox fans. Officially 10,454 were there to see the day game against the O's but as time has passed and Williams' greatness had grown, the number of New Englanders who swear they were there that incredible day now numbers in the hundreds of thousands.

In his very last at bat, facing Jack Fisher in the 8th inning, the 42-year old Williams turned on a 1-1 fastball and sent it sailing into the Red Sox bullpen for a home run. The Red Sox faithful went wild, but Ted being Ted, just kept his head down as he circled the bases, his 521st regular season round-tripper.

For a pure hitter and a perfectionist like the incomparable Teddy Ballgame, it was the best way, maybe the only way, for him to say good-bye to the game.

| | 1 | 2 | 3 | 4 | 5 | 6 | 7 | 8 | 9 | | R | H | E |
|---|---|---|---|---|---|---|---|---|---|---|---|---|---|
| Baltimore Orioles | 0 | 2 | 0 | 0 | 1 | 1 | 0 | 0 | 0 | | 4 | 9 | 1 |
| Boston Red Sox | 2 | 0 | 0 | 0 | 0 | 0 | 0 | 1 | 2 | | 5 | 6 | 1 |

Two outs when winning run scored.
E--Coughtry, Klaus. DP--Baltimore 1. LOB--Baltimore 6, Boston 7. 2B--Stephens, Robinson, Wertz. HR--Triandos, Williams. SF--Clinton, Gentile.

| Baltimore Orioles | IP | H | R | ER | BB | SO |
|---|---|---|---|---|---|---|
| Steve Barber | 0.1 | 0 | 2 | 2 | 3 | 0 |
| Jack Fisher (L) | 8.1 | 6 | 3 | 2 | 3 | 5 |

| Boston Red Sox | IP | H | R | ER | BB | SO |
|---|---|---|---|---|---|---|
| Billy Muffett | 7.0 | 9 | 4 | 4 | 0 | 4 |
| Fornieles (W) | 2.0 | 0 | 0 | 0 | 0 | 2 |

HBP--Pagliaroni by Barber. WP--Barber, Muffett. Time--2:18. Attendance--10,454.
Umpires--HP, Hurley. 1B, Rice. 2B, Stevens. 3B, Drummond.

# October 13 1960

**Pittsburgh Pirates**     10
**New York Yankees**     9

**October 13 1960, Forbes Field, Pittsburgh**

Many a boyhood dream has centered a round hitting a game-winning, series-ending homer. In the 1960 World Series the Pittsburgh Pirates' Bill Mazeroski had the chance to make that dream a reality. It was Game 7 and the Yankees and the Pirates had played a very strange Series. Pittsburgh had taken Games 1, 4 and 5 6-4, 3-2 and 5-2, respectively. The Yankees had won Games 2, 3 and 6 by 16-3, 10-0, and 12-0 margins, respectively, so if there were lots of runs, New York would win, if it was close, the Pirates were favored. The Pirates should have already won the game when Mazeroski came to the plate with the game standing at 9-9 in the bottom of the 9th. They had led 4-1 after five innings and 9-7 after 8, but the Yankees had come back to tie it with a pair of runs off Bob Friend.

With the pressure mounting Mazeroski, a player noted for his fine glovework, not his power hit a towering fly ball off New York's Ralph Terry that cleared the left field wall. 10-9. Series over. Pittsburgh wins. And Bill Mazeroski became the envy of every kid in America by becoming the first player in baseball history to clinch a World Series championship with a home run. Truly, the stuff of childhood dreams.

| | 1 | 2 | 3 | 4 | 5 | 6 | 7 | 8 | 9 | R | H | E |
|---|---|---|---|---|---|---|---|---|---|---|---|---|
| **New York Yankees** | 0 | 0 | 0 | 0 | 1 | 4 | 0 | 2 | 2 | 9 | 13 | 1 |
| **Pittsburgh Pirates** | 2 | 2 | 0 | 0 | 0 | 0 | 0 | 5 | 1 | 10 | 11 | 0 |

E--Maris. DP--Yankees 3 (Stafford to Blanchard to Skowron;
Richardson to Kubek to Skowron; Kubek to Richardson to Skowron).
LOB--Yankees 6, Pirates 1. Scoring Position--Yankees 5-for-10, Pirates 5-for-8.
2B--Boyer. HR--Berra, Skowron, Nelson, Mazeroski, Smith.
S--Skinner. GDP--Clemente, Mazeroski, Law.

| New York Yankees | IP | H | R | ER | BB | K |
|---|---|---|---|---|---|---|
| Bob Turley | 1.0 | 2 | 3 | 3 | 1 | 0 |
| Bill Stafford | 1.0 | 2 | 1 | 1 | 1 | 0 |
| Bobby Shantz | 5.0 | 4 | 3 | 3 | 1 | 0 |
| Jim Coates (BS) | 0.2 | 2 | 2 | 2 | 0 | 0 |
| Ralph Terry (L) | 0.1 | 1 | 1 | 1 | 0 | 0 |

| Pittsburgh Pirates | IP | H | R | ER | BB | K |
|---|---|---|---|---|---|---|
| Vern Law | 5.0 | 4 | 3 | 3 | 1 | 0 |
| Roy Face (BS) | 3.0 | 6 | 4 | 4 | 1 | 0 |
| Bob Friend | 0.0 | 2 | 2 | 2 | 0 | 0 |
| Harvey Haddix (BS, W) | 1.0 | 1 | 0 | 0 | 0 | 0 |

Turley pitched to one batter in the 2nd.
Law pitched to two batters in the 6th.
Shantz pitched to three batters in the 8th.
Friend pitched to two batters in the 9th.
Terry pitched to one batter in the 9th.
Time--2:36. Attendance--36,683.
Umpires--HP, Jackowski. 1B, Chylak. 2B, Boggess. 3B, Stevens.

# October 1 1961

| New York Yankees | 1 |
|---|---|
| Boston Red Sox | 0 |

**October 1 1961, Yankee Stadium, New York**

He was smoking more than ever. His hair was falling out in clumps. But this is the day it would finally end. After Mickey Mantle's injuries had forced him out of the 1961 home run race, the Yankees' Roger Maris was left to chase Babe Ruth alone. Because the Babe and his records were so respected, Maris' pursuit of 61 and history was met with mixed emotions.

Commissioner Bowie Kuhn, a friend of Ruth's, had already decreed that any records set in 1961 would be tainted with an asterisk because of the expanded schedules. A record set in 154 games was fine, but if it needed 155-62, it would be devalued.

And the pressure had told against Maris. But up against the Red Sox on the final day of the season, with the American League pennant already secured, Maris parked a Tracy Stallard fastball into the right field seats in the 4th inning, to finally break baseball's most treasured and most visible record. It was almost irrelevant that it was the only run of the game.

"Holy cow!" exclaimed Yankees broadcaster and former shortstop Phil "The Scooter" Rizzuto. In a moment almost too huge for words, it couldn't have been said any better.

| | 1 | 2 | 3 | 4 | 5 | 6 | 7 | 8 | 9 | | R | H | E |
|---|---|---|---|---|---|---|---|---|---|---|---|---|---|
| Boston Red Sox | 0 | 0 | 0 | 0 | 0 | 0 | 0 | 0 | 0 | | 0 | 4 | 0 |
| New York Yankees | 0 | 0 | 0 | 1 | 0 | 0 | 0 | 0 | x | | 1 | 5 | 0 |

LOB--Boston 5, New York 5. 3B--Nixon. HR--Maris.
SH--Stallard. SB--Geiger.

| Boston Red Sox, | IP | H | R | ER | BB | SO |
|---|---|---|---|---|---|---|
| Tracy Stallard (L) | 7.0 | 5 | 1 | 1 | 1 | 5 |
| Chet Nichols | 1.0 | 0 | 0 | 0 | 0 | 0 |

| New York Yankees | IP | H | R | ER | BB | SO |
|---|---|---|---|---|---|---|
| Bill Stafford (W) | 6.0 | 3 | 0 | 0 | 1 | 7 |
| Hal Reniff | 1.0 | 0 | 0 | 0 | 0 | 1 |
| Luis Arroyo (S) | 2.0 | 1 | 0 | 0 | 0 | 1 |

WP--Stallard. Time--1:57. Attendance--23,154.
Umpires--HP, Kinnamon. 1B, Flaherty. 2B, Honochick. 3B, Salerno.

# September 12 1962

Washington Senators    2
Baltimore Orioles    1

**September 12 1962, Memorial Stadium, Baltimore**

The 1962 season was a disaster for Mickey Vernon and the second-year Washington Senators. They were on their way to finishing dead last in the American League with a dismal 60-101 record. And, at first glance, the '62 campaign wasn't any brighter for the Washington right-hander Tom Cheney. Cheney finished the year with a 7-9 losing record and though he posted a team-best 3.17 ERA, he couldn't help the Senators escape their mediocrity.

However, on September 12, Cheney and his Washington teammates forgot their problems for a day as Cheney set a new major league single-game strikeout record, fanning 21 Baltimore Orioles' in a 16-inning marathon that the Senators eventually won, 2-1.

| | 1 | 2 | 3 | 4 | 5 | 6 | 7 | 8 | 9 | 10 | 11 | 12 | 13 | 14 | 15 | 16 | R | H | E |
|---|---|---|---|---|---|---|---|---|---|---|---|---|---|---|---|---|---|---|---|
| Washington Senators | 1 | 0 | 0 | 0 | 0 | 0 | 0 | 0 | 0 | 0 | 0 | 0 | 0 | 0 | 0 | 1 | 2 | 10 | 0 |
| Baltimore Orioles | 0 | 0 | 0 | 0 | 0 | 0 | 1 | 0 | 0 | 0 | 0 | 0 | 0 | 0 | 0 | 0 | 1 | 10 | 2 |

E--Adair, Breeding. LOB--Washington 13, Baltimore 13.
2B--Hinton, Hicks, Adair, Snyder, Gentile, Breeding. HR--Zipfel.
SH--Cheney. SB--Adair. CS--Kennedy.

| Washington Senators | IP | H | R | ER | BB | SO |
|---|---|---|---|---|---|---|
| Tom Cheney (W) | 16.0 | 10 | 1 | 1 | 4 | 21 |

| Baltimore Orioles | IP | H | R | ER | BB | SO |
|---|---|---|---|---|---|---|
| Milt Pappa | 7.0 | 4 | 1 | 1 | 3 | 4 |
| Dick Hall (L) | 8.1 | 5 | 1 | 1 | 1 | 4 |
| Billy Hoeft | 0.1 | 1 | 0 | 0 | 0 | 0 |
| Wes Stock | 0.1 | 0 | 0 | 0 | 1 | 0 |

WP--Cheney. Balk--Pappas. Time--3:59. Attendance--4,098.
Umpires--HP, McKinley. 1B, Chylak. 2B, Umont. 3B, Stewart.

# October 14 1965

**Los Angeles Dodgers**     2
**Minnesota Twins**     0

**October 14 1965, Metropolitan Stadium, Minnesota**

Sandy Koufax and 1965 will always be associated with pitching domination.

The Dodgers' lefty dominated the National League throughout the season as Los Angeles beat out San Francisco to the win National League pennant. Koufax finished the year with 26 wins, 382 strikeouts, a 2.04 ERA and, eventually, the Cy Young Award.

His momentum didn't stop there. After winning Game 5 of the World Series, Koufax was again the Dodgers' starter in a crucial Game 7 against the AL champion Twins. From the get-go Koufax was awesome and when the dust settled he had allowed no runs and just three hits in a complete game masterpiece.

The Dodgers were crowned World Champions and the magical Koufax finished the series with an unbelievable 0.38 ERA and was voted the World Series MVP.

| | 1 | 2 | 3 | 4 | 5 | 6 | 7 | 8 | 9 | R | H | E |
|---|---|---|---|---|---|---|---|---|---|---|---|---|
| Los Angeles Dodgers | 0 | 0 | 0 | 2 | 0 | 0 | 0 | 0 | 0 | 2 | 7 | 0 |
| Minnesota Twins | 0 | 0 | 0 | 0 | 0 | 0 | 0 | 0 | 0 | 0 | 3 | 1 |

E--Oliva. LOB--Dodgers 9, Twins 6.
Scoring Position--Dodgers 1-for-12, Twins 0-for-3.
2B--Fairly, Roseboro, Quilici . 3B--Parker. HR--Johnson.
S--Davis. CS--Wills.

| Los Angeles Dodgers | IP | H | R | ER | BB | K |
|---|---|---|---|---|---|---|
| Sandy Koufax (W) | 9.0 | 3 | 0 | 0 | 3 | 10 |

| Minnesota Twins | IP | H | R | ER | BB | K |
|---|---|---|---|---|---|---|
| Jim Kaat (L) | 3.0 | 5 | 2 | 2 | 1 | 2 |
| Al Worthington | 2.0 | 0 | 0 | 0 | 1 | 0 |
| Johnny Klippstein | 1.2 | 2 | 0 | 0 | 1 | 2 |
| Jim Merritt | 1.1 | 0 | 0 | 0 | 0 | 1 |
| Jim Perry | 1.0 | 0 | 0 | 0 | 1 | 1 |

Kaat pitched to four batters in the 4th.
HBP--Davis by Klippstein. Time--2:27. Attendance--50,596.
Umpires--HP, Hurley. 1B, Venzon. 2B, Flaherty. 3B, Sudol.

# April 8 1974

**Atlanta Braves**  7
**Los Angeles Dodgers**  4

**April 8 1974, Fulton County Stadium, Atlanta**

After enduring racial abuse and death threats, the Braves Hank Aaron was finally there, ready to step out of the Babe's shadow and become the game's home run king. Just as Roger Maris had suffered from threatening Ruth's single-season home run record, Aaron too had been under the media scrutiny as he closed in on the Bambino's lifetime total of 714. Because Ruth and the numbers intrinsically linked with his name are so revered by ball fans, the breaking of them isn't always met with universal jubilation. The press and fans alike hounded Maris. Aaron, too. But unlike Maris, Aaron was also black.

But instead of succumbing to the letters of hate, Aaron used them as fuel for his fire. On Opening Day 1974 he equaled Ruth's mark, hitting his 714th career homer against the Reds. Although the Braves wanted him to sit down the rest of the road trip, the Commissioner ordered him to play. Aaron did not homer again, so returned to Atlanta still tied.

He didn't have to wait long to go one better. At the Braves home opener, in front of a sold-out Fulton County Stadium, Aaron sealed his place in the game's storied history. In the fourth inning he hit a powerful line drive off the Dodgers' Al Downing that flew towards left-center, clearing the 385-ft sign, landing in the Atlanta bullpen, for number 715. Aaron, who felt that he hadn't received the respect his talents and accomplishments deserved, was vindicated.

He went on to hit 755 homers, a record that still stands today.

|  | 1 | 2 | 3 | 4 | 5 | 6 | 7 | 8 | 9 | R | H | E |
|---|---|---|---|---|---|---|---|---|---|---|---|---|
| Los Angeles Dodgers | 0 | 0 | 3 | 0 | 0 | 1 | 0 | 0 | 0 | 4 | 7 | 6 |
| Atlanta Braves | 0 | 1 | 0 | 4 | 0 | 2 | 0 | 0 | x | 7 | 4 | 0 |

E--Russell 2, Lopes, Buckner, Ferguson, Cey.
LOB--Los Angeles 5, Atlanta 7. 2B--Russell, Wynn, Baker.
HR--Aaron. SH--Garr. SF--Garr.

| Los Angeles Dodgers | IP | H | R | ER | BB | SO |
|---|---|---|---|---|---|---|
| Al Downing (L) | 3 | 2 | 5 | 2 | 4 | 2 |
| Mike Marshall | 3 | 2 | 2 | 1 | 1 | 1 |
| Charlie Hough | 2 | 0 | 0 | 0 | 2 | 1 |

| Atlanta Braves | IP | H | R | ER | BB | SO |
|---|---|---|---|---|---|---|
| Ron Reed (W) | 6 | 7 | 4 | 4 | 1 | 4 |
| Buzz Capra (S) | 3 | 0 | 0 | 0 | 1 | 6 |

Downing pitched to four batters in the 4th.
WP--Reed. Time--2:27. Attendance--53,775.
Umpires--HP, Sudol. 1B, Weyer. 2B, Pulli. 3B, Davidson.

# September 28 1975

| | |
|---|---|
| **Oakland Athletics** | 5 |
| **California Angels** | 0 |

**September 28 1975, Oakland Coliseum, Oakland**

The Oakland A's pitching staff of the 1970s was always regarded as one of the league's strongest and while they might not have always been a unified group away from the mound, when it came to game time they were always awfully tough to beat.

On the final day of the 1975 regular season, with the American League West title already safe, the A's pitchers highlighted their individual dominance and team unity as Vida Blue, Paul Linblad, Glenn Abbott and reliever Rollie Fingers combined to toss the very first multi-pitcher no-hit game in baseball history.

The A's defeated the Angels, 5-0, thanks to a pair of homers from "Mr October" Reggie Jackson. Starter Blue went five strong innings, giving up a couple of walks before handing the ball to Abbott and Lindblad for one inning each.Fingers closed it out with two strong innings.

| | 1 | 2 | 3 | 4 | 5 | 6 | 7 | 8 | 9 | | R | H | E |
|---|---|---|---|---|---|---|---|---|---|---|---|---|---|
| California Angels | 0 | 0 | 0 | 0 | 0 | 0 | 0 | 0 | 0 | | 0 | 0 | 1 |
| Oakland Athletics | 2 | 0 | 1 | 0 | 0 | 0 | 2 | 0 | x | | 5 | 9 | 1 |

E--Hampton, Campaneris. DP--Oakland 1.
LOB--California 2, Oakland 8. 2B--Bando.
HR--Jackson 2. SB--Stanton, Bando, Hopkins.

| California Angels | IP | H | R | ER | BB | SO |
|---|---|---|---|---|---|---|
| Gary Ross (L) | 5.0 | 6 | 3 | 3 | 1 | 4 |
| Sid Monge | 2.0 | 2 | 2 | 2 | 1 | 1 |
| Joe Pactwa | 1.0 | 1 | 0 | 0 | 1 | 0 |

| Oakland Athletics | IP | H | R | ER | BB | SO |
|---|---|---|---|---|---|---|
| Vida Blue (W) | 5.0 | 0 | 0 | 0 | 2 | 2 |
| Glenn Abbott | 1.0 | 0 | 0 | 0 | 0 | 0 |
| Paul Lindblad | 1.0 | 0 | 0 | 0 | 0 | 1 |
| Rollie Fingers | 2.0 | 0 | 0 | 0 | 0 | 2 |

Time--1:59. Attendance--22,131. Umpires--HP,
Kunkel. 1B, Phillips. 2B, DiMuro.

# October 22 1975

Boston Red Sox 7
Cincinnati Reds 6

**October 22 1975, Fenway Park, Boston**

With the Red Sox trailing 3-2 in games and the World Series in the balance, Boston catcher Carlton Fisk came to bat in the bottom of the 12th with the game tied 6-6. If Boston was finally going to reverse the curse, something had to happen now, this at bat.

Fortunately for Red Sox fans, Fisk got a big piece of reliever Pat Darcy's 0-1 fastball and began to watch the ball soar into the Massachusetts night, hugging the leftfield line as it went. It was clearly going to be long enough, but would it count? In what is one of the game's most popular, and replayed, moments, Pudge Fisk began to try to steer the ball fair, waving his arms frantically, as if he had some control over its flight and final destination. The ball caromed off the foul pole, the home run was fair, and Fisk had won the game, assuring that the 1975 World Series would be remembered as one of the greatest of all time.

As for the Babe's supposed curse? Boston lost Game 7, 4-3 with a single run in the 9th inning.

| | 1 | 2 | 3 | 4 | 5 | 6 | 7 | 8 | 9 | 10 | 11 | 12 | | R | H | E |
|---|---|---|---|---|---|---|---|---|---|---|---|---|---|---|---|---|
| Reds | 0 | 0 | 0 | 0 | 3 | 0 | 2 | 1 | 0 | 0 | 0 | 0 | | 6 | 14 | 0 |
| Red Sox | 3 | 0 | 0 | 0 | 0 | 0 | 0 | 3 | 0 | 0 | 0 | 1 | | 7 | 10 | 1 |

E--Burleson. DP--Reds 1 (Foster to Bench), Red Sox 1 (Evans).
LOB--Reds 11, Red Sox 9. Scoring Position--Reds 3-for-13, Red Sox 2-for-10.
2B--Foster, Doyle, Evans. 3B--Griffey. HR--Geronimo, Fisk, Lynn, Carbo.
S--Tiant. SB--Concepcion.

| Cincinnati Reds | IP | H | R | ER | BB | K |
|---|---|---|---|---|---|---|
| Gary Nolan, | 2.0 | 3 | 3 | 3 | 0 | 2 |
| Fred Norman, | 0.2 | 1 | 0 | 0 | 2 | 0 |
| Jack Billingham, | 1.1 | 1 | 0 | 0 | 1 | 1 |
| Clay Carroll, | 1.0 | 1 | 0 | 0 | 0 | 0 |
| Pedro Borbon, | 2.0 | 1 | 2 | 2 | 2 | 1 |
| Rawly Eastwick (BS) | 1.0 | 2 | 1 | 1 | 1 | 2 |
| Will McEnaney | 1.0 | 0 | 0 | 0 | 1 | 0 |
| Pat Darcy (L) | 2.0 | 1 | 1 | 1 | 0 | 1 |

| Boston Red Sox | IP | H | R | ER | BB | K |
|---|---|---|---|---|---|---|
| Luis Tiant | 7.0 | 11 | 6 | 6 | 2 | 5 |
| Roger Moret | 1.0 | 0 | 0 | 0 | 0 | 0 |
| Dick Drago | 3.0 | 1 | 0 | 0 | 0 | 1 |
| Rick Wise (W) | 1.0 | 2 | 0 | 0 | 0 | 1 |

Tiant pitched to one batter in the 8th.
Borbon pitched to two batters in the 8th.
Eastwick pitched to two batters in the 9th.
Darcy pitched to one batter in the 12th.
HBP--Rose by Drago. Time--4:01. Attendance--35,205.
Umpires--HP, Davidson. 1B, Frantz. 2B, Colosi. 3B, Barnett.

# October 2 1982

**Kansas City Royals**      5
**Oakland Athletics**      4

**October 2 1982, Royals Stadium, Kansas City**

When talk turns to those records that may never be broken, DiMaggio's 56-game hit streak is always high on every list, but Rickey Henderson's unbelievable 1982 season that saw him steal a 130 bases may prove to be just as tough to surpass as DiMaggio's majestic number.

Since Henderson set the single-season record only the Cardinals' Vince Coleman in 1985 and '87 has come anywhere near Henderson's 130 thefts, with 110 and 109 respectively. The A's outfielder passed Lou Brock's previous mark of 118 on August 27 and reached the final game of the season with 127 stolen bases. Never one to ease up and take his foot off the gas, the intensely focused Henderson proceeded to steal three bases against the Royals' starter Vida Blue to finish the year with 130 steals from the 149 games he had played.

For all his efforts on the final day of the season, the A's still ended up on the short side of a 5-4 game.

| | 1 | 2 | 3 | 4 | 5 | 6 | 7 | 8 | 9 | | R | H | E |
|---|---|---|---|---|---|---|---|---|---|---|---|---|---|
| Oakland Athletics | 0 | 0 | 0 | 2 | 0 | 0 | 2 | 0 | 0 | | 4 | 9 | 1 |
| Kansas City Royals | 1 | 0 | 0 | 1 | 1 | 0 | 0 | 2 | x | | 5 | 10 | 0 |

E--Davis. DP--Oakland 1, Kansas City 2.
LOB--Oakland 10, Kansas City 8.
2B--Washington, Lopes. 3B--Wilson, Moore.
HR--Armas. S--White 2, Martin. SF--Geronimo.
SB--Lopes, Wilson, Brett, Henderson 3, Washington.

| Oakland Athletics | IP | H | R | ER | BB | SO |
|---|---|---|---|---|---|---|
| Matt Keough | 6.0 | 8 | 3 | 3 | 3 | 3 |
| Tom Underwood (L) | 1.1 | 1 | 2 | 1 | 0 | 0 |
| Dave Beard | 0.2 | 1 | 0 | 0 | 0 | 0 |

| Kansas City Royals | IP | H | R | ER | BB | SO |
|---|---|---|---|---|---|---|
| Vida Blue | 4.0 | 4 | 2 | 2 | 7 | 5 |
| Mike Armstrong | 2.0 | 0 | 0 | 0 | 0 | 4 |
| Dan Quisenberry (W) | 3.0 | 5 | 2 | 2 | 0 | 1 |

WP--Keough 2. Time--2:50. Attendance--23,787.

# September 11 1985

**Cincinnati Reds**       2
**San Diego Padres**      0

**September 11 1985, Riverfront Stadium, Cincinnati**

Pete Rose had made a career and established a reputation by playing hard, all-out, all the time. So it was probably no real surprise that when it came to breaking Ty Cobb's long-standing record of 4,191 hits, Charlie Hustle didn't waste any time.

With a sell-out crowd at Riverfront waiting expectantly, Rose slapped a first inning line drive off the Padres' Eric Show. As usual he sprinted down the line to first base, took his usual wide turn as if to try for second, stopped and ran back to first.

Rose had passed Cobb and was now the game's undisputed hit king. The crowd exploded and his team congratulated their favorite son. Rose then hugged his son, Pete Jr, who had run onto the field to be with his record-breaking father who was now in tears.

"I was doing all right until I looked up and started thinking about my father," said Rose. "I saw him up there and right behing him was Ty Cobb." Pete Rose would continue to play until 1986, finishing with an incredible 4256 runs, still the major league record.

| | 1 | 2 | 3 | 4 | 5 | 6 | 7 | 8 | 9 | R | H | E |
|---|---|---|---|---|---|---|---|---|---|---|---|---|
| San Diego Padres | 0 | 0 | 0 | 0 | 0 | 0 | 0 | 0 | 0 | 0 | 5 | 1 |
| Cincinnati Reds | 0 | 0 | 1 | 0 | 0 | 0 | 1 | 0 | x | 2 | 8 | 0 |

E--Show. DP--San Diego 1, Cincinnati 1. LOB--San Diego 4, Cincinnati 11.
2B--Bell, Diaz, Browning. 3B--Rose. SF--Esasky. SB--Gwynn.

| San Diego Padres | IP | H | R | ER | BB | SO |
|---|---|---|---|---|---|---|
| Eric Show (L) | 7.0 | 7 | 2 | 2 | 5 | 1 |
| Roy Lee Jackson | 0.1 | 1 | 0 | 0 | 1 | 0 |
| Gene Walter | 0.2 | 0 | 0 | 0 | 0 | 2 |

| Cincinnati Reds | IP | H | R | ER | BB | SO |
|---|---|---|---|---|---|---|
| Tom Browning (W) | 8.1 | 5 | 0 | 0 | 0 | 6 |
| John Franc | 0.1 | 0 | 0 | 0 | 0 | 0 |
| Ted Power (S) | 0.1 | 0 | 0 | 0 | 0 | 0 |

Time--2:17. Attendance--47,237.
Umpires--HP, Weyer. 1B, Montague. 2B, Brocklander. 3B, Rennert.

# April 29 1986

**Boston Red Sox**     3
**Seattle Mariners**     1

**April 29 1986, Fenway Park, Boston**

It was the year of the Rocket.

In one of the most dominant seasons ever by a pitcher, the Red Sox's ace Roger Clemens went 24-4 with a 2.48 ERA, winning both the AL Cy Young and MVP awards, leading Boston to a division title, a pennant and a shot at the World Series. Clemens' dominance and his ability to overpower hitters with his mid-90's fastball was never more apparent than on an April night at Fenway when he fanned 20 Seattle Mariners to become baseball's nine-inning strikeout king. In a performance of awesome power and control, Clemens gave up just three hits, one run and no walks to accompany his unbelievable 20 strikeouts, as the Sox defeated the Mariners 3-1.

In setting the nine-inning mark, Clemens surpassed the previous mark, held by Steve Carlton, Tom Seaver and Nolan Ryan. Remarkably, 10 years later Clemens would repeat the feat when, still a Red Sox, he fanned 20 Tigers in a 4-0 Boston victory at Tiger Stadium.

The mark has since been equaled by the Chicago Cubs' rookie phenom Kerry Wood.

| | 1 | 2 | 3 | 4 | 5 | 6 | 7 | 8 | 9 | R | H | E |
|---|---|---|---|---|---|---|---|---|---|---|---|---|
| **Seattle Mariners** | 0 | 0 | 0 | 0 | 0 | 0 | 1 | 0 | 0 | 1 | 3 | 1 |
| **Boston Red Sox** | 0 | 0 | 0 | 0 | 0 | 0 | 3 | 0 | x | 3 | 8 | 1 |

E--Tartabull, Baylor. DP--Seattle 1. LOB--Seattle 2, Boston 7.
2B--Buckner. HR--Thomas, Evans. CS--Rice, Evans.

| Seattle Mariners | IP | H | R | ER | BB | SO |
|---|---|---|---|---|---|---|
| Mike Moore (L) | 7.1 | 8 | 3 | 3 | 4 | 4 |
| Matt Young | 0.1 | 0 | 0 | 0 | 0 | 0 |
| Karl Best | 0.1 | 0 | 0 | 0 | 0 | 1 |

| Boston Red Sox | IP | H | R | ER | BB | SO |
|---|---|---|---|---|---|---|
| Roger Clemens (W) | 9.0 | 3 | 1 | 1 | 0 | 20 |

Time--2:39. Attendance--13,414.
Umpires--HP, Voltaggio. 1B, Welke. 2B, Phillips. 3B, McCoy.

# October 25 1986

**New York Mets** 6
**Boston Red Sox** 5

**October 25 1986, Shea Stadium, New York**

It has, unfairly, become famous as the biggest error in World Series history and serves only to strengthen the belief in New England that the Curse of the Bambino is well and truly alive. If Fred Merkle was baseball's original goat then Bill Buckner became the World Series' most famous.

In the 10th inning of Game 6 of the 1986 World Series, the Red Sox were up 5-3 on the Mets and seemingly ready to win their first world championship since 1918. But the Mets rallied. They tied the score up, and with one on and two out, Mookie Wilson hit what appeared to be a harmless grounder off Bob Stanley to first. And then it happened. First baseman Buckner, who seemed to have it covered, somehow let the ball trickle under his glove, between his legs and into right field. The Mets' Ray Knight scored the winning run from second to win the game 6-5. After a day's rain delay, Game 7 was played at Shea Stadium and the Red Sox would eventually lose it 8-5 – throwing away a three-run lead after five innings – and the Series too.

It was a bungled routine play on the game's biggest stage and Buckner became about as popular in Beantown as the Boston Strangler. Ironically, it was Knight who thought he had lost the game when his 7th inning throwing error had give Boston the lead. Baseball had once again thrown up the most improbable, and unforgettable, of endings.

| | 1 | 2 | 3 | 4 | 5 | 6 | 7 | 8 | 9 | 10 | | R | H | E |
|---|---|---|---|---|---|---|---|---|---|---|---|---|---|---|
| **Boston Red Sox** | 1 | 1 | 0 | 0 | 0 | 0 | 1 | 0 | 0 | 2 | | 5 | 13 | 3 |
| **New York Mets** | 0 | 0 | 0 | 0 | 2 | 0 | 0 | 1 | 0 | 3 | | 6 | 8 | 2 |

E--Knight, Buckner, Evans, Gedman, Elster. DP--Red Sox 1 (Barrett to Owen to Buckner), Mets 1 (Backman to Elster to Hernandez). LOB--Red Sox 14, Mets 8.
Scoring Position--Red Sox 4-for-12, Mets 2-for-11. 2B--Boggs, Evans.
HR--Henderson. S--Owen, Dykstra, Backman. SF--Carter.
GDP--Gedman, Heep. SB--Strawberry 2.

| Boston Red Sox | IP | H | R | ER | BB | K | ERA |
|---|---|---|---|---|---|---|---|
| Roger Clemens, | 7.0 | 4 | 2 | 1 | 2 | 8 | 3.18 |
| Calvin Schiraldi (BS,, 1; L,, 0-1) | 2.2 | 4 | 4 | 3 | 2 | 1 | 7.36 |
| Bob Stanley (BS,, 1) | 0.0 | 0 | 0 | 0 | 0 | 0 | 0.00 |

| New York Mets | IP | H | R | ER | BB | K | ERA |
|---|---|---|---|---|---|---|---|
| Bobby Ojeda | 6.0 | 8 | 2 | 2 | 2 | 3 | 2.08 |
| Roger McDowell | 1.2 | 2 | 1 | 0 | 3 | 1 | 2.84 |
| Jesse Orosco | 0.1 | 0 | 0 | 0 | 0 | 0 | 0.00 |
| Rick Aguilera (W,, 1-0) | 2.0 | 3 | 2 | 2 | 0 | 3 | 12.00 |

Stanley pitched to two batters in the 10th.
WP--Stanley. HBP--Buckner by Aguilera. Time--4:02. Attendance--55,078.
Umpires--HP, Ford. 1B, Kibler. 2B, Evans. 3B, Wendelstedt.

# September 23 1988

| Oakland Athletics | 9 |
|---|---|
| Milwaukee Brewers | 8 |

**September 23 1988, County Stadium, Milwaukee**

As one-half of the awesome slugging combo, the Bash Brothers, the A's Jose Canseco had a truly special 1988 season. Alongside partner Mark McGwire, Canseco's power and speed helped Oakland to the AL West title, a pennant and a place in the World Series.

The A's would lose the World Series in five games to the Dodgers, but during the regular season Canseco underscored his potential as he became the first player ever to hit 40 home runs and swipe 40 bases in a single-season. He hit 42 dingers for the year and on September 23, Canseco stole the two bases he required against the Milwaukee Brewers, in a 9-8 Oakland victory. Home number 40 had arrived against the Texas Rangers a week earlier in the final homestand.

Since Canseco made history that day in 1988, both the Mariners' Alex Rodriguez and the Giants' Barry Bonds have equalled his 40-40 feat.

| | 1 | 2 | 3 | 4 | 5 | 6 | 7 | 8 | 9 | 10 | 11 | 12 | 13 | 14 | R | H | E |
|---|---|---|---|---|---|---|---|---|---|---|---|---|---|---|---|---|---|
| Oakland Athletics | 2 | 0 | 0 | 0 | 2 | 0 | 1 | 3 | 0 | 0 | 0 | 0 | 0 | 1 | 9 | 14 | 2 |
| Milwaukee Brewers | 0 | 0 | 0 | 0 | 2 | 0 | 0 | 1 | 5 | 0 | 0 | 0 | 0 | 0 | 8 | 11 | 1 |

E--Phillips, Molitor, Steinbach. LOB--Oakland 10,Milwaukee 11.
2B--Weiss, Steinbach. HR--McGwire,Canseco, Deer.
S--Gallego. SF--Yount, Jennings.
SB--Canseco 2, Weiss, Surhoff, Sheffield 2, Jose, Steinbach.

| Oakland Athletics | IP | H | R | ER | BB | SO |
|---|---|---|---|---|---|---|
| Curt Young | 7.0 | 3 | 2 | 2 | 3 | 1 |
| Eric Plunk | 1.0 | 2 | 1 | 1 | 0 | 1 |
| Greg Cadaret | 0.1 | 2 | 4 | 4 | 2 | 0 |
| Dennis Eckersley | 0.2 | 3 | 1 | 1 | 0 | 1 |
| Rick Honeycutt | 1.0 | 1 | 0 | 0 | 0 | 1 |
| Gene Nelson (W) | 3.0 | 0 | 0 | 0 | 1 | 3 |
| Todd Burns (S) | 1.0 | 0 | 0 | 0 | 0 | 1 |

| Milwaukee Brewers | IP | H | R | ER | BB | SO |
|---|---|---|---|---|---|---|
| Juan Nieves | 4.0 | 6 | 4 | 3 | 5 | 4 |
| Odell Jones | 3.1 | 4 | 3 | 3 | 0 | 2 |
| Chuck Crim | 3.2 | 3 | 1 | 1 | 0 | 3 |
| Chris Bosio (L) | 3.0 | 1 | 1 | 1 | 1 | 3 |

Nieves pitched to four batters in the 5th.
HBP--Leonard by Young. Time--5:04. Attendance--24,163.
Umpires--HP, Reed. 1B, Garcia. 2B, Hirschbeck. 3B, Joyce.

# October 15 1988

**Los Angeles Dodgers**   5
**Oakland Athletics**   4

**October 15 1988, Dodger Stadium, Los Angeles**

It seemed like a classic mismatch. Baseball's premier closer, on top of his game, against an injured pinch-hitter, too lame to start the game.

In the 9th inning of Game 1 of the 1988 all-Californian World Series, the A's Dennis Eckersley was facing the Dodgers' Kirk Gibson. Eck had just come off a stellar 45 save season and a dominating performance in the American League Championship Series sweep of the Red Sox.

Suffering from an injured hamstring and a damaged knee, Gibson could barely stand-up. But the National League MVP, in his first season as a Dodger following his collusion free agency departure from Detroit, was famous for his toughness, as would be expected from a standout college defensive back (with Michigan State).

But with Los Angeles down 4-3, with two outs and a runner – Mike Davis – on first, Gibson did the impossible for a man who didn't look capable of playing tee-ball. Waiting on Eckersley's famed slider, he went to a full count, and then got the pitch he had been looking for. Despite his weakened knee, Gibson somehow managed to launch the ball toward right field. And it kept going. When the ball disappeared for a two-run homer to clinch the game, Gibson and Dodger Stadium came to life. He hobbled around the base paths, punching the air, while the crowd erupted, now one of baseball's most durable images.

It was a classic tale of triumph over adversity. When CBS announcer Jack Buck called the home run, he echoed the thoughts of everybody watching. "I don't believe what I just saw," he cried. Twelve years after the event, many still don't.

| | 1 | 2 | 3 | 4 | 5 | 6 | 7 | 8 | 9 | | R | H | E |
|---|---|---|---|---|---|---|---|---|---|---|---|---|---|
| Oakland Athletics | 0 | 4 | 0 | 0 | 0 | 0 | 0 | 0 | 0 | | 4 | 7 | 0 |
| Los Angeles Dodgers | 2 | 0 | 0 | 0 | 0 | 1 | 0 | 0 | 2 | | 5 | 7 | 0 |

DP--Athletics 1 (Lansford to McGwire). LOB--Athletics 10, Dodgers 5.
Scoring Position--Athletics 1-for-11, Dodgers 3-for-6. 2B--Henderson.
HR--Canseco, Hatcher, Gibson. GDP--Hamilton. SB--Canseco, Sax, Davis.

| Oakland Athletics | IP | H | R | ER | BB | K |
|---|---|---|---|---|---|---|
| Dave Stewart | 8.0 | 6 | 3 | 3 | 2 | 5 |
| Dennis Eckersley (BS; L) | 0.2 | 1 | 2 | 2 | 1 | 1 |

| Los Angeles Dodgers | IP | H | R | ER | BB | K |
|---|---|---|---|---|---|---|
| Tim Belcher | 2.0 | 3 | 4 | 4 | 4 | 3 |
| Tim Leary | 3.0 | 3 | 0 | 0 | 1 | 3 |
| Brian Holton | 2.0 | 0 | 0 | 0 | 1 | 0 |
| Alejandro Pena (W) | 2.0 | 1 | 0 | 0 | 0 | 3 |

Balk--Stewart. WP--Stewart. HBP--Canseco by Belcher, Sax by Stewart. Time--3:04. Attendance--55,983. Umpires--HP, Harvey. 1B, Merrill. 2B, Froemming. 3B, Cousins.

193

# September 28 1988

**San Diego Padres**     2
**Los Angeles Dodgers**     1

September 28 1988, Jack Murphy Stadium, San Diego

The 1998 season was one of destiny for the Los Angeles Dodgers. They rose to first in the National League West division in May and stayed there for the rest of the campaign, due to some inspired performances that eventually resulted in a World Series triumph over the Oakland A's.

The most inspirational of all the Dodgers that year was "The Bulldog," Orel Hershiser. From August 30 to the end of the regular season, the staff ace tossed an unbelievable 59 consecutive scoreless innings to break the 20-year Major League record of another Dodger pitching icon, Don Drysdale. The highlight of Hershiser's six straight shutouts was his final-day 10-inning showing against the San Diego Padres, to bring the streak to 59 innings without conceding a run. Against the Padres, Hershiser gave up just four hits as the Dodgers eventually lost a 16-inning marathon, 2-1.

Hershiser would finish the year with a 23-8 record, a 2.26 ERA and was a no-brainer for the NL Cy Young Award, which he won as a unanimous selection.

| | 1 | 2 | 3 | 4 | 5 | 6 | 7 | 8 | 9 | 10 | 11 | 12 | 13 | 14 | 15 | 16 | R | H | E |
|---|---|---|---|---|---|---|---|---|---|---|---|---|---|---|---|---|---|---|---|
| Los Angeles | 0 | 0 | 0 | 0 | 0 | 0 | 0 | 0 | 0 | 0 | 0 | 0 | 0 | 0 | 0 | 1 | 1 | 6 | 0 |
| San Diego | 0 | 0 | 0 | 0 | 0 | 0 | 0 | 0 | 0 | 0 | 0 | 0 | 0 | 0 | 0 | 2 | 2 | 5 | 1 |

SD - RBI- Parent 2, HR- Parent , Sac- Santiago, SB- Gonzalez, Passed Ball- Santiago Team LOB-10
LA - 2B- Griffen, 3B- Woodsen, Sac-Hershiser, SB- Gwynn, Thon, Team LOB-11

| Los Angeles | IP | H | R | ER | BB | SO |
|---|---|---|---|---|---|---|
| Hershiser | 10 | 4 | 0 | 0 | 1 | 3 |
| Orosco | 1 | 0 | 0 | 0 | 4 | 0 |
| Crews | 2 | 0 | 0 | 0 | 0 | 2 |
| K.Howell | 2⅔ | 0 | 1 | 1 | 3 | 3 |
| Horton(L) | 0 | 1 | 1 | 1 | 0 | 0 |

| San Diego | IP | H | R | ER | BB | SO |
|---|---|---|---|---|---|---|
| Hawkins | 10 | 4 | 0 | 0 | 2 | 6 |
| Ma.Davis | 2 | 0 | 0 | 0 | 0 | 4 |
| McCullers | 3 | 1 | 0 | 0 | 0 | 4 |
| Leiper(W) | 1 | 1 | 1 | 0 | 0 | 0 |

Horton pitched to one batter in the 16th
HBP - Griffen by Hawkins
Time: 4:24. Attendance: 22,596
Umpires:     West, Runge, Engel, Williams

# June 29 1990

**St Louis Cardinals**    6
**Los Angeles Dodgers**    0

**June 29 1990, Dodger Stadium, Los Angeles**

The 1990 season was undoubtedly the year of the no-hitter. In total nine no-hit games were pitched that year, including Nolan Ryan's 6th Vs Oakland on June 11. Perhaps the most remarkable however, were the no-hitters tossed by the A's Dave Stewart and the Dodgers' Fernando Valenzuela. In an unbelievable twist of fate, both Stewart's and Valenzuela's efforts were achieved on the very same day, the first time this had occured in major league history. Stewart led his A's to a 5-0 win over the Blue Jays, while Valenzuela's was helping Los Angeles to a 6-0 victory against the St. Louis Cardinals.

The two pitchers had very different fortunes the rest of the year. Stewart went 22-11 with a 2.56 ERA in the regular season and made it to the World Series, while Valenzuela finished with a 13-13 record and a 4.59 ERA as the Dodgers failed to make in into postseason play.

| | 1 | 2 | 3 | 4 | 5 | 6 | 7 | 8 | 9 | | R | H | E |
|---|---|---|---|---|---|---|---|---|---|---|---|---|---|
| **St Louis Cardinals** | 0 | 0 | 0 | 0 | 0 | 0 | 0 | 0 | 0 | | 0 | 0 | 3 |
| **Los Angeles Dodgers** | 1 | 0 | 0 | 0 | 1 | 1 | 2 | 1 | 0 | | 6 | 12 | 1 |

Errors--Guererro, Gibson, McGee, Zeile. DP--St. Louis 1, Los Angeles 1. LOB--St. Louis 3, Los Angeles 9. HR--Brooks, Samuel. SF--Brooks. S--Javier 2. CS--Samuel.

| St. Louis Cardinals | IP | H | R | ER | BB | SO |
|---|---|---|---|---|---|---|
| Jose DeLeon (L) | 6.2 | 9 | 5 | 4 | 3 | 5 |
| Ricky Horton | 1.1 | 3 | 1 | 1 | 1 | 2 |

| Los Angeles Dodgers | IP | H | R | ER | BB | SO |
|---|---|---|---|---|---|---|
| Fernando Valenzuela (W) | 9.0 | 0 | 0 | 0 | 3 | 7 |

WP--DeLeon 3. Time: 2:41  Attendance: 38,583.
Umpires--HP, Layne. 1B, Hallion. 2B, Winters. 3B, Runge.

195

# May 1 1991

**Texas Rangers**     3
**Toronto Blue Jays**     0

**May 1 1991, Arlington Stadium, Texas**

On the same day that Rickey Henderson became the all-time stolen base king, stealing his 939th base to pass Lou Brock's old record, Texan legend Nolan Ryan also made headlines when he hurled his 7th career no-hitter. Against the Toronto Blue Jays, Ryan was his usual dominant self, overpowering hitters with his outstanding arsenal of pitches. In a 3-0 victory for the Texas Rangers, Ryan fanned 16 Blue Jays on his way to another pitching gem and another baseball record.

Nolan Ryan's other no-hit games came in 1973, 1974, 1975, 1981 and 1990, with the two no-hitters in '73 coming just two months apart in May and July. Ryan's reign as the no-hit specialist seems safe. Only the long-retired Sandy Koufax comes close to Ryan's seven lifetime with a still outstanding four career no-hitters.

|  | 1 | 2 | 3 | 4 | 5 | 6 | 7 | 8 | 9 | R | H | E |
|---|---|---|---|---|---|---|---|---|---|---|---|---|
| Toronto Blue Jays | 0 | 0 | 0 | 0 | 0 | 0 | 0 | 0 | 0 | 0 | 0 | 3 |
| Texas Rangers | 0 | 0 | 3 | 0 | 0 | 0 | 0 | 0 | x | 3 | 8 | 1 |

E--Gruber, Myers, Lee, Palmeiro. LOB--Toronto 2, Texas 8. 2B--Gonzalez, Stanley. HR--Sierra. SH--Huson. SB--Pettis. CS--Gonzalez.

| Toronto Blue Jays | IP | H | R | ER | BB | SO |
|---|---|---|---|---|---|---|
| Jimmy Key (L) | 6.0 | 5 | 3 | 3 | 1 | 5 |
| Bob MacDonald | 1.0 | 2 | 0 | 0 | 0 | 2 |
| Willie Fraser | 1.0 | 1 | 0 | 0 | 0 | 0 |

| Texas Rangers, | IP | H | R | ER | BB | SO |
|---|---|---|---|---|---|---|
| Nolan Ryan (W) | 9.0 | 0 | 0 | 0 | 2 | 16 |

HBP--Gonzalez by Fraser. Time--2:25. Attendance--33,439.
Umpires--HP, Tschida. 1B, Coble. 2B, Shulock. 3B, Johnson.

# October 26 1991

**Minnesota Twins** 4
**Atlanta Braves** 3

**October 26 1991, Hubert H. Humphrey Metrodome, Minnesota**

There is probably no more popular figure in Minnesota sports that the Twins' Kirby Puckett and his popularity reached an all-time high during the 1991 World Series against the Braves. It was already a great story as both the Twins and the Braves had finished dead last in their division the season before and no team had ever gone from worst to first in successive seasons.

In one of baseball's closest ever World championships, the Braves were leading the Twins 3-2 heading into Game 6, having already played five dramatic games with three decided by just one run, including a 12-inning thriller in Game 3. With the score tied 3-3 in the 11th inning, Puckett was at the plate when the Braves sent in reliever Charlie Leibrandt from the bullpen. Having already made an incredible defensive play and driven in a couple of runs, Puck was hot. And he got hotter. He smoked Leibrandt's pitch for a solo dinger to end the game and force a Game 7. The Twins won that Game 7, again in extra-innings and by one run, to capture the World Series.

Amazingly, the Twins would win two World Series in four years, each time going to seven games and each is the only Series ever to have the home team won each game.

| | 1 | 2 | 3 | 4 | 5 | 6 | 7 | 8 | 9 | 10 | 11 | | R | H | E |
|---|---|---|---|---|---|---|---|---|---|---|---|---|---|---|---|
| Braves | 0 | 0 | 0 | 0 | 2 | 0 | 1 | 0 | 0 | 0 | 0 | | 3 | 9 | 1 |
| Twins | 2 | 0 | 0 | 0 | 1 | 0 | 0 | 0 | 0 | 0 | 1 | | 4 | 9 | 0 |

E--Hunter. DP--Braves 2 (Bream to Belliard; Blauser to Lemke to Bream), Twins 2 (Gagne to Hrbek; Gagne). LOB--Braves 7, Twins 5.
Scoring Position--Braves 1-for-4, Twins 1-for-9. 2B--Mack. 3B--Puckett.
HR--Pendleton, Puckett. SF--Puckett. GDP--Smith, Gladden, Hrbek.
SB--Gladden, Puckett. CS--Mitchell.

| Atlanta Braves | IP | H | R | ER | BB | K |
|---|---|---|---|---|---|---|
| Steve Avery | 6.0 | 6 | 3 | 3 | 1 | 3 |
| Mike Stanton | 2.0 | 2 | 0 | 0 | 0 | 1 |
| Alejandro Pena | 2.0 | 0 | 0 | 0 | 0 | 2 |
| Charlie Leibrandt (L) | 0.0 | 1 | 1 | 1 | 0 | 0 |

| Minnesota Twins | IP | H | R | ER | BB | K |
|---|---|---|---|---|---|---|
| Scott Erickson | 6.0 | 5 | 3 | 3 | 2 | 2 |
| Mark Guthrie (H) | 0.1 | 1 | 0 | 0 | 1 | 1 |
| Carl Willis (BS) | 2.2 | 1 | 0 | 0 | 0 | 1 |
| Rick Aguilera (W) | 2.0 | 2 | 0 | 0 | 0 | 0 |

Erickson pitched to one batter in the 7th.
Leibrandt pitched to one batter in the 11th.
WP--Guthrie. HBP--Smith by Erickson. Time--3:36. Attendance--55,155.
Umpires--HP, Montague. 1B, Denkinger. 2B, Wendelstedt. 3B, Coble.

# October 23 1993

**Toronto Blue Jays**     8
**Philadelphia Phillies**     6

October 23 1993, SkyDome, Toronto

Not since Pittsburgh's Bill Mazeroski in 1960 had the decisive game of a World Series ended with a "walk-off" home run. On October 23 1993, Toronto's Joe Carter was presented with the opportunity to emulate Mazeroski's dramatic achievement.

It was the 9th inning of Game 6 in the '93 World Series between Carter's Blue Jays and the Phillies. With Toronto behind 6-5 in the bottom of the inning, Carter came into face reliever Mitch Williams. Williams, dubbed the Wild Thing, had given up three runs in Game 4 to give the Blue Jays a 3-1 lead in the Series. Unbelievably, he did it again.

Carter got all over his 2-2 slider and drove it into the Skydome's leftfield seats for the Series deciding dinger. Toronto became the first repeat winners since the New York Yankees in 1977-78.

Williams was traded to the Houston Astros before the start of the following season, but was never the same pitcher again.

|  | 1 | 2 | 3 | 4 | 5 | 6 | 7 | 8 | 9 | R | H | E |
|---|---|---|---|---|---|---|---|---|---|---|---|---|
| Philadelphia Phillies | 0 | 0 | 0 | 1 | 0 | 0 | 5 | 0 | 0 | 6 | 7 | 0 |
| Toronto Blue Jays | 3 | 0 | 0 | 1 | 1 | 0 | 0 | 0 | 3 | 8 | 10 | 2 |

E--Alomar, Sprague. LOB--Phillies 9, Blue Jays 7.
Scoring Position--Phillies 4-for-7, Blue Jays 2-for-4.
2B--Daulton, Olerud, Alomar. 3B--Molitor. HR--Dykstra, Molitor, Carter.
SF--Carter, Sprague, Incaviglia. SB--Dykstra, Duncan.

| Philadelphia Phillies | IP | H | R | ER | BB | K | ERA |
|---|---|---|---|---|---|---|---|
| Terry Mulholland | 5.0 | 7 | 5 | 5 | 1 | 1 | 6.75 |
| Roger Mason | 2.1 | 1 | 0 | 0 | 0 | 2 | 1.17 |
| David West | 0.0 | 0 | 0 | 0 | 1 | 0 | 27.00 |
| Larry Andersen (H,, 1) | 0.2 | 0 | 0 | 0 | 1 | 0 | 12.27 |
| Mitch Williams (BS,, 2; L,, 0-2) | 0.1 | 2 | 3 | 3 | 1 | 0 | 20.25 |

| Toronto Blue Jays | IP | H | R | ER | BB | K | ERA |
|---|---|---|---|---|---|---|---|
| Dave Stewart | 6.0 | 4 | 4 | 4 | 4 | 2 | 6.75 |
| Danny Cox (BS,, 1) | 0.1 | 3 | 2 | 2 | 1 | 1 | 8.10 |
| Al Leiter | 1.2 | 0 | 0 | 0 | 1 | 2 | 7.71 |
| Duane Ward (W,, 1-0) | 1.0 | 0 | 0 | 0 | 0 | 0 | 1.93 |

Stewart pitched to three batters in the 7th.
West pitched to one batter in the 8th.
HBP--Fernandez by Andersen. Time--3:27. Attendance--52,195.
Umpires--HP, DeMuth. 1B, Phillips. 2B, Runge. 3B, Johnson.

# September 6 1995

**Baltimore Orioles**      4
**California Angels**      2

**September 6 1995, Camden Yards, Baltimore**

It was the perfect tonic with the self-inflicted wounds of the previous season's strikes still clearly visible. The simplicity of the message was perfect. Here was a ballplayer who put on his uniform and played hard. And then did it the next day. And the next. It was about work ethic, responsibility and respect for the game. All the things the strike had threatened to negate.

When Cal Ripken Jr passed Lou Gehrig's mark of 2,130 consecutive games, baseball could finally put a period at the end of the labor negotiations that had turned so may fans off the game they loved. Ripken's record, his dignity and his passion for baseball had started the healing process between players and fans. He was giving some of the love back.

The game became official in the middle of the fifth inning with the Angels trailing by two runs. One pitch later, the numbers counting Ripken's streak on the warehouse housing the team offices, changed from 2130 to 2131. Ripken received a 20-minute ovation, the climax being his lap of honor, before the game resumed. The evening had evoked Gehrig and his huge contributions to the game but had also shown us the future. We knew baseball was going to be just fine again.

If anyone needed proof of Ripken's continued importance to Baltimore, the shortstop homered on an emotional night. He finally took a seat on September 25 1998, some 2,632 games without a rest.

| | 1 | 2 | 3 | 4 | 5 | 6 | 7 | 8 | 9 | | R | H | E |
|---|---|---|---|---|---|---|---|---|---|---|---|---|---|
| California Angels | 1 | 0 | 0 | 0 | 0 | 0 | 0 | 1 | 0 | | 2 | 6 | 1 |
| Baltimore Orioles | 1 | 0 | 0 | 2 | 0 | 0 | 1 | 0 | x | | 4 | 9 | 0 |

E--Phillips. DP--Baltimore 1. LOB--California 5, Baltimore 7.
2B--Salmon, Easley, Baines. 3B--Edmonds.
HR--Palmeiro 2, Salmon, Bonilla, Ripken

| California Angels | IP | H | R | ER | BB | SO |
|---|---|---|---|---|---|---|
| Shawn Boskie (L) | 5.0 | 6 | 3 | 3 | 1 | 4 |
| Mike Bielecki | 1.0 | 1 | 0 | 0 | 0 | 2 |
| Bob Patterson | 0.2 | 1 | 1 | 1 | 0 | 1 |
| Mike James | 1.1 | 1 | 0 | 0 | 0 | 1 |

| Baltimore Orioles | IP | H | R | ER | BB | SO |
|---|---|---|---|---|---|---|
| Mike Mussina (W) | 7.2 | 5 | 2 | 2 | 2 | 7 |
| Terry Clark | 0.0 | 1 | 0 | 0 | 0 | 0 |
| Jesse Orosco (S) | 1.1 | 0 | 0 | 0 | 0 | 2 |

Clark pitched to one batter in the 8th.
Time--3:35. Attendance--46,272.
Umpires--HP, Barron. 1B, Kosc. 2B, Morrison. 3B, Clark.

# June 12 1997

**San Francisco Giants**     4
**Texas Rangers**     3

**June 12 1997, The Ballpark in Arlington, Texas**

Since 1901 and the inception of the American League, baseball had always kept its two distinct leagues apart during regular season play, meeting only, from 1903 onwards, to decide the game's World Championship. Rivalries grew between ballclubs in both the American and National leagues but these were wars drawn on divisional lines, the AL's New York Yankees and Boston Red Sox, the NL's New York (the San Francisco) Giants and Brooklyn (Los Angeles) Dodgers, while the possibility of a Mets-Yankees subway series was just a thing of dreams.

But in 1997 that all changed. After the labor strikes of 1994, Major League Baseball, bruised and battered, sought to revive fan loyalty and get the turnstiles moving again. And so interleague play was born. The first matchup saw the National League Giants meet the American League Rangers at the ballpark in Arlington for the inaugural interleague game of baseball's modern era.

A three-run seventh-inning turned out to be the decisive one for the Giants. The game attracted 46,507 fans, who watched the game played under American League rules, i.e. with the designated hitter batting for the pitcher. In games played in National League parks, the American League pitchers would have to bat.

| | 1 | 2 | 3 | 4 | 5 | 6 | 7 | 8 | 9 | | R | H | E |
|---|---|---|---|---|---|---|---|---|---|---|---|---|---|
| San Francisco Giants | 0 | 0 | 1 | 0 | 0 | 0 | 3 | 0 | 0 | | 4 | 9 | 1 |
| Texas Rangers | 0 | 1 | 0 | 0 | 0 | 2 | 0 | 0 | 0 | | 3 | 8 | 0 |

E--Kent. DP--Texas 1. LOB--San Francisco 5, Texas 7.
2B--Bonds, Javier, Greer. 3B--McLemore. HR--Javier.
SF--Hill. SB--Greer, Buford. CS--Snow.

| San Francisco Giants | IP | H | R | ER | BB | SO |
|---|---|---|---|---|---|---|
| Mark Gardner (W) | 8.0 | 8 | 3 | 2 | 1 | 4 |
| Rod Beck (S) | 1.0 | 0 | 0 | 0 | 0 | 0 |

| Texas Rangers | IP | H | R | ER | BB | SO |
|---|---|---|---|---|---|---|
| Darren Oliver (L) | 7.2 | 8 | 4 | 4 | 1 | 2 |
| Xavier Hernandez | 1.1 | 1 | 0 | 0 | 0 | 1 |

HBP--Bonds by Oliver. Time--2:23. Attendance--46,507.
Umpires--HP, McKean. 1B, Hendry. 2B, Joyce. 3B, Hickox.

# May 6 1998

| | |
|---|---|
| **Chicago Cubs** | 2 |
| **Houston Astros** | 0 |

**May 6 1998, Wrigley Field, Chicago**

On May 6 1998, the Cubs' rookie pitcher Kerry Wood conjured up images of those other Texas-connected fireballers, Roger Clemens and Nolan Ryan, when he equaled the Rocketman's single-game nine-inning strikeout record against the powerful Houston Astros.

Facing the dynamic Killer Bees – Craig Biggio, Jeff Bagwell and Derek Bell – Wood tore through the Astros' line-up, using his high-90's heater and a vicious curveball that left the Houston hitters weak at the knees. When the game was over, the 20-year old Wood had fanned 20 Astros in 122 pitches. But his dominance didn't stop there. Wood also allowed just one hit – and that a bobble that many scorers might have called an error – no walks and no runs. Only two balls left the infield all day, making his awesome performance one of the most dominant in major league history.

Wood captured the NL Rookie of the Year Award in 1998 and made his big league return in 2000 after missing '99 through Tommy John surgery.

| | 1 | 2 | 3 | 4 | 5 | 6 | 7 | 8 | 9 | | R | H | E |
|---|---|---|---|---|---|---|---|---|---|---|---|---|---|
| Houston Astros | 0 | 0 | 0 | 0 | 0 | 0 | 0 | 0 | 0 | | 0 | 1 | 1 |
| Chicago Cubs | 0 | 1 | 0 | 0 | 0 | 2 | 0 | 1 | x | | 2 | 8 | 0 |

E--DClark. DP--1 Astros 1. LOB--Astros 2, Cubs 6.
2B--Grace, Blauser. SF-Rodriguez. RBI-Rodriguez, Hernandez.
GIDP-Morandini. CS-Hernandez

| Houston Astros | IP | H | R | ER | BB | SO |
|---|---|---|---|---|---|---|
| Shane Reynolds (L) | 8.0 | 8 | 2 | 1 | 2 | 10 |

| Chicago Cubs | IP | H | R | ER | BB | SO |
|---|---|---|---|---|---|---|
| Kerry Wood (W) | 9 | 1 | 0 | 0 | 0 | 20 |

HBP--Biggio by Wood. Time--2:19. Attendance--15,758.
Umpires--HP, Meals. 1B, Tata. 2B, Davis. 3B, Bell.

# September 8 1998

**St. Louis Cardinals**    **6**
**Chicago Cubs**    **3**

**September 8 1998, Busch Stadium, St. Louis**

It was time for baseball's most revered record to fall. After chasing Roger Maris, number 61 and immortality all season long, St. Louis slugger Mark McGwire was finally knocking on the door. Ready to set a new mark of excellence. A fresh record for fans to drool over. Number 62.

Coming into the game with 61 home runs on the season, McGwire was edgy. The anticipation was immense. In the 1st inning, he walked. Around Busch Stadium, enough air was exhaled to fill the Breitling Orbiter balloon. In the 4th inning, facing the Cubs' Steve Trachsel, McGwire, with that huge, unforgiving cut of his, went first pitch swinging. He caught some of the ball and while it was no Ruthian blast, it was enough. The low, zinging line drive had the trajectory of a scorched 1-iron, clearing the leftfield wall in record time. With Sammy Sosa on hand to congratulate him, along with seemingly the entire population of St. Louis, Big Mac touched 'em all. The homer was measured at only 341 feet, McGwire's shortest dinger of the season, but it didn't matter. It was 62. It was history.

| | 1 | 2 | 3 | 4 | 5 | 6 | 7 | 8 | 9 | | R | H | E |
|---|---|---|---|---|---|---|---|---|---|---|---|---|---|
| Chicago Cubs | 2 | 0 | 0 | 0 | 0 | 0 | 0 | 1 | 0 | | 3 | 12 | 1 |
| St. Louis Cardinals | 0 | 0 | 0 | 1 | 0 | 5 | 0 | 0 | x | | 6 | 5 | 0 |

E--Hill. DP--St. Louis 1. LOB--Chicago 13, St. Louis 1. 2B--Hill. HR--McGwire, R.Lankford, Gant.

| Chicago Cubs | IP | H | R | ER | BB | SO |
|---|---|---|---|---|---|---|
| Steve Trachsel (L) | 5.2 | 5 | 6 | 6 | 2 | 6 |
| Terry Mulholland | 1.1 | 0 | 0 | 0 | 0 | 1 |
| Don Wengert | 0.2 | 0 | 0 | 0 | 1 | 1 |
| Felix Heredia | 0.1 | 0 | 0 | 0 | 0 | 0 |

| St. Louis Cardinals | IP | H | R | ER | BB | SO |
|---|---|---|---|---|---|---|
| Mercker (W) | 6.0 | 8 | 2 | 2 | 3 | 2 |
| Croushore | 0.2 | 1 | 0 | 0 | 2 | 0 |
| Painter | 0.2 | 2 | 1 | 1 | 0 | 0 |
| Frascatore | 0.2 | 0 | 0 | 0 | 0 | 0 |
| Acevedo (S) | 1.0 | 1 | 0 | 0 | 0 | 1 |

WP--Mercker. BALKS--Trachsel, Mercker. Time--2:46. Attendance--43,688. Umpires--HP, Rippley. 1B, Poncino. 2B, Winters. 3B, Darling.

# September 27 1998

**St. Louis Cardinals** 6
**Montreal Expos** 3

September 27 1998, Busch Stadium, St. Louis

After surpassing Roger Maris' 61 in '61 on September 8, Mark McGwire was now no longer chasing history, rather a new number of his own.

It was a simple case of Big Mac trying to hit as may homers as possible before the season's end. Entering the final game of the 1998 regular season, the record-breaking slugger had reached 68 dingers. Facing the Montreal Expos, Big Mac launched number 69 in the third inning off Mike Thurman and for a final encore in the 7th inning hit his final round-tripper of the year off Carl Pavano for number 70 and a new single-season home run record. Like his historic 62nd, the homer was far from one of McGwire's longer blasts, measuring in at 370 feet. But who cared?

It was the perfect exclamation point to the most magnificent of seasons.

| | 1 | 2 | 3 | 4 | 5 | 6 | 7 | 8 | 9 | | R | H | E |
|---|---|---|---|---|---|---|---|---|---|---|---|---|---|
| St. Louis Cardinals | 1 | 1 | 1 | 0 | 0 | 0 | 3 | 0 | x | | 6 | 9 | 2 |
| Montreal Expos | 0 | 0 | 2 | 1 | 0 | 0 | 0 | 0 | 0 | | 3 | 9 | 1 |

E--Andrews, Tatis, Ordaz. DP--St. Louis 1. LOB--Montreal 9, St. Louis 5. 2B--Barrett, Drew, Gant. HR--Cabrera, McGwire 2, Tatis. SB--Jordan. CS--McEwing.

| St. Louis Cardinals | IP | H | R | ER | BB | SO |
|---|---|---|---|---|---|---|
| MattMorris | 4.0 | 6 | 3 | 3 | 3 | 2 |
| John Frascatore (W) | 3.0 | 3 | 0 | 0 | 0 | 2 |
| Curtis King | 1.0 | 0 | 0 | 0 | 0 | 1 |
| Juan Acevedo (S) | 1.0 | 0 | 0 | 0 | 0 | 0 |

| Montreal Expos | IP | H | R | ER | BB | SO |
|---|---|---|---|---|---|---|
| Mike Thurman | 5.0 | 6 | 3 | 3 | 1 | 3 |
| Carl Pavano (L) | 2.0 | 3 | 3 | 3 | 0 | 2 |
| Anthony Telford | 1.0 | 0 | 0 | 0 | 0 | 1 |

HBP--McEwing by Thurman. WP--Morris. Time--2:33. Attendance--46,110. Umpires--HP, Rieker. 1B, West. 2B, Danley. 3B, Gorman.

# April 23 1999

**St. Louis Cardinals** 12
**Los Angeles Dodgers** 5

**April 23 1999, Dodger Stadium, Los Angeles**

In recent years Major League Baseball has witnessed an offensive explosion, with homers being swatted and runs being piled on the scoreboards at a greater frequency than ever before. Perhaps no other game epitomized this new-found explosiveness than a St. Louis Cardinals game against the Los Angeles Dodgers on April 23 1999.

In the 3rd inning, with the bases loaded, St. Louis third baseman Fernando Tatis launched a grand slam off Los Angeles starter Chan Ho Park. Nothing too unusual about that, with some 4,777 grand slams being hit in the majors before Tatis' blast. But the Cardinals' inning continued and with two men out, Tatis again arrived at the plate with another bases loaded situation.

Having waited 2,424 at bats for his first grand salami, Tatis didn't have to wait long for his second. He took Park deep again to become the only player in baseball history to hit two slams in the same inning. St. Louis scored 11 runs in the 3rd and Tatis entered the record books a second time, his eight RBIs the most ever in a single inning.

| | 1 | 2 | 3 | 4 | 5 | 6 | 7 | 8 | 9 | | R | H | E |
|---|---|---|---|---|---|---|---|---|---|---|---|---|---|
| St. Louis Cardinals | 0 | 0 | 11 | 0 | 0 | 1 | 0 | 0 | 0 | | 12 | 11 | 0 |
| Los Angeles Dodgers | 1 | 1 | 0 | 0 | 0 | 0 | 2 | 1 | 0 | | 5 | 11 | 3 |

E--Bragg, Karros, Vizcaino 2. Left On Base--St. Louis, 8. Los Angeles 8.
2B--Drew, Bragg, Hansen. HR--Tatis 2, Marrero, Drew.
RBI--Tatis 8, Marrero, Renteria, Drew, McEwing, Sheffield,
Hundley, Young, Hollansworth, Beltre.
S--Jimenez, Vizcaino. SF--Sheffield, Hundley. SB--Marrero.

| St. Louis Cardinals | IP | H | R | ER | BB | SO |
|---|---|---|---|---|---|---|
| Jimenez(W) | 7.0 | 9 | 4 | 3 | 1 | 6 |
| Aybar | 2.0 | 2 | 1 | 1 | 0 | 2 |
| Los Angeles Dodgers | IP | H | R | ER | BB | SO |
| Park (L) | 2.2 | 8 | 11 | 6 | 3 | 2 |
| Perez | 4.1 | 3 | 1 | 1 | 0 | 4 |
| Kubenka | 2 | 0 | 0 | 0 | 2 | 1 |

HBP--Renteria by Park, Grudzielanek by Aybar. Time--3:05. Attendance--46,687.
Umpires--HP, Bonin. 1B, Nelson. 2B, Pulli. 3B, Williams.
Ejections- LA Manager Johnson by Bonin (3rd)

# November 4 2001

**Arizona Diamonbacks**    3
**New York Yankees**    2

**November 4 2001, Bank One Ballpark, Phoenix**

The 2001 World Series will be remembered as one of the most dramatic series in baseball history.

The upstart Diamondbacks, in only their forth year of existence, were trying to achieve what the Mets, Braves and Padres had failed to do in the last three years. Beat Joe Torre's dogged New York Yankees to the World Championship. After a great start at home, the D-backs took a 2–0 lead into Yankee Stadium. They left staring defeat in the face.

The Yankees won Game 3 then proceeded to clinch Games 4 and 5 in the most incredible fashion as they won both games in extra innings after being down to their final out before two clutch hits breathed new life into their challenge.

Game 6 was then won easily by Arizona setting up a Game 7. And this time it was the D-backs who would perform the ninth inning heroics. Trailing 2-1 in the bottom of the ninth, Mark Grace singled off Mariano Rivera before Tony Womack tied the game with an RBI double. Luis Gonzalez then completed the comeback with a bloop single to center to give the state of Arizona its first World Championship. "We went through sports' greatest dynasty to win our first World Series," said co-MVP Curt Schilling, who shared the award with Randy Johnson.

| | 1 | 2 | 3 | 4 | 5 | 6 | 7 | 8 | 9 | | R | H | E |
|---|---|---|---|---|---|---|---|---|---|---|---|---|---|
| NY Yankees | 0 | 0 | 0 | 0 | 0 | 0 | 1 | 1 | 0 | | 2 | 6 | 3 |
| Arizona | 0 | 0 | 0 | 0 | 0 | 1 | 0 | 0 | 2 | | 3 | 11 | 0 |

Yankees–2B–O'Neill. HR–Soriano. RBI–Martinez, Soriano. E–Clemens, Soriano, Rivera. LOB–3.
Diamondbacks–2B–Bautista, Womack. SF–Knoblauch. RBI–Bautista, Womack, Gonzalez. LOB–11.
CS–Womack

| New York Yankees | IP | H | R | ER | BB | SO |
|---|---|---|---|---|---|---|
| Clemens | 6⅓ | 7 | 1 | 1 | 1 | 10 |
| Stanton | ⅔ | 0 | 0 | 0 | 0 | 0 |
| Rivera (L) | 1⅓ | 4 | 2 | 2 | 0 | 3 |

| Arizona Diamondbacks | IP | H | R | ER | BB | SO |
|---|---|---|---|---|---|---|
| Schilling | 7⅓ | 6 | 2 | 2 | 0 | 9 |
| Batista | ⅓ | 0 | 0 | 0 | 0 | 0 |
| Johnson (W) | 1⅓ | 0 | 0 | 0 | 0 | 1 |

HBP–Counsell (by Rivera). Time–3:20. Att–49,589.
Umpires–HP, Rippley. 1B, M Hirschbeck. 2B,Scott. 3B, Rapuano.

# The Facts & Stats

# CAREER REGULAR SEASON

## Career Games

| Player | Games |
|---|---|
| Pete Rose | 3562 |
| Carl Yastrzemski | 3308 |
| Hank Aaron | 3298 |
| Ty Cobb | 3034 |
| Eddie Murray | 3026 |
| Stan Musial | 3026 |
| Cal Ripken Jr. | 3001 |
| Willie Mays | 2992 |
| Rickey Henderson | 2979 |
| Dave Winfield | 2973 |
| Rusty Staub | 2951 |
| Brooks Robinson | 2896 |
| Robin Yount | 2856 |
| Al Kaline | 2834 |
| Harold Baines | 2830 |
| Eddie Collins | 2826 |
| Reggie Jackson | 2820 |
| Frank Robinson | 2808 |
| Honus Wagner | 2792 |
| Tris Speaker | 2789 |

## Career Batting Average

[minimum 3000 plate appearances]

| Player | Avg |
|---|---|
| Ty Cobb | .366 |
| Rogers Hornsby | .358 |
| Joe Jackson | .356 |
| Lefty O'Doul | .349 |
| Ed Delahanty | .346 |
| Tris Speaker | .345 |
| Ted Williams | .344 |
| Billy Hamilton | .344 |
| Dan Brouthers | .342 |
| Babe Ruth | .342 |
| Dave Orr | .342 |
| Harry Heilmann | .342 |
| Pete Browning | .341 |
| Willie Keeler | .341 |
| Bill Terry | .341 |
| George Sisler | .340 |
| Lou Gehrig | .340 |
| Jake Stenzel | .339 |
| Tony Gwynn | .338 |
| Jesse Burkett | .338 |

## Career .300-Average Seasons

[minimum 500 plate appearances each season]

| Player | Num |
|---|---|
| Tris Speaker | 18 |
| Stan Musial | 17 |
| Ty Cobb | 16 |
| Eddie Collins | 15 |
| Pete Rose | 14 |
| Honus Wagner | 14 |
| Hank Aaron | 13 |
| Luke Appling | 13 |
| Frankie Frisch | 13 |
| Tony Gwynn | 13 |
| Willie Keeler | 13 |
| Babe Ruth | 13 |
| Paul Waner | 13 |
| Ted Williams | 13 |
| Wade Boggs | 12 |
| Rod Carew | 12 |
| Lou Gehrig | 12 |
| Harry Heilmann | 12 |
| Rogers Hornsby | 12 |
| Paul Molitor | 12 |
| Al Simmons | 12 |
| George Sisler | 12 |

## Most Consecutive .300-Average Seasons

[minimum 500 plate appearances each season]

| Player | Years | Number |
|---|---|---|
| Honus Wagner | 1899-12 | 14 |
| Willie Keeler | 1894-06 | 13 |
| Stan Musial | 1946-58 | 13 |
| Lou Gehrig | 1926-37 | 12 |
| Harry Heilmann | 1919-30 | 12 |
| Paul Waner | 1926-37 | 12 |
| Ed Delahanty | 1892-02 | 11 |
| Frankie Frisch | 1921-31 | 11 |
| Jesse Burkett | 1893-02 | 10 |
| Tony Gwynn | 1984-93 | 10 |
| Joe Medwick | 1933-42 | 10 |
| Tris Speaker | 1909-18 | 10 |
| Wade Boggs | 1983-91 | 9 |
| Joe Kelley | 1893-01 | 9 |
| Pete Rose | 1965-73 | 9 |
| Bill Terry | 1927-35 | 9 |
| George Van Haltren | 1893-01 | 9 |
| Arky Vaughan | 1932-40 | 9 |
| Rod Carew | 1971-78 | 8 |
| Roberto Clemente | 1960-67 | 8 |
| Eddie Collins | 1909-16 | 8 |
| Hugh Duffy | 1890-97 | 8 |
| Babe Ruth | 1926-33 | 8 |
| Tris Speaker | 1920-27 | 8 |

# CAREER REGULAR SEASON

## Career At-bats

| Player | At-bats |
|---|---|
| Pete Rose | 14053 |
| Hank Aaron | 12364 |
| Carl Yastrzemski | 11988 |
| Cal Ripken Jr. | 11551 |
| Ty Cobb | 11434 |
| Eddie Murray | 11336 |
| Robin Yount | 11008 |
| Dave Winfield | 11003 |
| Stan Musial | 10972 |
| Willie Mays | 10881 |
| Paul Molitor | 10835 |
| Rickey Henderson | 10710 |
| Brooks Robinson | 10654 |
| Honus Wagner | 10430 |
| George Brett | 10349 |
| Lou Brock | 10332 |
| Luis Aparicio | 10230 |
| Tris Speaker | 10195 |
| Al Kaline | 10116 |
| Rabbit Maranville | 10078 |

## Career Runs

| Player | Runs |
|---|---|
| Rickey Henderson | 2248 |
| Ty Cobb | 2245 |
| Hank Aaron | 2174 |
| Babe Ruth | 2174 |
| Pete Rose | 2165 |
| Willie Mays | 2062 |
| Stan Musial | 1949 |
| Lou Gehrig | 1888 |
| Tris Speaker | 1882 |
| Mel Ott | 1859 |
| Frank Robinson | 1829 |
| Eddie Collins | 1821 |
| Carl Yastrzemski | 1816 |
| Ted Williams | 1798 |
| Paul Molitor | 1782 |
| Charlie Gehringer | 1774 |
| Jimmie Foxx | 1751 |
| Honus Wagner | 1736 |
| Jesse Burkett | 1720 |
| Cap Anson | 1719 |
| Willie Keeler | 1719 |

## Career 100-Run Seasons

| Player | Number |
|---|---|
| Hank Aaron | 15 |
| Lou Gehrig | 13 |
| Rickey Henderson | 13 |
| Charlie Gehringer | 12 |
| Willie Mays | 12 |
| Babe Ruth | 12 |
| Ty Cobb | 11 |
| Jimmie Foxx | 11 |
| Billy Hamilton | 11 |
| Stan Musial | 11 |
| George Van Haltren | 11 |
| Ed Delahanty | 10 |
| Mike Griffin | 10 |
| Bid McPhee | 10 |
| Pete Rose | 10 |
| Sam Thompson | 10 |
| Earl Averill | 9 |
| Jesse Burkett | 9 |
| Hugh Duffy | 9 |
| Dummy Hoy | 9 |
| Arlie Latham | 9 |
| Mickey Mantle | 9 |
| Mel Ott | 9 |
| Harry Stovey | 9 |
| Frank Thomas | 9 |
| Paul Waner | 9 |
| Ted Williams | 9 |

## Career Hits

| Player | Hits |
|---|---|
| Pete Rose | 4256 |
| Ty Cobb | 4190 |
| Hank Aaron | 3771 |
| Stan Musial | 3630 |
| Tris Speaker | 3514 |
| Carl Yastrzemski | 3419 |
| Honus Wagner | 3415 |
| Paul Molitor | 3319 |
| Eddie Collins | 3312 |
| Willie Mays | 3283 |
| Eddie Murray | 3255 |
| Nap Lajoie | 3242 |
| Cal Ripken Jr. | 3184 |
| George Brett | 3154 |
| Paul Waner | 3152 |
| Robin Yount | 3142 |
| Tony Gwynn | 3141 |
| Dave Winfield | 3110 |
| Rod Carew | 3053 |
| Lou Brock | 3023 |

# CAREER REGULAR SEASON

## Career 200-Hit Seasons

| Player | Number |
|---|---|
| Pete Rose | 10 |
| Ty Cobb | 9 |
| Lou Gehrig | 8 |
| Willie Keeler | 8 |
| Paul Waner | 8 |
| Wade Boggs | 7 |
| Charlie Gehringer | 7 |
| Rogers Hornsby | 7 |
| Jesse Burkett | 6 |
| Steve Garvey | 6 |
| Stan Musial | 6 |
| Sam Rice | 6 |
| Al Simmons | 6 |
| George Sisler | 6 |
| Bill Terry | 6 |
| Tony Gwynn | 5 |
| Chuck Klein | 5 |
| Kirby Puckett | 5 |
| Lou Brock | 4 |
| Rod Carew | 4 |
| Roberto Clemente | 4 |
| Harry Heilmann | 4 |
| Joe Jackson | 4 |
| Nap Lajoie | 4 |
| Heinie Manush | 4 |
| Joe Medwick | 4 |
| Paul Molitor | 4 |
| Vada Pinson | 4 |
| Jim Rice | 4 |
| Tris Speaker | 4 |
| Jack Tobin | 4 |
| Lloyd Waner | 4 |

## Career Singles

| Player | Singles |
|---|---|
| Pete Rose | 3215 |
| Ty Cobb | 3053 |
| Eddie Collins | 2641 |
| Willie Keeler | 2513 |
| Honus Wagner | 2422 |
| Rod Carew | 2404 |
| Tris Speaker | 2383 |
| Tony Gwynn | 2378 |
| Paul Molitor | 2366 |
| Nap Lajoie | 2340 |
| Hank Aaron | 2294 |
| Jesse Burkett | 2272 |
| Sam Rice | 2272 |
| Carl Yastrzemski | 2262 |
| Wade Boggs | 2253 |
| Stan Musial | 2253 |
| Cap Anson | 2247 |
| Lou Brock | 2247 |
| Paul Waner | 2246 |
| Robin Yount | 2182 |

## Career Doubles

| Player | Doubles |
|---|---|
| Tris Speaker | 792 |
| Pete Rose | 746 |
| Ty Cobb | 725 |
| Stan Musial | 725 |
| George Brett | 665 |
| Nap Lajoie | 657 |
| Carl Yastrzemski | 646 |
| Honus Wagner | 640 |
| Hank Aaron | 624 |
| Paul Molitor | 605 |
| Cal Ripken Jr. | 603 |
| Paul Waner | 603 |
| Robin Yount | 583 |
| Wade Boggs | 578 |
| Charlie Gehringer | 574 |
| Eddie Murray | 560 |
| Tony Gwynn | 543 |
| Harry Heilmann | 542 |
| Rogers Hornsby | 541 |

## Career Triples

| Player | Triples |
|---|---|
| Sam Crawford | 309 |
| Ty Cobb | 295 |
| Honus Wagner | 252 |
| Jake Beckley | 243 |
| Roger Connor | 233 |
| Tris Speaker | 222 |
| Fred Clarke | 220 |
| Dan Brouthers | 205 |
| Joe Kelley | 194 |
| Paul Waner | 190 |
| Bid McPhee | 188 |
| Eddie Collins | 186 |
| Ed Delahanty | 185 |
| Sam Rice | 184 |
| Jesse Burkett | 182 |
| Edd Roush | 182 |
| Ed Konetchy | 181 |
| Buck Ewing | 178 |
| Rabbit Maranville | 177 |
| Stan Musial | 177 |

# CAREER REGULAR SEASON

## Career Home Runs

| Player | HR |
|---|---|
| Hank Aaron | 755 |
| Babe Ruth | 714 |
| Willie Mays | 660 |
| Frank Robinson | 586 |
| Mark McGwire | 583 |
| Harmon Killebrew | 573 |
| Barry Bonds | 567 |
| Reggie Jackson | 563 |
| Mike Schmidt | 548 |
| Mickey Mantle | 536 |
| Jimmie Foxx | 534 |
| Willie McCovey | 521 |
| Ted Williams | 521 |
| Ernie Banks | 512 |
| Eddie Mathews | 512 |
| Mel Ott | 511 |
| Eddie Murray | 504 |
| Lou Gehrig | 493 |
| Stan Musial | 475 |
| Willie Stargell | 475 |

## Home Runs – Left-handed

| Player | HR |
|---|---|
| Babe Ruth | 714 |
| Barry Bonds | 567 |
| Reggie Jackson | 563 |
| Willie McCovey | 521 |
| Ted Williams | 521 |
| Eddie Mathews | 512 |
| Mel Ott | 511 |
| Lou Gehrig | 493 |
| Stan Musial | 475 |
| Willie Stargell | 475 |
| Ken Griffey Jr. | 460 |
| Carl Yastrzemski | 452 |
| Fred McGriff | 448 |
| Rafael Palmeiro | 447 |
| Billy Williams | 426 |
| Darrell Evans | 414 |
| Duke Snider | 407 |
| Graig Nettles | 390 |
| Harold Baines | 384 |
| Norm Cash | 377 |

## Home Runs – Right-handed

| Player | HR |
|---|---|
| Hank Aaron | 755 |
| Willie Mays | 660 |
| Frank Robinson | 586 |
| Mark McGwire | 583 |
| Harmon Killebrew | 573 |
| Mike Schmidt | 548 |
| Jimmie Foxx | 534 |
| Ernie Banks | 512 |
| Dave Winfield | 465 |
| Jose Canseco | 446 |
| Sammy Sosa | 450 |
| Dave Kingman | 442 |
| Andre Dawson | 438 |
| Cal Ripken Jr. | 431 |
| Al Kaline | 399 |
| Dale Murphy | 398 |
| Juan Gonzalez | 397 |
| Joe Carter | 396 |
| Johnny Bench | 389 |
| Dwight Evans | 385 |

## Home Runs – Switch-Hitter

| Player | HR |
|---|---|
| Mickey Mantle | 536 |
| Eddie Murray | 504 |
| Chili Davis | 350 |
| Reggie Smith | 314 |
| Bobby Bonilla | 287 |
| Ruben Sierra | 263 |
| Ted Simmons | 248 |
| Ken Singleton | 246 |
| Mickey Tettleton | 245 |
| Ken Caminiti | 239 |
| Howard Johnson | 228 |
| Chipper Jones | 227 |
| Devon White | 208 |
| Bernie Williams | 207 |
| Roberto Alomar | 190 |
| Todd Hundley | 184 |
| Tim Raines | 169 |
| Roy Smalley | 163 |
| Tony Phillips | 160 |
| Pete Rose | 160 |
| Roy White | 160 |

# CAREER REGULAR SEASON

## Career 30-Home Run Seasons

| Player | Number |
|---|---|
| Hank Aaron | 15 |
| Babe Ruth | 13 |
| Mike Schmidt | 13 |
| Jimmie Foxx | 12 |
| Barry Bonds | 11 |
| Willie Mays | 11 |
| Frank Robinson | 11 |
| Mark McGwire | 11 |
| Lou Gehrig | 10 |
| Harmon Killebrew | 10 |
| Eddie Mathews | 10 |
| Mickey Mantle | 9 |
| Fred McGriff | 9 |
| Albert Belle | 8 |
| Jose Canseco | 8 |
| Mel Ott | 8 |
| Rafael Palmeiro | 8 |
| Mike Piazza | 8 |
| Sammy Sosa | 8 |
| Ted Williams | 8 |
| Ernie Banks | 7 |
| Rocky Colavito | 7 |
| Joe DiMaggio | 7 |
| Ken Griffey Jr. | 7 |
| Reggie Jackson | 7 |
| Ralph Kiner | 7 |
| Dave Kingman | 7 |
| Willie McCovey | 7 |
| Frank Thomas | 7 |

| Player | Number |
|---|---|
| Rocky Colavito | 3 |
| Andres Galarraga | 3 |
| Frank Howard | 3 |
| Ted Kluszewski | 3 |
| Johnny Mize | 3 |
| Manny Ramirez | 3 |
| Mike Schmidt | 3 |
| Greg Vaughn | 3 |
| Carl Yastrzemski | 3 |

## Career 40-Home Run Seasons

| Player | Number |
|---|---|
| Babe Ruth | 11 |
| Hank Aaron | 8 |
| Harmon Killebrew | 8 |
| Ken Griffey Jr. | 7 |
| Willie Mays | 6 |
| Mark McGwire | 6 |
| Ernie Banks | 5 |
| Jimmie Foxx | 5 |
| Lou Gehrig | 5 |
| Juan Gonzalez | 5 |
| Ralph Kiner | 5 |
| Duke Snider | 5 |
| Barry Bonds | 5 |
| Sammy Sosa | 5 |
| Hank Greenberg | 4 |
| Mickey Mantle | 4 |
| Eddie Mathews | 4 |
| Alex Rodriguez | 4 |
| Frank Thomas | 4 |
| Jeff Bagwell | 3 |
| Albert Belle | 3 |
| Jay Buhner | 3 |
| Jose Canseco | 3 |
| Vinny Castilla | 3 |

## Career Total Bases

| Player | TB |
|---|---|
| Hank Aaron | 6856 |
| Stan Musial | 6134 |
| Willie Mays | 6066 |
| Ty Cobb | 5856 |
| Babe Ruth | 5793 |
| Pete Rose | 5752 |
| Carl Yastrzemski | 5539 |
| Eddie Murray | 5397 |
| Frank Robinson | 5373 |
| Dave Winfield | 5221 |
| Cal Ripken Jr. | 5168 |
| Tris Speaker | 5101 |
| Lou Gehrig | 5060 |
| George Brett | 5044 |
| Mel Ott | 5041 |
| Jimmie Foxx | 4956 |
| Ted Williams | 4884 |
| Honus Wagner | 4862 |
| Paul Molitor | 4854 |
| Al Kaline | 4852 |

## Career Slugging Percentage

[minimum 3000 plate appearances]

| Player | Slg |
|---|---|
| Babe Ruth | .690 |
| Ted Williams | .634 |
| Lou Gehrig | .632 |
| Jimmie Foxx | .609 |
| Hank Greenberg | .605 |
| Manny Ramirez | .594 |
| Mark McGwire | .588 |
| Vladimir Guerrero | .587 |
| Barry Bonds | .585 |
| Mike Piazza | .579 |
| Joe DiMaggio | .579 |
| Frank Thomas | .577 |
| Rogers Hornsby | .577 |
| Larry Walker | .572 |
| Alex Rodriguez | .571 |
| Juan Gonzalez | .568 |
| Ken Griffey Jr. | .566 |
| Albert Belle | .564 |
| Johnny Mize | .562 |
| Brian Giles | .560 |

# CAREER REGULAR SEASON

## Career Runs Batted In

| Player | RBI |
|---|---|
| Hank Aaron | 2297 |
| Babe Ruth | 2213 |
| Lou Gehrig | 1995 |
| Stan Musial | 1951 |
| Ty Cobb | 1937 |
| Jimmie Foxx | 1922 |
| Eddie Murray | 1917 |
| Willie Mays | 1903 |
| Cap Anson | 1879 |
| Mel Ott | 1860 |
| Carl Yastrzemski | 1844 |
| Ted Williams | 1839 |
| Dave Winfield | 1833 |
| Al Simmons | 1827 |
| Frank Robinson | 1812 |
| Honus Wagner | 1732 |
| Reggie Jackson | 1702 |
| Cal Ripken Jr. | 1695 |
| Tony Perez | 1652 |
| Ernie Banks | 1636 |

## Career 100-RBI Seasons

| Player | Number |
|---|---|
| Jimmie Foxx | 13 |
| Lou Gehrig | 13 |
| Babe Ruth | 13 |
| Al Simmons | 12 |
| Hank Aaron | 11 |
| Goose Goslin | 11 |
| Barry Bonds | 10 |
| Joe Carter | 10 |
| Willie Mays | 10 |
| Stan Musial | 10 |
| Albert Belle | 9 |
| Joe DiMaggio | 9 |
| Harmon Killebrew | 9 |
| Mel Ott | 9 |
| Mike Schmidt | 9 |
| Frank Thomas | 9 |
| Honus Wagner | 9 |
| Ted Williams | 9 |
| Ernie Banks | 8 |
| Joe Cronin | 8 |
| Hugh Duffy | 8 |
| Juan Gonzalez | 8 |
| Ken Griffey Jr. | 8 |
| Harry Heilmann | 8 |
| Bob Johnson | 8 |
| Johnny Mize | 8 |
| Rafael Palmeiro | 8 |

| Player | Number |
|---|---|
| Jim Rice | 8 |
| Sam Thompson | 8 |
| Dave Winfield | 8 |

## Career Walks

| Player | BB |
|---|---|
| Rickey Henderson | 2141 |
| Babe Ruth | 2062 |
| Ted Williams | 2019 |
| Joe Morgan | 1865 |
| Carl Yastrzemski | 1845 |
| Mickey Mantle | 1733 |
| Barry Bonds | 1724 |
| Mel Ott | 1708 |
| Eddie Yost | 1614 |
| Darrell Evans | 1605 |
| Stan Musial | 1599 |
| Pete Rose | 1566 |
| Harmon Killebrew | 1559 |
| Lou Gehrig | 1508 |
| Mike Schmidt | 1507 |
| Eddie Collins | 1499 |
| Willie Mays | 1464 |
| Jimmie Foxx | 1452 |
| Eddie Mathews | 1444 |
| Frank Robinson | 1420 |

## Career Intentional Walks

| Player | IBB |
|---|---|
| Barry Bonds | 355 |
| Hank Aaron | 293 |
| Willie McCovey | 260 |
| George Brett | 229 |
| Willie Stargell | 227 |
| Eddie Murray | 222 |
| Frank Robinson | 218 |
| Tony Gwynn | 203 |
| Mike Schmidt | 201 |
| Ernie Banks | 198 |
| Ken Griffey Jr. | 193 |
| Rusty Staub | 193 |
| Willie Mays | 192 |
| Carl Yastrzemski | 190 |
| Chili Davis | 188 |
| Ted Simmons | 188 |
| Harold Baines | 187 |
| Billy Williams | 182 |
| Wade Boggs | 180 |
| Dave Winfield | 172 |

# CAREER REGULAR SEASON

## Career Strikeouts

| Player | K |
| --- | --- |
| Reggie Jackson | 2597 |
| Jose Canseco | 1942 |
| Willie Stargell | 1936 |
| Mike Schmidt | 1883 |
| Tony Perez | 1867 |
| Andres Galarraga | 1858 |
| Dave Kingman | 1816 |
| Bobby Bonds | 1757 |
| Dale Murphy | 1748 |
| Lou Brock | 1730 |
| Mickey Mantle | 1710 |
| Harmon Killebrew | 1699 |
| Chili Davis | 1698 |
| Fred McGriff | 1698 |
| Dwight Evans | 1697 |
| Sammy Sosa | 1690 |
| Dave Winfield | 1686 |
| Rickey Henderson | 1631 |
| Gary Gaetti | 1599 |
| Mark McGwire | 1596 |

## Career Stolen Bases

| Player | SB |
| --- | --- |
| Rickey Henderson | 1395 |
| Lou Brock | 938 |
| Billy Hamilton | 912 |
| Ty Cobb | 892 |
| Tim Raines | 808 |
| Vince Coleman | 752 |
| Eddie Collins | 744 |
| Arlie Latham | 739 |
| Max Carey | 738 |
| Honus Wagner | 722 |
| Joe Morgan | 689 |
| Willie Wilson | 668 |
| Tom Brown | 657 |
| Bert Campaneris | 649 |
| Otis Nixon | 620 |
| George Davis | 616 |
| Dummy Hoy | 594 |
| Maury Wills | 586 |
| George Van Haltren | 583 |
| Ozzie Smith | 580 |

## Career Games - Pitchers

| Player | G |
| --- | --- |
| Jesse Orosco | 1131 |
| Dennis Eckersley | 1071 |
| Hoyt Wilhelm | 1070 |
| Kent Tekulve | 1050 |
| Lee Smith | 1022 |
| Goose Gossage | 1002 |
| John Franco | 998 |
| Lindy McDaniel | 987 |
| Dan Plesac | 946 |
| Rollie Fingers | 944 |
| Gene Garber | 931 |
| Cy Young | 906 |
| Mike Jackson | 902 |
| Sparky Lyle | 899 |
| Jim Kaat | 898 |
| Paul Assenmacher | 884 |
| Jeff Reardon | 880 |
| Don McMahon | 874 |
| Phil Niekro | 864 |
| Charlie Hough | 858 |

## Career Games Started

| Player | GS |
| --- | --- |
| Cy Young | 815 |
| Nolan Ryan | 773 |
| Don Sutton | 756 |
| Phil Niekro | 716 |
| Steve Carlton | 709 |
| Tommy John | 700 |
| Gaylord Perry | 690 |
| Bert Blyleven | 685 |
| Pud Galvin | 681 |
| Walter Johnson | 666 |
| Warren Spahn | 665 |
| Tom Seaver | 647 |
| Jim Kaat | 625 |
| Frank Tanana | 616 |
| Early Wynn | 612 |
| Robin Roberts | 609 |
| Pete Alexander | 599 |
| Fergie Jenkins | 594 |
| Tim Keefe | 593 |
| Dennis Martinez | 562 |
| Kid Nichols | 562 |

# CAREER REGULAR SEASON

## Career Complete Games

| Player | CG |
|---|---|
| Cy Young | 749 |
| Pud Galvin | 640 |
| Tim Keefe | 553 |
| Kid Nichols | 533 |
| Walter Johnson | 531 |
| Mickey Welch | 525 |
| Old Hoss Radbourn | 489 |
| John Clarkson | 485 |
| Tony Mullane | 469 |
| Jim McCormick | 466 |
| Gus Weyhing | 450 |
| Pete Alexander | 437 |
| Christy Mathewson | 434 |
| Jack Powell | 422 |
| Eddie Plank | 410 |
| Will White | 394 |
| Amos Rusie | 393 |
| Vic Willis | 388 |
| Warren Spahn | 382 |
| Jim Whitney | 377 |

## Career Innings Pitched

| Player | IP |
|---|---|
| Cy Young | 7356.0 |
| Pud Galvin | 5941.1 |
| Walter Johnson | 5914.1 |
| Phil Niekro | 5404.1 |
| Nolan Ryan | 5386.0 |
| Gaylord Perry | 5350.1 |
| Don Sutton | 5282.1 |
| Warren Spahn | 5243.2 |
| Steve Carlton | 5217.1 |
| Pete Alexander | 5190.0 |
| Kid Nichols | 5056.1 |
| Tim Keefe | 5047.2 |
| Bert Blyleven | 4970.0 |
| Mickey Welch | 4802.0 |
| Tom Seaver | 4782.2 |
| Christy Mathewson | 4780.2 |
| Tommy John | 4710.1 |
| Robin Roberts | 4688.2 |
| Early Wynn | 4564.0 |
| John Clarkson | 4536.1 |

## Career 300-Inning Seasons

| Player | Num |
|---|---|
| Cy Young | 16 |
| Kid Nichols | 12 |
| Pud Galvin | 11 |
| Christy Mathewson | 11 |
| Tim Keefe | 10 |
| Pete Alexander | 9 |
| Walter Johnson | 9 |
| Joe McGinnity | 9 |
| Mickey Welch | 9 |
| Gus Weyhing | 9 |
| John Clarkson | 8 |
| Jim McCormick | 8 |
| Tony Mullane | 8 |
| Old Hoss Radbourn | 8 |
| Amos Rusie | 8 |
| Jim Whitney | 8 |
| Vic Willis | 8 |
| Charlie Buffinton | 7 |
| Mark Baldwin | 6 |
| Ted Breitenstein | 6 |
| Bob Caruthers | 6 |
| Charlie Getzien | 6 |
| Pink Hawley | 6 |
| Silver King | 6 |
| George Mullin | 6 |
| Gaylord Perry | 6 |
| Jack Powell | 6 |
| Robin Roberts | 6 |
| Jack Taylor | 6 |
| Will White | 6 |

# CAREER REGULAR SEASON

## Career Earned Run Average
*[minimum 1500 innings]*

| Player | ERA |
| --- | --- |
| Ed Walsh | 1.82 |
| Addie Joss | 1.89 |
| Three Finger Brown | 2.06 |
| Monte Ward | 2.10 |
| Christy Mathewson | 2.13 |
| Rube Waddell | 2.16 |
| Walter Johnson | 2.17 |
| Orval Overall | 2.23 |
| Tommy Bond | 2.25 |
| Will White | 2.28 |
| Ed Reulbach | 2.28 |
| Jim Scott | 2.30 |
| Eddie Plank | 2.35 |
| Larry Corcoran | 2.36 |
| George McQuillan | 2.38 |
| Eddie Cicotte | 2.38 |
| Ed Killian | 2.38 |
| Doc White | 2.39 |
| Nap Rucker | 2.42 |
| Jeff Tesreau | 2.43 |

## Career Wins

| Player | W |
| --- | --- |
| Cy Young | 510 |
| Walter Johnson | 417 |
| Pete Alexander | 373 |
| Christy Mathewson | 373 |
| Warren Spahn | 363 |
| Pud Galvin | 360 |
| Kid Nichols | 360 |
| Tim Keefe | 342 |
| Steve Carlton | 329 |
| John Clarkson | 329 |
| Eddie Plank | 326 |
| Nolan Ryan | 324 |
| Don Sutton | 324 |
| Phil Niekro | 318 |
| Gaylord Perry | 314 |
| Tom Seaver | 311 |
| Old Hoss Radbourn | 309 |
| Mickey Welch | 308 |
| Lefty Grove | 300 |
| Early Wynn | 300 |

## Career Wins-RH Pitcher

| Player | W |
| --- | --- |
| Cy Young | 510 |
| Walter Johnson | 417 |
| Pete Alexander | 373 |
| Christy Mathewson | 373 |
| Pud Galvin | 360 |
| Kid Nichols | 360 |
| Tim Keefe | 342 |
| John Clarkson | 329 |
| Nolan Ryan | 324 |
| Don Sutton | 324 |
| Phil Niekro | 318 |
| Gaylord Perry | 314 |
| Tom Seaver | 311 |
| Old Hoss Radbourn | 309 |
| Mickey Welch | 308 |
| Early Wynn | 300 |
| Bert Blyleven | 287 |
| Tony Mullane | 287 |
| Robin Roberts | 286 |
| Fergie Jenkins | 284 |

## Career Wins-LH Pitcher

| Player | W |
| --- | --- |
| Warren Spahn | 363 |
| Steve Carlton | 329 |
| Eddie Plank | 326 |
| Lefty Grove | 300 |
| Tommy John | 288 |
| Jim Kaat | 283 |
| Eppa Rixey | 266 |
| Carl Hubbell | 253 |
| Herb Pennock | 241 |
| Frank Tanana | 240 |
| Whitey Ford | 236 |
| Tom Glavine | 224 |
| Jerry Koosman | 222 |
| Jerry Reuss | 220 |
| Earl Whitehill | 218 |
| Mickey Lolich | 217 |
| Wilbur Cooper | 216 |
| Billy Pierce | 211 |
| Vida Blue | 209 |
| Hal Newhouser | 207 |

# CAREER REGULAR SEASON

## Career 20-Win Seasons

| Player | Num |
|---|---|
| Cy Young | 15 |
| Christy Mathewson | 13 |
| Warren Spahn | 13 |
| Walter Johnson | 12 |
| Kid Nichols | 11 |
| Pud Galvin | 10 |
| Pete Alexander | 9 |
| Old Hoss Radbourn | 9 |
| Mickey Welch | 9 |
| John Clarkson | 8 |
| Lefty Grove | 8 |
| Jim McCormick | 8 |
| Joe McGinnity | 8 |
| Tony Mullane | 8 |
| Jim Palmer | 8 |
| Eddie Plank | 8 |
| Amos Rusie | 8 |
| Vic Willis | 8 |
| Charlie Buffinton | 7 |
| Clark Griffith | 7 |
| Fergie Jenkins | 7 |
| Tim Keefe | 7 |
| Bob Lemon | 7 |
| Gus Weyhing | 7 |

## Most Consecutive 20-Win Seasons

| Player | Years | Num |
|---|---|---|
| Christy Mathewson | 1903-14 | 12 |
| Walter Johnson | 1910-19 | 10 |
| Kid Nichols | 1890-99 | 10 |
| Cy Young | 1891-99 | 9 |
| John Clarkson | 1885-92 | 8 |
| Jim McCormick | 1879-86 | 8 |
| Joe McGinnity | 1899-06 | 8 |
| Lefty Grove | 1927-33 | 7 |
| Tim Keefe | 1883-89 | 7 |
| Old Hoss Radbourn | 1881-87 | 7 |
| Mickey Welch | 1883-89 | 7 |
| Gus Weyhing | 1887-93 | 7 |
| Three Finger Brown | 1906-11 | 6 |
| Bob Caruthers | 1885-90 | 6 |
| Pud Galvin | 1879-84 | 6 |
| Clark Griffith | 1894-99 | 6 |
| Fergie Jenkins | 1967-72 | 6 |
| Robin Roberts | 1950-55 | 6 |
| Amos Rusie | 1890-95 | 6 |
| Warren Spahn | 1956-61 | 6 |

## Career 30-Win Seasons

| Player | Num |
|---|---|
| Kid Nichols | 7 |
| John Clarkson | 6 |
| Tim Keefe | 6 |
| Tony Mullane | 5 |
| Amos Rusie | 5 |
| Will White | 5 |
| Cy Young | 5 |
| Tommy Bond | 4 |
| Larry Corcoran | 4 |
| Silver King | 4 |
| Christy Mathewson | 4 |
| Jim McCormick | 4 |
| Mickey Welch | 4 |
| Gus Weyhing | 4 |
| Pete Alexander | 3 |
| Bob Caruthers | 3 |
| Pud Galvin | 3 |
| Bill Hutchison | 3 |
| Bobby Mathews | 3 |
| Ed Morris | 3 |
| Old Hoss Radbourn | 3 |

## Career Losses

| Player | L |
|---|---|
| Cy Young | 316 |
| Pud Galvin | 305 |
| Nolan Ryan | 292 |
| Walter Johnson | 279 |
| Phil Niekro | 274 |
| Gaylord Perry | 265 |
| Jack Powell | 256 |
| Don Sutton | 256 |
| Eppa Rixey | 251 |
| Bert Blyleven | 250 |
| Robin Roberts | 245 |
| Warren Spahn | 245 |
| Steve Carlton | 244 |
| Early Wynn | 244 |
| Jim Kaat | 237 |
| Frank Tanana | 236 |
| Gus Weyhing | 234 |
| Tommy John | 231 |
| Bob Friend | 230 |
| Ted Lyons | 230 |

# CAREER REGULAR SEASON

## Career Losses-RH Pitcher

| Player | L |
|---|---|
| Cy Young | 316 |
| Pud Galvin | 305 |
| Nolan Ryan | 292 |
| Walter Johnson | 279 |
| Phil Niekro | 274 |
| Gaylord Perry | 265 |
| Jack Powell | 256 |
| Don Sutton | 256 |
| Bert Blyleven | 250 |
| Robin Roberts | 245 |
| Early Wynn | 244 |
| Gus Weyhing | 234 |
| Bob Friend | 230 |
| Ted Lyons | 230 |
| Fergie Jenkins | 226 |
| Tim Keefe | 226 |
| Red Ruffing | 225 |
| Bobo Newsom | 222 |
| Jack Quinn | 218 |
| Sad Sam Jones | 217 |

## Career Losses-LH Pitcher

| Player | L |
|---|---|
| Eppa Rixey | 251 |
| Warren Spahn | 245 |
| Steve Carlton | 244 |
| Jim Kaat | 237 |
| Frank Tanana | 236 |
| Tommy John | 231 |
| Jerry Koosman | 209 |
| Claude Osteen | 195 |
| Eddie Plank | 194 |
| Mickey Lolich | 191 |
| Jerry Reuss | 191 |
| Tom Zachary | 191 |
| Earl Whitehill | 185 |
| Curt Simmons | 183 |
| Wilbur Cooper | 178 |
| Rube Marquard | 177 |
| Larry French | 171 |
| Billy Pierce | 169 |
| Ted Breitenstein | 166 |
| Herb Pennock | 162 |

## Career Strikeouts

| Player | K |
|---|---|
| Nolan Ryan | 5714 |
| Steve Carlton | 4136 |
| Roger Clemens | 3717 |
| Bert Blyleven | 3701 |
| Tom Seaver | 3640 |
| Don Sutton | 3574 |
| Gaylord Perry | 3534 |
| Walter Johnson | 3509 |
| Randy Johnson | 3412 |
| Phil Niekro | 3342 |
| Fergie Jenkins | 3192 |
| Bob Gibson | 3117 |
| Jim Bunning | 2855 |
| Mickey Lolich | 2832 |
| Cy Young | 2803 |
| Frank Tanana | 2773 |
| David Cone | 2655 |
| Warren Spahn | 2583 |
| Bob Feller | 2581 |
| Jerry Koosman | 2556 |

## Career Shutouts

| Player | ShO |
|---|---|
| Walter Johnson | 110 |
| Pete Alexander | 90 |
| Christy Mathewson | 79 |
| Cy Young | 76 |
| Eddie Plank | 69 |
| Warren Spahn | 63 |
| Nolan Ryan | 61 |
| Tom Seaver | 61 |
| Bert Blyleven | 60 |
| Don Sutton | 58 |
| Pud Galvin | 57 |
| Ed Walsh | 57 |
| Bob Gibson | 56 |
| Three Finger Brown | 55 |
| Steve Carlton | 55 |
| Jim Palmer | 53 |
| Gaylord Perry | 53 |
| Juan Marichal | 52 |
| Rube Waddell | 50 |
| Vic Willis | 50 |

# CAREER REGULAR SEASON

## Most No-Hitters

[excludes no-hitters broken up, or combined with other pitchers, or lasting less than nine innings]

| Player | Num |
|---|---|
| Nolan Ryan | 7 |
| Sandy Koufax | 4 |
| Larry Corcoran | 3 |
| Bob Feller | 3 |
| Cy Young | 3 |
| Al Atkinson | 2 |
| Ted Breitenstein | 2 |
| Jim Bunning | 2 |
| Steve Busby | 2 |
| Carl Erskine | 2 |
| Bob Forsch | 2 |
| Pud Galvin | 2 |
| Ken Holtzman | 2 |
| Addie Joss | 2 |
| Dutch Leonard | 2 |
| Jim Maloney | 2 |
| Christy Mathewson | 2 |
| Allie Reynolds | 2 |
| Frank Smith | 2 |
| Warren Spahn | 2 |
| Bill Stoneman | 2 |
| Adonis Terry | 2 |
| Virgil Trucks | 2 |
| Johnny Vander Meer | 2 |
| Don Wilson | 2 |

## Career Walks Allowed

| Player | BB |
|---|---|
| Nolan Ryan | 2795 |
| Steve Carlton | 1833 |
| Phil Niekro | 1809 |
| Early Wynn | 1775 |
| Bob Feller | 1764 |
| Bobo Newsom | 1732 |
| Amos Rusie | 1704 |
| Charlie Hough | 1665 |
| Gus Weyhing | 1566 |
| Red Ruffing | 1541 |
| Bump Hadley | 1442 |
| Warren Spahn | 1434 |
| Earl Whitehill | 1431 |
| Tony Mullane | 1408 |
| Sad Sam Jones | 1396 |
| Jack Morris | 1390 |
| Tom Seaver | 1390 |
| Gaylord Perry | 1379 |
| Bobby Witt | 1375 |
| Mike Torrez | 1371 |

## Career Saves

| Player | Sv |
|---|---|
| Lee Smith | 478 |
| John Franco | 422 |
| Dennis Eckersley | 390 |
| Jeff Reardon | 367 |
| Randy Myers | 347 |
| Rollie Fingers | 341 |
| John Wetteland | 330 |
| Rick Aguilera | 318 |
| Trevor Hoffman | 314 |
| Tom Henke | 311 |
| Goose Gossage | 310 |
| Jeff Montgomery | 304 |
| Doug Jones | 303 |
| Bruce Sutter | 300 |
| Roberto Hernandez | 294 |
| Robb Nen | 271 |
| Rod Beck | 266 |
| Todd Worrell | 256 |
| Dave Righetti | 252 |
| Dan Quisenberry | 244 |

# CAREER WORLD SERIES

## Games

| Player | G |
| --- | --- |
| Yogi Berra | 75 |
| Mickey Mantle | 65 |
| Elston Howard | 54 |
| Hank Bauer | 53 |
| Gil McDougald | 53 |
| Phil Rizzuto | 52 |
| Joe DiMaggio | 51 |
| Frankie Frisch | 50 |
| Pee Wee Reese | 44 |
| Roger Maris | 41 |
| Babe Ruth | 41 |
| Carl Furillo | 40 |
| Jim Gilliam | 39 |
| Gil Hodges | 39 |
| Bill Skowron | 39 |
| Bill Dickey | 38 |
| Jackie Robinson | 38 |
| Tony Kubek | 37 |
| Joe Collins | 36 |
| Bobby Richardson | 36 |
| Duke Snider | 36 |

## Career Batting Average

[minimum 50 plate appearances]

| Player | Avg |
| --- | --- |
| Pepper Martin | .418 |
| Paul Molitor | .418 |
| Hal McRae | .400 |
| Lou Brock | .391 |
| Marquis Grissom | .390 |
| Thurman Munson | .373 |
| George Brett | .373 |
| Hank Aaron | .364 |
| Home Run Baker | .363 |
| Roberto Clemente | .362 |
| Lou Gehrig | .361 |
| Reggie Jackson | .357 |
| Carl Yastrzemski | .352 |
| Earle Combs | .350 |
| Stan Hack | .348 |
| Roberto Alomar | .347 |
| Joe Jackson | .345 |
| Jimmie Foxx | .344 |
| Rickey Henderson | .339 |
| Julian Javier | .333 |
| Billy Martin | .333 |

## Career At-bats

| Player | AB |
| --- | --- |
| Yogi Berra | 259 |
| Mickey Mantle | 230 |
| Joe DiMaggio | 199 |
| Frankie Frisch | 197 |
| Gil McDougald | 190 |
| Hank Bauer | 188 |
| Phil Rizzuto | 183 |
| Elston Howard | 171 |
| Pee Wee Reese | 169 |
| Roger Maris | 152 |
| Jim Gilliam | 147 |
| Tony Kubek | 146 |
| Bill Dickey | 145 |
| Jackie Robinson | 137 |
| Bill Skowron | 133 |
| Duke Snider | 133 |
| Gil Hodges | 131 |
| Bobby Richardson | 131 |
| Pete Rose | 130 |
| Goose Goslin | 129 |
| Bob Meusel | 129 |
| Babe Ruth | 129 |

## Career Runs

| Player | R |
| --- | --- |
| Mickey Mantle | 42 |
| Yogi Berra | 41 |
| Babe Ruth | 37 |
| Lou Gehrig | 30 |
| Joe DiMaggio | 27 |
| Roger Maris | 26 |
| Elston Howard | 25 |
| Gil McDougald | 23 |
| Derek Jeter | 22 |
| Jackie Robinson | 22 |
| Hank Bauer | 21 |
| Reggie Jackson | 21 |
| Phil Rizzuto | 21 |
| Duke Snider | 21 |
| Gene Woodling | 21 |
| Eddie Collins | 20 |
| Pee Wee Reese | 20 |
| Bill Dickey | 19 |
| Frank Robinson | 19 |
| Bill Skowron | 19 |

# CAREER WORLD SERIES

## Career Hits

| Player | H |
|---|---|
| Yogi Berra | 71 |
| Mickey Mantle | 59 |
| Frankie Frisch | 58 |
| Joe DiMaggio | 54 |
| Hank Bauer | 46 |
| Pee Wee Reese | 46 |
| Gil McDougald | 45 |
| Phil Rizzuto | 45 |
| Lou Gehrig | 43 |
| Eddie Collins | 42 |
| Elston Howard | 42 |
| Babe Ruth | 42 |
| Bobby Richardson | 40 |
| Bill Skowron | 39 |
| Duke Snider | 38 |
| Bill Dickey | 37 |
| Goose Goslin | 37 |
| Steve Garvey | 36 |
| Gil Hodges | 35 |
| Reggie Jackson | 35 |
| Tony Kubek | 35 |
| Pete Rose | 35 |

## Career Singles

| Player | 1B |
|---|---|
| Yogi Berra | 49 |
| Frankie Frisch | 45 |
| Joe DiMaggio | 40 |
| Phil Rizzuto | 40 |
| Pee Wee Reese | 39 |
| Hank Bauer | 34 |
| Eddie Collins | 33 |
| Mickey Mantle | 33 |
| Gil McDougald | 33 |
| Tony Kubek | 31 |
| Bobby Richardson | 31 |
| Bill Dickey | 30 |
| Steve Garvey | 29 |
| Elston Howard | 29 |
| Red Rolfe | 28 |
| Gil Hodges | 27 |
| Pete Rose | 27 |
| Bill Skowron | 26 |
| Marquis Grissom | 25 |
| Jim Gilliam | 24 |
| Goose Goslin | 24 |

## Career Doubles

| Player | 2B |
|---|---|
| Yogi Berra | 10 |
| Frankie Frisch | 10 |
| Jack Barry | 9 |
| Pete Fox | 9 |
| Carl Furillo | 9 |
| Lou Gehrig | 8 |
| Lonnie Smith | 8 |
| Duke Snider | 8 |
| Home Run Baker | 7 |
| Lou Brock | 7 |
| Eddie Collins | 7 |
| Rick Dempsey | 7 |
| Hank Greenberg | 7 |
| Chick Hafey | 7 |
| Elston Howard | 7 |
| Reggie Jackson | 7 |
| Marty Marion | 7 |
| Pepper Martin | 7 |
| Danny Murphy | 7 |
| Stan Musial | 7 |
| Terry Pendleton | 7 |
| Jackie Robinson | 7 |
| Devon White | 7 |

## Career Total Bases

| Player | TB |
|---|---|
| Mickey Mantle | 123 |
| Yogi Berra | 117 |
| Babe Ruth | 96 |
| Lou Gehrig | 87 |
| Joe DiMaggio | 84 |
| Duke Snider | 79 |
| Hank Bauer | 75 |
| Frankie Frisch | 74 |
| Reggie Jackson | 74 |
| Gil McDougald | 72 |
| Bill Skowron | 69 |
| Elston Howard | 66 |
| Goose Goslin | 64 |
| Pee Wee Reese | 59 |
| Lou Brock | 57 |
| Roger Maris | 56 |
| Billy Martin | 56 |
| Bill Dickey | 55 |
| Gil Hodges | 54 |
| Phil Rizzuto | 54 |

# CAREER WORLD SERIES

## Career Triples

| Player | 3B |
| --- | --- |
| Bill Johnson | 4 |
| Tommy Leach | 4 |
| Tris Speaker | 4 |
| Hank Bauer | 3 |
| Bobby Brown | 3 |
| Dave Concepcion | 3 |
| Buck Freeman | 3 |
| Frankie Frisch | 3 |
| Lou Gehrig | 3 |
| Dan Gladden | 3 |
| Mark Lemke | 3 |
| Billy Martin | 3 |
| Tim McCarver | 3 |
| Bob Meusel | 3 |
| Freddy Parent | 3 |
| Chick Stahl | 3 |
| Devon White | 3 |
| Many at 2 | |

## Career Home Runs

| Player | HR |
| --- | --- |
| Mickey Mantle | 18 |
| Babe Ruth | 15 |
| Yogi Berra | 12 |
| Duke Snider | 11 |
| Lou Gehrig | 10 |
| Reggie Jackson | 10 |
| Joe DiMaggio | 8 |
| Frank Robinson | 8 |
| Bill Skowron | 8 |
| Hank Bauer | 7 |
| Goose Goslin | 7 |
| Gil McDougald | 7 |
| Lenny Dykstra | 6 |
| Roger Maris | 6 |
| Al Simmons | 6 |
| Reggie Smith | 6 |
| Johnny Bench | 5 |
| Bill Dickey | 5 |
| Hank Greenberg | 5 |
| Gil Hodges | 5 |
| Elston Howard | 5 |
| Charlie Keller | 5 |
| Billy Martin | 5 |

## Career Slugging Percentage

[minimum 50 plate appearances]

| Player | Slg |
| --- | --- |
| Reggie Jackson | .755 |
| Babe Ruth | .744 |
| Lou Gehrig | .731 |
| Lenny Dykstra | .700 |
| Al Simmons | .658 |
| Lou Brock | .655 |
| Pepper Martin | .636 |
| Paul Molitor | .636 |
| Hank Greenberg | .624 |
| Charlie Keller | .611 |
| Jimmie Foxx | .609 |
| Scott Brosius | .609 |
| Rickey Henderson | .607 |
| Dave Henderson | .606 |
| Fred McGriff | .605 |
| Hank Aaron | .600 |
| Joe Carter | .596 |
| Duke Snider | .594 |
| Dwight Evans | .580 |
| Steve Yeager | .579 |

## Career Runs Batted In

| Player | RBI |
| --- | --- |
| Mickey Mantle | 40 |
| Yogi Berra | 39 |
| Lou Gehrig | 35 |
| Babe Ruth | 33 |
| Joe DiMaggio | 30 |
| Bill Skowron | 29 |
| Duke Snider | 26 |
| Hank Bauer | 24 |
| Bill Dickey | 24 |
| Reggie Jackson | 24 |
| Gil McDougald | 24 |
| Hank Greenberg | 22 |
| Gil Hodges | 21 |
| David Justice | 21 |
| Goose Goslin | 19 |
| Elston Howard | 19 |
| Tony Lazzeri | 19 |
| Billy Martin | 19 |
| Home Run Baker | 18 |
| Charlie Keller | 18 |
| Roger Maris | 18 |

# CAREER WORLD SERIES

## Career Walks

| Player | BB |
|---|---|
| Mickey Mantle | 43 |
| Babe Ruth | 33 |
| Yogi Berra | 32 |
| Phil Rizzuto | 30 |
| Lou Gehrig | 26 |
| Mickey Cochrane | 26 |
| David Justice | 25 |
| Jim Gilliam | 23 |
| Jackie Robinson | 21 |
| Gil McDougald | 20 |
| Joe DiMaggio | 19 |
| Gene Woodling | 19 |
| Roger Maris | 18 |
| Pee Wee Reese | 18 |
| Bernie Williams | 18 |
| Gil Hodges | 17 |
| Gene Tenace | 17 |
| Ross Youngs | 17 |
| Paul O'Neill | 16 |
| Pete Rose | 16 |

## Career Stolen Bases

| Player | SB |
|---|---|
| Lou Brock | 14 |
| Eddie Collins | 14 |
| Frank Chance | 10 |
| Davey Lopes | 10 |
| Phil Rizzuto | 10 |
| Frankie Frisch | 9 |
| Honus Wagner | 9 |
| Johnny Evers | 8 |
| Roberto Alomar | 7 |
| Rickey Henderson | 7 |
| Pepper Martin | 7 |
| Joe Morgan | 7 |
| Joe Tinker | 7 |
| Vince Coleman | 6 |
| Chuck Knoblauch | 6 |
| Kenny Lofton | 6 |
| Jackie Robinson | 6 |
| Jimmy Slagle | 6 |
| Bobby Tolan | 6 |
| Omar Vizquel | 6 |
| Maury Wills | 6 |
| Many at | 5 |

## Career Pitcher Games

| Player | G |
|---|---|
| Whitey Ford | 22 |
| Mike Stanton | 20 |
| Mariano Rivera | 18 |
| Rollie Fingers | 16 |
| Allie Reynolds | 15 |
| Bob Turley | 15 |
| Clay Carroll | 14 |
| Clem Labine | 13 |
| Jeff Nelson | 13 |
| Mark Wohlers | 13 |
| Waite Hoyt | 12 |
| Catfish Hunter | 12 |
| Art Nehf | 12 |
| Paul Derringer | 11 |
| Carl Erskine | 11 |
| Rube Marquard | 11 |
| Christy Mathewson | 11 |
| Vic Raschi | 11 |
| Chief Bender | 10 |
| Pedro Borbon | 10 |
| Don Gullett | 10 |
| Don Larsen | 10 |
| Herb Pennock | 10 |
| Dan Quisenberry | 10 |
| Red Ruffing | 10 |
| Dave Stewart | 10 |

## Career Games Started

| Player | GS |
|---|---|
| Whitey Ford | 22 |
| Waite Hoyt | 11 |
| Christy Mathewson | 11 |
| Chief Bender | 10 |
| Red Ruffing | 10 |
| Bob Gibson | 9 |
| Catfish Hunter | 9 |
| Art Nehf | 9 |
| Allie Reynolds | 9 |
| George Earnshaw | 8 |
| Tom Glavine | 8 |
| Rube Marquard | 8 |
| Jim Palmer | 8 |
| Vic Raschi | 8 |
| John Smoltz | 8 |
| Dave Stewart | 8 |
| Don Sutton | 8 |
| Bob Turley | 8 |
| Many at | 7 |

# CAREER WORLD SERIES

## Career Complete Games

| Player | CG |
| --- | --- |
| Christy Mathewson | 10 |
| Chief Bender | 9 |
| Bob Gibson | 8 |
| Red Ruffing | 8 |
| Whitey Ford | 7 |
| Waite Hoyt | 6 |
| George Mullin | 6 |
| Art Nehf | 6 |
| Eddie Plank | 6 |
| Three Finger Brown | 5 |
| Joe Bush | 5 |
| Wild Bill Donovan | 5 |
| George Earnshaw | 5 |
| Walter Johnson | 5 |
| Carl Mays | 5 |
| Deacon Phillippe | 5 |
| Allie Reynolds | 5 |
| Many at | 4 |

## Career Innings Pitched

| Player | IP |
| --- | --- |
| Whitey Ford | 146.0 |
| Christy Mathewson | 101.2 |
| Red Ruffing | 85.2 |
| Chief Bender | 85.0 |
| Waite Hoyt | 83.2 |
| Bob Gibson | 81.0 |
| Art Nehf | 79.0 |
| Allie Reynolds | 77.1 |
| Jim Palmer | 64.2 |
| Catfish Hunter | 63.0 |
| George Earnshaw | 62.2 |
| Joe Bush | 60.2 |
| Vic Raschi | 60.1 |
| Rube Marquard | 58.2 |
| Tom Glavine | 58.1 |
| George Mullin | 58.0 |
| Three Finger Brown | 57.2 |
| Carl Mays | 57.1 |
| Sandy Koufax | 57.0 |
| Dave Stewart | 57.0 |

## Career Earned Run Average

[minimum 25 innings]

| Player | ERA |
| --- | --- |
| Jack Billingham | 0.36 |
| Harry Brecheen | 0.83 |
| Babe Ruth | 0.87 |
| Sherry Smith | 0.89 |
| Sandy Koufax | 0.95 |
| Hippo Vaughn | 1.00 |
| Monte Pearson | 1.01 |
| Christy Mathewson | 1.06 |
| Babe Adams | 1.29 |
| Eddie Plank | 1.32 |
| Rollie Fingers | 1.35 |
| Wild Bill Hallahan | 1.36 |
| Jesse Barnes | 1.45 |
| Roger Clemens | 1.56 |
| Orval Overall | 1.58 |
| George Earnshaw | 1.58 |
| Spud Chandler | 1.62 |
| Mickey Lolich | 1.67 |
| Jesse Haines | 1.67 |
| Mariano Rivera | 1.67 |

## Career Wins

| Player | W |
| --- | --- |
| Whitey Ford | 10 |
| Bob Gibson | 7 |
| Allie Reynolds | 7 |
| Red Ruffing | 7 |
| Chief Bender | 6 |
| Lefty Gomez | 6 |
| Waite Hoyt | 6 |
| Three Finger Brown | 5 |
| Jack Coombs | 5 |
| Lefty Grove | 5 |
| Catfish Hunter | 5 |
| Christy Mathewson | 5 |
| Herb Pennock | 5 |
| Vic Raschi | 5 |
| Many at | 4 |

223

# CAREER WORLD SERIES

## Career Losses

| Player | L |
|---|---|
| Whitey Ford | 8 |
| Joe Bush | 5 |
| Rube Marquard | 5 |
| Christy Mathewson | 5 |
| Eddie Plank | 5 |
| Schoolboy Rowe | 5 |
| Many at | 4 |

## Career Saves

| Player | Sv |
|---|---|
| Mariano Rivera | 8 |
| Rollie Fingers | 6 |
| Johnny Murphy | 4 |
| Allie Reynolds | 4 |
| John Wetteland | 4 |
| Roy Face | 3 |
| Will McEnaney | 3 |
| Tug McGraw | 3 |
| Herb Pennock | 3 |
| Kent Tekulve | 3 |
| Todd Worrell | 3 |
| Many at | 2 |

## Career Strikeouts

| Player | K |
|---|---|
| Whitey Ford | 94 |
| Bob Gibson | 92 |
| Allie Reynolds | 62 |
| Sandy Koufax | 61 |
| Red Ruffing | 61 |
| Chief Bender | 59 |
| George Earnshaw | 56 |
| John Smoltz | 52 |
| Waite Hoyt | 49 |
| Christy Mathewson | 48 |
| Bob Turley | 46 |
| Jim Palmer | 44 |
| Roger Clemens | 43 |
| Vic Raschi | 43 |
| Jack Morris | 40 |
| Tom Glavine | 38 |
| Don Gullett | 37 |
| Don Drysdale | 36 |
| Lefty Grove | 36 |
| George Mullin | 36 |
| Three Finger Brown | 35 |
| Mort Cooper | 35 |
| Orel Hershiser | 35 |
| Walter Johnson | 35 |
| Rube Marquard | 35 |
| Dave McNally | 35 |
| Orval Overall | 35 |

# SINGLE SEASON

## Single Season Rankings Batting

[since 1900; minimum 500 plate appearances]

| Year | Player | Avg |
|------|--------|-----|
| 1901 | Nap Lajoie | .426 |
| 1924 | Rogers Hornsby | .424 |
| 1922 | George Sisler | .420 |
| 1911 | Ty Cobb | .420 |
| 1912 | Ty Cobb | .410 |
| 1911 | Joe Jackson | .408 |
| 1920 | George Sisler | .407 |
| 1941 | Ted Williams | .406 |
| 1925 | Rogers Hornsby | .403 |
| 1923 | Harry Heilmann | .403 |
| 1922 | Rogers Hornsby | .401 |
| 1930 | Bill Terry | .401 |
| 1922 | Ty Cobb | .401 |
| 1929 | Lefty O'Doul | .398 |
| 1927 | Harry Heilmann | 398 |
| 1921 | Rogers Hornsby | .397 |
| 1912 | Joe Jackson | .395 |
| 1921 | Harry Heilmann | .394 |
| 1923 | Babe Ruth | .393 |
| 1925 | Harry Heilmann | .393 |

## Single Season Rankings Hits

[since 1900]

| Year | Player | H |
|------|--------|---|
| 1920 | George Sisler | 257 |
| 1929 | Lefty O'Doul | 254 |
| 1930 | Bill Terry | 254 |
| 1925 | Al Simmons | 253 |
| 1922 | Rogers Hornsby | 250 |
| 1930 | Chuck Klein | 250 |
| 1911 | Ty Cobb | 248 |
| 1922 | George Sisler | 246 |
| 2001 | Ichiro Suzuki | 242 |
| 1930 | Babe Herman | 241 |
| 1928 | Heinie Manush | 241 |
| 1985 | Wade Boggs | 240 |
| 2000 | Darin Erstad | 240 |
| 1977 | Rod Carew | 239 |
| 1986 | Don Mattingly | 238 |
| 1921 | Harry Heilmann | 237 |
| 1937 | Joe Medwick | 237 |
| 1927 | Paul Waner | 237 |
| 1921 | Jack Tobin | 236 |
| 1921 | Rogers Hornsby | 235 |

## Single Season Rankings Runs

[since 1900]

| Year | Player | R |
|------|--------|---|
| 1921 | Babe Ruth | 177 |
| 1936 | Lou Gehrig | 167 |
| 1931 | Lou Gehrig | 163 |
| 1928 | Babe Ruth | 163 |
| 1930 | Chuck Klein | 158 |
| 1920 | Babe Ruth | 158 |
| 1927 | Babe Ruth | 158 |
| 1929 | Rogers Hornsby | 156 |
| 2000 | Jeff Bagwell | 152 |
| 1930 | Kiki Cuyler | 155 |
| 1930 | Woody English | 152 |
| 1932 | Chuck Klein | 152 |
| 1929 | Lefty O'Doul | 152 |
| 1930 | Al Simmons | 152 |
| 1937 | Joe DiMaggio | 151 |
| 1932 | Jimmie Foxx | 151 |
| 1923 | Babe Ruth | 151 |
| 1930 | Babe Ruth | 150 |
| 1949 | Ted Williams | 150 |
| 1927 | Lou Gehrig | 149 |
| 1931 | Babe Ruth | 149 |

## Single Season Rankings Singles

[since 1900]

| Year | Player | 1B |
|------|--------|-----|
| 1927 | Lloyd Waner | 198 |
| 2001 | Ichiro Suzuki | 192 |
| 1985 | Wade Boggs | 187 |
| 1980 | Willie Wilson | 184 |
| 1969 | Matty Alou | 183 |
| 1925 | Sam Rice | 182 |
| 1951 | Richie Ashburn | 181 |
| 1901 | Jesse Burkett | 181 |
| 1929 | Lefty O'Doul | 181 |
| 1973 | Pete Rose | 181 |
| 1929 | Lloyd Waner | 181 |
| 1974 | Rod Carew | 180 |
| 1971 | Ralph Garr | 180 |
| 1928 | Lloyd Waner | 180 |
| 1921 | Jack Tobin | 179 |
| 1962 | Maury Wills | 179 |
| 1964 | Curt Flood | 178 |
| 1922 | George Sisler | 178 |
| 1937 | Paul Waner | 178 |
| 1984 | Tony Gwynn | 177 |
| 1930 | Bill Terry | 177 |

# SINGLE SEASON

## Single Season Rankings Doubles

[since 1900]

| Year | Player | 2B |
|------|--------|----|
| 1931 | Earl Webb | 67 |
| 1926 | George Burns | 64 |
| 1936 | Joe Medwick | 64 |
| 1934 | Hank Greenberg | 63 |
| 1932 | Paul Waner | 62 |
| 1936 | Charlie Gehringer | 60 |
| 2000 | Todd Helton | 59 |
| 1930 | Chuck Klein | 59 |
| 1923 | Tris Speaker | 59 |
| 2000 | Carlos Delgado | 57 |
| 1935 | Billy Herman | 57 |
| 1936 | Billy Herman | 57 |
| 1999 | Craig Biggio | 56 |
| 1950 | George Kell | 56 |
| 1937 | Joe Medwick | 56 |
| 2001 | Lance Berkman | 55 |
| 1936 | Gee Walker | 55 |
| 1997 | Mark Grudzielanek | 54 |
| 2001 | Todd Helton | 54 |
| 1977 | Hal McRae | 54 |
| 1993 | John Olerud | 54 |
| 1996 | Alex Rodriguez | 54 |

## Single Season Rankings Triples

[since 1900]

| Year | Player | 3B |
|------|--------|----|
| 1912 | Chief Wilson | 36 |
| 1914 | Sam Crawford | 26 |
| 1925 | Kiki Cuyler | 26 |
| 1912 | Joe Jackson | 26 |
| 1903 | Sam Crawford | 25 |
| 1911 | Larry Doyle | 25 |
| 1915 | Tom Long | 25 |
| 1911 | Ty Cobb | 24 |
| 1917 | Ty Cobb | 24 |
| 1912 | Ty Cobb | 23 |
| 1927 | Earle Combs | 23 |
| 1930 | Adam Comorosky | 23 |
| 1913 | Sam Crawford | 23 |
| 1949 | Dale Mitchell | 23 |
| 1903 | Bill Bradley | 22 |
| 1930 | Earle Combs | 22 |
| 1902 | Sam Crawford | 22 |
| 1911 | Birdie Cree | 22 |
| 1922 | Jake Daubert | 22 |
| 1906 | Elmer Flick | 22 |
| 1902 | Tommy Leach | 22 |
| 1911 | Mike Mitchell | 22 |
| 1920 | Hi Myers | 22 |
| 1913 | Tris Speaker | 22 |
| 1945 | Snuffy Stirnweiss | 22 |
| 1900 | Honus Wagner | 22 |
| 1926 | Paul Waner | 22 |

## Single Season Rankings Home Runs

[since 1900]

| Year | Player | HR |
|------|--------|----|
| 2001 | Barry Bonds | 73 |
| 1998 | Mark McGwire | 70 |
| 1998 | Sammy Sosa | 66 |
| 1999 | Mark McGwire | 65 |
| 1999 | Sammy Sosa | 63 |
| 1961 | Roger Maris | 61 |
| 1927 | Babe Ruth | 60 |
| 1921 | Babe Ruth | 59 |
| 1932 | Jimmie Foxx | 58 |
| 1938 | Hank Greenberg | 58 |
| 1997 | Mark McGwire | 58 |
| 2001 | Luis Gonzalez | 57 |
| 1997 | Ken Griffey Jr. | 56 |
| 1998 | Ken Griffey Jr. | 56 |
| 1930 | Hack Wilson | 56 |
| 1949 | Ralph Kiner | 54 |
| 1961 | Mickey Mantle | 54 |
| 1920 | Babe Ruth | 54 |
| 1928 | Babe Ruth | 54 |
| 1961 | Mickey Mantle | 54 |
| 1920 | Babe Ruth | 54 |
| 1928 | Babe Ruth | 54 |

# SINGLE SEASON

## Single Season Rankings Home Runs-RH Batter

[since 1900]

| Year | Player | HR |
|------|--------|-----|
| 1998 | Mark McGwire | 70 |
| 1998 | Sammy Sosa | 66 |
| 1999 | Mark McGwire | 65 |
| 2001 | Sammy Sosa | 64 |
| 1999 | Sammy Sosa | 63 |
| 1932 | Jimmie Foxx | 58 |
| 1938 | Hank Greenberg | 58 |
| 1997 | Mark McGwire | 58 |
| 1930 | Hack Wilson | 56 |
| 1949 | Ralph Kiner | 54 |
| 1977 | George Foster | 52 |
| 1965 | Willie Mays | 52 |
| 1996 | Mark McGwire | 52 |
| 2001 | Alex Rodriguez | 52 |
| 1990 | Cecil Fielder | 51 |
| 1947 | Ralph Kiner | 51 |
| 1955 | Willie Mays | 51 |
| 1995 | Albert Belle | 50 |
| 1938 | Jimmie Foxx | 50 |
| 2000 | Sammy Sosa | 50 |
| 1998 | Greg Vaughn | 50 |

## Single Season Rankings Home Runs-LH Batter

[since 1900]

| Year | Player | HR |
|------|--------|-----|
| 2001 | Barry Bonds | 73 |
| 1961 | Roger Maris | 61 |
| 1927 | Babe Ruth | 60 |
| 1921 | Babe Ruth | 59 |
| 2001 | Luis Gonzalez | 57 |
| 1997 | Ken Griffey Jr. | 56 |
| 1998 | Ken Griffey Jr. | 56 |
| 1920 | Babe Ruth | 54 |
| 1928 | Babe Ruth | 54 |
| 1947 | Johnny Mize | 51 |
| 1996 | Brady Anderson | 50 |
| 2000 | Barry Bonds | 49 |
| 1934 | Lou Gehrig | 49 |
| 1936 | Lou Gehrig | 49 |
| 2001 | Shawn Green | 49 |
| 1996 | Ken Griffey Jr. | 49 |
| 1954 | Ted Kluszewski | 49 |
| 1930 | Babe Ruth | 49 |
| 2001 | Jim Thome | 49 |
| 1997 | Larry Walker | 49 |

## Single Season Rankings Home Runs-Switch Hitter

[since 1900]

| Year | Player | HR |
|------|--------|-----|
| 1961 | Mickey Mantle | 54 |
| 1956 | Mickey Mantle | 52 |
| 1999 | Chipper Jones | 45 |
| 1958 | Mickey Mantle | 42 |
| 1996 | Ken Caminiti | 40 |
| 1960 | Mickey Mantle | 40 |
| 1991 | Howard Johnson | 38 |
| 2001 | Chipper Jones | 38 |
| 1955 | Mickey Mantle | 37 |
| 1987 | Howard Johnson | 36 |
| 1989 | Howard Johnson | 36 |
| 2000 | Chipper Jones | 36 |
| 1934 | Ripper Collins | 35 |
| 1964 | Mickey Mantle | 35 |
| 1979 | Ken Singleton | 35 |
| 2001 | Lance Berkman | 34 |
| 1993 | Bobby Bonilla | 34 |
| 1998 | Tony Clark | 34 |
| 2001 | Jose Cruz | 34 |
| 2000 | Carl Everett | 34 |
| 1998 | Chipper Jones | 34 |
| 1957 | Mickey Mantle | 34 |

## Single Season Rankings Total Bases

[since 1900]

| Year | Player | TB |
|------|--------|-----|
| 1921 | Babe Ruth | 457 |
| 1922 | Rogers Hornsby | 450 |
| 1927 | Lou Gehrig | 447 |
| 1930 | Chuck Klein | 445 |
| 1932 | Jimmie Foxx | 438 |
| 1948 | Stan Musial | 429 |
| 2001 | Sammy Sosa | 425 |
| 1930 | Hack Wilson | 423 |
| 1932 | Chuck Klein | 420 |
| 1930 | Lou Gehrig | 419 |
| 2001 | Luis Gonzalez | 419 |
| 1937 | Joe DiMaggio | 418 |
| 1927 | Babe Ruth | 417 |
| 1930 | Babe Herman | 416 |
| 1998 | Sammy Sosa | 416 |
| 2001 | Barry Bonds | 411 |
| 1931 | Lou Gehrig | 410 |
| 1934 | Lou Gehrig | 409 |
| 1929 | Rogers Hornsby | 409 |
| 1997 | Larry Walker | 409 |
| 2000 | Todd Helton | 405 |

# SINGLE SEASON

## Single Season Rankings
## Slugging Percentage

[since 1900; minimum 500 plate appearances]

| Year | Player | Slg |
|------|--------|-----|
| 2001 | Barry Bonds | .863 |
| 1920 | Babe Ruth | .847 |
| 1921 | Babe Ruth | .846 |
| 1927 | Babe Ruth | .772 |
| 1927 | Lou Gehrig | .765 |
| 1923 | Babe Ruth | .764 |
| 1925 | Rogers Hornsby | .756 |
| 1998 | Mark McGwire | .752 |
| 1932 | Jimmie Foxx | .749 |
| 1924 | Babe Ruth | .739 |
| 1926 | Babe Ruth | .737 |
| 2001 | Sammy Sosa | .737 |
| 1941 | Ted Williams | .735 |
| 1930 | Babe Ruth | .732 |
| 1957 | Ted Williams | .731 |
| 1996 | Mark McGwire | .730 |
| 1994 | Frank Thomas | .729 |
| 1930 | Hack Wilson | .723 |
| 1922 | Rogers Hornsby | .722 |
| 1930 | Lou Gehrig | .721 |

## Single Season Rankings RBI

[since 1900]

| Year | Player | RBI |
|------|--------|-----|
| 1930 | Hack Wilson | 191 |
| 1931 | Lou Gehrig | 184 |
| 1937 | Hank Greenberg | 183 |
| 1938 | Jimmie Foxx | 175 |
| 1927 | Lou Gehrig | 175 |
| 1930 | Lou Gehrig | 174 |
| 1921 | Babe Ruth | 171 |
| 1935 | Hank Greenberg | 170 |
| 1930 | Chuck Klein | 170 |
| 1932 | Jimmie Foxx | 169 |
| 1937 | Joe DiMaggio | 167 |
| 1934 | Lou Gehrig | 165 |
| 1999 | Manny Ramirez | 165 |
| 1930 | Al Simmons | 165 |
| 1927 | Babe Ruth | 164 |
| 1933 | Jimmie Foxx | 163 |
| 1931 | Babe Ruth | 163 |
| 1936 | Hal Trosky | 162 |
| 1937 | Lou Gehrig | 159 |
| 1949 | Vern Stephens | 159 |
| 1949 | Ted Williams | 159 |
| 1929 | Hack Wilson | 159 |

## Single Season Rankings Walks

[since 1900]

| Year | Player | BB |
|------|--------|-----|
| 2001 | Barry Bonds | 177 |
| 1923 | Babe Ruth | 170 |
| 1998 | Mark McGwire | 162 |
| 1947 | Ted Williams | 162 |
| 1949 | Ted Williams | 162 |
| 1946 | Ted Williams | 156 |
| 1996 | Barry Bonds | 151 |
| 1956 | Eddie Yost | 151 |
| 1920 | Babe Ruth | 150 |
| 1999 | Jeff Bagwell | 149 |
| 1949 | Eddie Joost | 149 |
| 1945 | Eddie Stanky | 148 |
| 1969 | Jimmy Wynn | 148 |
| 1911 | Jimmy Sheckard | 147 |
| 1957 | Mickey Mantle | 146 |
| 1997 | Barry Bonds | 145 |
| 1969 | Harmon Killebrew | 145 |
| 1921 | Babe Ruth | 145 |
| 1941 | Ted Williams | 145 |
| 1942 | Ted Williams | 145 |

## Single Season Rankings
## Intentional Walks

[since 1900]

| Year | Player | IBB |
|------|--------|-----|
| 1969 | Willie McCovey | 45 |
| 1993 | Barry Bonds | 43 |
| 1970 | Willie McCovey | 40 |
| 2001 | Sammy Sosa | 37 |
| 2001 | Barry Bonds | 35 |
| 1997 | Barry Bonds | 34 |
| 1993 | John Olerud | 33 |
| 1957 | Ted Williams | 33 |
| 1992 | Barry Bonds | 32 |
| 1989 | Kevin Mitchell | 32 |
| 1985 | George Brett | 31 |
| 1996 | Barry Bonds | 30 |
| 1998 | Barry Bonds | 29 |
| 1970 | Frank Howard | 29 |
| 1987 | Dale Murphy | 29 |
| 1967 | Adolfo Phillips | 29 |
| 1995 | Frank Thomas | 29 |
| 1960 | Ernie Banks | 28 |
| 1998 | Mark McGwire | 28 |
| 1997 | Jeff Bagwell | 27 |
| 1988 | Will Clark | 27 |
| 1968 | Roberto Clemente | 27 |

# SINGLE SEASON

## Single Season Rankings Stolen Bases

[since 1900]

| Year | Player | SB |
|------|--------|-----|
| 1982 | Rickey Henderson | 130 |
| 1974 | Lou Brock | 118 |
| 1985 | Vince Coleman | 110 |
| 1987 | Vince Coleman | 109 |
| 1983 | Rickey Henderson | 108 |
| 1986 | Vince Coleman | 107 |
| 1962 | Maury Wills | 104 |
| 1980 | Rickey Henderson | 100 |
| 1980 | Ron LeFlore | 97 |
| 1915 | Ty Cobb | 96 |
| 1980 | Omar Moreno | 96 |
| 1965 | Maury Wills | 94 |
| 1988 | Rickey Henderson | 93 |
| 1983 | Tim Raines | 90 |
| 1912 | Clyde Milan | 88 |
| 1986 | Rickey Henderson | 87 |
| 1911 | Ty Cobb | 83 |
| 1979 | Willie Wilson | 83 |

## Single Season Rankings Pitching Games

[since 1900]

| Year | Player | G |
|------|--------|-----|
| 1974 | Mike Marshall | 106 |
| 1979 | Kent Tekulve | 94 |
| 1973 | Mike Marshall | 92 |
| 1978 | Kent Tekulve | 91 |
| 1969 | Wayne Granger | 90 |
| 1979 | Mike Marshall | 90 |
| 1987 | Kent Tekulve | 90 |
| 1987 | Mark Eichhorn | 89 |
| 1997 | Julian Tavarez | 89 |
| 1997 | Mike Myers | 88 |
| 1998 | Sean Runyan | 88 |
| 1968 | Wilbur Wood | 88 |
| 1987 | Rob Murphy | 87 |
| 1982 | Kent Tekulve | 85 |
| 1987 | Frank Williams | 85 |
| 1987 | Mitch Williams | 85 |
| 1965 | Ted Abernathy | 84 |
| 1997 | Stan Belinda | 84 |
| 2001 | Graeme Lloyd | 84 |
| 1985 | Dan Quisenberry | 84 |
| 1979 | Enrique Romo | 84 |
| 1980 | Dick Tidrow | 84 |

## Single Season Rankings Games Started

[since 1900]

| Year | Player | GS |
|------|--------|-----|
| 1904 | Jack Chesbro | 51 |
| 1908 | Ed Walsh | 49 |
| 1972 | Wilbur Wood | 49 |
| 1903 | Joe McGinnity | 48 |
| 1973 | Wilbur Wood | 48 |
| 1915 | Dave Davenport | 46 |
| 1904 | Christy Mathewson | 46 |
| 1904 | Rube Waddell | 46 |
| 1907 | Ed Walsh | 46 |
| 1902 | Vic Willis | 46 |
| 1916 | Pete Alexander | 45 |
| 1971 | Mickey Lolich | 45 |
| 1904 | Jack Powell | 45 |
| 1917 | Pete Alexander | 44 |
| 1908 | Christy Mathewson | 44 |
| 1904 | Joe McGinnity | 44 |
| 1904 | George Mullin | 44 |
| 1979 | Phil Niekro | 44 |
| 1923 | George Uhle | 44 |
| 1914 | Cy Falkenberg | 43 |
| 1901 | Joe McGinnity | 43 |
| 1977 | Phil Niekro | 43 |
| 1904 | Eddie Plank | 43 |
| 1915 | Dick Rudolph | 43 |
| 1901 | Luther Taylor | 43 |
| 1904 | Vic Willis | 43 |
| 1975 | Wilbur Wood | 43 |
| 1902 | Cy Young | 43 |

# SINGLE SEASON

## Single Season Rankings
## Complete Games
[since 1900]

| Year | Player | CG |
|------|--------|-----|
| 1904 | Jack Chesbro | 48 |
| 1902 | Vic Willis | 45 |
| 1903 | Joe McGinnity | 44 |
| 1904 | George Mullin | 42 |
| 1908 | Ed Walsh | 42 |
| 1901 | Noodles Hahn | 41 |
| 1902 | Cy Young | 41 |
| 1905 | Irv Young | 41 |
| 1904 | Cy Young | 40 |
| 1902 | Bill Dinneen | 39 |
| 1901 | Joe McGinnity | 39 |
| 1904 | Jack Taylor | 39 |
| 1904 | Rube Waddell | 39 |
| 1904 | Vic Willis | 39 |
| 1916 | Pete Alexander | 38 |
| 1910 | Walter Johnson | 38 |
| 1904 | Oscar Jones | 38 |
| 1904 | Joe McGinnity | 38 |
| 1904 | Jack Powell | 38 |
| 1901 | Cy Young | 38 |

## Single Season Rankings Wins
[since 1900]

| Year | Player | W |
|------|--------|-----|
| 1904 | Jack Chesbro | 41 |
| 1908 | Ed Walsh | 40 |
| 1908 | Christy Mathewson | 37 |
| 1913 | Walter Johnson | 36 |
| 1904 | Joe McGinnity | 35 |
| 1912 | Joe Wood | 34 |
| 1916 | Pete Alexander | 33 |
| 1912 | Walter Johnson | 33 |
| 1904 | Christy Mathewson | 33 |
| 1901 | Cy Young | 33 |
| 1902 | Cy Young | 32 |
| 1915 | Pete Alexander | 31 |
| 1920 | Jim Bagby | 31 |
| 1910 | Jack Coombs | 31 |
| 1931 | Lefty Grove | 31 |
| 1905 | Christy Mathewson | 31 |
| 1903 | Joe McGinnity | 31 |
| 1968 | Denny McLain | 31 |
| 1917 | Pete Alexander | 30 |
| 1934 | Dizzy Dean | 30 |
| 1903 | Christy Mathewson | 30 |

## Single Season Rankings
## Innings Pitched
[since 1900]

| Year | Player | IP |
|------|--------|-----|
| 1908 | Ed Walsh | 464.0 |
| 1904 | Jack Chesbro | 454.2 |
| 1903 | Joe McGinnity | 434.0 |
| 1907 | Ed Walsh | 422.1 |
| 1902 | Vic Willis | 410.0 |
| 1904 | Joe McGinnity | 408.0 |
| 1912 | Ed Walsh | 393.0 |
| 1915 | Dave Davenport | 392.2 |
| 1908 | Christy Mathewson | 390.2 |
| 1904 | Jack Powell | 390.1 |
| 1902 | Togie Pittinger | 389.1 |
| 1916 | Pete Alexander | 389.0 |
| 1917 | Pete Alexander | 388.0 |
| 1902 | Cy Young | 384.2 |
| 1904 | Rube Waddell | 383.0 |
| 1904 | George Mullin | 382.1 |
| 1901 | Joe McGinnity | 382.0 |
| 1904 | Cy Young | 380.0 |
| 1905 | Irv Young | 378.0 |
| 1914 | Cy Falkenberg | 377.1 |

## Single Season Rankings Earned Run
[since 1900; minimum 150 innings]

| Year | Player | ERA |
|------|--------|-----|
| 1914 | Dutch Leonard | 0.96 |
| 1906 | Three Finger Brown | 1.04 |
| 1968 | Bob Gibson | 1.12 |
| 1909 | Christy Mathewson | 1.14 |
| 1913 | Walter Johnson | 1.14 |
| 1907 | Jack Pfiester | 1.15 |
| 1908 | Addie Joss | 1.16 |
| 1907 | Carl Lundgren | 1.17 |
| 1915 | Pete Alexander | 1.22 |
| 1908 | Cy Young | 1.26 |
| 1910 | Ed Walsh | 1.27 |
| 1918 | Walter Johnson | 1.27 |
| 1905 | Christy Mathewson | 1.28 |
| 1910 | Jack Coombs | 1.30 |
| 1909 | Three Finger Brown | 1.31 |
| 1902 | Jack Taylor | 1.33 |
| 1910 | Walter Johnson | 1.36 |
| 1912 | Walter Johnson | 1.39 |
| 1907 | Three Finger Brown | 1.39 |
| 1909 | Harry Krause | 1.39 |

# SINGLE SEASON

## Single Season Rankings Losses
[since 1900]

| Year | Player | L |
|------|--------|---|
| 1905 | Vic Willis | 29 |
| 1910 | George Bell | 27 |
| 1933 | Paul Derringer | 27 |
| 1901 | Luther Taylor | 27 |
| 1906 | Gus Dorner | 26 |
| 1901 | Pete Dowling | 26 |
| 1909 | Bob Groom | 26 |
| 1904 | Jack Townsend | 26 |
| 1935 | Ben Cantwell | 25 |
| 1903 | Patsy Flaherty | 25 |
| 1905 | Fred Glade | 25 |
| 1909 | Walter Johnson | 25 |
| 1904 | Oscar Jones | 25 |
| 1907 | Stoney McGlynn | 25 |
| 1905 | Harry McIntire | 25 |
| 1920 | Scott Perry | 25 |
| 1908 | Bugs Raymond | 25 |
| 1928 | Red Ruffing | 25 |
| 1904 | Vic Willis | 25 |
| 1906 | Irv Young | 25 |

## Single Season Rankings Saves
[since 1900]

| Year | Player | Sv |
|------|--------|----|
| 1990 | Bobby Thigpen | 57 |
| 1998 | Trevor Hoffman | 53 |
| 1993 | Randy Myers | 53 |
| 1998 | Rod Beck | 51 |
| 1992 | Dennis Eckersley | 51 |
| 2001 | Mariano Rivera | 50 |
| 1993 | Rod Beck | 48 |
| 1990 | Dennis Eckersley | 48 |
| 1998 | Jeff Shaw | 48 |
| 1991 | Lee Smith | 47 |
| 1998 | Tom Gordon | 46 |
| 1991 | Bryan Harvey | 46 |
| 1995 | Jose Mesa | 46 |
| 1986 | Dave Righetti | 46 |
| 1993 | Lee Smith | 46 |
| 2000 | Antonio Alfonseca | 45 |
| 1988 | Dennis Eckersley | 45 |
| 1993 | Bryan Harvey | 45 |
| 1993 | Jeff Montgomery | 45 |
| 1997 | Randy Myers | 45 |
| 2001 | Robb Nen | 45 |
| 1983 | Dan Quisenberry | 45 |
| 1999 | Mariano Rivera | 45 |
| 2001 | Kazuhiro Sasaki | 45 |

| Year | Player | Sv |
|------|--------|----|
| 1984 | Bruce Sutter | 45 |
| 1993 | Duane Ward | 45 |

## Single Season Rankings Strikeouts
[since 1900]

| Year | Player | K |
|------|--------|---|
| 1973 | Nolan Ryan | 383 |
| 1965 | Sandy Koufax | 382 |
| 2001 | Randy Johnson | 364 |
| 1974 | Nolan Ryan | 367 |
| 1999 | Randy Johnson | 364 |
| 1904 | Rube Waddell | 349 |
| 1946 | Bob Feller | 348 |
| 2000 | Randy Johnson | 347 |
| 1977 | Nolan Ryan | 341 |
| 1998 | Randy Johnson | 329 |
| 1972 | Nolan Ryan | 329 |
| 1976 | Nolan Ryan | 327 |
| 1965 | Sam McDowell | 325 |
| 1997 | Curt Schilling | 319 |
| 1966 | Sandy Koufax | 317 |
| 1910 | Walter Johnson | 313 |
| 1999 | Pedro Martinez | 313 |
| 1979 | J.R. Richard | 313 |

## Single Season Rankings Shutouts
[since 1900]

| Year | Player | ShO |
|------|--------|-----|
| 1916 | Pete Alexander | 16 |
| 1912 | George Boehler | 15 |
| 1910 | Jack Coombs | 13 |
| 1968 | Bob Gibson | 13 |
| 1915 | Pete Alexander | 12 |
| 1964 | Dean Chance | 11 |
| 1913 | Walter Johnson | 11 |
| 1963 | Sandy Koufax | 11 |
| 1908 | Christy Mathewson | 11 |
| 1908 | Ed Walsh | 11 |
| 1942 | Mort Cooper | 10 |
| 1915 | Dave Davenport | 10 |
| 1946 | Bob Feller | 10 |
| 1933 | Carl Hubbell | 10 |
| 1948 | Bob Lemon | 10 |
| 1965 | Juan Marichal | 10 |
| 1975 | Jim Palmer | 10 |
| 1985 | John Tudor | 10 |
| 1906 | Ed Walsh | 10 |
| 1912 | Joe Wood | 10 |
| 1904 | Cy Young | 10 |

# SINGLE SEASON WORLD SERIES

## Batting 4-Game World Series

[minimum 12 plate appearances]

| Year | Player | Avg |
|------|--------|-----|
| 1990 | Billy Hatcher | .750 |
| 1928 | Babe Ruth | .625 |
| 1998 | Ricky Ledee | .600 |
| 1990 | Chris Sabo | .563 |
| 1928 | Lou Gehrig | .545 |
| 1914 | Hank Gowdy | .545 |
| 1999 | Bret Boone | .538 |
| 1976 | Johnny Bench | .533 |
| 1932 | Lou Gehrig | .529 |
| 1976 | Thurman Munson | .529 |
| 1998 | Tony Gwynn | .500 |
| 1927 | Mark Koenig | .500 |
| 1938 | Joe Marty | .500 |
| 1954 | Vic Wertz | .500 |
| 1989 | Rickey Henderson | .474 |
| 1998 | Scott Brosius | .471 |
| 1938 | Stan Hack | .471 |
| 1938 | Phil Cavarretta | .462 |
| 1932 | Riggs Stephenson | .444 |
| 1932 | Bill Dickey | .438 |
| 1914 | Johnny Evers | .438 |
| 1939 | Charlie Keller | .438 |
| 1989 | Carney Lansford | .438 |

## Runs 4-Game World Series

| Year | Player | R |
|------|--------|---|
| 1932 | Lou Gehrig | 9 |
| 1928 | Babe Ruth | 9 |
| 1932 | Earle Combs | 8 |
| 1939 | Charlie Keller | 8 |
| 1927 | Earle Combs | 6 |
| 1990 | Billy Hatcher | 6 |
| 1989 | Dave Henderson | 6 |
| 1932 | Babe Ruth | 6 |
| 1954 | Hank Thompson | 6 |
| 1989 | Jose Canseco | 5 |
| 1928 | Lou Gehrig | 5 |
| 1932 | Billy Herman | 5 |
| 1999 | Chuck Knoblauch | 5 |
| 1927 | Mark Koenig | 5 |
| 1989 | Carney Lansford | 5 |
| 1928 | Bob Meusel | 5 |
| 1927 | Lloyd Waner | 5 |
| Many at | | 4 |

## Hits 4-Game World Series

| Year | Player | H |
|------|--------|---|
| 1928 | Babe Ruth | 10 |
| 1932 | Lou Gehrig | 9 |
| 1990 | Billy Hatcher | 9 |
| 1989 | Rickey Henderson | 9 |
| 1927 | Mark Koenig | 9 |
| 1976 | Thurman Munson | 9 |
| 1990 | Chris Sabo | 9 |
| 1976 | Johnny Bench | 8 |
| 1998 | Scott Brosius | 8 |
| 1998 | Tony Gwynn | 8 |
| 1938 | Stan Hack | 8 |
| 1932 | Riggs Stephenson | 8 |
| 1954 | Vic Wertz | 8 |
| 1999 | Bret Boone | 7 |
| 1954 | Al Dark | 7 |
| 1932 | Bill Dickey | 7 |
| 1914 | Johnny Evers | 7 |
| 1939 | Charlie Keller | 7 |
| 1989 | Carney Lansford | 7 |
| 1954 | Don Mueller | 7 |

## Doubles 4-Game World Series

| Year | Player | 2B |
|------|--------|-----|
| 1999 | Bret Boone | 4 |
| 1990 | Billy Hatcher | 4 |
| 1914 | Hank Gowdy | 3 |
| 1998 | Ricky Ledee | 3 |
| 1990 | Joe Oliver | 3 |
| 1928 | Babe Ruth | 3 |
| Many at | | 2 |

## Triples 4-Game World Series

| Year | Player | 3B |
|------|--------|-----|
| 1963 | Tommy Davis | 2 |
| 1927 | Lou Gehrig | 2 |
| 1989 | Rickey Henderson | 2 |
| Many at | | 1 |

# SINGLE SEASON WORLD SERIES

## Home Runs 4-Game World Series

| Year | Player | HR |
|------|--------|-----|
| 1928 | Lou Gehrig | 4 |
| 1932 | Lou Gehrig | 3 |
| 1939 | Charlie Keller | 3 |
| 1928 | Babe Ruth | 3 |
| 1976 | Johnny Bench | 2 |
| 1998 | Scott Brosius | 2 |
| 1999 | Chad Curtis | 2 |
| 1939 | Bill Dickey | 2 |
| 1989 | Dave Henderson | 2 |
| 1932 | Tony Lazzeri | 2 |
| 1954 | Dusty Rhodes | 2 |
| 1966 | Frank Robinson | 2 |
| 1927 | Babe Ruth | 2 |
| 1932 | Babe Ruth | 2 |
| 1990 | Chris Sabo | 2 |
| 1998 | Greg Vaughn | 2 |

Many at 1

## Total Bases 4-Game World Series

| Year | Player | TB |
|------|--------|-----|
| 1928 | Babe Ruth | 22 |
| 1928 | Lou Gehrig | 19 |
| 1932 | Lou Gehrig | 19 |
| 1939 | Charlie Keller | 19 |
| 1976 | Johnny Bench | 17 |
| 1989 | Rickey Henderson | 17 |
| 1990 | Chris Sabo | 16 |
| 1990 | Billy Hatcher | 15 |
| 1954 | Vic Wertz | 15 |
| 1998 | Scott Brosius | 14 |
| 1914 | Hank Gowdy | 14 |
| 1989 | Dave Henderson | 12 |
| 1966 | Frank Robinson | 12 |
| 1927 | Babe Ruth | 12 |
| 1999 | Bret Boone | 11 |
| 1938 | Frankie Crosetti | 11 |
| 1932 | Kiki Cuyler | 11 |
| 1938 | Joe Gordon | 11 |
| 1998 | Tony Gwynn | 11 |
| 1927 | Mark Koenig | 11 |
| 1989 | Carney Lansford | 11 |
| 1932 | Tony Lazzeri | 11 |
| 1976 | Joe Morgan | 11 |
| 1932 | Babe Ruth | 11 |

## Runs Batted In 4-Game World Series

| Year | Player | RBI |
|------|--------|-----|
| 1928 | Lou Gehrig | 9 |
| 1932 | Lou Gehrig | 8 |
| 1954 | Dusty Rhodes | 7 |
| 1927 | Babe Ruth | 7 |
| 1989 | Terry Steinbach | 7 |
| 1976 | Johnny Bench | 6 |
| 1998 | Scott Brosius | 6 |
| 1932 | Ben Chapman | 6 |
| 1938 | Frankie Crosetti | 6 |
| 1938 | Joe Gordon | 6 |
| 1939 | Charlie Keller | 6 |
| 1932 | Babe Ruth | 6 |
| 1990 | Eric Davis | 5 |
| 1939 | Bill Dickey | 5 |
| 1932 | Tony Lazzeri | 5 |
| 1999 | Tino Martinez | 5 |
| 1938 | Joe Marty | 5 |
| 1990 | Chris Sabo | 5 |

Many at 4

## Innings Pitched 4-Game World Series

| Year | Player | IP |
|------|--------|-----|
| 1928 | Waite Hoyt | 18.0 |
| 1963 | Sandy Koufax | 18.0 |
| 1914 | Dick Rudolph | 18.0 |
| 1938 | Red Ruffing | 18.0 |
| 1989 | Dave Stewart | 16.0 |
| 1939 | Paul Derringer | 15.1 |
| 1990 | Jose Rijo | 15.1 |
| 1950 | Jim Konstanty | 15.0 |
| 1998 | Kevin Brown | 14.1 |
| 1954 | Bob Lemon | 13.1 |
| 1928 | Bill Sherdel | 13.1 |
| 1989 | Mike Moore | 13.0 |
| 1990 | Dave Stewart | 13.0 |
| 1963 | Whitey Ford | 12.0 |
| 1966 | Dave McNally | 11.1 |
| 1914 | Joe Bush | 11.0 |
| 1914 | Bill James | 11.0 |
| 1938 | Bill Lee | 11.0 |
| 1950 | Robin Roberts | 11.0 |
| 1939 | Bucky Walters | 11.0 |

# SINGLE SEASON WORLD SERIES

## Stolen Bases 4-Game World Series

| Year | Player | SB |
|------|--------|-----|
| 1989 | Rickey Henderson | 3 |
| 1990 | Rickey Henderson | 3 |
| 1999 | Derek Jeter | 3 |
| 1989 | Brett Butler | 2 |
| 1914 | Charlie Deal | 2 |
| 1928 | Frankie Frisch | 2 |
| 1976 | Cesar Geronimo | 2 |
| 1932 | Billy Jurges | 2 |
| 1928 | Tony Lazzeri | 2 |
| 1914 | Rabbit Maranville | 2 |
| 1928 | Bob Meusel | 2 |
| 1976 | Joe Morgan | 2 |

Many at 1

## Wins 4-Game World Series

| Year | Player | W |
|------|--------|-----|
| 1928 | Waite Hoyt | 2 |
| 1914 | Bill James | 2 |
| 1963 | Sandy Koufax | 2 |
| 1989 | Mike Moore | 2 |
| 1990 | Jose Rijo | 2 |
| 1914 | Dick Rudolph | 2 |
| 1938 | Red Ruffing | 2 |
| 1989 | Dave Stewart | 2 |

Many at 1

## Earned Run 4-Game World Series

[minimum 8 innings]

| Year | Player | ERA |
|------|--------|-----|
| 1966 | Wally Bunker | 0.00 |
| 1963 | Don Drysdale | 0.00 |
| 1950 | Whitey Ford | 0.00 |
| 1914 | Bill James | 0.00 |
| 1966 | Jim Palmer | 0.00 |
| 1939 | Monte Pearson | 0.00 |
| 1950 | Vic Raschi | 0.00 |
| 1914 | Dick Rudolph | 0.50 |
| 1990 | Jose Rijo | 0.59 |
| 1954 | Johnny Antonelli | 0.84 |
| 1927 | Wilcy Moore | 0.84 |
| 1950 | Allie Reynolds | 0.87 |
| 1932 | Lefty Gomez | 1.00 |
| 1938 | Monte Pearson | 1.00 |
| 1927 | Herb Pennock | 1.00 |
| 1914 | Eddie Plank | 1.00 |
| 1939 | Red Ruffing | 1.00 |
| 1963 | Johnny Podres | 1.08 |
| 1928 | Waite Hoyt | 1.50 |
| 1963 | Sandy Koufax | 1.50 |

## Saves 4-Game World Series

| Year | Player | Sv |
|------|--------|-----|
| 1938 | Red Ruffing | 1.50 |
| 1998 | Mariano Rivera | 3 |
| 1976 | Will McEnaney | 2 |
| 1932 | Herb Pennock | 2 |
| 1999 | Mariano Rivera | 2 |
| 1954 | Johnny Antonelli | 1 |
| 1989 | Dennis Eckersley | 1 |
| 1927 | Wilcy Moore | 1 |
| 1938 | Johnny Murphy | 1 |
| 1990 | Randy Myers | 1 |
| 1963 | Ron Perranoski | 1 |
| 1950 | Allie Reynolds | 1 |
| 1954 | Hoyt Wilhelm | 1 |

## Batting 5-Game World Series

[minimum 15 plate appearances]

| Year | Player | Avg |
|------|--------|-----|
| 1941 | Joe Gordon | .500 |
| 1970 | Paul Blair | .474 |
| 1922 | Heine Groh | .474 |
| 2000 | Paul O'Neill | .474 |
| 1922 | Frankie Frisch | .471 |
| 1907 | Harry Steinfeldt | .471 |
| 1929 | Hack Wilson | .471 |
| 1969 | Al Weis | .455 |
| 1913 | Home Run Baker | .450 |
| 1984 | Alan Trammell | .450 |
| 1915 | Duffy Lewis | .444 |
| 1915 | Fred Luderus | .438 |
| 1910 | Eddie Collins | .429 |
| 1970 | Brooks Robinson | .429 |
| 1908 | Frank Chance | .421 |
| 1913 | Eddie Collins | .421 |
| 1929 | Jimmy Dykes | .421 |
| 1984 | Kurt Bevacqua | .412 |
| 1910 | Home Run Baker | .409 |
| 2000 | Derek Jeter | .409 |
| 1929 | Mickey Cochrane | .400 |
| 1937 | Tony Lazzeri | .400 |
| 1907 | Claude Rossman | .400 |
| 1969 | Ron Swoboda | .400 |
| 2000 | Todd Zeile | .400 |

# SINGLE SEASON WORLD SERIES

## Runs 5-Game World Series

| Year | Player | R |
|------|--------|---|
| 1910 | Home Run Baker | 6 |
| 1916 | Harry Hooper | 6 |
| 2000 | Derek Jeter | 6 |
| 1970 | Lee May | 6 |
| 1910 | Danny Murphy | 6 |
| 1970 | Boog Powell | 6 |
| 1929 | Al Simmons | 6 |
| 1984 | Lou Whitaker | 6 |
| 1970 | Paul Blair | 5 |
| 1929 | Mickey Cochrane | 5 |
| 1910 | Eddie Collins | 5 |
| 1913 | Eddie Collins | 5 |
| 1910 | Harry Davis | 5 |
| 1908 | Johnny Evers | 5 |
| 1929 | Jimmie Foxx | 5 |
| 1988 | Mickey Hatcher | 5 |
| 1961 | Elston Howard | 5 |
| 1941 | Charlie Keller | 5 |
| 1913 | Rube Oldring | 5 |
| 1970 | Brooks Robinson | 5 |
| 1970 | Frank Robinson | 5 |
| 1942 | Red Rolfe | 5 |
| 1937 | George Selkirk | 5 |
| 1910 | Jimmy Sheckard | 5 |
| 1970 | Bobby Tolan | 5 |
| 1984 | Alan Trammell | 5 |

## Doubles 5-Game World Series

| Year | Player | 2B |
|------|--------|----|
| 1910 | Eddie Collins | 4 |
| 1983 | Rick Dempsey | 4 |
| 1910 | Home Run Baker | 3 |
| 1913 | Jack Barry | 3 |
| 1949 | Jerry Coleman | 3 |
| 1910 | Harry Davis | 3 |
| 1961 | Elston Howard | 3 |
| 1916 | Hal Janvrin | 3 |
| 1910 | Danny Murphy | 3 |
| 1910 | Wildfire Schulte | 3 |
| 1949 | Gene Woodling | 3 |
| Many at | | 2 |

## Triples 5-Game World Series

| Year | Player | 3B |
|------|--------|----|
| 1949 | Bobby Brown | 2 |
| 1913 | Eddie Collins | 2 |
| 2000 | Paul O'Neill | 2 |
| Many at 1 | | |

## Hits 5-Game World Series

| Year | Player | H |
|------|--------|---|
| 1910 | Home Run Baker | 9 |
| 1913 | Home Run Baker | 9 |
| 1970 | Paul Blair | 9 |
| 1910 | Eddie Collins | 9 |
| 1922 | Heine Groh | 9 |
| 2000 | Derek Jeter | 9 |
| 1937 | Jo-Jo Moore | 9 |
| 2000 | Paul O'Neill | 9 |
| 1961 | Bobby Richardson | 9 |
| 1970 | Brooks Robinson | 9 |
| 1984 | Alan Trammell | 9 |
| 1908 | Frank Chance | 8 |
| 1913 | Eddie Collins | 8 |
| 1929 | Jimmy Dykes | 8 |
| 1922 | Frankie Frisch | 8 |
| 1974 | Steve Garvey | 8 |
| 1915 | Duffy Lewis | 8 |
| 2000 | Tino Martinez | 8 |
| 1942 | Phil Rizzuto | 8 |
| 1907 | Claude Rossman | 8 |
| 1907 | Harry Steinfeldt | 8 |
| 1984 | Alan Wiggins | 8 |
| 1929 | Hack Wilson | 8 |
| 2000 | Todd Zeile | 8 |

## Home Runs 5-Game World Series

| Year | Player | HR |
|------|--------|----|
| 1969 | Donn Clendenon | 3 |
| 1984 | Kurt Bevacqua | 2 |
| 1961 | Johnny Blanchard | 2 |
| 1929 | Jimmie Foxx | 2 |
| 1916 | Larry Gardner | 2 |
| 1984 | Kirk Gibson | 2 |
| 1929 | Mule Haas | 2 |
| 1988 | Mickey Hatcher | 2 |
| 1915 | Harry Hooper | 2 |
| 2000 | Derek Jeter | 2 |
| 1942 | Charlie Keller | 2 |
| 1970 | Lee May | 2 |
| 1983 | Joe Morgan | 2 |
| 1983 | Eddie Murray | 2 |
| 1933 | Mel Ott | 2 |
| 2000 | Mike Piazza | 2 |
| 1970 | Boog Powell | 2 |
| 1970 | Brooks Robinson | 2 |
| 1970 | Frank Robinson | 2 |
| 1929 | Al Simmons | 2 |
| 1984 | Alan Trammell | 2 |
| 1922 | Aaron Ward | 2 |

## Total Bases 5-Game World Series

| Year | Player | TB |
|------|--------|-----|
| 2000 | Derek Jeter | 19 |
| 1970 | Brooks Robinson | 17 |
| 1984 | Alan Trammell | 16 |
| 1984 | Kurt Bevacqua | 15 |
| 1969 | Donn Clendenon | 15 |
| 1970 | Lee May | 15 |
| 2000 | Paul O'Neill | 15 |
| 1929 | Jimmie Foxx | 14 |
| 1988 | Mickey Hatcher | 14 |
| 2000 | Mike Piazza | 14 |
| 1910 | Eddie Collins | 13 |
| 1941 | Joe Gordon | 13 |
| 1915 | Harry Hooper | 13 |
| 1983 | Joe Morgan | 13 |
| 1910 | Danny Murphy | 13 |
| 1933 | Mel Ott | 13 |
| 1929 | Al Simmons | 13 |
| 1910 | Home Run Baker | 12 |
| 1913 | Home Run Baker | 12 |
| 1913 | Eddie Collins | 12 |
| 1983 | Rick Dempsey | 12 |
| 1984 | Kirk Gibson | 12 |
| 1915 | Duffy Lewis | 12 |
| 1915 | Fred Luderus | 12 |
| 1970 | Boog Powell | 12 |
| 1970 | Frank Robinson | 12 |

## Runs Batted In 5-Game World Series

| Year | Player | RBI |
|------|--------|-----|
| 1910 | Danny Murphy | 9 |
| 1970 | Lee May | 8 |
| 1913 | Home Run Baker | 7 |
| 1984 | Kirk Gibson | 7 |
| 1961 | Hector Lopez | 7 |
| 1922 | Irish Meusel | 7 |
| 1913 | Wally Schang | 7 |
| 1916 | Larry Gardner | 6 |
| 1929 | Mule Haas | 6 |
| 1915 | Fred Luderus | 6 |
| 1970 | Brooks Robinson | 6 |
| 1937 | George Selkirk | 6 |
| 1984 | Alan Trammell | 6 |
| 1949 | Bobby Brown | 5 |
| 1988 | Jose Canseco | 5 |
| 1929 | Jimmie Foxx | 5 |
| 1941 | Joe Gordon | 5 |
| 1988 | Mickey Hatcher | 5 |
| 1941 | Charlie Keller | 5 |
| 1942 | Charlie Keller | 5 |
| 1942 | Whitey Kurowski | 5 |
| 1915 | Duffy Lewis | 5 |
| 1970 | Boog Powell | 5 |
| 1929 | Al Simmons | 5 |
| 1961 | Bill Skowron | 5 |

## Stolen Bases 5-Game World Series

| Year | Player | SB |
|------|--------|-----|
| 1907 | Jimmy Slagle | 6 |
| 1908 | Frank Chance | 5 |
| 1910 | Eddie Collins | 4 |
| 1907 | Frank Chance | 3 |
| 1913 | Eddie Collins | 3 |
| 1905 | Art Devlin | 3 |
| 1907 | Johnny Evers | 3 |
| 1984 | Kirk Gibson | 3 |
| 1907 | Davy Jones | 3 |
| 1905 | George Browne | 2 |
| 1908 | Ty Cobb | 2 |
| 1905 | Bill Dahlen | 2 |
| 1988 | Mike Davis | 2 |
| 1905 | Mike Donlin | 2 |
| 1908 | Johnny Evers | 2 |
| 1905 | Topsy Hartsel | 2 |
| 1910 | Topsy Hartsel | 2 |
| 1908 | Solly Hofman | 2 |
| 1984 | Chet Lemon | 2 |
| 1974 | Davey Lopes | 2 |
| 1913 | Red Murray | 2 |
| 1942 | Phil Rizzuto | 2 |
| 1908 | Wildfire Schulte | 2 |
| 1908 | Joe Tinker | 2 |

# SINGLE SEASON WORLD SERIES

## Earned Run 5-Game World Series

[minimum 10 innings]

| Year | Player | ERA |
|---|---|---|
| 1908 | Three Finger Brown | 0.00 |
| 1961 | Whitey Ford | 0.00 |
| 1933 | Carl Hubbell | 0.00 |
| 1905 | Christy Mathewson | 0.00 |
| 1905 | Joe McGinnity | 0.00 |
| 1949 | Allie Reynolds | 0.00 |
| 1943 | Spud Chandler | 0.50 |
| 1916 | Babe Ruth | 0.64 |
| 1984 | Andy Hawkins | 0.75 |
| 1907 | Ed Reulbach | 0.75 |
| 1929 | Guy Bush | 0.82 |
| 1933 | Jack Russell | 0.87 |
| 1913 | Christy Mathewson | 0.95 |
| 1913 | Eddie Plank | 0.95 |
| 1908 | Orval Overall | 0.98 |
| 1988 | Orel Hershiser | 1.00 |
| 1907 | Orval Overall | 1.00 |
| 1905 | Chief Bender | 1.06 |
| 1983 | Scott McGregor | 1.06 |
| 1969 | Mike Cuellar | 1.13 |

## Innings Pitched 5-Game World Series

| Year | Player | IP |
|---|---|---|
| 1910 | Jack Coombs | 27.0 |
| 1905 | Christy Mathewson | 27.0 |
| 1907 | Wild Bill Donovan | 21.0 |
| 1933 | Carl Hubbell | 20.0 |
| 1913 | Christy Mathewson | 19.0 |
| 1913 | Eddie Plank | 19.0 |
| 1910 | Chief Bender | 18.2 |
| 1908 | Orval Overall | 18.1 |
| 1942 | Johnny Beazley | 18.0 |
| 1913 | Chief Bender | 18.0 |
| 1910 | Three Finger Brown | 18.0 |
| 1943 | Spud Chandler | 18.0 |
| 1915 | Rube Foster | 18.0 |
| 1937 | Lefty Gomez | 18.0 |
| 1988 | Orel Hershiser | 18.0 |
| 1984 | Jack Morris | 18.0 |
| 1907 | Orval Overall | 18.0 |
| 1941 | Whit Wyatt | 18.0 |
| 1915 | Pete Alexander | 17.2 |
| 1969 | Jerry Koosman | 17.2 |
| 1942 | Red Ruffing | 17.2 |
| 1916 | Ernie Shore | 17.2 |

## Saves 5-Game World Series

| Year | Player | Sv |
|---|---|---|
| 1974 | Rollie Fingers | 2 |
| 1984 | Willie Hernandez | 2 |
| 1983 | Tippy Martinez | 2 |
| 2000 | Mariano Rivera | 2 |
| Many at 1 | | |

## Wins 5-Game World Series

| Year | Player | W |
|---|---|---|
| 1910 | Jack Coombs | 3 |
| 1905 | Christy Mathewson | 3 |
| 1942 | Johnny Beazley | 2 |
| 1913 | Chief Bender | 2 |
| 1908 | Three Finger Brown | 2 |
| 1943 | Spud Chandler | 2 |
| 1961 | Whitey Ford | 2 |
| 1915 | Rube Foster | 2 |
| 1937 | Lefty Gomez | 2 |
| 1988 | Orel Hershiser | 2 |
| 1933 | Carl Hubbell | 2 |
| 1969 | Jerry Koosman | 2 |
| 1984 | Jack Morris | 2 |
| 1908 | Orval Overall | 2 |
| 1916 | Ernie Shore | 2 |
| 2000 | Mike Stanton | 2 |
| Many at 1 | | |

## Batting 6-Game World Series

[minimum 18 plate appearances]

| Year | Player | Avg |
|---|---|---|
| 1953 | Billy Martin | .500 |
| 1993 | Paul Molitor | .500 |
| 1917 | Dave Robertson | .500 |
| 1993 | Roberto Alomar | .480 |
| 1980 | Amos Otis | .478 |
| 1951 | Monte Irvin | .458 |
| 1936 | Jake Powell | .455 |
| 1992 | Pat Borders | .450 |
| 1977 | Reggie Jackson | .450 |
| 1996 | Marquis Grissom | .444 |
| 1944 | George McQuinn | .438 |
| 1953 | Yogi Berra | .429 |
| 1978 | Bill Russell | .423 |
| 1951 | Al Dark | .417 |
| 1978 | Bucky Dent | .417 |
| 1981 | Steve Garvey | .417 |
| 1923 | Aaron Ward | .417 |
| 1980 | Bob Boone | .412 |
| 1944 | Emil Verban | .412 |
| 1917 | Eddie Collins | .409 |

# SINGLE SEASON WORLD SERIES

## Runs 6-Game World Series

| Year | Player | R |
|------|--------|---|
| 1977 | Reggie Jackson | 10 |
| 1993 | Paul Molitor | 10 |
| 1993 | Lenny Dykstra | 9 |
| 1978 | Roy White | 9 |
| 1936 | Jake Powell | 8 |
| 1923 | Babe Ruth | 8 |
| 1993 | Devon White | 8 |
| 1911 | Home Run Baker | 7 |
| 1978 | Davey Lopes | 7 |
| 1977 | Reggie Smith | 7 |
| 1953 | Hank Bauer | 6 |
| 1953 | Roy Campanella | 6 |
| 1993 | Joe Carter | 6 |
| 1993 | Rickey Henderson | 6 |
| 1959 | Jim Landis | 6 |
| 1995 | Kenny Lofton | 6 |
| 1981 | Davey Lopes | 6 |
| 1980 | Mike Schmidt | 6 |
| 1936 | George Selkirk | 6 |
| 1951 | Gene Woodling | 6 |

## Hits 6-Game World Series

| Year | Player | H |
|------|--------|---|
| 1993 | Roberto Alomar | 12 |
| 1996 | Marquis Grissom | 12 |
| 1953 | Billy Martin | 12 |
| 1993 | Paul Molitor | 12 |
| 1951 | Monte Irvin | 11 |
| 1980 | Amos Otis | 11 |
| 1917 | Dave Robertson | 11 |
| 1978 | Bill Russell | 11 |
| 1951 | Al Dark | 10 |
| 1978 | Bucky Dent | 10 |
| 1993 | Mariano Dunca | 10 |
| 1935 | Pete Fox | 10 |
| 1923 | Frankie Frisch | 10 |
| 1981 | Steve Garvey | 10 |
| 1959 | Charlie Neal | 10 |
| 1936 | Jake Powell | 10 |
| 1936 | Red Rolfe | 10 |
| 1923 | Aaron Ward | 10 |
| 1911 | Home Run Baker | 9 |
| 1953 | Yogi Berra | 9 |
| 1992 | Pat Borders | 9 |
| 1980 | Larry Bowa | 9 |
| 1980 | George Brett | 9 |
| 1917 | Eddie Collins | 9 |
| 1936 | Joe DiMaggio | 9 |
| 1996 | Cecil Fielder | 9 |

| Year | Player | H |
|------|--------|---|
| 1959 | Nellie Fox | 9 |
| 1977 | Steve Garvey | 9 |
| 1935 | Charlie Gehringer | 9 |
| 1995 | Marquis Grissom | 9 |
| 1959 | Gil Hodges | 9 |
| 1977 | Reggie Jackson | 9 |
| 1978 | Reggie Jackson | 9 |
| 1959 | Ted Kluszewski | 9 |
| 1980 | Hal McRae | 9 |

## Doubles 6-Game World Series

| Year | Player | 2B |
|------|--------|----|
| 1930 | Chick Hafey | 5 |
| 1911 | Jack Barry | 4 |
| 1948 | Lou Boudreau | 4 |
| 1906 | Frank Isbell | 4 |
| Many at 3 | | |

## Triples 6-Game World Series

| Year | Player | 3B |
|------|--------|----|
| 1953 | Billy Martin | 2 |
| 1923 | Bob Meusel | 2 |
| 1993 | Paul Molitor | 2 |
| 1906 | George Rohe | 2 |
| 1993 | Devon White | 2 |
| Many at 1 | | |

## Home Runs 6-Game World Series

| Year | Player | HR |
|------|--------|----|
| 1977 | Reggie Jackson | 5 |
| 1980 | Willie Aikens | 4 |
| 1993 | Lenny Dykstra | 4 |
| 1995 | Ryan Klesko | 3 |
| 1959 | Ted Kluszewski | 3 |
| 1978 | Davey Lopes | 3 |
| 1980 | Amos Otis | 3 |
| 1923 | Babe Ruth | 3 |
| 1977 | Reggie Smith | 3 |
| Many at 2 | | |

# SINGLE SEASON WORLD SERIES

## Total Bases 6-Game World Series

| Year | Player | TB |
|------|--------|----|
| 1977 | Reggie Jackson | 25 |
| 1993 | Paul Molitor | 24 |
| 1953 | Billy Martin | 23 |
| 1980 | Willie Aikens | 22 |
| 1980 | Amos Otis | 22 |
| 1993 | Lenny Dykstra | 21 |
| 1959 | Ted Kluszewski | 19 |
| 1923 | Babe Ruth | 19 |
| 1959 | Charlie Neal | 18 |
| 1911 | Home Run Baker | 17 |
| 1953 | Jim Gilliam | 17 |
| 1978 | Davey Lopes | 17 |
| 1993 | Devon White | 17 |
| 1993 | Roberto Alomar | 16 |
| 1980 | George Brett | 16 |
| 1951 | Al Dark | 16 |
| 1996 | Marquis Grissom | 16 |
| 1981 | Pedro Guerrero | 16 |
| 1978 | Reggie Jackson | 16 |
| 1936 | George Selkirk | 16 |
| 1930 | Al Simmons | 16 |
| 1977 | Reggie Smith | 16 |

## Runs Batted In 6-Game World Series

| Year | Player | RBI |
|------|--------|-----|
| 1959 | Ted Kluszewski | 10 |
| 1993 | Tony Fernandez | 9 |
| 1980 | Willie Aikens | 8 |
| 1993 | Joe Carter | 8 |
| 1993 | Lenny Dykstra | 8 |
| 1977 | Reggie Jackson | 8 |
| 1978 | Reggie Jackson | 8 |
| 1953 | Billy Martin | 8 |
| 1923 | Bob Meusel | 8 |
| 1993 | Paul Molitor | 8 |
| 1978 | Bucky Dent | 7 |
| 1993 | Jim Eisenreich | 7 |
| 1936 | Lou Gehrig | 7 |
| 1981 | Pedro Guerrero | 7 |
| 1936 | Tony Lazzeri | 7 |
| 1978 | Davey Lopes | 7 |
| 1953 | Mickey Mantle | 7 |
| 1951 | Gil McDougald | 7 |
| 1978 | Thurman Munson | 7 |
| 1980 | Amos Otis | 7 |
| 1980 | Mike Schmidt | 7 |
| 1981 | Bob Watson | 7 |
| 1993 | Devon White | 7 |

## Stolen Bases 6-Game World Series

| Year | Player | SB |
|------|--------|----|
| 1995 | Kenny Lofton | 6 |
| 1992 | Otis Nixon | 5 |
| 1992 | Deion Sanders | 5 |
| 1993 | Roberto Alomar | 4 |
| 1993 | Lenny Dykstra | 4 |
| 1981 | Davey Lopes | 4 |
| 1992 | Roberto Alomar | 3 |
| 1980 | Larry Bowa | 3 |
| 1917 | Eddie Collins | 3 |
| 1993 | Mariano Duncan | 3 |
| 1995 | Marquis Grissom | 3 |
| 1906 | Joe Tinker | 3 |

Many at 2

## Earned Run 6-Game World Series
[minimum 12 innings]

| Year | Player | ERA |
|------|--------|-----|
| 1917 | Rube Benton | 0.00 |
| 1951 | Ed Lopat | 0.50 |
| 1935 | Lon Warneke | 0.54 |
| 1996 | John Smoltz | 0.64 |
| 1981 | Tommy John | 0.69 |
| 1959 | Larry Sherry | 0.71 |
| 1930 | George Earnshaw | 0.72 |
| 1906 | Nick Altrock | 1.00 |
| 1918 | Carl Mays | 1.00 |
| 1918 | Hippo Vaughn | 1.00 |
| 1911 | Chief Bender | 1.04 |
| 1918 | Babe Ruth | 1.06 |
| 1948 | Johnny Sain | 1.06 |
| 1923 | Joe Bush | 1.08 |
| 1944 | Mort Cooper | 1.13 |
| 1918 | Lefty Tyler | 1.17 |
| 1906 | Ed Walsh | 1.20 |
| 1995 | Tom Glavine | 1.29 |
| 1911 | Jack Coombs | 1.35 |
| 1930 | Lefty Grove | 1.42 |

## Innings Pitched 6-Game World Series

| Year | Player | IP |
|------|--------|-----|
| 1917 | Red Faber | 27.0 |
| 1911 | Christy Mathewson | 27.0 |
| 1918 | Hippo Vaughn | 27.0 |
| 1911 | Chief Bender | 26.0 |
| 1930 | George Earnshaw | 25.0 |
| 1917 | Eddie Cicotte | 23.0 |
| 1918 | Lefty Tyler | 23.0 |
| 1935 | Schoolboy Rowe | 21.0 |

# SINGLE SEASON WORLD SERIES

## Innings Pitched 6-Game World Series cont.

| Year | Player | IP |
|---|---|---|
| 1911 | Jack Coombs | 20.0 |
| 1906 | Three Finger Brown | 19.2 |
| 1930 | Lefty Grove | 19.0 |
| 1906 | Nick Altrock | 18.0 |
| 1935 | Tommy Bridges | 18.0 |
| 1944 | Denny Galehouse | 18.0 |
| 1951 | Ed Lopat | 18.0 |
| 1918 | Carl Mays | 18.0 |
| 1977 | Mike Torrez | 18.0 |
| 1923 | Herb Pennock | 17.1 |
| 1992 | Tom Glavine | 17.0 |
| 1930 | Burleigh Grimes | 17.0 |
| 1918 | Babe Ruth | 17.0 |
| 1948 | Johnny Sain | 17.0 |

## Wins 6-Game World Series

| Year | Player | W |
|---|---|---|
| 1917 | Red Faber | 3 |
| 1911 | Chief Bender | 2 |
| 1935 | Tommy Bridges | 2 |
| 1980 | Steve Carlton | 2 |
| 1930 | George Earnshaw | 2 |
| 1995 | Tom Glavine | 2 |
| 1936 | Lefty Gomez | 2 |
| 1930 | Lefty Grove | 2 |
| 1992 | Jimmy Key | 2 |
| 1948 | Bob Lemon | 2 |
| 1951 | Ed Lopat | 2 |
| 1918 | Carl Mays | 2 |
| 1923 | Herb Pennock | 2 |
| 1918 | Babe Ruth | 2 |
| 1959 | Larry Sherry | 2 |
| 1977 | Mike Torrez | 2 |
| 1906 | Ed Walsh | 2 |
| 1992 | Duane Ward | 2 |
| 1935 | Lon Warneke | 2 |
| Many at 1 | | |

## Saves 6-Game World Series

| Year | Player | Sv |
|---|---|---|
| 1996 | John Wetteland | 4 |
| 1981 | Goose Gossage | 2 |
| 1992 | Tom Henke | 2 |
| 1980 | Tug McGraw | 2 |
| 1959 | Larry Sherry | 2 |
| 1993 | Duane Ward | 2 |
| 1995 | Mark Wohlers | 2 |
| Many at 1 | | |

## Batting 7-Game World Series
[minimum 21 plate appearances]

| Year | Player | Avg |
|---|---|---|
| 1979 | Phil Garner | .500 |
| 1947 | Johnny Lindell | .500 |
| 1931 | Pepper Martin | .500 |
| 1964 | Tim McCarver | .478 |
| 1968 | Lou Brock | .464 |
| 1925 | Max Carey | .458 |
| 1925 | Joe Harris | .440 |
| 1972 | Tony Perez | .435 |
| 1986 | Marty Barrett | .433 |
| 1945 | Phil Cavarretta | .423 |
| 1973 | Rusty Staub | .423 |
| 1955 | Yogi Berra | .417 |
| 1991 | Mark Lemke | .417 |
| 1926 | Tommy Thevenow | .417 |
| 1967 | Lou Brock | .414 |
| 1971 | Roberto Clemente | .414 |
| 1982 | Robin Yount | .414 |
| 1958 | Bill Bruton | .412 |
| 1946 | Harry Walker | .412 |
| 1946 | Bobby Doerr | .409 |
| 1987 | Tony Pena | .409 |

## Runs 7-Game World Series

| Year | Player | R |
|---|---|---|
| 1967 | Lou Brock | 8 |
| 1947 | Bill Johnson | 8 |
| 1909 | Tommy Leach | 8 |
| 1960 | Mickey Mantle | 8 |
| 1964 | Mickey Mantle | 8 |
| 1934 | Pepper Martin | 8 |
| 1960 | Bobby Richardson | 8 |
| 1997 | Jim Thome | 8 |
| 1997 | Matt Williams | 8 |
| 1945 | Phil Cavarretta | 7 |
| 1909 | Fred Clarke | 7 |
| 1945 | Doc Cramer | 7 |
| 1997 | Darren Daulton | 7 |
| 1965 | Ron Fairly | 7 |
| 1945 | Hank Greenberg | 7 |
| 1924 | George Kelly | 7 |
| 1925 | Eddie Moore | 7 |
| 1960 | Bill Skowron | 7 |
| 1979 | Willie Stargell | 7 |
| 1975 | Carl Yastrzemski | 7 |

# SINGLE SEASON WORLD SERIES

## Hits 7-Game World Series

| Year | Player | H |
|------|--------|---|
| 1986 | Marty Barrett | 13 |
| 1968 | Lou Brock | 13 |
| 1964 | Bobby Richardson | 13 |
| 1967 | Lou Brock | 12 |
| 1971 | Roberto Clemente | 12 |
| 1979 | Phil Garner | 12 |
| 1931 | Pepper Martin | 12 |
| 1925 | Sam Rice | 12 |
| 1960 | Bill Skowron | 12 |
| 1979 | Willie Stargell | 12 |
| 1982 | Robin Yount | 12 |

Many at 11

## Doubles 7-Game World Series

| Year | Player | 2B |
|------|--------|----|
| 1934 | Pete Fox | 6 |
| 1925 | Max Carey | 4 |
| 1909 | Jim Delahanty | 4 |
| 1924 | Frankie Frisch | 4 |
| 1982 | Jim Gantner | 4 |
| 1979 | Phil Garner | 4 |
| 1982 | Dane Iorg | 4 |
| 1909 | Tommy Leach | 4 |
| 1931 | Pepper Martin | 4 |
| 1946 | Stan Musial | 4 |
| 1997 | Bip Roberts | 4 |
| 1982 | Lonnie Smith | 4 |
| 1979 | Willie Stargell | 4 |
| 1940 | Bill Werber | 4 |

Many at 3

## Triples 7-Game World Series

| Year | Player | 3B |
|------|--------|----|
| 1947 | Bill Johnson | 3 |
| 1991 | Mark Lemke | 3 |
| 1991 | Dan Gladden | 2 |
| 1968 | Tim McCarver | 2 |
| 1960 | Bobby Richardson | 2 |
| 1925 | Pie Traynor | 2 |

Many at 1

## Home Runs 7-Game World Series

| Year | Player | HR |
|------|--------|----|
| 1958 | Hank Bauer | 4 |
| 1926 | Babe Ruth | 4 |
| 1952 | Duke Snider | 4 |
| 1955 | Duke Snider | 4 |
| 1972 | Gene Tenace | 4 |
| 1957 | Hank Aaron | 3 |
| 1997 | Moises Alou | 3 |
| 1956 | Yogi Berra | 3 |
| 1924 | Goose Goslin | 3 |
| 1925 | Goose Goslin | 3 |
| 1925 | Joe Harris | 3 |
| 1956 | Mickey Mantle | 3 |
| 1960 | Mickey Mantle | 3 |
| 1964 | Mickey Mantle | 3 |
| 1952 | Johnny Mize | 3 |
| 1975 | Tony Perez | 3 |
| 1991 | Lonnie Smith | 3 |
| 1979 | Willie Stargell | 3 |
| 1967 | Carl Yastrzemski | 3 |

Many at 2

## Total Bases 7-Game World Series

| Year | Player | TB |
|------|--------|----|
| 1979 | Willie Stargell | 25 |
| 1968 | Lou Brock | 24 |
| 1952 | Duke Snider | 24 |
| 1957 | Hank Aaron | 22 |
| 1958 | Hank Bauer | 22 |
| 1971 | Roberto Clemente | 22 |
| 1924 | Goose Goslin | 22 |
| 1925 | Joe Harris | 22 |
| 1955 | Duke Snider | 21 |
| 1972 | Gene Tenace | 21 |
| 1967 | Carl Yastrzemski | 21 |
| 1997 | Moises Alou | 20 |
| 1956 | Yogi Berra | 20 |
| 1965 | Ron Fairly | 20 |
| 1960 | Mickey Mantle | 20 |
| 1991 | Terry Pendleton | 20 |
| 1960 | Bobby Richardson | 20 |
| 1960 | Bill Skowron | 20 |
| 1967 | Lou Brock | 19 |
| 1924 | Bucky Harris | 19 |
| 1986 | Dave Henderson | 19 |
| 1968 | Al Kaline | 19 |
| 1952 | Mickey Mantle | 19 |
| 1964 | Mickey Mantle | 19 |
| 1931 | Pepper Martin | 19 |

241

# SINGLE SEASON WORLD SERIES

## Runs Batted In 7-Game World Series

| Year | Player | RBI |
|------|--------|-----|
| 1960 | Bobby Richardson | 12 |
| 1960 | Mickey Mantle | 11 |
| 1997 | Sandy Alomar Jr. | 10 |
| 1956 | Yogi Berra | 10 |
| 1997 | Moises Alou | 9 |
| 1986 | Gary Carter | 9 |
| 1986 | Dwight Evans | 9 |
| 1972 | Gene Tenace | 9 |
| 1958 | Hank Bauer | 8 |
| 1960 | Yogi Berra | 8 |
| 1982 | Keith Hernandez | 8 |
| 1956 | Gil Hodges | 8 |
| 1968 | Al Kaline | 8 |
| 1964 | Mickey Mantle | 8 |
| 1945 | Bill Nicholson | 8 |
| 1968 | Jim Northrup | 8 |
| 1931 | Al Simmons | 8 |
| 1952 | Duke Snider | 8 |
| 1957 | Hank Aaron | 7 |
| 2001 | Danny Bautista | 7 |
| 1909 | Fred Clarke | 7 |
| 1987 | Dan Gladden | 7 |
| 1924 | Goose Goslin | 7 |
| 1934 | Hank Greenberg | 7 |
| 1945 | Hank Greenberg | 7 |
| 1924 | Bucky Harris | 7 |
| 1947 | Johnny Lindell | 7 |
| 1967 | Roger Maris | 7 |
| 1975 | Tony Perez | 7 |
| 1958 | Bill Skowron | 7 |
| 1955 | Duke Snider | 7 |
| 1979 | Willie Stargell | 7 |
| 1964 | Tom Tresh | 7 |
| 2001 | Matt Williams | 7 |

## Stolen Bases 7-Game World Series

| Year | Player | SB |
|------|--------|-----|
| 1967 | Lou Brock | 7 |
| 1968 | Lou Brock | 7 |
| 1987 | Vince Coleman | 6 |
| 1909 | Honus Wagner | 6 |
| 1931 | Pepper Martin | 5 |
| 1972 | Bobby Tolan | 5 |
| 1997 | Omar Vizquel | 5 |
| 1991 | Chuck Knoblauch | 4 |
| 1973 | Bert Campaneris | 3 |
| 1925 | Max Carey | 3 |
| 1909 | Fred Clarke | 3 |
| 1975 | Dave Concepcion | 3 |
| 1965 | Willie Davis | 3 |
| 1968 | Curt Flood | 3 |
| 1909 | Dots Miller | 3 |
| 1947 | Pee Wee Reese | 3 |
| 1986 | Darryl Strawberry | 3 |
| 1965 | Maury Wills | 3 |
| 1986 | Mookie Wilson | 3 |

Many at 2

## Earned Run 7-Game World Series

[minimum 14 innings]

| Year | Player | ERA |
|------|--------|-----|
| 1960 | Whitey Ford | 0.00 |
| 1920 | Duster Mails | 0.00 |
| 1965 | Sandy Koufax | 0.38 |
| 1946 | Harry Brecheen | 0.45 |
| 1931 | Wild Bill Hallahan | 0.49 |
| 1985 | Bret Saberhagen | 0.50 |
| 1920 | Sherry Smith | 0.53 |
| 1965 | Claude Osteen | 0.64 |
| 1957 | Lew Burdette | 0.67 |
| 1920 | Stan Coveleski | 0.67 |
| 1971 | Steve Blass | 1.00 |
| 1934 | Paul Dean | 1.00 |
| 1967 | Bob Gibson | 1.00 |
| 1955 | Johnny Podres | 1.00 |
| 2001 | Randy Johnson | 1.04 |
| 1926 | Jesse Haines | 1.08 |
| 1957 | Whitey Ford | 1.13 |
| 1991 | Jack Morris | 1.17 |
| 1926 | Waite Hoyt | 1.20 |
| 1926 | Herb Pennock | 1.23 |
| 1991 | John Smoltz | 1.26 |

# SINGLE SEASON WORLD SERIES

## Innings Pitched 7-Game World Series

| Year | Player | IP |
|------|--------|-----|
| 1909 | George Mullin | 32.0 |
| 1958 | Warren Spahn | 28.2 |
| 1909 | Babe Adams | 27.0 |
| 1957 | Lew Burdette | 27.0 |
| 1920 | Stan Coveleski | 27.0 |
| 1964 | Bob Gibson | 27.0 |
| 1967 | Bob Gibson | 27.0 |
| 1968 | Bob Gibson | 27.0 |
| 1968 | Mickey Lolich | 27.0 |
| 1934 | Dizzy Dean | 26.0 |
| 1931 | Lefty Grove | 26.0 |
| 1925 | Walter Johnson | 26.0 |
| 1940 | Bobo Newsom | 26.0 |
| 1962 | Ralph Terry | 25.0 |
| 1975 | Luis Tiant | 25.0 |
| 1931 | George Earnshaw | 24.0 |
| 1924 | Walter Johnson | 24.0 |
| 1965 | Sandy Koufax | 24.0 |
| 1967 | Jim Lonborg | 24.0 |
| 1962 | Jack Sanford | 23.1 |

## Saves 7-Game World Series

| Year | Player | Sv |
|------|--------|-----|
| 1960 | Roy Face | 3 |
| 1979 | Kent Tekulve | 3 |
| 1991 | Rick Aguilera | 2 |
| 1972 | Rollie Fingers | 2 |
| 1973 | Rollie Fingers | 2 |
| 1973 | Darold Knowles | 2 |
| 1982 | Bob McClure | 2 |
| 1997 | Robb Nen | 2 |
| 1986 | Jesse Orosco | 2 |
| 1982 | Bruce Sutter | 2 |
| 1987 | Todd Worrell | 2 |
| Many at 1 | | |

## Wins 7-Game World Series

| Year | Player | W |
|------|--------|-----|
| 1909 | Babe Adams | 3 |
| 1946 | Harry Brecheen | 3 |
| 1957 | Lew Burdette | 3 |
| 1920 | Stan Coveleski | 3 |
| 1967 | Bob Gibson | 3 |
| 2001 | Randy Johnson | 3 |
| 1968 | Mickey Lolich | 3 |
| Many at 2 | | |

## Strikeouts 7-Game World Series

| Year | Player | k |
|------|--------|-----|
| 1968 | Bob Gibson | 35 |
| 1964 | Bob Gibson | 31 |
| 1965 | Sandy Koufax | 29 |
| 1967 | Bob Gibson | 26 |
| 2001 | Curt Schilling | 26 |
| 1945 | Hal Newhouser | 22 |
| 1968 | Mickey Lolich | 21 |
| 1931 | George Earnshaw | 20 |
| 1924 | Walter Johnson | 20 |
| 1909 | George Mullin | 20 |
| 2001 | Roger Clemens | 19 |
| 2001 | Randy Johnson | 19 |
| 1962 | Jack Sanford | 19 |
| 1952 | Vic Raschi | 18 |
| 1952 | Allie Reynolds | 18 |
| 1973 | Tom Seaver | 18 |
| 1958 | Warren Spahn | 18 |
| 1926 | Pete Alexander | 17 |
| 1934 | Dizzy Dean | 17 |
| 1986 | Bruce Hurst | 17 |
| 1940 | Bobo Newsom | 17 |

# SINGLE SEASON/SINGLE GAME

## Most Consecutive Games Played

| | |
|---|---|
| Cal Ripken, Jr. | 2,632 |
| Lou Gehrig | 2,130 |
| Everett Scott | 1,307 |
| Steve Garvey | 1,207 |
| Billy Williams | 1,117 |
| Joe Sewell | 1,103 |
| Stan Musial | 895 |
| Eddie Yost | 829 |
| Gus Suhr | 822 |
| Nellie Fox | 798 |

## Most Home Runs Leading Off Game - Career

| | |
|---|---|
| Rickey Henderson | 78 |

## Most Grand Slams - Career

| | |
|---|---|
| Lou Gehrig | 23 |

## Most Consecutive Wins - Pitchers

| | | |
|---|---|---|
| Carl Hubbell, NYG | 1936-37 | 24 |

## Longest Hitting Streaks

| | | |
|---|---|---|
| Joe DiMaggio, NYY | 1941 | 56 |
| Willie Keeler, BalN | 1897 | 44 |
| Pete Rose, Cin | 1978 | 44 |
| Bill Dahlen, ChC | 1894 | 42 |
| George Sisler, StLA | 1922 | 41 |
| Ty Cobb, Det | 1911 | 40 |
| Paul Molitor, MilA | 1987 | 39 |
| Tommy Holmes, BosN | 1945 | 37 |
| Billy Hamilton, PhiN | 1894 | 36 |
| Fred Clarke, Lou | 1895 | 35 |
| Ty Cobb, Det | 1917 | 35 |

## Most Consecutive Hits

| | | |
|---|---|---|
| Pinky Higgins, BosA | 1938 | 12 |
| Walt Dropo, Det | 1952 | 12 |
| Tris Speaker, Cle | 1920 | 11 |
| Johnny Pesky, BosA | 1946 | 11 |
| 14 with 10 | | |

## Most Consecutive Games With a Home Run

| | | |
|---|---|---|
| Dale Long, Pit | 1956 | 8 |
| Don Mattingly, NYY | 1987 | 8 |
| Ken Griffey, Jr., Sea | 1993 | 8 |

## Most Grand Slams

| | | |
|---|---|---|
| Don Mattingly, NYY | 1987 | 6 |

## Single Game Regular Season Records

### Most Hits (9 Inning Game)

| | | |
|---|---|---|
| Wilbert Robinson, BalN | 1892 | 7 |
| Rennie Stennet, Pit | 1975 | 7 |

### Most Runs

| | | |
|---|---|---|
| Guy Hecker, Lou | 1886 | 7 |

### Most Doubles

| | |
|---|---|
| Many players with | 4 |

### Most Triples

| | | |
|---|---|---|
| George Strief, Phi | 1885 | 4 |
| Bill Joyce, NYG | 1897 | 4 |

### Most Homers

| | | |
|---|---|---|
| Bobby Lowe, BosN | 1894 | 4 |
| Ed Delahanty, PhiN | 1896 | 4 |
| Lou Gehrig, NYY | 1932 | 4 |
| Chuck Klein, PhiN | 1936 | 4 (10 inn) |
| Pat Seerey, CWS | 1948 | 4 (11 inn) |
| Gil Hodges, Brk | 1950 | 4 |
| Joe Adcock, Mil | 1954 | 4 |
| Rocky Colavito, Cle | 1959 | 4 |
| Willie Mays, SF | 1961 | 4 |
| Mike Schmidt, Phi | 1976 | 4 (10 inn) |
| Bob Horner, Atl | 1986 | 4 |
| Mark Whiten, StL | 1993 | 4 |

### Most Grand Slams

| | | |
|---|---|---|
| Tony Lazzeri, NYY | 1936 | 2 |
| Jim Tabor, BosA | 1939 | 2 |
| Rudy York, BosA | 1946 | 2 |
| Jim Gentile, Bal | 1961 | 2 |
| Tony Cloninger, Atl | 1966 | 2 |
| Jim Northrup, Det | 1968 | 2 |
| Frank Robinson, Bal | 1970 | 2 |
| Robin Ventura, CWS | 1995 | 2 |
| Chris Hoiles, Bal | 1998 | 2 |
| Fernando Tatis, StL | 1999 | 2 |
| Nomar Garciaparra | 1999 | 2 |

### Most Total Bases

| | | |
|---|---|---|
| Joe Adcock, Mil | 1954 | 18 |

### Most RBIs

| | | |
|---|---|---|
| Jim Bottomley, StLN | 1924 | 12 |
| Mark Whiten, StL | 1993 | 12 |

# SINGLE GAME

## Most Stolen Bases (Since 1900)

| Player | Year | No. |
|---|---|---|
| Eddie Collins, PhiA | 1912 | 6 |
| Otis Nixon, Atl | 1991 | 6 |
| Eric Young, Col | 1996 | 6 |

## Most Runs Allowed

| Player | Year | No. |
|---|---|---|
| Dave Rowe, Cle | 1882 | 35 |

## Most Hits Allowed

| Player | Year | No. |
|---|---|---|
| John Wadsworth, Lou | 1894 | 26 |

## Most Strikeouts (9 inning game)

| Player | Year | No. |
|---|---|---|
| Roger Clemens, Bos | 1986 | 20 |
| Roger Clemens, Bos | 1996 | 20 |
| Kerry Wood, ChC | 1998 | 20 |

## Most Walks (9 inning game)

| Player | Year | No. |
|---|---|---|
| Bill George, NYG | 1887 | 16 |
| George Van Haltren, ChC | 1887 | 16 |
| Henry Gruber, Cle | 1890 | 16 |
| Bruno Haas, Phi | 1915 | 16 |

## Single Game World Series Records

### Most Grand Slams

| | | |
|---|---|---|
| 17 players | | 1 |

### Most Hits

| Player | Date | No. |
|---|---|---|
| Paul Molitor, Mil | 10/12/82 | 5 |

### Most Runs

| Player | Date | No. |
|---|---|---|
| Babe Ruth, NYY | 10/06/26 | 4 |
| Earle Combs, NYY | 10/02/32 | 4 |
| Frank Crosetti, NYY | 10/02/36 | 4 |
| Enos Slaughter, StLN | 10/10/46 | 4 |
| Reggie Jackson, NYY | 10/18/77 | 4 |
| Kirby Puckett, Min | 10/24/87 | 4 |
| Carney Lansford, Oak | 10/27/89 | 4 |
| Lenny Dykstra, Phi | 10/20/93 | 4 |

### Most Doubles

| Player | Date | No. |
|---|---|---|
| Frank Isbell, CWS | 10/13/06 | 4 |

# SINGLE GAME

## Single Game World Series Records cont.

### Most Triples

| Player | Date | No. |
|---|---|---|
| Tommy Leach, Pit | 10/01/03 | 2 |
| Patsy Dougherty, BosA | 10/07/03 | 2 |
| Dutch Ruether, Cin | 10/01/19 | 2 |
| Bobby Richardson, NYY | 10/12/60 | 2 |
| Tommy Davis, LA | 10/03/63 | 2 |
| Mark Lemke, Atl | 10/24/91 | 2 |

### Most Home runs

| Player | Date | No. |
|---|---|---|
| Babe Ruth,NYY | 10/06/26 | 3 |
| Babe Ruth,NYY | 10/09/28 | 3 |
| Reggie Jackson,NYY | 10/18/77 | 3 |

### Most Total Bases

| Player | Date | No. |
|---|---|---|
| Babe Ruth, NYY | 10/06/26 | 12 |
| Babe Ruth, NYY | 10/09/28 | 12 |
| Reggie Jackson,NYY | 10/18/77 | 12 |

### Most RBIs

| Player | Date | No. |
|---|---|---|
| Bobby Richardson, NYY | 10/08/60 | 6 |

### Most Stolen Bases

| Player | Date | No. |
|---|---|---|
| Honus Wagner, Pit | 10/11/09 | 3 |
| Willie Davis, LA | 10/11/65 | 3 |
| Lou Brock, StL | 10/12/67 | 3 |
| Lou Brock, StL | 10/05/68 | 3 |

### Most Runs Allowed

| Player | Date | No. |
|---|---|---|
| Bill Kennedy, Pit | 10/07/03 | 10 |

### Most Hits Allowed

| Player | Date | No. |
|---|---|---|
| Walter Johnson, Was | 10/15/25 | 15 |

### Most Strikeouts

| Player | Date | No. |
|---|---|---|
| Bob Gibson, StL | 10/02/68 | 17 |

### Most Walks

| Player | Date | No. |
|---|---|---|
| Bill Bevans, NYY | 10/03/47 | 10 |

# SINGLE SEASON

## Joe DiMaggio's 56 Game Hit Streak-1941

| No. | Date | Pitcher |
|-----|------|---------|
| 1 | 05-15-1941 | Eddie Smith |
| 2 | 05-16-1941 | Thornton Lee |
| 3 | 05-17-1941 | Johnny Rigney |
| 4 | 05-18-1941 | Bob Harris |
| 5 | 05-19-1941 | Denny Galehouse |
| 6 | 05-20-1941 | Elden Auker |
| 7 | 05-21-1941 | Schoolboy Rowe |
| 8 | 05-22-1941 | Archie McKain |
| 9 | 05-23-1941 | Dick Newsome |
| 10 | 05-24-1941 | Earl Johnson |
| 11 | 05-25-1941 | Lefty Grove |
| 12 | 05-27-1941 | Ken Chase |
| 13 | 05-28-1941 | Sid Hudson |
| 14 | 05-29-1941 | Steve Sundra |
| 15 | 05-30-1941 | Earl Johnson |
| 16 | 05-30-1941 | Mickey Harris |
| 17 | 06-01-1941 | Al Milnar |
| 18 | 06-01-1941 | Mel Harder |
| 19 | 06-02-1941 | Bob Feller |
| 20 | 06-03-1941 | Dizzy Trout |
| 21 | 06-05-1941 | Hal Newhouser |
| 22 | 06-07-1941 | Bob Muncrief |
| 23 | 06-08-1941 | Elden Auker |
| 24 | 06-08-1941 | George Caster |
| 25 | 06-10-1941 | Johnny Rigney |
| 26 | 06-12-1941 | Thornton Lee |
| 27 | 06-14-1941 | Bob Feller |
| 28 | 06-15-1941 | Jim Bagby |
| 29 | 06-16-1941 | Al Milnar |
| 30 | 06-17-1941 | Johnny Rigney |
| 31 | 06-18-1941 | Thornton Lee |
| 32 | 06-19-1941 | Eddie Smith |
| 33 | 06-20-1941 | Bobo Newsom |
| 34 | 06-21-1941 | Dizzy Trout |
| 35 | 06-22-1941 | Hal Newhouser |
| 36 | 06-24-1941 | Bob Muncrief |
| 37 | 06-25-1941 | Denny Galehouse |
| 38 | 06-26-1941 | Elden Auker |
| 39 | 06-27-1941 | Chubby Dean |
| 40 | 06-28-1941 | Johnny Babich |
| 41 | 06-29-1941 | Dutch Leonard |
| 42 | 06-29-1941 | Red Anderson |
| 43 | 07-01-1941 | Mickey Harris |
| 44 | 07-01-1941 | Jack Wilson |
| 45 | 07-02-1941 | Dick Newsome |
| 46 | 07-05-1941 | Phil Marchildon |
| 47 | 07-06-1941 | Johnny Babich |
| 48 | 07-06-1941 | Jack Knott |
| 49 | 07-10-1941 | Johnny Niggeling |
| 50 | 07-11-1941 | Bob Harris |
| 51 | 07-12-1941 | Elden Auker |
| 52 | 07-13-1941 | Ted Lyons |
| 53 | 07-13-1941 | Thornton Lee |
| 54 | 07-14-1941 | Johnny Rigney |
| 55 | 07-15-1941 | Eddie Smith |
| 56 | 07-16-1941 | Al Milnar |

# SINGLE SEASON

## Rickey Henderson's
## 130 Stolen Bases -1982

| No. | Date | Pitcher | Base | Inning |
|-----|------|---------|------|--------|
| 1 | 04-08-82 | Mike Witt | 2nd | 1st |
| 2 | 04-08-82 | Luis Sanchez | 2nd | 14th |
| 3 | 04-09-82 | Gaylord Perry | 2nd | 7th |
| 4 | 04-11-82 | Floyd Bannister | 2nd | 5th |
| 5 | 04-11-82 | Ed VandeBerg | 2nd | 12th |
| 6 | 04-13-82 | Terry Felton | 2nd | 8th |
| 7 | 04-14-82 | Brad Havens | 2nd | 1st |
| 8 | 04-14-82 | Terry Felton | 3rd | 4th |
| 9 | 04-15-82 | Al Williams | 2nd | 4th |
| 10 | 04-16-82 | Floyd Bannister | 2nd | 1st |
| 11 | 04-17-82 | Mike Moore | 2nd | 2nd |
| 12 | 04-17-82 | Larry Andersen | 2nd | 4th |
| 13 | 04-18-82 | Ed Nunez | 2nd | 6th |
| 14 | 04-20-82 | Al Williams | 2nd | 5th |
| 15 | 04-21-82 | Darrell Jackson | 3rd | 1st |
| 16 | 04-23-82 | Ken Forsch | 3rd | 1st |
| 17 | 04-23-82 | Ken Forsch | 2nd | 3rd |
| 18 | 04-28-82 | Mike Flanagan | 3rd | 2nd |
| 19 | 04-28-82 | Scott McGregor | 3rd | 3rd |
| 20 | 04-29-82 | Dennis Martinez | 2nd | 1st |
| 21 | 04-29-82 | Dennis Martinez | 2nd | 2nd |
| 22 | 04-30-82 | John Denny | 2nd | 5th |
| 23 | 05-01-82 | Ed Whitson | 2nd | 9th |
| 24 | 05-01-82 | Ed Whitson | 3rd | 9th |
| 25 | 05-02-82 | Rick Waits | 2nd | 3rd |
| 26 | 05-03-82 | Tommy John | 2nd | 5th |
| 27 | 05-06-82 | John Denny | 2nd | 1st |
| 28 | 05-06-82 | John Denny | 3rd | 1st |
| 29 | 05-08-82 | Len Barker | 2nd | 1st |
| 30 | 05-08-82 | Len Barker | 3rd | 1st |
| 31 | 05-08-82 | Dan Spillner | 2nd | 9th |
| 32 | 05-09-82 | Lary Sorensen, | 2nd | 9th |
| 33 | 05-10-82 | Tim Stoddard | 3rd | 9th |
| 34 | 05-11-82 | Scott McGregor | 2nd | 1st |
| 35 | 05-11-82 | Scott McGregor | 2nd | 3rd |
| 36 | 05-15-82 | George Frazier | 3rd | 7th |
| 37 | 05-16-82 | George Frazier | 2nd | 5th |
| 38 | 05-16-82 | GeorgeFrazier | 3rd | 5th |
| 39 | 05-19-82 | Dan Petry | 2nd | 1st |
| 40 | 05-22-82 | Bob Ojeda | 2nd | 1st |
| 41 | 05-22-82 | Bob Ojeda | 3rd | 1st |
| 42 | 05-23-82 | Dennis Eckersley | 2nd | 3rd |
| 43 | 05-26-82 | Bob McClure | 2nd | 7th |
| 44 | 05-26-82 | Dwight Bernard | 2nd | 9th |
| 45 | 05-26-82 | Dwight Bernard | 3rd | 9th |
| 46 | 05-30-82 | Pat Underwood | 2nd | 1st |
| 47 | 05-30-82 | Pat Underwood | 3rd | 1st |
| 48 | 05-30-82 | Pat Underwood | 2nd | 3rd |
| 49 | 05-30-82 | Pat Underwood | 3rd | 3rd |
| 50 | 06-01-82 | Chuck Rainey | 2nd | 1st |
| 51 | 06-01-82 | Chuck Rainey | 2nd | 3rd |
| 52 | 06-04-82 | Moose Haas | 2nd | 3rd |
| 53 | 06-06-82 | Pete Vuckovich | 3rd | 1st |
| 54 | 06-06-82 | Pete Vuckovich | 2nd | 3rd |
| 55 | 06-08-82 | Dennis Lamp | 2nd | 5th |
| 56 | 06-08-82 | Jerry Koosman | 2nd | 7th |
| 57 | 06-08-82 | Jerry Koosman | 3rd | 7th |
| 58 | 06-09-82 | LaMarr Hoyt | 2nd | 3rd |
| 59 | 06-13-82 | Luis Leal | 2nd | 2nd |
| 60 | 06-13-82 | Roy Jackson | 2nd | 7th |
| 61 | 06-13-82 | Roy Jackson | 3rd | 7th |
| 62 | 06-13-82 | Dale Murray | 2nd | 8th |
| 63 | 06-14-82 | Jerry Garvin | 2nd | 7th |
| 64 | 06-15-82 | LaMarr Hoyt | 2nd | 1st |
| 65 | 06-18-82 | Jerry Garvin | 2nd | 1st |
| 66 | 06-18-82 | Roy Jackson | 2nd | 7th |
| 67 | 06-22-82 | Dan Quisenberry | 2nd | 8th |
| 68 | 06-22-82 | Dan Quisenberry | 3rd | 8th |
| 69 | 06-25-82 | Frank Tanana | 2nd | 1st |
| 70 | 06-25-82 | Frank Tanana | 2nd | 3rd |
| 71 | 06-26-82 | Steve Comer | 2nd | 8th |
| 72 | 06-29-82 | Don Hood | 3rd | 5th |
| 73 | 06-30-82 | Paul Splittorff | 2nd | 1st |
| 74 | 07-02-82 | Charlie Hough | 2nd | 3rd |
| 75 | 07-02-82 | Charlie Hough | 3rd | 9th |
| 76 | 07-03-82 | Rick Honeycutt | 2nd | 5th |
| 77 | 07-04-82 | Doc Medich | 2nd | 2nd |
| 78 | 07-06-82 | Len Barker | 2nd | 1st |
| 79 | 07-06-82 | Len Barker | 2nd | 5th |
| 80 | 07-08-82 | Doyle Alexander | 2nd | 1st |
| 81 | 07-08-82 | Doyle Alexander | 2nd | 1st |
| 82 | 07-09-82 | Scott McGregor | 3rd | 1st |
| 83 | 07-10-82 | Dennis Martinez | 3rd | 1st |
| 84 | 07-11-82 | Storm Davis | 2nd | 3rd |

## Rickey Henderson's 130 Stolen Bases -1982 cont.

| No. | Date | Pitcher | Base | Inning |
|-----|------|---------|------|--------|
| 85 | 07-15-82 | Mike Morgan | 2nd | 5th |
| 86 | 07-16-82 | Roger Erickson | 2nd | 1st |
| 87 | 07-19-82 | Lary Sorensen | 2nd | 3rd |
| 88 | 07-20-82 | Ed Whitson | 2nd | 7th |
| 89 | 07-20-82 | Ed Whitson | 3rd | 7th |
| 90 | 07-24-82 | Scott McGregor | 2nd | 6th |
| 91 | 07-24-82 | Scott McGregor | 3rd | 6th |
| 92 | 07-25-82 | Dennis Martinez | 2nd | 7th |
| 93 | 07-26-82 | Ken Forsch | 2nd | 1st |
| 94 | 07-26-82 | Andy Hassler | Home | 8th |
| 95 | 07-27-82 | Dave Goltz | 2nd | 9th |
| 96 | 07-29-82 | Brad Havens | 3rd | 1st |
| 97 | 07-30-82 | Al Williams | 2nd | 1st |
| 98 | 07-30-82 | Al Williams | 3rd | 1st |
| 99 | 07-30-82 | Ron Davis | 2nd | 8th |
| 100 | 08-02-82 | Mike Stanton | 2nd | 7th |
| 101 | 08-04-82 | Jim Beattie | 2nd | 1st |
| 102 | 08-04-82 | Rich Bordi | 2nd | 1st |
| 103 | 08-04-82 | Rich Bordi | 3rd | 1st |
| 104 | 08-06-82 | Frank Viola | 2nd | 6th |
| 105 | 08-08-82 | Brad Havens | 2nd | 3rd |
| 106 | 08-11-82 | Floyd Bannister | 2nd | 2nd |
| 107 | 08-11-82 | Floyd Bannister | 3rd | 5th |
| 108 | 08-14-82 | Steve Renko | 2nd | 5th |
| 109 | 08-15-82 | Ken Forsch | 2nd | 3rd |
| 110 | 08-17-82 | Moose Haas | 2nd | 1st |
| 111 | 08-19-82 | Jim Slaton | 2nd | 7th |
| 112 | 08-21-82 | Chuck Rainey | 2nd | 1st |
| 113 | 08-21-82 | Chuck Rainey | 2nd | 3rd |
| 114 | 08-21-82 | Luis Aponte | 2nd | 8th |
| 115 | 08-23-82 | Dan Petry | 2nd | 3rd |
| 116 | 08-24-82 | Jerry Ujdur | 2nd | 1st |
| 117 | 08-24-82 | Jerry Ujdur | 3rd | 1st |
| 118 | 08-26-82 | Mike Caldwell | 2nd | 1st |
| 119 | 08-27-82 | Doc Medich | 2nd | 3rd |
| 120 | 08-27-82 | Doc Medich | 2nd | 6th |
| 121 | 08-27-82 | Doc Medich | 2nd | 8th |
| 122 | 08-27-82 | Doc Medich | 3rd | 8th |
| 123 | 08-30-82 | Mark Clear | 3rd | 8th |
| 124 | 09-03-82 | Jerry Ujdur | 2nd | 1st |
| 125 | 09-25-82 | Dennis Leonard | 2nd | 4th |
| 126 | 09-28-82 | Jim Farr | 2nd | 6th |
| 127 | 10-01-82 | Bill Castro | 2nd | 3rd |
| 128 | 10-02-82 | Vida Blue | 2nd | 2nd |
| 129 | 10-02-82 | Vida Blue | 2nd | 4th |
| 130 | 10-02-82 | Vida Blue | 3rd | 4th |

# SINGLE SEASON

## Barry Bonds'
## 73 Home Runs–2001

| No. | Date | Pitcher | Length(ft) |
|---|---|---|---|
| 1 | 04-02-01 | Woody Williams | 420 |
| 2 | 04-12-01 | Adam Eaton | 417 |
| 3 | 04-13-01 | Jamey Wright | 440 |
| 4 | 04-14-01 | Jimmy Haynes | 410 |
| 5 | 04-15-01 | Dave Weathers | 390 |
| 6 | 04-17-01 | Terry Adams | 417 |
| 7 | 04-18-01 | Chan Ho Park | 420 |
| 8 | 04-20-01 | Jimmy Haynes | 410 |
| 9 | 04-24-01 | Jim Brower | 380 |
| 10 | 04-26-01 | Scott Sullivan | 430 |
| 11 | 04-29-01 | Manny Aybar | 370 |
| 12 | 05-02-01 | Todd Ritchie | 420 |
| 13 | 05-03-01 | Jimmy Anderson | 400 |
| 14 | 05-04-01 | Bruce Chen | 360 |
| 15 | 05-11-01 | Steve Trachsel | 410 |
| 16 | 05-17-01 | Chuck Smith. | 420 |
| 17 | 05-18-01 | Mike Remlinger | 391 |
| 18 | 05-19-01 | Odalis Perez | 416 |
| 19 | 05-19-01 | Jose Cabrera | 440 |
| 20 | 05-19-01 | Jason Marquis | 410 |
| 21 | 05-20-01 | John Burkett | 415 |
| 22 | 05-20-01 | Mike Remlinger | 436 |
| 23 | 05-21-01 | Curt Schilling | 430 |
| 24 | 05-22-01 | Russ Springer | 410 |
| 25 | 05-24-01 | John Thomson | 400 |
| 26 | 05-27-01 | Denny Neagle | 390 |
| 27 | 05-30-01 | Robert Ellis | 420 |
| 28 | 05-30-01 | Robert Ellis | 410 |
| 29 | 06-01-01 | Shawn Chacon | 420 |
| 30 | 06-04-01 | Bobby J. Jones | 410 |
| 31 | 06-05-01 | Wascar Serrano | 410 |
| 32 | 06-07-01 | Brian Lawrence | 450 |
| 33 | 06-12-01 | Pat Rapp | 320 |
| 34 | 06-14-01 | Lou Pote | 430 |
| 35 | 06-15-01 | Mark Mulder | 380 |

| No. | Date | Pitcher | Length(ft |
|---|---|---|---|
| 36 | 06-15-01 | Mark Mulder | 375 |
| 37 | 06-19-01 | Adam Eaton | 375 |
| 38 | 06-20-01 | Rodney Myers | 347 |
| 39 | 06-23-01 | Darryl Kile | 380 |
| 40 | 07-12-01 | Paul Abbott | 429 |
| 41 | 07-18-01 | Mike Hampton | 320 |
| 42 | 07-18-01 | Mike Hampton | 360 |
| 43 | 07-26-01 | Curt Schilling | 375 |
| 44 | 07-26-01 | Curt Schilling | 370 |
| 45 | 07-27-01 | Brian Anderson | 440 |
| 46 | 08-01-01 | Joe Beimel | 400 |
| 47 | 08-04-01 | Nelson Figueroa | 405 |
| 48 | 08-07-01 | Danny Graves | 430 |
| 49 | 08-09-01 | Scott Winchester | 350 |
| 50 | 08-11-01 | Joe Borowski | 396 |
| 51 | 08-14-01 | Ricky Bones | 410 |
| 52 | 08-16-01 | A.J. Burnett | 380 |
| 53 | 08-16-01 | Vic Darensbourg | 430 |
| 54 | 08-18-01 | Jason Marquis | 415 |
| 55 | 08-23-01 | Graeme Lloyd | 380 |
| 56 | 08-27-01 | Kevin Appier | 375 |
| 57 | 08-31-01 | John Thomson | 400 |
| 58 | 09-03-01 | Jason Jennings | 435 |
| 59 | 09-04-01 | Miguel Batista | 420 |
| 60 | 09-06-01 | Albie Lopez | 420 |
| 61 | 09-09-01 | Scott Elarton | 488 |
| 62 | 09-09-01 | Scott Elarton | 361 |
| 63 | 09-09-01 | Todd Belitz | 394 |
| 64 | 09-20-01 | Wade Miller | 410 |
| 65 | 09-23-01 | J Middlebrook | 411 |
| 66 | 09-23-01 | J Middlebrook | 365 |
| 67 | 09-24-01 | James Baldwin | 360 |
| 68 | 09-28-01 | J Middlebrook | 440 |
| 69 | 09-29-01 | Chuck McElroy | 435 |
| 70 | 10-04-01 | Wilfredo Rodriguez | 454 |
| 71 | 10-05-01 | Chan Ho Park | 442 |
| 72 | 10-05-01 | Chan Ho Park | 407 |
| 73 | 10-07-01 | Dennis Springer | 380 |

# PERFECT GAMES (since 1900)

| Pitcher | Game | Score | Date |
|---|---|---|---|
| David Cone | New York vs. Montreal | 6-0 | July 18,1999 |
| David Wells | New York vs.Minnesota | 4-0 | May 17,1998 |
| Kenny Rogers | Texas vs. California | 4-0 | July 28,1994 |
| Dennis Martinez | Montreal vs. Los Angeles | 2-0 | July 28,1991 |
| Tom Browning | Cincinnati vs. Los Angeles | 1-0 | Sept. 16,1988 |
| Mike Witt | California vs. Texas | 1-0 | Sept. 30,1984 |
| Len Barker | Cleveland vs. Toronto | 3-0 | May 15,1981 |
| Catfish Hunter | Oakland vs. Minnesota | 4-0 | May 8,1968 |
| Sandy Koufax | Los Angeles vs.Chicago | 1-0 | Sept. 9,1965 |
| Jim Bunning | Philadelphia vs. New York | 6-0 | June 21,1964 |
| *Don Larsen | New York (AL) vs.Brooklyn (NL) | 2-0 | Oct. 8,1956 |
| Charles Robertson | Chicago vs. Detroit | 2-0 | April 30,1922 |
| Addie Joss | Cleveland vs. Chicago | 1-0 | Oct. 2,1908 |
| Cy Young | Boston vs. Philadelphia | 3-0 | May 5,1904 |

* World Series

# HALL OF FAME

## Highest voting percentage

| Year | Player | Total Ballots | Votes Received | % Votes | Omitted Ballots |
|------|--------|---------------|----------------|---------|-----------------|
| 1992 | Tom Seaver | 430 | 425 | 98.8 | 5 |
| 1999 | Nolan Ryan | 497 | 491 | 98.79 | 6 |
| 1936 | Ty Cobb | 226 | 222 | 98.2 | 4 |
| 1999 | George Brett | 497 | 488 | 98.19 | 9 |
| 1982 | Hank Aaron | 415 | 406 | 97.8 | 9 |
| 1995 | Mike Schmidt | 460 | 444 | 96.5 | 16 |
| 1989 | Johnny Bench | 447 | 431 | 96.4 | 16 |
| 1994 | Steve Carlton | 455 | 436 | 95.8 | 19 |
| 1936 | Honus Wagner | 226 | 215 | 95.1 | 11 |
| 1936 | Babe Ruth | 226 | 215 | 95.1 | 11 |
| 1979 | Willie Mays | 432 | 409 | 94.7 | 23 |
| 1988 | Carl Yastrzemski | 447 | 423 | 94.6 | 24 |
| 1962 | Bob Feller | 160 | 150 | 93.8 | 10 |
| 1993 | Reggie Jackson | 423 | 396 | 93.6 | 27 |
| 1966 | Ted Williams | 302 | 282 | 93.4 | 20 |
| 1969 | Stan Musial | 340 | 317 | 93.2 | 23 |
| 1990 | Jim Palmer | 444 | 411 | 92.6 | 33 |
| 1983 | Brooks Robinson | 374 | 344 | 92.0 | 30 |
| 1936 | Christy Mathewson | 226 | 205 | 90.7 | 21 |
| 1991 | Rod Carew | 443 | 401 | 90.5 | 42 |
| 1982 | Frank Robinson | 415 | 370 | 89.2 | 45 |
| 1955 | Joe DiMaggio | 251 | 223 | 89.2 | 28 |
| 1980 | Al Kaline | 385 | 340 | 88.3 | 45 |
| 1974 | Mickey Mantle | 365 | 322 | 88.2 | 43 |
| 1951 | Mel Ott | 226 | 197 | 87.1 | 29 |
| 1947 | Carl Hubbell | 161 | 140 | 86.9 | 21 |
| 1967 | Red Ruffing | 306 | 266 | 86.9 | 40 |
| 1972 | Sandy Koufax | 396 | 344 | 86.8 | 52 |
| 1976 | Robin Roberts | 388 | 337 | 86.8 | 51 |
| 1952 | Henry Heilmann | 234 | 203 | 86.7 | 31 |
| 2001 | Dave Winfield | 515 | 435 | 84.5 | – |
| 1987 | Willie Stargell | 427 | 352 | 82.4 | 75 |

# HALL OF FAME

## First-Ballot Inductees

| Player | Year |
|--------|------|
| George Brett | 1999 |
| Nolan Ryan | 1999 |
| Robin Yount | 1999 |
| Mike Schmidt | 1995 |
| Steve Carlton | 1994 |
| Reggie Jackson | 1993 |
| Tom Seaver | 1992 |
| Rod Carew | 1991 |
| Joe Morgan | 1990 |
| Jim Palmer | 1990 |
| Carl Yastrzemski | 1989 |
| Johnny Bench | 1989 |
| Willie Stargell | 1988 |
| Willie McCovey | 1986 |
| Lou Brock | 1985 |
| Brooks Robinson | 1983 |
| Frank Robinson | 1982 |
| Hank Aaron | 1982 |
| Bob Gibson | 1981 |
| Al Kaline | 1980 |
| Willie Mays | 1979 |
| Ernie Banks | 1977 |
| Mickey Mantle | 1974 |
| Warren Spahn | 1973 |
| Sandy Koufax | 1972 |
| Stan Musial | 1969 |
| Ted Williams | 1966 |
| Bob Feller | 1962 |
| Jackie Robinson | 1962 |

# HALL OF FAME

**1936**
Ty Cobb
Walter Johnson
Christy Mathewson
Babe Ruth
Honus Wagner

**1937**
Morgan Bulkeley
Ban Johnson
Nap Lajoie
Connie Mack
John McGraw
Tris Speaker
George Wright
Cy Young

**1938**
Pete Alexander
Alexander
Cartwright
Henry Chadwick

**1939**
Cap Anson
Eddie Collins
Charlie Comiskey
Candy Cummings
Buck Ewing
Lou Gehrig
Willie Keeler
Old Hoss Radbourn
George Sisler
Al Spalding

**1940**
None

**1941**
None

**1942**
Rogers Hornsby

**1943 None**

**1944**
Kenesaw Landis

**1945**
Roger Bresnahan
Dan Brouthers
Fred Clarke
Jimmy Collins
Ed Delahanty
Hugh Duffy
Hughie Jennings
King Kelly
Jim O'Rourke
Wilbert Robinson

**1946**
Jesse Burkett
Frank Chance
Jack Chesbro
Johnny Evers
Clark Griffith
Tommy McCarthy
Joe McGinnity
Eddie Plank
Joe Tinker
Rube Waddell
Ed Walsh

**1947**
Mickey Cochrane
Frankie Frisch
Lefty Grove
Carl Hubbell

**1948**
Herb Pennock
Pie Traynor

**1949**
Three Finger
Brown
Charlie Gehringer
Kid Nichols

**1950**
None

**1951**
Jimmie Foxx
Mel Ott

**1952**
Harry Heilmann
Paul Waner

**1953**
Ed Barrow
Chief Bender
Tom Connolly
Dizzy Dean
Bill Klem
Al Simmons
Bobby Wallace
Harry Wright

**1954**
Bill Dickey
Rabbit Maranville
Bill Terry

**1955**
Home Run Baker
Joe DiMaggio
Gabby Hartnett
Ted Lyons
Ray Schalk
Dazzy Vance

**1956**
Joe Cronin
Hank Greenberg

**1957**
Sam Crawford
Joe McCarthy

**1958**
None

**1959**
Zack Wheat

**1960 None**

**1961**
Max Carey
Billy Hamilton

**1962**
Bob Feller
Bill McKechnie
Jackie Robinson

**1963**
John Clarkson
Elmer Flick
Sam Rice
Eppa Rixey

**1964**
Luke Appling
Red Faber
Burleigh Grimes
Miller Huggins
Tim Keefe
Heinie Manush
Monte Ward

**1965**
Pud Galvin

**1966**
Casey Stengel
Ted Williams

**1967**
Branch Rickey
Red Ruffing
Lloyd Waner

**1968**
Kiki Cuyler
Goose Goslin
Joe Medwick

**1969**
Roy Campanella
Stan Coveleski
Waite Hoyt
Stan Musial

**1970**
Lou Boudreau
Earle Combs
Ford Frick
Jesse Haines

# HALL OF FAME

**1971**
Dave Bancroft
Jake Beckley
Chick Hafey
Harry Hooper
Joe Kelley
Rube Marquard
Satchel Paige
George Weiss

**1972**
Yogi Berra
Josh Gibson
Lefty Gomez
Will Harridge
Sandy Koufax
Buck Leonard
Early Wynn
Ross Youngs

**1973**
Roberto Clemente
Billy Evans
Monte Irvin
George Kelly
Warren Spahn
Mickey Welch

**1974**
Cool Papa Bell
Jim Bottomley
Jocko Conlan
Whitey Ford
Mickey Mantle
Sam Thompson

**1975**
Earl Averill
Bucky Harris
Billy Herman
Judy Johnson
Ralph Kiner

**1976**
Oscar Charleston
Roger Connor
Cal Hubbard
Bob Lemon
Freddy Lindstrom
Robin Roberts

**1977**
Ernie Banks
Martin Dihigo
Pop Lloyd
Al Lopez
Amos Rusie
Joe Sewell

**1978**
Addie Joss
Larry MacPhail
Eddie Mathews

**1979**
Warren Giles
Willie Mays
Hack Wilson

**1980**
Al Kaline
Chuck Klein
Duke Snider
Tom Yawkey

**1981**
Rube Foster
Bob Gibson
Johnny Mize

**1982**
Hank Aaron
Happy Chandler
Travis Jackson
Frank Robinson

**1983**
Walter Alston
George Kell
Juan Marichal
Brooks Robinson

**1984**
Luis Aparicio
Don Drysdale
Rick Ferrell
Harmon Killebrew
Pee Wee Reese

**1985**
Lou Brock
Enos Slaughter
Arky Vaughan
Hoyt Wilhelm

**1986**
Bobby Doerr
Ernie Lombardi
Willie McCovey
Edd Roush

**1987**
Ray Dandridge
Catfish Hunter
Billy Williams

**1988**
Willie Stargell

**1989**
Al Barlick
Johnny Bench
Red Schoendienst
Carl Yastrzemski

**1990**
Joe Morgan
Jim Palmer

**1991**
Rod Carew
Fergie Jenkins
Tony Lazzeri
Gaylord Perry
Bill Veeck,Jr.

**1992**
Rollie Fingers
Bill McGowan
Hal Newhouser
Tom Seaver

**1993**
Reggie Jackson

**1994**
Steve Carlton
Leo Durocher
Phil Rizzuto

**1995**
Richie Ashburn
Leon Day
William Hulbert
Mike Schmidt
Vic Willis

**1996**
Jim Bunning
Willie Foster
Ned Hanlon
Earl Weaver

**1997**
Nellie Fox
Tom Lasorda
Phil Niekro
Willie Wells

**1998**
George Davis
Larry Doby
Lee MacPhail
Bullet Joe Rogan
Don Sutton

**1999**
George Brett
Nolan Ryan
Robin Yount

**2000**
Sparky Anderson
Carlton Fisk
Bid McPhee
Tony Perez
Turkey Stearnes

**2001**
Bill Mazeroski
Kirby Puckett
Hilton Smith
Dave Winfield

# AMERICAN LEAGUE

| TEAM | TYPE | YEAR(S) |
|------|------|---------|
| **EAST** | | |
| Blue Jays | Division: | 1985, 1989, 1991, 1992, 1993 |
| | League: | 1992, 1993 |
| | World: | 1992, 1993 |
| Devil Rays | Division: | None |
| | League: | None |
| | World: | None |
| Orioles | Division: | 1969, 1970, 1971, 1973, 1974, 1979, 1983, 1997 |
| | League: | 1944, 1966, 1969, 1970, 1971, 1979, 1983 |
| | World: | 1966, 1970, 1983 |
| Red Sox | Division: | 1975, 1986, 1988, 1990, 1995 |
| | League: | 1903, 1904, 1912, 1915, 1916, 1918, 1946, 1967, 1975, 1986 |
| | World: | 1903, 1912, 1915, 1916, 1918 |
| Yankees | Division: | 1976, 1977, 1978, 1980, 1994, 1996, 1998, 1999, 2000, 2001 |
| | League: | 1921, 1922, 1923, 1926, 1927, 1928, 1932, 1936, 1937, 1938, 1939, 1941, 1942, 1943, 1947, 1949, 1950, 1951, 1952, 1953, 1955, 1956, 1957, 1958, 1960, 1961, 1962, 1963, 1964, 1976, 1977, 1978, 1981, 1996, 1998, 1999, 2000, 2001 |
| | World: | 1923, 1927, 1928, 1932, 1936, 1937, 1938, 1939, 1941, 1943, 1947, 1949, 1950, 1951, 1952, 1953, 1956, 1958, 1961, 1962, 1977, 1978, 1996, 1998, 1999, 2000 |
| **CENTRAL** | | |
| Indians | Division: | 1995, 1996, 1997, 1998, 1999, 2001 |
| | League: | 1920, 1948, 1954, 1995, 1997 |
| | World: | 1920, 1948 |
| Royals | Division: | 1976, 1977, 1978, 1980, 1984, 1985 |
| | League: | 1980, 1985 |
| | World: | 1985 |
| Tigers | Division: | 1972, 1984, 1987 |
| | League: | 1907, 1908, 1909, 1934, 1935, 1940, 1945, 1968, 1984 |
| | World: | 1935, 1945, 1968, 1984 |
| Twins | Division: | 1969, 1970, 1987, 1991 |
| | League: | 1924, 1925, 1933, 1965, 1987, 1991 |
| | World: | 1924, 1987, 1991 |
| White Sox | Division: | 1983, 1993, 1994, 2000 |
| | League: | 1901, 1906, 1917, 1919, 1959 |
| | World: | 1906, 1917 |
| **WEST** | | |
| Angels | Division: | 1979, 1982, 1986 |
| | League: | None |
| | World: | None |
| Athletics | Division: | 1971, 1972, 1973, 1974, 1975, 1981, 1988, 1989, 1990, 1992, 2000 |
| | League: | 1902, 1905, 1910, 1911, 1913, 1914, 1929, 1930, 1931, 1972, 1973, 1974, 1988, 1989, 1990, |
| | World: | 1910, 1911, 1913, 1929, 1930, 1972, 1973, 1974, 1989 |
| Mariners | Division: | 1995, 1997, 2001 |
| | League: | None |
| | World: | None |
| Rangers | Division: | 1994, 1996, 1998, 1999 |
| | League: | None |
| | World: | None |

# NATIONAL LEAGUE

| TEAM | TYPE | YEAR(S) |
|------|------|---------|
| **EAST** | | |
| Braves | Division: | 1969, 1982, 1991, 1992, 1993, 1995, 1996, 1997, 1998, 1999, 2000, 2001 |
| | League: | 1877, 1878, 1883, 1891, 1892, 1893, 1897, 1898, 1914, 1948, 1957, 1958, 1991, 1992, 1995, 1996, 1999 |
| | World: | 1914, 1957, 1995 |
| Expos | Division: | 1994 |
| | League: | None |
| | World: | None |
| | World: | 1905, 1921, 1922, 1933, 1954 |
| Marlins | Division: | None |
| | League: | 1997 |
| | World: | 1997 |
| Mets | Division: | 1969, 1973, 1986, 1988 |
| | League: | 1969, 1973, 1986, 2000 |
| | World: | 1969, 1986 |
| Phillies | Division: | 1976, 1977, 1978, 1980, 1983, 1993 |
| | League: | 1915, 1950, 1980, 1983, 1993 |
| | World: | 1980 |
| **CENTRAL** | | |
| Astros | Division: | 1980, 1986, 1997, 1998, 1999, 2001 |
| | League: | None |
| | World: | None |
| Brewers | Division: | 1981, 1982 |
| | League: | 1982 |
| | World: | None |
| Cardinals | Division: | 1981, 1982, 1985, 1987, 1996, 2000 |
| | League: | 1885, 1886, 1887, 1888, 1926, 1928, 1930, 1931, 1934, 1942, 1943, 1944, 1946, 1964, 1967, 1968, 1982, 1985, 1987 |
| | World: | 1926, 1931, 1934, 1942, 1944, 1946, 1964, 1967, 1982 |
| Cubs | Division: | 1984, 1989 |
| | League: | 1876, 1880, 1881, 1882, 1885, 1886, 1906, 1907, 1908, 1910, 1918, 1929, 1932, 1935, 1938, 1945 |
| | World: | 1907, 1908 |
| Pirates | Division: | 1970, 1971, 1972, 1974, 1975, 1979, 1990, 1991, 1992 |
| | League: | 1901, 1902, 1903, 1909, 1925, 1927, 1960, 1971, 1979 |
| | World: | 1909, 1925, 1960, 1971, 1979 |
| Reds | Division: | 1970, 1972, 1973, 1975, 1976, 1979, 1981, 1990, 1994, 1995 |
| | League: | 1882, 1919, 1939, 1940, 1961, 1970, 1972, 1975, 1976, 1990 |
| | World: | 1919, 1940, 1975, 1976, 1990 |
| **WEST** | | |
| Diamondbacks | Division: | 1999, 2001 |
| | League: | 2001 |
| | World: | 2001 |
| Dodgers | Division: | 1974, 1977, 1978, 1983, 1985, 1988, 1994, 1995 |
| | League: | 1889, 1890, 1899, 1900, 1916, 1920, 1941, 1947, 1949, 1952, 1953, 1955, 1956, 1959, 1963, 1965, 1966, 1974, 1977, 1978, 1981, 1988 |
| | World: | 1955, 1959, 1963, 1965, 1981, 1988 |
| Giants | Division: | 1971, 1987, 1989, 1997, 2000 |
| | League: | 1888, 1889, 1904, 1905, 1911, 1912, 1913, 1917, 1921, 1922, 1923, 1924, 1933, 1936, 1937, 1951, 1954, 1962, 1989 |
| Padres | Division: | 1984, 1996, 1998 |
| | League: | 1984, 1998 |
| | World: | None |
| Rockies | Division: | None |
| | League: | None |
| | World: | None |

# FINAL STANDINGS

## 1876 National League

| Team | W | L | Pct | GB |
|---|---|---|---|---|
| Chicago | 52 | 14 | .788 | -- |
| St. Louis | 45 | 19 | .703 | 6.0 |
| Hartford | 47 | 21 | .691 | 6.0 |
| Boston | 39 | 31 | .557 | 15.0 |
| Louisville | 30 | 36 | .455 | 22.0 |
| New York | 21 | 35 | .375 | 26.0 |
| Philadelphia | 14 | 45 | .237 | 34.5 |
| Cincinnati | 9 | 56 | .138 | 42.5 |

## 1877 National League

| Team | W | L | Pct | GB |
|---|---|---|---|---|
| Boston | 42 | 18 | .700 | -- |
| Louisville | 35 | 25 | .583 | 7.0 |
| Hartford | 31 | 27 | .534 | 10.0 |
| St. Louis | 28 | 32 | .467 | 14.0 |
| Chicago | 26 | 33 | .441 | 15.5 |
| Cincinnati | 15 | 42 | .263 | 25.5 |

## 1878 National League

| Team | W | L | Pct | GB |
|---|---|---|---|---|
| Boston | 41 | 19 | .683 | -- |
| Cincinnati | 37 | 23 | .617 | 4.0 |
| Providence | 33 | 27 | .550 | 8.0 |
| Chicago | 30 | 30 | .500 | 11.0 |
| Indianapolis | 24 | 36 | .400 | 17.0 |
| Milwaukee | 15 | 45 | .250 | 26.0 |

## 1879 National League

| Team | W | L | Pct | GB |
|---|---|---|---|---|
| Providence | 59 | 25 | .702 | -- |
| Boston | 54 | 30 | .643 | 5.0 |
| Buffalo | 46 | 32 | .590 | 10.0 |
| Chicago | 46 | 33 | .582 | 10.5 |
| Cincinnati | 43 | 37 | .538 | 14.0 |
| Cleveland | 27 | 55 | .329 | 31.0 |
| Syracuse | 22 | 48 | .314 | 30.0 |
| Troy | 19 | 56 | .253 | 35.5 |

## 1880 National League

| Team | W | L | Pct | GB |
|---|---|---|---|---|
| Chicago | 67 | 17 | .798 | -- |
| Providence | 52 | 32 | .619 | 15.0 |
| Cleveland | 47 | 37 | .560 | 20.0 |
| Troy | 41 | 42 | .494 | 25.5 |
| Worcester | 40 | 43 | .482 | 26.5 |
| Boston | 40 | 44 | .476 | 27.0 |
| Buffalo | 24 | 58 | .293 | 42.0 |
| Cincinnati | 21 | 59 | .263 | 44.0 |

## 1881 National League

| Team | W | L | Pct | GB |
|---|---|---|---|---|
| Chicago | 56 | 28 | .667 | -- |
| Providence | 47 | 37 | .560 | 9.0 |
| Buffalo | 45 | 38 | .542 | 10.5 |
| Detroit | 41 | 43 | .488 | 15.0 |
| Troy | 39 | 45 | .464 | 17.0 |
| Boston | 38 | 45 | .458 | 17.5 |
| Cleveland | 36 | 48 | .429 | 20.0 |
| Worcester | 32 | 50 | .390 | 23.0 |

## 1882 National League

| Team | W | L | Pct | GB |
|---|---|---|---|---|
| Chicago | 55 | 29 | .655 | -- |
| Providence | 52 | 32 | .619 | 3.0 |
| Boston | 45 | 39 | .536 | 10.0 |
| Buffalo | 45 | 39 | .536 | 10.0 |
| Cleveland | 42 | 40 | .512 | 12.0 |
| Detroit | 42 | 41 | .506 | 12.5 |
| Troy | 35 | 48 | .422 | 19.5 |
| Worcester | 18 | 66 | .214 | 37.0 |

## 1882 National League

| Team | W | L | Pct | GB |
|---|---|---|---|---|
| Cincinnati | 55 | 25 | .688 | -- |
| Philadelphia | 41 | 34 | .547 | 11.5 |
| Louisville | 42 | 38 | .525 | 13.0 |
| Pittsburgh | 39 | 39 | .500 | 15.0 |
| St. Louis | 37 | 43 | .463 | 18.0 |
| Baltimore | 19 | 54 | .260 | 32.5 |

## 1883 National League

| Team | W | L | Pct | GB |
|---|---|---|---|---|
| Boston | 63 | 35 | .643 | -- |
| Chicago | 59 | 39 | .602 | 4.0 |
| Providence | 58 | 40 | .592 | 5.0 |
| Cleveland | 55 | 42 | .567 | 7.5 |
| Buffalo | 52 | 45 | .536 | 10.5 |
| New York | 46 | 50 | .479 | 16.0 |
| Detroit | 40 | 58 | .408 | 23.0 |
| Philadelphia | 17 | 81 | .173 | 46.0 |

## 1883 National League

| Team | W | L | Pct | GB |
|---|---|---|---|---|
| Philadelphia | 66 | 32 | .673 | -- |
| St. Louis | 65 | 33 | .663 | 1.0 |
| Cincinnati | 61 | 37 | .622 | 5.0 |
| New York | 54 | 42 | .563 | 11.0 |
| Louisville | 52 | 45 | .536 | 13.5 |
| Columbus | 32 | 65 | .330 | 33.5 |
| Pittsburgh | 31 | 67 | .316 | 35.0 |
| Baltimore | 28 | 68 | .292 | 37.0 |

## 1884 National League

| Team | W | L | Pct | GB |
|---|---|---|---|---|
| Providence | 84 | 28 | .750 | -- |
| Boston | 73 | 38 | .658 | 10.5 |
| Buffalo | 64 | 47 | .577 | 19.5 |
| Chicago | 62 | 50 | .554 | 22.0 |
| New York | 62 | 50 | .554 | 22.0 |
| Philadelphia | 39 | 73 | .348 | 45.0 |
| Cleveland | 35 | 77 | .313 | 49.0 |
| Detroit | 28 | 84 | .250 | 56.0 |

## 1884 Union Association

| Team | W | L | Pct | GB |
|---|---|---|---|---|
| St. Louis | 94 | 19 | .832 | -- |
| Milwaukee | 8 | 4 | .667 | 35.5 |
| Cincinnati | 69 | 36 | .657 | 21.0 |
| Baltimore | 58 | 47 | .552 | 32.0 |
| Boston | 58 | 51 | .532 | 34.0 |
| Chicago | 34 | 39 | .466 | 40.0 |
| Washington | 47 | 65 | .420 | 46.5 |
| Pittsburgh | 7 | 11 | .389 | 39.5 |
| Philadelphia | 21 | 46 | .313 | 50.0 |
| St. Paul | 2 | 6 | .250 | 39.5 |
| Altoona | 6 | 19 | .240 | 44.0 |
| Kansas City | 16 | 63 | .203 | 61.0 |
| Wilmington | 2 | 16 | .111 | 44.5 |

## 1884 American Association

| Team | W | L | Pct | GB |
|---|---|---|---|---|
| New York | 75 | 32 | .701 | -- |
| Columbus | 69 | 39 | .639 | 6.5 |
| Louisville | 68 | 40 | .630 | 7.5 |
| St. Louis | 67 | 40 | .626 | 8.0 |
| Cincinnati | 68 | 41 | .624 | 8.0 |
| Baltimore | 63 | 43 | .594 | 11.5 |
| Philadelphia | 61 | 46 | .570 | 14.0 |
| Toledo | 46 | 58 | .442 | 27.5 |
| Brooklyn | 40 | 64 | .385 | 33.5 |
| Richmond | 12 | 30 | .286 | 30.5 |
| Pittsburgh | 30 | 78 | .278 | 45.5 |
| Indianapolis | 29 | 78 | .271 | 46.0 |
| Washington | 12 | 51 | .190 | 41.0 |

258

# FINAL STANDINGS

## 1885 National League

| Team | W | L | Pct | GB |
|------|---|---|-----|-----|
| Chicago | 87 | 25 | .777 | -- |
| New York | 85 | 27 | .759 | 2.0 |
| Philadelphia | 56 | 54 | .509 | 30.0 |
| Providence | 53 | 57 | .482 | 33.0 |
| Boston | 46 | 66 | .411 | 41.0 |
| Detroit | 41 | 67 | .380 | 44.0 |
| Buffalo | 38 | 74 | .339 | 49.0 |
| St. Louis | 36 | 72 | .333 | 49.0 |

## 1885 American Association

| Team | W | L | Pct | GB |
|------|---|---|-----|-----|
| St. Louis | 79 | 33 | .705 | -- |
| Cincinnati | 63 | 49 | .563 | 16.0 |
| Pittsburgh | 56 | 55 | .505 | 22.5 |
| Philadelphia | 55 | 57 | .491 | 24.0 |
| Louisville | 53 | 59 | .473 | 26.0 |
| Brooklyn | 53 | 59 | .473 | 26.0 |
| New York | 44 | 64 | .407 | 33.0 |
| Baltimore | 41 | 68 | .376 | 36.5 |

## 1886 National League

| Team | W | L | Pct | GB |
|------|---|---|-----|-----|
| Chicago | 90 | 34 | .726 | -- |
| Detroit | 87 | 36 | .707 | 2.5 |

## 1886 American Association

| Team | W | L | Pct | GB |
|------|---|---|-----|-----|
| St. Louis | 93 | 46 | .669 | -- |
| Pittsburgh | 80 | 57 | .584 | 12.0 |
| Brooklyn | 76 | 61 | .555 | 16.0 |
| Louisville | 66 | 70 | .485 | 25.5 |
| Cincinnati | 65 | 73 | .471 | 27.5 |
| Philadelphia | 63 | 72 | .467 | 28.0 |
| New York | 53 | 82 | .393 | 38.0 |
| Baltimore | 48 | 83 | .366 | 41.0 |

## 1887 National League

| Team | W | L | Pct | GB |
|------|---|---|-----|-----|
| Detroit | 79 | 45 | .637 | -- |
| Philadelphia | 75 | 48 | .610 | 3.5 |
| Chicago | 71 | 50 | .587 | 6.5 |
| New York | 68 | 55 | .553 | 10.5 |
| Boston | 61 | 60 | .504 | 16.5 |
| Pittsburgh | 55 | 69 | .444 | 24.0 |
| Washington | 46 | 76 | .377 | 32.0 |
| Indianapolis | 37 | 89 | .294 | 43.0 |

## 1887 American Association

| Team | W | L | Pct | GB |
|------|---|---|-----|-----|
| St. Louis | 95 | 40 | .704 | -- |
| Cincinnati | 81 | 54 | .600 | 14.0 |
| Baltimore | 77 | 58 | .570 | 18.0 |
| Louisville | 76 | 60 | .559 | 19.5 |
| Philadelphia | 64 | 69 | .481 | 30.0 |
| Brooklyn | 60 | 74 | .448 | 34.5 |
| New York | 44 | 89 | .331 | 50.0 |
| Cleveland | 39 | 92 | .298 | 54.0 |

## 1888 National League

| Team | W | L | Pct | GB |
|------|---|---|-----|-----|
| New York | 84 | 47 | .641 | -- |
| Chicago | 77 | 58 | .570 | 9.0 |
| Philadelphia | 69 | 61 | .531 | 14.5 |
| Boston | 70 | 64 | .522 | 15.5 |
| Detroit | 68 | 63 | .519 | 16.0 |
| Pittsburgh | 66 | 68 | .493 | 19.5 |
| Indianapolis | 50 | 85 | .370 | 36.0 |
| Washington | 48 | 86 | .358 | 37.5 |

## 1888 American Association

| Team | W | L | Pct | GB |
|------|---|---|-----|-----|
| St. Louis | 92 | 43 | .681 | -- |
| Brooklyn | 88 | 52 | .629 | 6.5 |
| Philadelphia | 81 | 52 | .609 | 10.0 |
| Cincinnati | 80 | 54 | .597 | 11.5 |
| Baltimore | 57 | 80 | .416 | 36.0 |
| Cleveland | 50 | 82 | .379 | 40.5 |
| Louisville | 48 | 87 | .356 | 44.0 |
| Kansas City | 43 | 89 | .326 | 47.5 |

## 1889 National League

| Team | W | L | Pct | GB |
|------|---|---|-----|-----|
| New York | 83 | 43 | .659 | -- |
| Boston | 83 | 45 | .648 | 1.0 |
| Chicago | 67 | 65 | .508 | 19.0 |
| Philadelphia | 63 | 64 | .496 | 20.5 |
| Pittsburgh | 61 | 71 | .462 | 25.0 |
| Cleveland | 61 | 72 | .459 | 25.5 |
| Indianapolis | 59 | 75 | .440 | 28.0 |
| Washington | 41 | 83 | .331 | 41.0 |

## 1889 American Association

| Team | W | L | Pct | GB |
|------|---|---|-----|-----|
| Brooklyn | 93 | 44 | .679 | -- |
| St. Louis | 90 | 45 | .667 | 2.0 |
| Philadelphia | 75 | 58 | .564 | 16.0 |
| Cincinnati | 76 | 63 | .547 | 18.0 |
| Baltimore | 70 | 65 | .519 | 22.0 |
| Columbus | 60 | 78 | .435 | 33.5 |
| Kansas City | 55 | 82 | .401 | 38.0 |
| Louisville | 27 | 111 | .196 | 66.5 |

## 1890 National League

| Team | W | L | Pct | GB |
|------|---|---|-----|-----|
| Brooklyn | 86 | 43 | .667 | -- |
| Chicago | 84 | 53 | .613 | 6.0 |
| Philadelphia | 78 | 54 | .591 | 9.5 |
| Cincinnati | 77 | 55 | .583 | 10.5 |
| Boston | 76 | 57 | .571 | 12.0 |
| New York | 63 | 68 | .481 | 24.0 |
| Cleveland | 44 | 88 | .333 | 43.5 |
| Pittsburgh | 23 | 113 | .169 | 66.5 |

## 1890 Players League

| Team | W | L | Pct | GB |
|------|---|---|-----|-----|
| Boston | 81 | 48 | .628 | -- |
| Brooklyn | 76 | 56 | .576 | 6.5 |
| New York | 74 | 57 | .565 | 8.0 |
| Chicago | 75 | 62 | .547 | 10.0 |
| Philadelphia | 68 | 63 | .519 | 14.0 |
| Pittsburgh | 60 | 68 | .469 | 20.5 |
| Cleveland | 55 | 75 | .423 | 26.5 |
| Buffalo | 36 | 96 | .273 | 46.5 |

## 1890 American Association

| Team | W | L | Pct | GB |
|------|---|---|-----|-----|
| Louisville | 88 | 44 | .667 | -- |
| Columbus | 79 | 55 | .590 | 10.0 |
| St. Louis | 77 | 58 | .570 | 12.5 |
| Toledo | 68 | 64 | .515 | 20.0 |
| Rochester | 63 | 63 | .500 | 22.0 |
| Baltimore | 15 | 19 | .441 | 24.0 |
| Syracuse | 55 | 72 | .433 | 30.5 |
| Philadelphia | 54 | 78 | .409 | 34.0 |
| Brooklyn | 26 | 72 | .265 | 45.0 |

# FINAL STANDINGS

### 1891 National League

| Team | W | L | Pct | GB |
|---|---|---|---|---|
| Boston | 87 | 51 | .630 | -- |
| Chicago | 82 | 53 | .607 | 3.5 |
| New York | 71 | 61 | .538 | 13.0 |
| Philadelphia | 68 | 69 | .496 | 18.5 |
| Cleveland | 65 | 74 | .468 | 22.5 |
| Brooklyn | 61 | 76 | .445 | 25.5 |
| Cincinnati | 56 | 81 | .409 | 30.5 |
| Pittsburgh | 55 | 80 | .407 | 30.5 |

### 1891 American Association

| Team | W | L | Pct | GB |
|---|---|---|---|---|
| Boston | 93 | 42 | .689 | -- |
| St. Louis | 85 | 51 | .625 | 8.5 |
| Milwaukee | 21 | 15 | .583 | 22.5 |
| Baltimore | 71 | 64 | .526 | 22.0 |
| Philadelphia | 73 | 66 | .525 | 22.0 |
| Columbus | 61 | 76 | .445 | 33.0 |
| Cincinnati | 43 | 57 | .430 | 32.5 |
| Louisville | 54 | 83 | .394 | 40.0 |
| Washington | 44 | 91 | .326 | 49.0 |

### 1892 National League

| Team | W | L | Pct | GB |
|---|---|---|---|---|
| Boston | 102 | 48 | .680 | -- |
| Cleveland | 93 | 56 | .624 | 8.5 |
| Brooklyn | 95 | 59 | .617 | 9.0 |
| Philadelphia | 87 | 66 | .569 | 16.5 |
| Cincinnati | 82 | 68 | .547 | 20.0 |
| Pittsburgh | 80 | 73 | .523 | 23.5 |
| Chicago | 70 | 76 | .479 | 30.0 |
| New York | 71 | 80 | .470 | 31.5 |
| Louisville | 63 | 89 | .414 | 40.0 |
| Washington | 58 | 93 | .384 | 44.5 |
| St. Louis | 56 | 94 | .373 | 46.0 |
| Baltimore | 46 | 101 | .313 | 54.5 |

### 1893 National League

| Team | W | L | Pct | GB |
|---|---|---|---|---|
| Boston | 86 | 43 | .667 | -- |
| Pittsburgh | 81 | 48 | .628 | 5.0 |
| Cleveland | 73 | 55 | .570 | 12.5 |
| Philadelphia | 72 | 57 | .558 | 14.0 |
| New York | 68 | 64 | .515 | 19.5 |
| Cincinnati | 65 | 63 | .508 | 20.5 |
| Brooklyn | 65 | 63 | .508 | 20.5 |
| Baltimore | 60 | 70 | .462 | 26.5 |
| Chicago | 56 | 71 | .441 | 29.0 |
| St. Louis | 57 | 75 | .432 | 30.5 |
| Louisville | 50 | 75 | .400 | 34.0 |
| Washington | 40 | 89 | .310 | 46.0 |

### 1894 National League

| Team | W | L | Pct | GB |
|---|---|---|---|---|
| Baltimore | 89 | 39 | .695 | -- |
| New York | 88 | 44 | .667 | 3.0 |
| Boston | 83 | 49 | .629 | 8.0 |
| Philadelphia | 71 | 57 | .555 | 18.0 |
| Brooklyn | 70 | 61 | .534 | 20.5 |
| Cleveland | 68 | 61 | .527 | 21.5 |
| Pittsburgh | 65 | 65 | .500 | 25.0 |
| Chicago | 57 | 75 | .432 | 34.0 |
| St. Louis | 56 | 76 | .424 | 35.0 |
| Cincinnati | 55 | 75 | .423 | 35.0 |
| Washington | 45 | 87 | .341 | 46.0 |
| Louisville | 36 | 94 | .277 | 54.0 |

### 1895 National League

| Team | W | L | Pct | GB |
|---|---|---|---|---|
| Baltimore | 87 | 43 | .669 | -- |
| Cleveland | 84 | 46 | .646 | 3.0 |
| Philadelphia | 78 | 53 | .595 | 9.5 |
| Chicago | 72 | 58 | .554 | 15.0 |
| Brooklyn | 71 | 60 | .542 | 16.5 |
| Boston | 71 | 60 | .542 | 16.5 |
| Pittsburgh | 71 | 61 | .538 | 17.0 |
| Cincinnati | 66 | 64 | .508 | 21.0 |
| New York | 66 | 65 | .504 | 21.5 |
| Washington | 43 | 85 | .336 | 43.0 |
| St. Louis | 39 | 92 | .298 | 48.5 |
| Louisville | 35 | 96 | .267 | 52.5 |

### 1896 National League

| Team | W | L | Pct | GB |
|---|---|---|---|---|
| Baltimore | 90 | 39 | .698 | -- |
| Cleveland | 80 | 48 | .625 | 9.5 |
| Cincinnati | 77 | 50 | .606 | 12.0 |
| Boston | 74 | 57 | .565 | 17.0 |
| Chicago | 71 | 57 | .555 | 18.5 |
| Pittsburgh | 66 | 63 | .512 | 24.0 |
| New York | 64 | 67 | .489 | 27.0 |
| Philadelphia | 62 | 68 | .477 | 28.5 |
| Brooklyn | 58 | 73 | .443 | 33.0 |
| Washington | 58 | 73 | .443 | 33.0 |
| St. Louis | 40 | 90 | .308 | 50.5 |
| Louisville | 38 | 93 | .290 | 53.0 |

### 1897 National League

| Team | W | L | Pct | GB |
|---|---|---|---|---|
| Boston | 93 | 39 | .705 | -- |
| Baltimore | 90 | 40 | .692 | 2.0 |
| New York | 83 | 48 | .634 | 9.5 |
| Cincinnati | 76 | 56 | .576 | 17.0 |
| Cleveland | 69 | 62 | .527 | 23.5 |
| Brooklyn | 61 | 71 | .462 | 32.0 |
| Washington | 61 | 71 | .462 | 32.0 |
| Pittsburgh | 60 | 71 | .458 | 32.5 |
| Chicago | 59 | 73 | .447 | 34.0 |
| Philadelphia | 55 | 77 | .417 | 38.0 |
| Louisville | 52 | 78 | .400 | 40.0 |
| St. Louis | 29 | 102 | .221 | 63.5 |

### 1898 National League

| Team | W | L | Pct | GB |
|---|---|---|---|---|
| Boston | 102 | 47 | .685 | -- |
| Baltimore | 96 | 53 | .644 | 6.0 |
| Cincinnati | 92 | 60 | .605 | 11.5 |
| Chicago | 85 | 65 | .567 | 17.5 |
| Cleveland | 81 | 68 | .544 | 21.0 |
| Philadelphia | 78 | 71 | .523 | 24.0 |
| New York | 77 | 73 | .513 | 25.5 |
| Pittsburgh | 72 | 76 | .486 | 29.5 |
| Louisville | 70 | 81 | .464 | 33.0 |
| Brooklyn | 54 | 91 | .372 | 46.0 |
| Washington | 51 | 101 | .336 | 52.5 |
| St. Louis | 39 | 111 | .260 | 63.5 |

# FINAL STANDINGS

## 1899 National League

| Team | W | L | Pct | GB |
|---|---|---|---|---|
| Brooklyn | 101 | 47 | .682 | -- |
| Boston | 95 | 57 | .625 | 8.0 |
| Philadelphia | 94 | 58 | .618 | 9.0 |
| Baltimore | 86 | 62 | .581 | 15.0 |
| St. Louis | 84 | 67 | .556 | 18.5 |
| Cincinnati | 83 | 67 | .553 | 19.0 |
| Pittsburgh | 76 | 73 | .510 | 25.5 |
| Chicago | 75 | 73 | .507 | 26.0 |
| Louisville | 75 | 77 | .493 | 28.0 |
| New York | 60 | 90 | .400 | 42.0 |
| Washington | 54 | 98 | .355 | 49.0 |
| Cleveland | 20 | 134 | .130 | 84.0 |

## 1900 National League

| Team | W | L | Pct | GB |
|---|---|---|---|---|
| Brooklyn | 82 | 54 | .603 | -- |
| Pittsburgh | 79 | 60 | .568 | 4.5 |
| Philadelphia | 75 | 63 | .543 | 8.0 |
| Boston | 66 | 72 | .478 | 17.0 |
| Chicago | 65 | 75 | .464 | 19.0 |
| St. Louis | 65 | 75 | .464 | 19.0 |
| Cincinnati | 62 | 77 | .446 | 21.5 |
| New York | 60 | 78 | .435 | 23.0 |

## 1901 American League

| Team | W | L | Pct | GB |
|---|---|---|---|---|
| Chicago | 83 | 53 | .610 | -- |
| Boston | 79 | 57 | .581 | 4.0 |
| Detroit | 74 | 61 | .548 | 8.5 |
| Philadelphia | 74 | 62 | .544 | 9.0 |
| Baltimore | 68 | 65 | .511 | 13.5 |
| Washington | 61 | 72 | .459 | 20.5 |
| Cleveland | 54 | 82 | .397 | 29.0 |
| Milwaukee | 48 | 89 | .350 | 35.5 |

## 1901 National League

| Team | W | L | Pct | GB |
|---|---|---|---|---|
| Pittsburgh | 90 | 49 | .647 | -- |
| Philadelphia | 83 | 57 | .593 | 7.5 |
| Brooklyn | 79 | 57 | .581 | 9.5 |
| St. Louis | 76 | 64 | .543 | 14.5 |
| Boston | 69 | 69 | .500 | 20.5 |
| Chicago | 53 | 86 | .381 | 37.0 |
| New York | 52 | 85 | .380 | 37.0 |
| Cincinnati | 52 | 87 | .374 | 38.0 |

## 1902 American League

| Team | W | L | Pct | GB |
|---|---|---|---|---|
| Philadelphia | 83 | 53 | .610 | -- |
| St. Louis | 78 | 58 | .574 | 5.0 |
| Boston | 77 | 60 | .562 | 6.5 |
| Chicago | 74 | 60 | .552 | 8.0 |
| Cleveland | 69 | 67 | .507 | 14.0 |
| Washington | 61 | 75 | .449 | 22.0 |
| Detroit | 52 | 83 | .385 | 30.5 |
| Baltimore | 50 | 88 | .362 | 34.0 |

## 1902 National League

| Team | W | L | Pct | GB |
|---|---|---|---|---|
| Pittsburgh | 103 | 36 | .741 | -- |
| Brooklyn | 75 | 63 | .543 | 27.5 |
| Boston | 73 | 64 | .533 | 29.0 |
| Cincinnati | 70 | 70 | .500 | 33.5 |
| Chicago | 68 | 69 | .496 | 34.0 |
| St. Louis | 56 | 78 | .418 | 44.5 |
| Philadelphia | 56 | 81 | .409 | 46.0 |
| New York | 48 | 88 | .353 | 53.5 |

## 1903 American League

| Team | W | L | Pct | GB |
|---|---|---|---|---|
| Boston | 91 | 47 | .659 | -- |
| Philadelphia | 75 | 60 | .556 | 14.5 |
| Cleveland | 77 | 63 | .550 | 15.0 |
| New York | 72 | 62 | .537 | 17.0 |
| Detroit | 65 | 71 | .478 | 25.0 |
| St. Louis | 65 | 74 | .468 | 26.5 |
| Chicago | 60 | 77 | .438 | 30.5 |
| Washington | 43 | 94 | .314 | 47.5 |

## 1903 National League

| Team | W | L | Pct | GB |
|---|---|---|---|---|
| Pittsburgh | 91 | 49 | .650 | -- |
| New York | 84 | 55 | .604 | 6.5 |
| Chicago | 82 | 56 | .594 | 8.0 |
| Cincinnati | 74 | 65 | .532 | 16.5 |
| Brooklyn | 70 | 66 | .515 | 19.0 |
| Boston | 58 | 80 | .420 | 32.0 |
| Philadelphia | 49 | 86 | .363 | 39.5 |
| St. Louis | 43 | 94 | .314 | 46.5 |

## 1904 American League

| Team | W | L | Pct | GB |
|---|---|---|---|---|
| Boston | 95 | 59 | .617 | -- |
| New York | 92 | 59 | .609 | 1.5 |
| Chicago | 89 | 65 | .578 | 6.0 |
| Cleveland | 86 | 65 | .570 | 7.5 |
| Philadelphia | 81 | 70 | .536 | 12.5 |
| St. Louis | 65 | 87 | .428 | 29.0 |
| Detroit | 62 | 90 | .408 | 32.0 |
| Washington | 38 | 113 | .252 | 55.5 |

## 1904 National League

| Team | W | L | Pct | GB |
|---|---|---|---|---|
| New York | 106 | 47 | .693 | -- |
| Chicago | 93 | 60 | .608 | 13.0 |
| Cincinnati | 88 | 65 | .575 | 18.0 |
| Pittsburgh | 87 | 66 | .569 | 19.0 |
| St. Louis | 75 | 79 | .487 | 31.5 |
| Brooklyn | 56 | 97 | .366 | 50.0 |
| Boston | 55 | 98 | .359 | 51.0 |
| Philadelphia | 52 | 100 | .342 | 53.5 |

## 1905 American League

| Team | W | L | Pct | GB |
|---|---|---|---|---|
| Philadelphia | 92 | 56 | .622 | -- |
| Chicago | 92 | 60 | .605 | 2.0 |
| Detroit | 79 | 74 | .516 | 15.5 |
| Boston | 78 | 74 | .513 | 16.0 |
| Cleveland | 76 | 78 | .494 | 19.0 |
| New York | 71 | 78 | .477 | 21.5 |
| Washington | 64 | 87 | .424 | 29.5 |
| St. Louis | 54 | 99 | .353 | 40.5 |

## 1905 National League

| Team | W | L | Pct | GB |
|---|---|---|---|---|
| New York | 105 | 48 | .686 | -- |
| Pittsburgh | 96 | 57 | .627 | 9.0 |
| Chicago | 92 | 61 | .601 | 13.0 |
| Philadelphia | 83 | 69 | .546 | 21.5 |
| Cincinnati | 79 | 74 | .516 | 26.0 |
| St. Louis | 58 | 96 | .377 | 47.5 |
| Boston | 51 | 103 | .331 | 54.5 |
| Brooklyn | 48 | 104 | .316 | 56.5 |

# FINAL STANDINGS

## 1906 American League

| Team | W | L | Pct | GB |
|------|---|---|-----|-----|
| Chicago | 93 | 58 | .616 | -- |
| New York | 90 | 61 | .596 | 3.0 |
| Cleveland | 89 | 64 | .582 | 5.0 |
| Philadelphia | 78 | 67 | .538 | 12.0 |
| St. Louis | 76 | 73 | .510 | 16.0 |
| Detroit | 71 | 78 | .477 | 21.0 |
| Washington | 55 | 95 | .367 | 37.5 |
| Boston | 49 | 105 | .318 | 45.5 |

## 1906 National League

| Team | W | L | Pct | GB |
|------|---|---|-----|-----|
| Chicago | 116 | 36 | .763 | -- |
| New York | 96 | 56 | .632 | 20.0 |
| Pittsburgh | 93 | 60 | .608 | 23.5 |
| Philadelphia | 71 | 82 | .464 | 45.5 |
| Brooklyn | 66 | 86 | .434 | 50.0 |
| Cincinnati | 64 | 87 | .424 | 51.5 |
| St. Louis | 52 | 98 | .347 | 63.0 |
| Boston | 49 | 102 | .325 | 66.5 |

## 1907 American League

| Team | W | L | Pct | GB |
|------|---|---|-----|-----|
| Detroit | 92 | 58 | .613 | -- |
| Philadelphia | 88 | 57 | .607 | 1.5 |
| Chicago | 87 | 64 | .576 | 5.5 |
| Cleveland | 85 | 67 | .559 | 8.0 |
| New York | 70 | 78 | .473 | 21.0 |
| St. Louis | 69 | 83 | .454 | 24.0 |
| Boston | 59 | 90 | .396 | 32.5 |
| Washington | 49 | 102 | .325 | 43.5 |

## 1907 National League

| Team | W | L | Pct | GB |
|------|---|---|-----|-----|
| Chicago | 107 | 45 | .704 | -- |
| Pittsburgh | 91 | 63 | .591 | 17.0 |
| Philadelphia | 83 | 64 | .565 | 21.5 |
| New York | 82 | 71 | .536 | 25.5 |
| Brooklyn | 65 | 83 | .439 | 40.0 |
| Cincinnati | 66 | 87 | .431 | 41.5 |
| Boston | 58 | 90 | .392 | 47.0 |
| St. Louis | 52 | 101 | .340 | 55.5 |

## 1908 American League

| Team | W | L | Pct | GB |
|------|---|---|-----|-----|
| Detroit | 90 | 63 | 588 | -- |
| Cleveland | 90 | 64 | .584 | 0.5 |
| Chicago | 88 | 64 | .579 | 1.5 |
| St. Louis | 83 | 69 | .546 | 6.5 |
| Boston | 75 | 79 | .487 | 15.5 |
| Philadelphia | 68 | 85 | .444 | 22.0 |
| Washington | 67 | 85 | .441 | 22.5 |
| New York | 51 | 103 | .331 | 39.5 |

## 1908 National League

| Team | W | L | Pct | GB |
|------|---|---|-----|-----|
| Chicago | 99 | 55 | .643 | -- |
| Pittsburgh | 98 | 56 | .636 | 1.0 |
| New York | 98 | 56 | .636 | 1.0 |
| Philadelphia | 83 | 71 | .539 | 16.0 |
| Cincinnati | 73 | 81 | .474 | 26.0 |
| Boston | 63 | 91 | .409 | 36.0 |
| Brooklyn | 53 | 101 | .344 | 46.0 |
| St. Louis | 49 | 105 | .318 | 50.0 |

## 1909 American League

| Team | W | L | Pct | GB |
|------|---|---|-----|-----|
| Detroit | 98 | 54 | .645 | -- |
| Philadelphia | 95 | 58 | .621 | 3.5 |
| Boston | 88 | 63 | .583 | 9.5 |
| Chicago | 78 | 74 | .513 | 20.0 |
| New York | 74 | 77 | .490 | 23.5 |
| Cleveland | 71 | 82 | .464 | 27.5 |
| St. Louis | 61 | 89 | .407 | 36.0 |
| Washington | 42 | 110 | .276 | 56.0 |

## 1909 National League

| Team | W | L | Pct | GB |
|------|---|---|-----|-----|
| Pittsburgh | 110 | 42 | .724 | -- |
| Chicago | 104 | 49 | .680 | 6.5 |
| New York | 92 | 61 | .601 | 18.5 |
| Cincinnati | 77 | 76 | .503 | 33.5 |
| Philadelphia | 74 | 79 | .484 | 36.5 |
| Brooklyn | 55 | 98 | .359 | 55.5 |
| St. Louis | 54 | 98 | .355 | 56.0 |
| Boston | 45 | 108 | .294 | 65.5 |

## 1910 American League

| Team | W | L | Pct | GB |
|------|---|---|-----|-----|
| Philadelphia | 102 | 48 | .680 | -- |
| New York | 88 | 63 | .583 | 14.5 |
| Detroit | 86 | 68 | .558 | 18.0 |
| Boston | 81 | 72 | .529 | 22.5 |
| Cleveland | 71 | 81 | .467 | 32.0 |
| Chicago | 68 | 85 | .444 | 35.5 |
| Washington | 66 | 85 | .437 | 36.5 |
| St. Louis | 47 | 107 | .305 | 57.0 |

## 1910 National League

| Team | W | L | Pct | GB |
|------|---|---|-----|-----|
| Chicago | 104 | 50 | .675 | -- |
| New York | 91 | 63 | .591 | 13.0 |
| Pittsburgh | 86 | 67 | .562 | 17.5 |
| Philadelphia | 78 | 75 | .510 | 25.5 |
| Cincinnati | 75 | 79 | .487 | 29.0 |
| Brooklyn | 64 | 90 | .416 | 40.0 |
| St. Louis | 63 | 90 | .412 | 40.5 |
| Boston | 53 | 100 | .346 | 50.5 |

## 1911 American League

| Team | W | L | Pct | GB |
|------|---|---|-----|-----|
| Philadelphia | 101 | 50 | .669 | -- |
| Detroit | 89 | 65 | .578 | 13.5 |
| Cleveland | 80 | 73 | .523 | 22.0 |
| Chicago | 77 | 74 | .510 | 24.0 |
| Boston | 78 | 75 | .510 | 24.0 |
| New York | 76 | 76 | .500 | 25.5 |
| Washington | 64 | 90 | .416 | 38.5 |
| St. Louis | 45 | 107 | .296 | 56.5 |

## 1911 National League

| Team | W | L | Pct | GB |
|------|---|---|-----|-----|
| New York | 99 | 54 | .647 | -- |
| Chicago | 92 | 62 | .597 | 7.5 |
| Pittsburgh | 85 | 69 | .552 | 14.5 |
| Philadelphia | 79 | 73 | .520 | 19.5 |
| St. Louis | 75 | 74 | .503 | 22.0 |
| Cincinnati | 70 | 83 | .458 | 29.0 |
| Brooklyn | 64 | 86 | .427 | 33.5 |
| Boston | 44 | 107 | .291 | 54.0 |

# FINAL STANDINGS

## 1912 American League

| Team | W | L | Pct | GB |
|---|---|---|---|---|
| Boston | 105 | 47 | .691 | -- |
| Washington | 91 | 61 | .599 | 14.0 |
| Philadelphia | 90 | 62 | .592 | 15.0 |
| Chicago | 78 | 76 | .506 | 28.0 |
| Cleveland | 75 | 78 | .490 | 30.5 |
| Detroit | 69 | 84 | .451 | 36.5 |
| St. Louis | 53 | 101 | .344 | 53.0 |
| New York | 50 | 102 | .329 | 55.0 |

## 1912 National League

| Team | W | L | Pct | GB |
|---|---|---|---|---|
| New York | 103 | 48 | .682 | -- |
| Pittsburgh | 93 | 58 | .616 | 10.0 |
| Chicago | 91 | 59 | .607 | 11.5 |
| Cincinnati | 75 | 78 | .490 | 29.0 |
| Philadelphia | 73 | 79 | .480 | 30.5 |
| St. Louis | 63 | 90 | .412 | 41.0 |
| Brooklyn | 58 | 95 | .379 | 46.0 |
| Boston | 52 | 101 | .340 | 52.0 |

## 1913 American League

| Team | W | L | Pct | GB |
|---|---|---|---|---|
| Philadelphia | 96 | 57 | .627 | -- |
| Washington | 90 | 64 | .584 | 6.5 |
| Cleveland | 86 | 66 | .566 | 9.5 |
| Boston | 79 | 71 | .527 | 15.5 |
| Chicago | 78 | 74 | .513 | 17.5 |
| Detroit | 66 | 87 | .431 | 30.0 |
| New York | 57 | 94 | .377 | 38.0 |
| St. Louis | 57 | 96 | .373 | 39.0 |

## 1913 National League

| Team | W | L | Pct | GB |
|---|---|---|---|---|
| New York | 101 | 51 | .664 | -- |
| Philadelphia | 88 | 63 | .583 | 12.5 |
| Chicago | 88 | 65 | .575 | 13.5 |
| Pittsburgh | 78 | 71 | .523 | 21.5 |
| Boston | 69 | 82 | .457 | 31.5 |
| Brooklyn | 65 | 84 | .436 | 34.5 |
| Cincinnati | 64 | 89 | .418 | 37.5 |
| St. Louis | 51 | 99 | .340 | 49.0 |

## 1914 American League

| Team | W | L | Pct | GB |
|---|---|---|---|---|
| Philadelphia | 99 | 53 | .651 | -- |
| Boston | 91 | 62 | .595 | 8.5 |
| Washington | 81 | 73 | .526 | 19.0 |
| Detroit | 80 | 73 | .523 | 19.5 |
| St. Louis | 71 | 82 | .464 | 28.5 |
| Chicago | 70 | 84 | .455 | 30.0 |
| New York | 70 | 84 | .455 | 30.0 |
| Cleveland | 51 | 102 | .333 | 48.5 |

## 1914 National League

| Team | W | L | Pct | GB |
|---|---|---|---|---|
| Boston | 94 | 59 | .614 | -- |
| New York | 84 | 70 | .545 | 10.5 |
| St. Louis | 81 | 72 | .529 | 13.0 |
| Chicago | 78 | 76 | .506 | 6.5 |
| Brooklyn | 75 | 79 | .487 | 19.5 |
| Philadelphia | 74 | 80 | .481 | 20.5 |
| Pittsburgh | 69 | 85 | .448 | 25.5 |
| Cincinnati | 60 | 94 | .390 | 34.5 |

## 1914 Federal League

| Team | W | L | Pct | GB |
|---|---|---|---|---|
| Indianapolis | 88 | 65 | .575 | -- |
| Chicago | 87 | 67 | .565 | 1.5 |
| Baltimore | 84 | 70 | .545 | 4.5 |
| Buffalo | 80 | 71 | .530 | 7.0 |
| Brooklyn | 77 | 77 | .500 | 11.5 |
| Kansas City | 67 | 84 | .444 | 20.0 |
| Pittsburgh | 64 | 86 | .427 | 22.5 |
| St. Louis | 62 | 89 | .411 | 25.0 |

## 1915 American League

| Team | W | L | Pct | GB |
|---|---|---|---|---|
| Boston | 101 | 50 | .669 | -- |
| Detroit | 100 | 54 | .649 | 2.5 |
| Chicago | 93 | 61 | .604 | 9.5 |
| Washington | 85 | 68 | .556 | 17.0 |
| New York | 69 | 83 | .454 | 32.5 |
| St. Louis | 63 | 91 | .409 | 39.5 |
| Cleveland | 57 | 95 | .375 | 44.5 |
| Philadelphia | 43 | 109 | .283 | 58.5 |

## 1915 National League

| Team | W | L | Pct | GB |
|---|---|---|---|---|
| Philadelphia | 90 | 62 | .592 | -- |
| Boston | 83 | 69 | .546 | 7.0 |
| Brooklyn | 80 | 72 | .526 | 10.0 |
| Chicago | 73 | 80 | .477 | 17.5 |
| Pittsburgh | 73 | 81 | .474 | 18.0 |
| St. Louis | 72 | 81 | .471 | 18.5 |
| Cincinnati | 71 | 83 | .461 | 20.0 |
| New York | 69 | 83 | .454 | 21.0 |

## 1915 Federal League

| Team | W | L | Pct | GB |
|---|---|---|---|---|
| Chicago | 86 | 66 | .566 | -- |
| St. Louis | 87 | 67 | .565 | 0.0 |
| Pittsburgh | 86 | 67 | .562 | 0.5 |
| Kansas City | 81 | 72 | .529 | 5.5 |
| Newark | 80 | 72 | .526 | 6.0 |
| Buffalo | 74 | 78 | .487 | 12.0 |
| Brooklyn | 70 | 82 | .461 | 16.0 |
| Baltimore | 47 | 107 | .305 | 40.0 |

## 1916 American League

| Team | W | L | Pct | GB |
|---|---|---|---|---|
| Boston | 91 | 63 | .591 | -- |
| Chicago | 89 | 65 | .578 | 2.0 |
| Detroit | 87 | 67 | .565 | 4.0 |
| New York | 80 | 74 | .519 | 11.0 |
| St. Louis | 79 | 75 | .513 | 12.0 |
| Cleveland | 77 | 77 | .500 | 14.0 |
| Washington | 76 | 77 | .497 | 14.5 |
| Philadelphia | 36 | 117 | .235 | 54.5 |

## 1916 National League

| Team | W | L | Pct | GB |
|---|---|---|---|---|
| Brooklyn | 94 | 60 | .610 | -- |
| Philadelphia | 91 | 62 | .595 | 2.5 |
| Boston | 89 | 63 | .586 | 4.0 |
| New York | 86 | 66 | .566 | 7.0 |
| Chicago | 67 | 86 | .438 | 26.5 |
| Pittsburgh | 65 | 89 | .422 | 29.0 |
| Cincinnati | 60 | 93 | .392 | 33.5 |
| St. Louis | 60 | 93 | .392 | 33.5 |

263

# FINAL STANDINGS

## 1917 American League

| Team | W | L | Pct | GB |
|---|---|---|---|---|
| Chicago | 100 | 54 | .649 | -- |
| Boston | 90 | 62 | .592 | 9.0 |
| Cleveland | 88 | 66 | .571 | 12.0 |
| Detroit | 78 | 75 | .510 | 21.5 |
| Washington | 74 | 79 | .484 | 25.5 |
| New York | 71 | 82 | .464 | 28.5 |
| St. Louis | 57 | 97 | .370 | 43.0 |
| Philadelphia | 55 | 98 | .359 | 44.5 |

## 1917 National League

| Team | W | L | Pct | GB |
|---|---|---|---|---|
| New York | 98 | 56 | .636 | -- |
| Philadelphia | 87 | 65 | .572 | 10.0 |
| St. Louis | 82 | 70 | .539 | 15.0 |
| Cincinnati | 78 | 76 | .506 | 20.0 |
| Chicago | 74 | 80 | .481 | 24.0 |
| Boston | 72 | 81 | .471 | 25.5 |
| Brooklyn | 70 | 81 | .464 | 26.5 |
| Pittsburgh | 51 | 103 | .331 | 47.0 |

## 1918 American League

| Team | W | L | Pct | GB |
|---|---|---|---|---|
| Boston | 75 | 51 | .595 | -- |
| Cleveland | 73 | 54 | .575 | 2.5 |
| Washington | 72 | 56 | .563 | 4.0 |
| New York | 60 | 63 | .488 | 13.5 |
| St. Louis | 58 | 64 | .475 | 15.0 |
| Chicago | 57 | 67 | .460 | 17.0 |
| Detroit | 55 | 71 | .437 | 20.0 |
| Philadelphia | 52 | 76 | .406 | 24.0 |

## 1918 National League

| Team | W | L | Pct | GB |
|---|---|---|---|---|
| Chicago | 84 | 45 | .651 | -- |
| New York | 71 | 53 | .573 | 10.5 |
| Cincinnati | 68 | 60 | .531 | 15.5 |
| Pittsburgh | 65 | 60 | .520 | 17.0 |
| Brooklyn | 57 | 69 | .452 | 25.5 |
| Philadelphia | 55 | 68 | .447 | 26.0 |
| Boston | 53 | 71 | .427 | 28.5 |
| St. Louis | 51 | 78 | .395 | 33.0 |

## 1919 American League

| Team | W | L | Pct | GB |
|---|---|---|---|---|
| Chicago | 88 | 52 | .629 | -- |
| Cleveland | 84 | 55 | .604 | 3.5 |
| New York | 80 | 59 | .576 | 7.5 |
| Detroit | 80 | 60 | .571 | 8.0 |
| St. Louis | 67 | 72 | .482 | 20.5 |
| Boston | 66 | 71 | .482 | 20.5 |
| Washington | 56 | 84 | .400 | 32.0 |
| Philadelphia | 36 | 104 | .257 | 52.0 |

## 1919 National League

| Team | W | L | Pct | GB |
|---|---|---|---|---|
| Cincinnati | 96 | 44 | .686 | -- |
| New York | 87 | 53 | .621 | 9.0 |
| Chicago | 75 | 65 | .536 | 21.0 |
| Pittsburgh | 71 | 68 | .511 | 24.5 |
| Brooklyn | 69 | 71 | .493 | 27.0 |
| Boston | 57 | 82 | .410 | 38.5 |
| St. Louis | 54 | 83 | .394 | 40.5 |
| Philadelphia | 47 | 90 | .343 | 47.5 |

## 1920 American League

| Team | W | L | Pct | GB |
|---|---|---|---|---|
| Cleveland | 98 | 56 | .636 | -- |
| Chicago | 96 | 58 | .623 | 2.0 |
| New York | 95 | 59 | .617 | 3.0 |
| St. Louis | 76 | 77 | .497 | 21.5 |
| Boston | 72 | 81 | .471 | 25.5 |
| Washington | 68 | 84 | .447 | 29.0 |
| Detroit | 61 | 93 | .396 | 37.0 |
| Philadelphia | 48 | 106 | .312 | 50.0 |

## 1920 National League

| Team | W | L | Pct | GB |
|---|---|---|---|---|
| Brooklyn | 93 | 61 | .604 | -- |
| New York | 86 | 68 | .558 | 7.0 |
| Cincinnati | 82 | 71 | .536 | 10.5 |
| Pittsburgh | 79 | 75 | .513 | 14.0 |
| Chicago | 75 | 79 | .487 | 18.0 |
| St. Louis | 75 | 79 | .487 | 18.0 |
| Boston | 62 | 90 | .408 | 30.0 |
| Philadelphia | 62 | 91 | .405 | 30.5 |

## 1921 American League

| Team | W | L | Pct | GB |
|---|---|---|---|---|
| New York | 98 | 55 | .641 | -- |
| Cleveland | 94 | 60 | .610 | 4.5 |
| St. Louis | 81 | 73 | .526 | 17.5 |
| Washington | 80 | 73 | .523 | 18.0 |
| Boston | 75 | 79 | .487 | 23.5 |
| Detroit | 71 | 82 | .464 | 27.0 |
| Chicago | 62 | 92 | .403 | 36.5 |
| Philadelphia | 53 | 100 | .346 | 45.0 |

## 1921 National League

| Team | W | L | Pct | GB |
|---|---|---|---|---|
| New York | 94 | 59 | .614 | -- |
| Pittsburgh | 90 | 63 | .588 | 4.0 |
| St. Louis | 87 | 66 | .569 | 7.0 |
| Boston | 79 | 74 | .516 | 15.0 |
| Brooklyn | 77 | 75 | .507 | 16.5 |
| Cincinnati | 70 | 83 | .458 | 24.0 |
| Chicago | 64 | 89 | .418 | 30.0 |
| Philadelphia | 51 | 103 | .331 | 43.5 |

## 1922 American League

| Team | W | L | Pct | GB |
|---|---|---|---|---|
| New York | 94 | 60 | .610 | -- |
| St. Louis | 93 | 61 | .604 | 1.0 |
| Detroit | 79 | 75 | .513 | 15.0 |
| Cleveland | 78 | 76 | .506 | 16.0 |
| Chicago | 77 | 77 | .500 | 17.0 |
| Washington | 69 | 85 | .448 | 25.0 |
| Philadelphia | 65 | 89 | .422 | 29.0 |
| Boston | 61 | 93 | .396 | 33.0 |

## 1922 National League

| Team | W | L | Pct | GB |
|---|---|---|---|---|
| New York | 93 | 61 | .604 | -- |
| Cincinnati | 86 | 68 | .558 | 7.0 |
| Pittsburgh | 85 | 69 | .552 | 8.0 |
| St. Louis | 85 | 69 | .552 | 8.0 |
| Chicago | 80 | 74 | .519 | 13.0 |
| Brooklyn | 76 | 78 | .494 | 17.0 |
| Philadelphia | 57 | 96 | .373 | 35.5 |
| Boston | 53 | 100 | .346 | 39.5 |

# FINAL STANDINGS

### 1923 American League

| Team | W | L | Pct | GB |
|---|---|---|---|---|
| New York | 98 | 54 | .645 | -- |
| Detroit | 83 | 71 | .539 | 16.0 |
| Cleveland | 82 | 71 | .536 | 16.5 |
| Washington | 75 | 78 | .490 | 23.5 |
| St. Louis | 74 | 78 | .487 | 24.0 |
| Philadelphia | 69 | 83 | .454 | 29.0 |
| Chicago | 69 | 85 | .448 | 30.0 |
| Boston | 61 | 91 | .401 | 37.0 |

### 1923 National League

| Team | W | L | Pct | GB |
|---|---|---|---|---|
| New York | 95 | 58 | .621 | -- |
| Cincinnati | 91 | 63 | .591 | 4.5 |
| Pittsburgh | 87 | 67 | .565 | 8.5 |
| Chicago | 83 | 71 | .539 | 12.5 |
| St. Louis | 79 | 74 | .516 | 16.0 |
| Brooklyn | 76 | 78 | .494 | 19.5 |
| Boston | 54 | 100 | .351 | 41.5 |
| Philadelphia | 50 | 104 | .325 | 45.5 |

### 1924 American League

| Team | W | L | Pct | GB |
|---|---|---|---|---|
| Washington | 92 | 62 | .597 | -- |
| New York | 89 | 63 | .586 | 2.0 |
| Detroit | 86 | 68 | .558 | 6.0 |
| St. Louis | 74 | 78 | .487 | 17.0 |
| Philadelphia | 71 | 81 | .467 | 20.0 |
| Cleveland | 67 | 86 | .438 | 24.5 |
| Boston | 67 | 87 | .435 | 25.0 |
| Chicago | 66 | 87 | .431 | 25.5 |

### 1924 National League

| Team | W | L | Pct | GB |
|---|---|---|---|---|
| New York | 93 | 60 | .608 | -- |
| Brooklyn | 92 | 62 | .597 | 1.5 |
| Pittsburgh | 90 | 63 | .588 | 3.0 |
| Cincinnati | 83 | 70 | .542 | 10.0 |
| Chicago | 81 | 72 | .529 | 12.0 |
| St. Louis | 65 | 89 | .422 | 28.5 |
| Philadelphia | 55 | 96 | .364 | 37.0 |
| Boston | 53 | 100 | .346 | 40.0 |

### 1925 American League

| Team | W | L | Pct | GB |
|---|---|---|---|---|
| Washington | 96 | 55 | .636 | -- |
| Philadelphia | 88 | 64 | .579 | 8.5 |
| St. Louis | 82 | 71 | .536 | 15.0 |
| Detroit | 81 | 73 | .526 | 16.5 |
| Chicago | 79 | 75 | .513 | 18.5 |
| Cleveland | 70 | 84 | .455 | 27.5 |
| New York | 69 | 85 | .448 | 28.5 |
| Boston | 47 | 105 | .309 | 49.5 |

### 1925 National League

| Team | W | L | Pct | GB |
|---|---|---|---|---|
| Pittsburgh | 95 | 58 | .621 | -- |
| New York | 86 | 66 | .566 | 8.5 |
| Cincinnati | 80 | 73 | .523 | 15.0 |
| St. Louis | 77 | 76 | .503 | 18.0 |
| Boston | 70 | 83 | .458 | 25.0 |
| Philadelphia | 68 | 85 | .444 | 27.0 |
| Brooklyn | 68 | 85 | .444 | 27.0 |
| Chicago | 68 | 86 | .442 | 27.5 |

### 1926 American League

| Team | W | L | Pct | GB |
|---|---|---|---|---|
| New York | 91 | 63 | .591 | -- |
| Cleveland | 88 | 66 | .571 | 3.0 |
| Philadelphia | 83 | 67 | .553 | 6.0 |
| Washington | 81 | 69 | .540 | 8.0 |
| Chicago | 81 | 72 | .529 | 9.5 |
| Detroit | 79 | 75 | .513 | 12.0 |
| St. Louis | 62 | 92 | .403 | 29.0 |
| Boston | 46 | 107 | .301 | 44.5 |

### 1926 National League

| Team | W | L | Pct | GB |
|---|---|---|---|---|
| St. Louis | 89 | 65 | .578 | -- |
| Cincinnati | 87 | 67 | .565 | 2.0 |
| Pittsburgh | 84 | 69 | .549 | 4.5 |
| Chicago | 82 | 72 | .532 | 7.0 |
| New York | 74 | 77 | .490 | 13.5 |
| Brooklyn | 71 | 82 | .464 | 17.5 |
| Boston | 66 | 86 | .434 | 22.0 |
| Philadelphia | 58 | 93 | .384 | 29.5 |

### 1927 American League

| Team | W | L | Pct | GB |
|---|---|---|---|---|
| New York | 110 | 44 | .714 | -- |
| Philadelphia | 91 | 63 | .591 | 19.0 |
| Washington | 85 | 69 | .552 | 25.0 |
| Detroit | 82 | 71 | .536 | 27.5 |
| Chicago | 70 | 83 | .458 | 39.5 |
| Cleveland | 66 | 87 | .431 | 43.5 |
| St. Louis | 59 | 94 | .386 | 50.5 |
| Boston | 51 | 103 | .331 | 59.0 |

### 1927 National League

| Team | W | L | Pct | GB |
|---|---|---|---|---|
| Pittsburgh | 94 | 60 | .610 | -- |
| St. Louis | 92 | 61 | .601 | 1.5 |
| New York | 92 | 62 | .597 | 2.0 |
| Chicago | 85 | 68 | .556 | 8.5 |
| Cincinnati | 75 | 78 | .490 | 18.5 |
| Brooklyn | 65 | 88 | .425 | 28.5 |
| Boston | 60 | 94 | .390 | 34.0 |
| Philadelphia | 51 | 103 | .331 | 43.0 |

### 1928 American League

| Team | W | L | Pct | GB |
|---|---|---|---|---|
| New York | 101 | 53 | .656 | -- |
| Philadelphia | 98 | 55 | .641 | 2.5 |
| St. Louis | 82 | 72 | .532 | 19.0 |
| Washington | 75 | 79 | .487 | 26.0 |
| Chicago | 72 | 82 | .468 | 29.0 |
| Detroit | 68 | 86 | .442 | 33.0 |
| Cleveland | 62 | 92 | .403 | 39.0 |
| Boston | 57 | 96 | .373 | 43.5 |

### 1928 National League

| Team | W | L | Pct | GB |
|---|---|---|---|---|
| St. Louis | 95 | 59 | .617 | -- |
| New York | 93 | 61 | .604 | 2.0 |
| Chicago | 91 | 63 | .591 | 4.0 |
| Pittsburgh | 85 | 67 | .559 | 9.0 |
| Cincinnati | 78 | 74 | .513 | 16.0 |
| Brooklyn | 77 | 76 | .503 | 17.5 |
| Boston | 50 | 103 | .327 | 44.5 |
| Philadelphia | 43 | 109 | .283 | 51.0 |

265

# FINAL STANDINGS

### 1929 American League

| Team | W | L | Pct | GB |
|---|---|---|---|---|
| Philadelphia | 104 | 46 | .693 | -- |
| New York | 88 | 66 | .571 | 18.0 |
| Cleveland | 81 | 71 | .533 | 24.0 |
| St. Louis | 79 | 73 | .520 | 26.0 |
| Washington | 71 | 81 | .467 | 34.0 |
| Detroit | 70 | 84 | .455 | 36.0 |
| Chicago | 59 | 93 | .388 | 46.0 |
| Boston | 58 | 96 | .377 | 48.0 |

### 1929 National League

| Team | W | L | Pct | GB |
|---|---|---|---|---|
| Chicago | 98 | 54 | .645 | -- |
| Pittsburgh | 88 | 65 | .575 | 10.5 |
| New York | 84 | 67 | .556 | 13.5 |
| St. Louis | 78 | 74 | .513 | 20.0 |
| Philadelphia | 71 | 82 | .464 | 27.5 |
| Brooklyn | 70 | 83 | .458 | 28.5 |
| Cincinnati | 66 | 88 | .429 | 33.0 |
| Boston | 56 | 98 | .364 | 43.0 |

### 1930 American League

| Team | W | L | Pct | GB |
|---|---|---|---|---|
| Philadelphia | 102 | 52 | .662 | -- |
| Washington | 94 | 60 | .610 | 8.0 |
| New York | 86 | 68 | .558 | 16.0 |
| Cleveland | 81 | 73 | .526 | 21.0 |
| Detroit | 75 | 79 | .487 | 27.0 |
| St. Louis | 64 | 90 | .416 | 38.0 |
| Chicago | 62 | 92 | .403 | 40.0 |
| Boston | 52 | 102 | .338 | 50.0 |

### 1930 National League

| Team | W | L | Pct | GB |
|---|---|---|---|---|
| St. Louis | 92 | 62 | .597 | -- |
| Chicago | 90 | 64 | .584 | 2.0 |
| New York | 87 | 67 | .565 | 5.0 |
| Brooklyn | 86 | 68 | .558 | 6.0 |
| Pittsburgh | 80 | 74 | .519 | 12.0 |
| Boston | 70 | 84 | .455 | 22.0 |
| Cincinnati | 59 | 95 | .383 | 33.0 |
| Philadelphia | 52 | 102 | .338 | 40.0 |

### 1931 American League

| Team | W | L | Pct | GB |
|---|---|---|---|---|
| Philadelphia | 107 | 45 | .704 | -- |
| New York | 94 | 59 | .614 | 13.5 |
| Washington | 92 | 62 | .597 | 16.0 |
| Cleveland | 78 | 76 | .506 | 30.0 |
| St. Louis | 63 | 91 | .409 | 45.0 |
| Boston | 62 | 90 | .408 | 45.0 |
| Detroit | 61 | 93 | .396 | 47.0 |
| Chicago | 56 | 97 | .366 | 51.5 |

### 1931 National League

| Team | W | L | Pct | GB |
|---|---|---|---|---|
| St. Louis | 101 | 53 | .656 | -- |
| New York | 87 | 65 | .572 | 13.0 |
| Chicago | 84 | 70 | .545 | 17.0 |
| Brooklyn | 79 | 73 | .520 | 21.0 |
| Pittsburgh | 75 | 79 | .487 | 26.0 |
| Philadelphia | 66 | 88 | .429 | 35.0 |
| Boston | 64 | 90 | .416 | 37.0 |
| Cincinnati | 58 | 96 | .377 | 43.0 |

### 1932 American League

| Team | W | L | Pct | GB |
|---|---|---|---|---|
| New York | 107 | 47 | .695 | -- |
| Philadelphia | 94 | 60 | .610 | 13.0 |
| Washington | 93 | 61 | .604 | 4.0 |
| Cleveland | 87 | 65 | .572 | 19.0 |
| Detroit | 76 | 75 | .503 | 29.5 |
| St. Louis | 63 | 91 | .409 | 44.0 |
| Chicago | 49 | 102 | .325 | 56.5 |
| Boston | 43 | 111 | .279 | 64.0 |

### 1932 National League

| Team | W | L | Pct | GB |
|---|---|---|---|---|
| Chicago | 90 | 64 | .584 | -- |
| Pittsburgh | 86 | 68 | .558 | 4.0 |
| Brooklyn | 81 | 73 | .526 | 9.0 |
| Philadelphia | 78 | 76 | .506 | 12.0 |
| Boston | 77 | 77 | .500 | 13.0 |
| St. Louis | 72 | 82 | .468 | 18.0 |
| New York | 72 | 82 | .468 | 18.0 |
| Cincinnati | 60 | 94 | .390 | 30.0 |

### 1933 American League

| Team | W | L | Pct | GB |
|---|---|---|---|---|
| Washington | 99 | 53 | .651 | -- |
| New York | 91 | 59 | .607 | 7.0 |
| Philadelphia | 79 | 72 | .523 | 19.5 |
| Cleveland | 75 | 76 | .497 | 23.5 |
| Detroit | 75 | 79 | .487 | 25.0 |
| Chicago | 67 | 83 | .447 | 31.0 |
| Boston | 63 | 86 | .423 | 34.5 |
| St. Louis | 55 | 96 | .364 | 43.5 |

### 1933 National League

| Team | W | L | Pct | GB |
|---|---|---|---|---|
| New York | 91 | 61 | .599 | -- |
| Pittsburgh | 87 | 67 | .565 | 5.0 |
| Chicago | 86 | 68 | .558 | 6.0 |
| Boston | 83 | 71 | .539 | 9.0 |
| St. Louis | 82 | 71 | .536 | 9.5 |
| Brooklyn | 65 | 88 | .425 | 26.5 |
| Philadelphia | 60 | 92 | .395 | 31.0 |
| Cincinnati | 58 | 94 | .382 | 33.0 |

### 1934 American League

| Team | W | L | Pct | GB |
|---|---|---|---|---|
| Detroit | 101 | 53 | .656 | -- |
| New York | 94 | 60 | .610 | 7.0 |
| Cleveland | 85 | 69 | .552 | 16.0 |
| Boston | 76 | 76 | .500 | 24.0 |
| Philadelphia | 68 | 82 | .453 | 31.0 |
| St. Louis | 67 | 85 | .441 | 33.0 |
| Washington | 66 | 86 | .434 | 34.0 |
| Chicago | 53 | 99 | .349 | 47.0 |

### 1934 National League

| Team | W | L | Pct | GB |
|---|---|---|---|---|
| St. Louis | 95 | 58 | .621 | -- |
| New York | 93 | 60 | .608 | 2.0 |
| Chicago | 86 | 65 | .570 | 8.0 |
| Boston | 78 | 73 | .517 | 16.0 |
| Pittsburgh | 74 | 76 | .493 | 19.5 |
| Brooklyn | 71 | 81 | .467 | 23.5 |
| Philadelphia | 56 | 93 | .376 | 37.0 |
| Cincinnati | 52 | 99 | .344 | 42.0 |

# FINAL STANDINGS

## 1935 American League

| Team | W | L | Pct | GB |
|---|---|---|---|---|
| Detroit | 93 | 58 | .616 | -- |
| New York | 89 | 60 | .597 | 3.0 |
| Cleveland | 82 | 71 | .536 | 12.0 |
| Boston | 78 | 75 | .510 | 16.0 |
| Chicago | 74 | 78 | .487 | 19.5 |
| Washington | 67 | 86 | .438 | 27.0 |
| St. Louis | 65 | 87 | .428 | 28.5 |
| Philadelphia | 58 | 91 | .389 | 34.0 |

## 1935 National League

| Team | W | L | Pct | GB |
|---|---|---|---|---|
| Chicago | 100 | 54 | .649 | -- |
| St. Louis | 96 | 58 | .623 | 4.0 |
| New York | 91 | 62 | .595 | 8.5 |
| Pittsburgh | 86 | 67 | .562 | 13.5 |
| Brooklyn | 70 | 83 | .458 | 29.5 |
| Cincinnati | 68 | 85 | .444 | 31.5 |
| Philadelphia | 64 | 89 | .418 | 35.5 |
| Boston | 38 | 115 | .248 | 61.5 |

## 1936 American League

| Team | W | L | Pct | GB |
|---|---|---|---|---|
| New York | 102 | 51 | .667 | -- |
| Detroit | 83 | 71 | .539 | 19.5 |
| Chicago | 81 | 70 | .536 | 20.0 |
| Washington | 82 | 71 | .536 | 20.0 |
| Cleveland | 80 | 74 | .519 | 22.5 |
| Boston | 74 | 80 | .481 | 28.5 |
| St. Louis | 57 | 95 | .375 | 44.5 |
| Philadelphia | 53 | 100 | .346 | 49.0 |

## 1936 National League

| Team | W | L | Pct | GB |
|---|---|---|---|---|
| New York | 92 | 62 | .597 | -- |
| Chicago | 87 | 67 | .565 | 5.0 |
| St. Louis | 87 | 67 | .565 | 5.0 |
| Pittsburgh | 84 | 70 | .545 | 8.0 |
| Cincinnati | 74 | 80 | .481 | 18.0 |
| Boston | 71 | 83 | .461 | 21.0 |
| Brooklyn | 67 | 87 | .435 | 25.0 |
| Philadelphia | 54 | 100 | .351 | 38.0 |

## 1937 American League

| Team | W | L | Pct | GB |
|---|---|---|---|---|
| New York | 102 | 52 | .662 | -- |
| Detroit | 89 | 65 | .578 | 13.0 |
| Chicago | 86 | 68 | .558 | 16.0 |
| Cleveland | 83 | 71 | .539 | 19.0 |
| Boston | 80 | 72 | .526 | 21.0 |
| Washington | 73 | 80 | .477 | 28.5 |
| Philadelphia | 54 | 97 | .358 | 46.5 |
| St. Louis | 46 | 108 | .299 | 56.0 |

## 1937 National League

| Team | W | L | Pct | GB |
|---|---|---|---|---|
| New York | 95 | 57 | .625 | -- |
| Chicago | 93 | 61 | .604 | 3.0 |
| Pittsburgh | 86 | 68 | .558 | 10.0 |
| St. Louis | 81 | 73 | .526 | 15.0 |
| Boston | 79 | 73 | .520 | 16.0 |
| Brooklyn | 62 | 91 | .405 | 33.5 |
| Philadelphia | 61 | 92 | .399 | 34.5 |
| Cincinnati | 56 | 98 | .364 | 40.0 |

## 1938 American League

| Team | W | L | Pct | GB |
|---|---|---|---|---|
| New York | 99 | 53 | .651 | -- |
| Boston | 88 | 61 | .591 | 9.5 |
| Cleveland | 86 | 66 | .566 | 13.0 |
| Detroit | 84 | 70 | .545 | 16.0 |
| Washington | 75 | 76 | .497 | 23.5 |
| Chicago | 65 | 83 | .439 | 32.0 |
| St. Louis | 55 | 97 | .362 | 44.0 |
| Philadelphia | 53 | 99 | .349 | 46.0 |

## 1938 National League

| Team | W | L | Pct | GB |
|---|---|---|---|---|
| Chicago | 89 | 63 | .586 | -- |
| Pittsburgh | 86 | 64 | .573 | 2.0 |
| New York | 83 | 67 | .553 | 5.0 |
| Cincinnati | 82 | 68 | .547 | 6.0 |
| Boston | 77 | 75 | .507 | 12.0 |
| St. Louis | 71 | 80 | .470 | 17.5 |
| Brooklyn | 69 | 80 | .463 | 18.5 |
| Philadelphia | 45 | 105 | .300 | 43.0 |

## 1939 American League

| Team | W | L | Pct | GB |
|---|---|---|---|---|
| New York | 106 | 45 | .702 | -- |
| Boston | 89 | 62 | .589 | 17.0 |
| Cleveland | 87 | 67 | .565 | 20.5 |
| Chicago | 85 | 69 | .552 | 22.5 |
| Detroit | 81 | 73 | .526 | 26.5 |
| Washington | 65 | 87 | .428 | 41.5 |
| Philadelphia | 55 | 97 | .362 | 51.5 |
| St. Louis | 43 | 111 | .279 | 64.5 |

## 1939 National League

| Team | W | L | Pct | GB |
|---|---|---|---|---|
| Cincinnati | 97 | 57 | .630 | -- |
| St. Louis | 92 | 61 | .601 | 4.5 |
| Brooklyn | 84 | 69 | .549 | 12.5 |
| Chicago | 84 | 70 | .545 | 13.0 |
| New York | 77 | 74 | .510 | 18.5 |
| Pittsburgh | 68 | 85 | .444 | 28.5 |
| Boston | 63 | 88 | .417 | 32.5 |
| Philadelphia | 45 | 106 | .298 | 50.5 |

## 1940 American League

| Team | W | L | Pct | GB |
|---|---|---|---|---|
| Detroit | 90 | 64 | .584 | -- |
| Cleveland | 89 | 65 | .578 | 1.0 |
| New York | 88 | 66 | .571 | 2.0 |
| Boston | 82 | 72 | .532 | 8.0 |
| Chicago | 82 | 72 | .532 | 8.0 |
| St. Louis | 67 | 87 | .435 | 23.0 |
| Washington | 64 | 90 | .416 | 26.0 |
| Philadelphia | 54 | 100 | .351 | 36.0 |

## 1940 National League

| Team | W | L | Pct | GB |
|---|---|---|---|---|
| Cincinnati | 100 | 53 | .654 | -- |
| Brooklyn | 88 | 65 | .575 | 12.0 |
| St. Louis | 84 | 69 | .549 | 16.0 |
| Pittsburgh | 78 | 76 | .506 | 22.5 |
| Chicago | 75 | 79 | .487 | 25.5 |
| New York | 72 | 80 | .474 | 27.5 |
| Boston | 65 | 87 | .428 | 34.5 |
| Philadelphia | 50 | 103 | .327 | 50.0 |

# FINAL STANDINGS

## 1941 American League

| Team | W | L | Pct | GB |
|------|---|---|-----|-----|
| New York | 101 | 53 | .656 | -- |
| Boston | 84 | 70 | .545 | 17.0 |
| Chicago | 77 | 77 | .500 | 24.0 |
| Cleveland | 75 | 79 | .487 | 26.0 |
| Detroit | 75 | 79 | .487 | 26.0 |
| St. Louis | 70 | 84 | .455 | 31.0 |
| Washington | 70 | 84 | .455 | 31.0 |
| Philadelphia | 64 | 90 | .416 | 37.0 |

## 1941 National League

| Team | W | L | Pct | GB |
|------|---|---|-----|-----|
| Brooklyn | 100 | 54 | .649 | -- |
| St. Louis | 97 | 56 | .634 | 2.5 |
| Cincinnati | 88 | 66 | .571 | 12.0 |
| Pittsburgh | 81 | 73 | .526 | 19.0 |
| New York | 74 | 79 | .484 | 25.5 |
| Chicago | 70 | 84 | .455 | 30.0 |
| Boston | 62 | 92 | .403 | 38.0 |
| Philadelphia | 43 | 111 | .279 | 57.0 |

## 1942 American League

| Team | W | L | Pct | GB |
|------|---|---|-----|-----|
| New York | 103 | 51 | .669 | -- |
| Boston | 93 | 59 | .612 | 9.0 |
| St. Louis | 82 | 69 | .543 | 19.5 |
| Cleveland | 75 | 79 | .487 | 28.0 |
| Detroit | 73 | 81 | .474 | 30.0 |
| Chicago | 66 | 82 | .446 | 34.0 |
| Washington | 62 | 89 | .411 | 39.5 |
| Philadelphia | 55 | 99 | .357 | 48.0 |

## 1942 National League

| Team | W | L | Pct | GB |
|------|---|---|-----|-----|
| St. Louis | 106 | 48 | .688 | -- |
| Brooklyn | 104 | 50 | .675 | 2.0 |
| New York | 85 | 67 | .559 | 20.0 |
| Cincinnati | 76 | 76 | .500 | 29.0 |
| Pittsburgh | 66 | 81 | .449 | 36.5 |
| Chicago | 68 | 86 | .442 | 38.0 |
| Boston | 59 | 89 | .399 | 44.0 |
| Philadelphia | 42 | 109 | .278 | 62.5 |

## 1943 American League

| Team | W | L | Pct | GB |
|------|---|---|-----|-----|
| New York | 98 | 56 | .636 | -- |
| Washington | 84 | 69 | .549 | 13.5 |
| Cleveland | 82 | 71 | .536 | 15.5 |
| Chicago | 82 | 72 | .532 | 16.0 |
| Detroit | 78 | 76 | .506 | 20.0 |
| St. Louis | 72 | 80 | .474 | 25.0 |
| Boston | 68 | 84 | .447 | 29.0 |
| Philadelphia | 49 | 105 | .318 | 49.0 |

## 1943 National League

| Team | W | L | Pct | GB |
|------|---|---|-----|-----|
| St. Louis | 105 | 49 | .682 | -- |
| Cincinnati | 87 | 67 | .565 | 18.0 |
| Brooklyn | 81 | 72 | .529 | 23.5 |
| Pittsburgh | 80 | 74 | .519 | 25.0 |
| Chicago | 74 | 79 | .484 | 30.5 |
| Boston | 68 | 85 | .444 | 36.5 |
| Philadelphia | 64 | 90 | .416 | 41.0 |
| New York | 55 | 98 | .359 | 49.5 |

## 1944 American League

| Team | W | L | Pct | GB |
|------|---|---|-----|-----|
| St. Louis | 89 | 65 | .578 | -- |
| Detroit | 88 | 66 | .571 | 1.0 |
| New York | 83 | 71 | .539 | 6.0 |
| Boston | 77 | 77 | .500 | 12.0 |
| Cleveland | 72 | 82 | .468 | 17.0 |
| Philadelphia | 72 | 82 | .468 | 17.0 |
| Chicago | 71 | 83 | .461 | 18.0 |
| Washington | 64 | 90 | .416 | 25.0 |

## 1944 National League

| Team | W | L | Pct | GB |
|------|---|---|-----|-----|
| St. Louis | 105 | 49 | .682 | -- |
| Pittsburgh | 90 | 63 | .588 | 14.5 |
| Cincinnati | 89 | 65 | .578 | 16.0 |
| Chicago | 75 | 79 | .487 | 30.0 |
| New York | 67 | 87 | .435 | 38.0 |
| Boston | 65 | 89 | .422 | 40.0 |
| Brooklyn | 63 | 91 | .409 | 42.0 |
| Philadelphia | 61 | 92 | .399 | 43.5 |

## 1945 American League

| Team | W | L | Pct | GB |
|------|---|---|-----|-----|
| Detroit | 88 | 65 | .575 | -- |
| Washington | 87 | 67 | .565 | 1.5 |
| St. Louis | 81 | 70 | .536 | 6.0 |
| New York | 81 | 71 | .533 | 6.5 |
| Cleveland | 73 | 72 | .503 | 11.0 |
| Chicago | 71 | 78 | .477 | 15.0 |
| Boston | 71 | 83 | .461 | 17.5 |
| Philadelphia | 52 | 98 | .347 | 34.5 |

## 1945 National League

| Team | W | L | Pct | GB |
|------|---|---|-----|-----|
| Chicago | 98 | 56 | .636 | -- |
| St. Louis | 95 | 59 | .617 | 3.0 |
| Brooklyn | 87 | 67 | .565 | 11.0 |
| Pittsburgh | 82 | 72 | .532 | 16.0 |
| New York | 78 | 74 | .513 | 19.0 |
| Boston | 67 | 85 | .441 | 30.0 |
| Cincinnati | 61 | 93 | .396 | 37.0 |
| Philadelphia | 46 | 108 | .299 | 52.0 |

## 1946 American League

| Team | W | L | Pct | GB |
|------|---|---|-----|-----|
| Boston | 104 | 50 | .675 | -- |
| Detroit | 92 | 62 | .597 | 12.0 |
| New York | 87 | 67 | .565 | 17.0 |
| Washington | 76 | 78 | .494 | 28.0 |
| Chicago | 74 | 80 | .481 | 30.0 |
| Cleveland | 68 | 86 | .442 | 36.0 |
| St. Louis | 66 | 88 | .429 | 38.0 |
| Philadelphia | 49 | 105 | .318 | 55.0 |

## 1946 National League

| Team | W | L | Pct | GB |
|------|---|---|-----|-----|
| St. Louis | 98 | 58 | .628 | -- |
| Brooklyn | 96 | 60 | .615 | 2.0 |
| Chicago | 82 | 71 | .536 | 14.5 |
| Boston | 81 | 72 | .529 | 15.5 |
| Philadelphia | 69 | 85 | .448 | 28.0 |
| Cincinnati | 67 | 87 | .435 | 30.0 |
| Pittsburgh | 63 | 91 | .409 | 34.0 |
| New York | 61 | 93 | .396 | 36.0 |

# FINAL STANDINGS

**1947 American League**

| Team | W | L | Pct | GB |
|---|---|---|---|---|
| New York | 97 | 57 | .630 | -- |
| Detroit | 85 | 69 | .552 | 12.0 |
| Boston | 83 | 71 | .539 | 14.0 |
| Cleveland | 80 | 74 | .519 | 17.0 |
| Philadelphia | 78 | 76 | .506 | 19.0 |
| Chicago | 70 | 84 | .455 | 27.0 |
| Washington | 64 | 90 | .416 | 33.0 |
| St. Louis | 59 | 95 | .383 | 38.0 |

**1947 National League**

| Team | W | L | Pct | GB |
|---|---|---|---|---|
| Brooklyn | 94 | 60 | .610 | -- |
| St. Louis | 89 | 65 | .578 | 5.0 |
| Boston | 86 | 68 | .558 | 8.0 |
| New York | 81 | 73 | .526 | 13.0 |
| Cincinnati | 73 | 81 | .474 | 21.0 |
| Chicago | 69 | 85 | .448 | 25.0 |
| Philadelphia | 62 | 92 | .403 | 32.0 |
| Pittsburgh | 62 | 92 | .403 | 32.0 |

**1948 American League**

| Team | W | L | Pct | GB |
|---|---|---|---|---|
| Cleveland | 97 | 58 | .626 | -- |
| Boston | 96 | 59 | .619 | 1.0 |
| New York | 94 | 60 | .610 | 2.5 |
| Philadelphia | 84 | 70 | .545 | 12.5 |
| Detroit | 78 | 76 | .506 | 18.5 |
| St. Louis | 59 | 94 | .386 | 37.0 |
| Washington | 56 | 97 | .366 | 40.0 |
| Chicago | 51 | 101 | .336 | 44.5 |

**1948 National League**

| Team | W | L | Pct | GB |
|---|---|---|---|---|
| Boston | 91 | 62 | .595 | -- |
| St. Louis | 85 | 69 | .552 | 6.5 |
| Brooklyn | 84 | 70 | .545 | 7.5 |
| Pittsburgh | 83 | 71 | .539 | 8.5 |
| New York | 78 | 76 | .506 | 13.5 |
| Philadelphia | 66 | 88 | .429 | 25.5 |
| Cincinnati | 64 | 89 | .418 | 27.0 |
| Chicago | 64 | 90 | .416 | 27.5 |

**1949 American League**

| Team | W | L | Pct | GB |
|---|---|---|---|---|
| New York | 97 | 57 | .630 | -- |
| Boston | 96 | 58 | .623 | 1.0 |
| Cleveland | 89 | 65 | .578 | 8.0 |
| Detroit | 87 | 67 | .565 | 10.0 |
| Philadelphia | 81 | 73 | .526 | 16.0 |
| Chicago | 63 | 91 | .409 | 34.0 |
| St. Louis | 53 | 101 | .344 | 44.0 |
| Washington | 50 | 104 | .325 | 47.0 |

**1949 National League**

| Team | W | L | Pct | GB |
|---|---|---|---|---|
| Brooklyn | 97 | 57 | .630 | -- |
| St. Louis | 96 | 58 | .623 | 1.0 |
| Philadelphia | 81 | 73 | .526 | 16.0 |
| Boston | 75 | 79 | .487 | 22.0 |
| New York | 73 | 81 | .474 | 24.0 |
| Pittsburgh | 71 | 83 | .461 | 26.0 |
| Cincinnati | 62 | 92 | .403 | 35.0 |
| Chicago | 61 | 93 | .396 | 36.0 |

**1950 American League**

| Team | W | L | Pct | GB |
|---|---|---|---|---|
| New York | 98 | 56 | .636 | -- |
| Detroit | 95 | 59 | .617 | 3.0 |
| Boston | 94 | 60 | .610 | 4.0 |
| Cleveland | 92 | 62 | .597 | 6.0 |
| Washington | 67 | 87 | .435 | 31.0 |
| Chicago | 60 | 94 | .390 | 38.0 |
| St. Louis | 58 | 96 | .377 | 40.0 |
| Philadelphia | 52 | 102 | .338 | 46.0 |

**1950 National League**

| Team | W | L | Pct | GB |
|---|---|---|---|---|
| Philadelphia | 91 | 63 | .591 | -- |
| Brooklyn | 89 | 65 | .578 | 2.0 |
| New York | 86 | 68 | .558 | 5.0 |
| Boston | 83 | 71 | .539 | 8.0 |
| St. Louis | 78 | 75 | .510 | 12.5 |
| Cincinnati | 66 | 87 | .431 | 24.5 |
| Chicago | 64 | 89 | .418 | 26.5 |
| Pittsburgh | 57 | 96 | .373 | 33.5 |

**1951 American League**

| Team | W | L | Pct | GB |
|---|---|---|---|---|
| New York | 98 | 56 | .636 | -- |
| Cleveland | 93 | 61 | .604 | 5.0 |
| Boston | 87 | 67 | .565 | 11.0 |
| Chicago | 81 | 73 | .526 | 17.0 |
| Detroit | 73 | 81 | .474 | 25.0 |
| Philadelphia | 70 | 84 | .455 | 28.0 |
| Washington | 62 | 92 | .403 | 36.0 |
| St. Louis | 52 | 102 | .338 | 46.0 |

**1951 National League**

| Team | W | L | Pct | GB |
|---|---|---|---|---|
| New York | 98 | 59 | .624 | -- |
| Brooklyn | 97 | 60 | .618 | 1.0 |
| St. Louis | 81 | 73 | .526 | 15.5 |
| Boston | 76 | 78 | .494 | 20.5 |
| Philadelphia | 73 | 81 | .474 | 23.5 |
| Cincinnati | 68 | 86 | .442 | 28.5 |
| Pittsburgh | 64 | 90 | .416 | 32.5 |
| Chicago | 62 | 92 | .403 | 34.5 |

**1952 American League**

| Team | W | L | Pct | GB |
|---|---|---|---|---|
| New York | 95 | 59 | .617 | -- |
| Cleveland | 93 | 61 | .604 | 2.0 |
| Chicago | 81 | 73 | .526 | 14.0 |
| Philadelphia | 79 | 75 | .513 | 16.0 |
| Washington | 78 | 76 | .506 | 17.0 |
| Boston | 76 | 78 | .494 | 19.0 |
| St. Louis | 64 | 90 | .416 | 31.0 |
| Detroit | 50 | 104 | .325 | 45.0 |

**1952 National League**

| Team | W | L | Pct | GB |
|---|---|---|---|---|
| Brooklyn | 96 | 57 | .627 | -- |
| New York | 92 | 62 | .597 | 4.5 |
| St. Louis | 88 | 66 | .571 | 8.5 |
| Philadelphia | 87 | 67 | .565 | 9.5 |
| Chicago | 77 | 77 | .500 | 19.5 |
| Cincinnati | 69 | 85 | .448 | 27.5 |
| Boston | 64 | 89 | .418 | 32.0 |
| Pittsburgh | 42 | 112 | .273 | 54.5 |

269

# FINAL STANDINGS

### 1953 American League
| Team | W | L | Pct | GB |
|---|---|---|---|---|
| New York | 99 | 52 | .656 | -- |
| Cleveland | 92 | 62 | .597 | 8.5 |
| Chicago | 89 | 65 | .578 | 11.5 |
| Boston | 84 | 69 | .549 | 16.0 |
| Washington | 76 | 76 | .500 | 23.5 |
| Detroit | 60 | 94 | .390 | 40.5 |
| Philadelphia | 59 | 95 | .383 | 41.5 |
| St. Louis | 54 | 100 | .351 | 46.5 |

### 1953 National League
| Team | W | L | Pct | GB- |
|---|---|---|---|---|
| Brooklyn | 105 | 49 | .682 | -- |
| Milwaukee | 92 | 62 | .597 | 13.0 |
| Philadelphia | 83 | 71 | .539 | 22.0 |
| St. Louis | 83 | 71 | .539 | 22.0 |
| New York | 70 | 84 | .455 | 35.0 |
| Cincinnati | 68 | 86 | .442 | 37.0 |
| Chicago | 65 | 89 | .422 | 40.0 |
| Pittsburgh | 50 | 104 | .325 | 55.0 |

### 1954 American League
| Team | W | L | Pct | GB- |
|---|---|---|---|---|
| Cleveland | 111 | 43 | .721 | -- |
| New York | 103 | 51 | .669 | 8.0 |
| Chicago | 94 | 60 | .610 | 17.0 |
| Boston | 69 | 85 | .448 | 42.0 |
| Detroit | 68 | 86 | .442 | 43.0 |
| Washington | 66 | 88 | .429 | 45.0 |
| Baltimore | 54 | 100 | .351 | 57.0 |
| Philadelphia | 51 | 103 | .331 | 60.0 |

### 1954 National League
| Team | W | L | Pct | GB |
|---|---|---|---|---|
| New York | 97 | 57 | .630 | -- |
| Brooklyn | 92 | 62 | .597 | 5.0 |
| Milwaukee | 89 | 65 | .578 | 8.0 |
| Philadelphia | 75 | 79 | .487 | 22.0 |
| Cincinnati | 74 | 80 | .481 | 23.0 |
| St. Louis | 72 | 82 | .468 | 25.0 |
| Chicago | 64 | 90 | .416 | 33.0 |
| Pittsburgh | 53 | 101 | .344 | 44.0 |

### 1955 American League
| Team | W | L | Pct | GB |
|---|---|---|---|---|
| New York | 96 | 58 | .623 | -- |
| Cleveland | 93 | 61 | .604 | 3.0 |
| Chicago | 91 | 63 | .591 | 5.0 |
| Boston | 84 | 70 | .545 | 12.0 |
| Detroit | 79 | 75 | .513 | 17.0 |
| Kansas City | 63 | 91 | .409 | 33.0 |
| Baltimore | 57 | 97 | .370 | 39.0 |
| Washington | 53 | 101 | .344 | 43.0 |

### 1955 National League
| Team | W | L | Pct | GB |
|---|---|---|---|---|
| Brooklyn | 98 | 55 | .641 | -- |
| Milwaukee | 85 | 69 | .552 | 13.5 |
| New York | 80 | 74 | .519 | 18.5 |
| Philadelphia | 77 | 77 | .500 | 21.5 |
| Cincinnati | 75 | 79 | .487 | 23.5 |
| Chicago | 72 | 81 | .471 | 26.0 |
| St. Louis | 68 | 86 | .442 | 30.5 |
| Pittsburgh | 60 | 94 | .390 | 38.5 |

### 1956 American League
| Team | W | L | Pct | GB |
|---|---|---|---|---|
| New York | 97 | 57 | .630 | -- |
| Cleveland | 88 | 66 | .571 | 9.0 |
| Chicago | 85 | 69 | .552 | 12.0 |
| Boston | 84 | 70 | .545 | 13.0 |
| Detroit | 82 | 72 | .532 | 15.0 |
| Baltimore | 69 | 85 | .448 | 28.0 |
| Washington | 59 | 95 | .383 | 38.0 |
| Kansas City | 52 | 102 | .338 | 45.0 |

### 1956 National League
| Team | W | L | Pct | GB |
|---|---|---|---|---|
| Brooklyn | 93 | 61 | .604 | -- |
| Milwaukee | 92 | 62 | .597 | 1.0 |
| Cincinnati | 91 | 63 | .591 | 2.0 |
| St. Louis | 76 | 78 | .494 | 17.0 |
| Philadelphia | 71 | 83 | .461 | 22.0 |
| New York | 67 | 87 | .435 | 26.0 |
| Pittsburgh | 66 | 88 | .429 | 27.0 |
| Chicago | 60 | 94 | .390 | 33.0 |

### 1957 American League
| Team | W | L | Pct | GB |
|---|---|---|---|---|
| New York | 98 | 56 | .636 | -- |
| Chicago | 90 | 64 | .584 | 8.0 |
| Boston | 82 | 72 | .532 | 16.0 |
| Detroit | 78 | 76 | .506 | 20.0 |
| Baltimore | 76 | 76 | .500 | 21.0 |
| Cleveland | 76 | 77 | .497 | 21.5 |
| Kansas City | 59 | 94 | .386 | 38.5 |
| Washington | 55 | 99 | .357 | 43.0 |

### 1957 National League
| Team | W | L | Pct | GB |
|---|---|---|---|---|
| Milwaukee | 95 | 59 | .617 | -- |
| St. Louis | 87 | 67 | .565 | 8.0 |
| Brooklyn | 84 | 70 | .545 | 11.0 |
| Cincinnati | 80 | 74 | .519 | 15.0 |
| Philadelphia | 77 | 77 | .500 | 18.0 |
| New York | 69 | 85 | .448 | 26.0 |
| Chicago | 62 | 92 | .403 | 33.0 |
| Pittsburgh | 62 | 92 | .403 | 33.0 |

### 1958 American League
| Team | W | L | Pct | GB |
|---|---|---|---|---|
| New York | 92 | 62 | .597 | -- |
| Chicago | 82 | 72 | .532 | 10.0 |
| Boston | 79 | 75 | .513 | 13.0 |
| Cleveland | 77 | 76 | .503 | 14.5 |
| Detroit | 77 | 77 | .500 | 15.0 |
| Baltimore | 74 | 79 | .484 | 17.5 |
| Kansas City | 73 | 81 | .474 | 19.0 |
| Washington | 61 | 93 | .396 | 31.0 |

### 1958 National League
| Team | W | L | Pct | GB |
|---|---|---|---|---|
| Milwaukee | 92 | 62 | .597 | -- |
| Pittsburgh | 84 | 70 | .545 | 8.0 |
| San Francisco | 80 | 74 | .519 | 12.0 |
| Cincinnati | 76 | 78 | .494 | 16.0 |
| Chicago | 72 | 82 | .468 | 20.0 |
| St. Louis | 72 | 82 | .468 | 20.0 |
| Los Angeles | 71 | 83 | .461 | 21.0 |
| Philadelphia | 69 | 85 | .448 | 23.0 |

# FINAL STANDINGS

## 1959 American League

| Team | W | L | Pct | GB |
|---|---|---|---|---|
| Chicago | 94 | 60 | .610 | -- |
| Cleveland | 89 | 65 | .578 | 5.0 |
| New York | 79 | 75 | .513 | 15.0 |
| Detroit | 76 | 78 | .494 | 18.0 |
| Boston | 75 | 79 | .487 | 19.0 |
| Baltimore | 74 | 80 | .481 | 20.0 |
| Kansas City | 66 | 88 | .429 | 28.0 |
| Washington | 63 | 91 | .409 | 31.0 |

## 1959 National League

| Team | W | L | Pct | GB |
|---|---|---|---|---|
| Los Angeles | 88 | 68 | .564 | -- |
| Milwaukee | 86 | 70 | .551 | 2.0 |
| San Francisco | 83 | 71 | .539 | 4.0 |
| Pittsburgh | 78 | 76 | .506 | 9.0 |
| Chicago | 74 | 80 | .481 | 13.0 |
| Cincinnati | 74 | 80 | .481 | 13.0 |
| St. Louis | 71 | 83 | .461 | 16.0 |
| Philadelphia | 64 | 90 | .416 | 23.0 |

## 1960 American League

| Team | W | L | Pct | GB |
|---|---|---|---|---|
| New York | 97 | 57 | .630 | -- |
| Baltimore | 89 | 65 | .578 | 8.0 |
| Chicago | 87 | 67 | .565 | 10.0 |
| Cleveland | 76 | 78 | .494 | 21.0 |
| Washington | 73 | 81 | .474 | 24.0 |
| Detroit | 71 | 83 | .461 | 26.0 |
| Boston | 65 | 89 | .422 | 32.0 |
| Kansas City | 58 | 96 | .377 | 39.0 |

## 1960 National League

| Team | W | L | Pct | GB |
|---|---|---|---|---|
| Pittsburgh | 95 | 59 | .617 | -- |
| Milwaukee | 88 | 66 | .571 | 7.0 |
| St. Louis | 86 | 68 | .558 | 9.0 |
| Los Angeles | 82 | 72 | .532 | 13.0 |
| San Francisco | 79 | 75 | .513 | 16.0 |
| Cincinnati | 67 | 87 | .435 | 28.0 |
| Chicago | 60 | 94 | .390 | 35.0 |
| Philadelphia | 59 | 95 | .383 | 36.0 |

## 1961 American League

| Team | W | L | Pct | GB |
|---|---|---|---|---|
| New York | 109 | 53 | .673 | -- |
| Detroit | 101 | 61 | .623 | 8.0 |
| Baltimore | 95 | 67 | .586 | 14.0 |
| Chicago | 86 | 76 | .531 | 23.0 |
| Cleveland | 78 | 83 | .484 | 30.5 |
| Boston | 76 | 86 | .469 | 33.0 |
| Minnesota | 70 | 90 | .438 | 38.0 |
| Los Angeles | 70 | 91 | .435 | 38.5 |
| Washington | 61 | 100 | .379 | 47.5 |
| Kansas City | 61 | 100 | .379 | 47.5 |

## 1961 National League

| Team | W | L | Pct | GB |
|---|---|---|---|---|
| Cincinnati | 93 | 61 | .604 | -- |
| Los Angeles | 89 | 65 | .578 | 4.0 |
| San Francisco | 85 | 69 | .552 | 8.0 |
| Milwaukee | 83 | 71 | .539 | 10.0 |
| St. Louis | 80 | 74 | .519 | 13.0 |
| Pittsburgh | 75 | 79 | .487 | 18.0 |
| Chicago | 64 | 90 | .416 | 29.0 |
| Philadelphia | 47 | 107 | .305 | 46.0 |

## 1962 American League

| Team | W | L | Pct | GB |
|---|---|---|---|---|
| New York | 96 | 66 | .593 | -- |
| Minnesota | 91 | 71 | .562 | 5.0 |
| Los Angeles | 86 | 76 | .531 | 10.0 |
| Detroit | 85 | 76 | .528 | 10.5 |
| Chicago | 85 | 77 | .525 | 11.0 |
| Cleveland | 80 | 82 | .494 | 16.0 |
| Baltimore | 77 | 85 | .475 | 19.0 |
| Boston | 76 | 84 | .475 | 19.0 |
| Kansas City | 72 | 90 | .444 | 24.0 |
| Washington | 60 | 101 | .373 | 35.5 |

## 1962 National League

| Team | W | L | Pct | GB |
|---|---|---|---|---|
| San Francisco | 103 | 62 | .624 | -- |
| Los Angeles | 102 | 63 | .618 | 1.0 |
| Cincinnati | 98 | 64 | .605 | 3.5 |
| Pittsburgh | 93 | 68 | .578 | 8.0 |
| Milwaukee | 86 | 76 | .531 | 15.5 |
| St. Louis | 84 | 78 | .519 | 17.5 |
| Philadelphia | 81 | 80 | .503 | 20.0 |
| Houston | 64 | 96 | .400 | 36.5 |
| Chicago | 59 | 103 | .364 | 42.5 |
| New York | 40 | 120 | .250 | 60.5 |

## 1963 American League

| Team | W | L | Pct | GB |
|---|---|---|---|---|
| New York | 104 | 57 | .646 | -- |
| Chicago | 94 | 68 | .580 | 10.5 |
| Minnesota | 91 | 70 | .565 | 13.0 |
| Baltimore | 86 | 76 | .531 | 18.5 |
| Cleveland | 79 | 83 | .488 | 25.5 |
| Detroit | 79 | 83 | .488 | 25.5 |
| Boston | 76 | 85 | .472 | 28.0 |
| Kansas City | 73 | 89 | .451 | 31.5 |
| Los Angeles | 70 | 91 | .435 | 34.0 |
| Washington | 56 | 106 | .346 | 48.5 |

## 1963 National League

| Team | W | L | Pct | GB |
|---|---|---|---|---|
| Los Angeles | 99 | 63 | .611 | -- |
| St. Louis | 93 | 69 | .574 | 6.0 |
| San Francisco | 88 | 74 | .543 | 11.0 |
| Philadelphia | 87 | 75 | .537 | 12.0 |
| Cincinnati | 86 | 76 | .531 | 13.0 |
| Milwaukee | 84 | 78 | .519 | 15.0 |
| Chicago | 82 | 80 | .506 | 17.0 |
| Pittsburgh | 74 | 88 | .457 | 25.0 |
| Houston | 66 | 96 | .407 | 33.0 |
| New York | 51 | 111 | .315 | 48.0 |

## 1964 American League

| Team | W | L | Pct | GB |
|---|---|---|---|---|
| New York | 99 | 63 | .611 | -- |
| Chicago | 98 | 64 | .605 | 1.0 |
| Baltimore | 97 | 65 | .599 | 2.0 |
| Detroit | 85 | 77 | .525 | 14.0 |
| Los Angeles | 82 | 80 | .506 | 17.0 |
| Cleveland | 79 | 83 | .488 | 20.0 |
| Minnesota | 79 | 83 | .488 | 20.0 |
| Boston | 72 | 90 | .444 | 27.0 |
| Washington | 62 | 100 | .383 | 37.0 |
| Kansas City | 57 | 105 | .352 | 42.0 |

271

# FINAL STANDINGS

## 1964 National League

| Team | W | L | Pct | GB |
|---|---|---|---|---|
| St. Louis | 93 | 69 | .574 | -- |
| Cincinnati | 92 | 70 | .568 | 1.0 |
| Philadelphia | 92 | 70 | .568 | 1.0 |
| San Francisco | 90 | 72 | .556 | 3.0 |
| Milwaukee | 88 | 74 | .543 | 5.0 |
| Los Angeles | 80 | 82 | .494 | 13.0 |
| Pittsburgh | 80 | 82 | .494 | 13.0 |
| Chicago | 76 | 86 | .469 | 17.0 |
| Houston | 66 | 96 | .407 | 27.0 |
| New York | 53 | 109 | .327 | 40.0 |

## 1965 American League

| Team | W | L | Pct | GB |
|---|---|---|---|---|
| Minnesota | 102 | 60 | .630 | -- |
| Chicago | 95 | 67 | .586 | 7.0 |
| Baltimore | 94 | 68 | .580 | 8.0 |
| Detroit | 89 | 73 | .549 | 13.0 |
| Cleveland | 87 | 75 | .537 | 15.0 |
| New York | 77 | 85 | .475 | 25.0 |
| California | 75 | 87 | .463 | 27.0 |
| Washington | 70 | 92 | .432 | 32.0 |
| Boston | 62 | 100 | .383 | 40.0 |
| Kansas City | 59 | 103 | .364 | 43.0 |

## 1965 National League

| Team | W | L | Pct | GB |
|---|---|---|---|---|
| Los Angeles | 97 | 65 | .599 | -- |
| San Francisco | 95 | 67 | .586 | 2.0 |
| Pittsburgh | 90 | 72 | .556 | 7.0 |
| Cincinnati | 89 | 73 | .549 | 8.0 |
| Milwaukee | 86 | 76 | .531 | 11.0 |
| Philadelphia | 85 | 76 | .528 | 11.5 |
| St. Louis | 80 | 81 | .497 | 16.5 |
| Chicago | 72 | 90 | .444 | 25.0 |
| Houston | 65 | 97 | .401 | 32.0 |
| New York | 50 | 112 | .309 | 47.0 |

## 1966 American League

| Team | W | L | Pct | GB |
|---|---|---|---|---|
| Baltimore | 97 | 63 | .606 | -- |
| Minnesota | 89 | 73 | .549 | 9.0 |
| Detroit | 88 | 74 | .543 | 10.0 |
| Chicago | 83 | 79 | .512 | 15.0 |
| Cleveland | 81 | 81 | .500 | 17.0 |
| California | 80 | 82 | .494 | 18.0 |
| Kansas City | 74 | 86 | .463 | 23.0 |
| Washington | 71 | 88 | .447 | 25.5 |
| Boston | 72 | 90 | .444 | 26.0 |
| New York | 70 | 89 | .440 | 26.5 |

## 1966 National League

| Team | W | L | Pct | GB |
|---|---|---|---|---|
| Los Angeles | 95 | 67 | .586 | -- |
| San Francisco | 93 | 68 | .578 | 1.5 |
| Pittsburgh | 92 | 70 | .568 | 3.0 |
| Philadelphia | 87 | 75 | .537 | 8.0 |
| Atlanta | 85 | 77 | .525 | 10.0 |
| St. Louis | 83 | 79 | .512 | 12.0 |
| Cincinnati | 76 | 84 | .475 | 18.0 |
| Houston | 72 | 90 | .444 | 23.0 |
| New York | 66 | 95 | .410 | 28.5 |
| Chicago | 59 | 103 | .364 | 36.0 |

## 1967 American League

| Team | W | L | Pct | GB |
|---|---|---|---|---|
| Boston | 92 | 70 | .568 | -- |
| Detroit | 91 | 71 | .562 | 1.0 |
| Minnesota | 91 | 71 | .562 | 1.0 |
| Chicago | 89 | 73 | .549 | 3.0 |
| California | 84 | 77 | .522 | 7.5 |
| Baltimore | 76 | 85 | .472 | 15.5 |
| Washington | 76 | 85 | .472 | 15.5 |
| Cleveland | 75 | 87 | .463 | 17.0 |
| New York | 72 | 90 | .444 | 20.0 |
| Kansas City | 62 | 99 | .385 | 29.5 |

## 1967 National League

| Team | W | L | Pct | GB |
|---|---|---|---|---|
| St. Louis | 101 | 60 | .627 | -- |
| San Francisco | 91 | 71 | .562 | 10.5 |
| Chicago | 87 | 74 | .540 | 14.0 |
| Cincinnati | 87 | 75 | .537 | 14.5 |
| Philadelphia | 82 | 80 | .506 | 19.5 |
| Pittsburgh | 81 | 81 | .500 | 20.5 |
| Atlanta | 77 | 85 | .475 | 24.5 |
| Los Angeles | 73 | 89 | .451 | 28.5 |
| Houston | 69 | 93 | .426 | 32.5 |
| New York | 61 | 101 | .377 | 40.5 |

## 1968 American League

| Team | W | L | Pct | GB |
|---|---|---|---|---|
| Detroit | 103 | 59 | .636 | -- |
| Baltimore | 91 | 71 | .562 | 12.0 |
| Cleveland | 86 | 75 | .534 | 16.5 |
| Boston | 86 | 76 | .531 | 17.0 |
| New York | 83 | 79 | .512 | 20.0 |
| Oakland | 82 | 80 | .506 | 21.0 |
| Minnesota | 79 | 83 | .488 | 24.0 |
| California | 67 | 95 | .414 | 36.0 |
| Chicago | 67 | 95 | .414 | 36.0 |
| Washington | 65 | 96 | .404 | 37.5 |

## 1968 National League

| Team | W | L | Pct | GB |
|---|---|---|---|---|
| St. Louis | 97 | 65 | .599 | -- |
| San Francisco | 88 | 74 | .543 | 9.0 |
| Chicago | 84 | 78 | .519 | 13.0 |
| Cincinnati | 83 | 79 | .512 | 14.0 |
| Atlanta | 81 | 81 | .500 | 16.0 |
| Pittsburgh | 80 | 82 | .494 | 17.0 |
| Los Angeles | 76 | 86 | .469 | 21.0 |
| Philadelphia | 76 | 86 | .469 | 21.0 |
| New York | 73 | 89 | .451 | 24.0 |
| Houston | 72 | 90 | .444 | 25.0 |

## 1969 American League East

| Team | W | L | Pct | GB |
|---|---|---|---|---|
| Baltimore | 109 | 53 | .673 | -- |
| Detroit | 90 | 72 | .556 | 19.0 |
| Boston | 87 | 75 | .537 | 22.0 |
| Washington | 86 | 76 | .531 | 23.0 |
| New York | 80 | 81 | .497 | 28.5 |
| Cleveland | 62 | 99 | .385 | 46.5 |

## 1969 American League West

| Team | W | L | Pct | GB |
|---|---|---|---|---|
| Minnesota | 97 | 65 | .599 | -- |
| Oakland | 88 | 74 | .543 | 9.0 |
| California | 71 | 91 | .438 | 26.0 |
| Kansas City | 69 | 93 | .426 | 28.0 |
| Chicago | 68 | 94 | .420 | 29.0 |
| Seattle | 64 | 98 | .395 | 33.0 |

# FINAL STANDINGS

### 1969 National League East
| Team | W | L | Pct | GB |
| --- | --- | --- | --- | --- |
| New York | 100 | 62 | .617 | -- |
| Chicago | 92 | 70 | .568 | 8.0 |
| Pittsburgh | 88 | 74 | .543 | 12.0 |
| St. Louis | 87 | 75 | .537 | 13.0 |
| Philadelphia | 63 | 99 | .389 | 37.0 |
| Montreal | 52 | 110 | .321 | 48.0 |

### 1969 National League West
| Team | W | L | Pct | GB |
| --- | --- | --- | --- | --- |
| Atlanta | 93 | 69 | .574 | -- |
| San Francisco | 90 | 72 | .556 | 3.0 |
| Cincinnati | 89 | 73 | .549 | 4.0 |
| Los Angeles | 85 | 77 | .525 | 8.0 |
| Houston | 81 | 81 | .500 | 12.0 |
| San Diego | 52 | 110 | .321 | 41.0 |

### 1970 American League East
| Team | W | L | Pct | GB |
| --- | --- | --- | --- | --- |
| Baltimore | 108 | 54 | .667 | -- |
| New York | 93 | 69 | .574 | 15.0 |
| Boston | 87 | 75 | .537 | 21.0 |
| Detroit | 79 | 83 | .488 | 29.0 |
| Cleveland | 76 | 86 | .469 | 32.0 |
| Washington | 70 | 92 | .432 | 38.0 |

### 1970 American League West
| Team | W | L | Pct | GB |
| --- | --- | --- | --- | --- |
| Minnesota | 98 | 64 | .605 | -- |
| Oakland | 89 | 73 | .549 | 9.0 |
| California | 86 | 76 | .531 | 12.0 |
| Kansas City | 65 | 97 | .401 | 33.0 |
| Milwaukee | 65 | 97 | .401 | 33.0 |
| Chicago | 56 | 106 | .346 | 42.0 |

### 1970 National League East
| Team | W | L | Pct | GB |
| --- | --- | --- | --- | --- |
| Pittsburgh | 89 | 73 | .549 | -- |
| Chicago | 84 | 78 | .519 | 5.0 |
| New York | 83 | 79 | .512 | 6.0 |
| St. Louis | 76 | 86 | .469 | 13.0 |
| Philadelphia | 73 | 88 | .453 | 15.5 |
| Montreal | 73 | 89 | .451 | 16.0 |

### 1970 National League West
| Team | W | L | Pct | GB |
| --- | --- | --- | --- | --- |
| Cincinnati | 102 | 60 | .630 | -- |
| Los Angeles | 87 | 74 | .540 | 14.5 |
| San Francisco | 86 | 76 | .531 | 16.0 |
| Houston | 79 | 83 | .488 | 23.0 |
| Atlanta | 76 | 86 | .469 | 26.0 |
| San Diego | 63 | 99 | .389 | 39.0 |

### 1970 American League East
| Team | W | L | Pct | GB |
| --- | --- | --- | --- | --- |
| Baltimore | 101 | 57 | .639 | -- |
| Detroit | 91 | 71 | .562 | 12.0 |
| Boston | 85 | 77 | .525 | 18.0 |
| New York | 82 | 80 | .506 | 21.0 |
| Washington | 63 | 96 | .396 | 38.5 |
| Cleveland | 60 | 102 | .370 | 43.0 |

### 1971 American League West
| Team | W | L | Pct | GB |
| --- | --- | --- | --- | --- |
| Oakland | 101 | 60 | .627 | -- |
| Kansas City | 85 | 76 | .528 | 16.0 |
| Chicago | 79 | 83 | .488 | 22.5 |
| California | 76 | 86 | .469 | 25.5 |
| Minnesota | 74 | 86 | .463 | 26.5 |
| Milwaukee | 69 | 92 | .429 | 32.0 |

### 1971 National League East
| Team | W | L | Pct | GB |
| --- | --- | --- | --- | --- |
| Pittsburgh | 97 | 65 | .599 | -- |
| St. Louis | 90 | 72 | .556 | 7.0 |
| Chicago | 83 | 79 | .512 | 14.0 |
| New York | 83 | 79 | .512 | 14.0 |
| Montreal | 71 | 90 | .441 | 25.5 |
| Philadelphia | 67 | 95 | .414 | 30.0 |

### 1971 National League West
| Team | W | L | Pct | GB |
| --- | --- | --- | --- | --- |
| San Francisco | 90 | 72 | .556 | -- |
| Los Angeles | 89 | 73 | .549 | 1.0 |
| Atlanta | 82 | 80 | .506 | 8.0 |
| Cincinnati | 79 | 83 | .488 | 11.0 |
| Houston | 79 | 83 | .488 | 11.0 |
| San Diego | 61 | 100 | .379 | 28.5 |

### 1972 American League East
| Team | W | L | Pct | GB |
| --- | --- | --- | --- | --- |
| Detroit | 86 | 70 | .551 | -- |
| Boston | 85 | 70 | .548 | 0.5 |
| Baltimore | 80 | 74 | .519 | 5.0 |
| New York | 79 | 76 | .510 | 6.5 |
| Cleveland | 72 | 84 | .462 | 14.0 |
| Milwaukee | 65 | 91 | .417 | 21.0 |

### 1972 American League West
| Team | W | L | Pct | GB |
| --- | --- | --- | --- | --- |
| Oakland | 93 | 62 | .600 | -- |
| Chicago | 87 | 67 | .565 | 5.5 |
| Minnesota | 77 | 77 | .500 | 15.5 |
| Kansas City | 76 | 78 | .494 | 16.5 |
| California | 75 | 80 | .484 | 18.0 |
| Texas | 54 | 100 | .351 | 38.5 |

### 1972 National League East
| Team | W | L | Pct | GB |
| --- | --- | --- | --- | --- |
| Pittsburgh | 96 | 59 | .619 | -- |
| Chicago | 85 | 70 | .548 | 11.0 |
| New York | 83 | 73 | .532 | 13.5 |
| St. Louis | 75 | 81 | .481 | 21.5 |
| Montreal | 70 | 86 | .449 | 26.5 |
| Philadelphia | 59 | 97 | .378 | 37.5 |

### 1972 National League West
| Team | W | L | Pct | GB |
| --- | --- | --- | --- | --- |
| Cincinnati | 95 | 59 | .617 | -- |
| Houston | 84 | 69 | .549 | 10.5 |
| Los Angeles | 85 | 70 | .548 | 10.5 |
| Atlanta | 70 | 84 | .455 | 25.0 |
| San Francisco | 69 | 86 | .445 | 26.5 |
| San Diego | 58 | 95 | .379 | 36.5 |

273

# FINAL STANDINGS

## 1973 American League East

| Team | W | L | Pct | GB |
|---|---|---|---|---|
| Baltimore | 97 | 65 | .599 | -- |
| Boston | 89 | 73 | .549 | 8.0 |
| Detroit | 85 | 77 | .525 | 12.0 |
| New York | 80 | 82 | .494 | 17.0 |
| Milwaukee | 74 | 88 | .457 | 23.0 |
| Cleveland | 71 | 91 | .438 | 26.0 |

## 1973 American League West

| Team | W | L | Pct | GB |
|---|---|---|---|---|
| Oakland | 94 | 68 | .580 | -- |
| Kansas City | 88 | 74 | .543 | 6.0 |
| Minnesota | 81 | 81 | .500 | 13.0 |
| California | 79 | 83 | .488 | 15.0 |
| Chicago | 77 | 85 | .475 | 17.0 |
| Texas | 57 | 105 | .352 | 37.0 |

## 1973 National League East

| Team | W | L | Pct | GB |
|---|---|---|---|---|
| New York | 82 | 79 | .509 | -- |
| St. Louis | 81 | 81 | .500 | 1.5 |
| Pittsburgh | 80 | 82 | .494 | 2.5 |
| Montreal | 79 | 83 | .488 | 3.5 |
| Chicago | 77 | 84 | .478 | 5.0 |
| Philadelphia | 71 | 91 | .438 | 11.5 |

## 1973 National League West

| Team | W | L | Pct | GB |
|---|---|---|---|---|
| Cincinnati | 99 | 63 | .611 | -- |
| Los Angeles | 95 | 66 | .590 | 3.5 |
| San Francisco | 88 | 74 | .543 | 11.0 |
| Houston | 82 | 80 | .506 | 17.0 |
| Atlanta | 76 | 85 | .472 | 22.5 |
| San Diego | 60 | 102 | .370 | 39.0 |

## 1974 American League East

| Team | W | L | Pct | GB |
|---|---|---|---|---|
| Baltimore | 91 | 71 | .562 | -- |
| New York | 89 | 73 | .549 | 2.0 |
| Boston | 84 | 78 | .519 | 7.0 |
| Cleveland | 77 | 85 | .475 | 14.0 |
| Milwaukee | 76 | 86 | .469 | 15.0 |
| Detroit | 72 | 90 | .444 | 19.0 |

## 1974 American League West

| Team | W | L | Pct | GB |
|---|---|---|---|---|
| Oakland | 90 | 72 | .556 | -- |
| Texas | 84 | 76 | .525 | 5.0 |
| Minnesota | 82 | 80 | .506 | 8.0 |
| Chicago | 80 | 80 | .500 | 9.0 |
| Kansas City | 77 | 85 | .475 | 13.0 |
| California | 68 | 94 | .420 | 22.0 |

## 1974 National League East

| Team | W | L | Pct | GB |
|---|---|---|---|---|
| Pittsburgh | 88 | 74 | .543 | -- |
| St. Louis | 86 | 75 | .534 | 1.5 |
| Philadelphia | 80 | 82 | .494 | 8.0 |
| Montreal | 79 | 82 | .491 | 8.5 |
| New York | 71 | 91 | .438 | 17.0 |
| Chicago | 66 | 96 | .407 | 22.0 |

## 1974 National League West

| Team | W | L | Pct | GB |
|---|---|---|---|---|
| Los Angeles | 102 | 60 | .630 | -- |
| Cincinnati | 98 | 64 | .605 | 4.0 |
| Atlanta | 88 | 74 | .543 | 14.0 |
| Houston | 81 | 81 | .500 | 21.0 |
| San Francisco | 72 | 90 | .444 | 30.0 |
| San Diego | 60 | 102 | .370 | 42.0 |

## 1975 American League East

| Team | W | L | Pct | GB |
|---|---|---|---|---|
| Boston | 95 | 65 | .594 | -- |
| Baltimore | 90 | 69 | .566 | 4.5 |
| New York | 83 | 77 | .519 | 12.0 |
| Cleveland | 79 | 80 | .497 | 15.5 |
| Milwaukee | 68 | 94 | .420 | 28.0 |
| Detroit | 57 | 102 | .358 | 37.5 |

## 1975 American League West

| Team | W | L | Pct | GB |
|---|---|---|---|---|
| Oakland | 98 | 64 | .605 | -- |
| Kansas City | 91 | 71 | .562 | 7.0 |
| Texas | 79 | 83 | .488 | 19.0 |
| Minnesota | 76 | 83 | .478 | 20.5 |
| Chicago | 75 | 86 | .466 | 22.5 |
| California | 72 | 89 | .447 | 25.5 |

## 1975 National League East

| Team | W | L | Pct | GB |
|---|---|---|---|---|
| Pittsburgh | 92 | 69 | .571 | -- |
| Philadelphia | 86 | 76 | .531 | 6.5 |
| New York | 82 | 80 | .506 | 10.5 |
| St. Louis | 82 | 80 | .506 | 10.5 |
| Chicago | 75 | 87 | .463 | 17.5 |
| Montreal | 75 | 87 | .463 | 17.5 |

## 1975 National League West

| Team | W | L | Pct | GB |
|---|---|---|---|---|
| Cincinnati | 108 | 54 | .667 | -- |
| Los Angeles | 88 | 74 | .543 | 20.0 |
| San Francisco | 80 | 81 | .497 | 27.5 |
| San Diego | 71 | 91 | .438 | 37.0 |
| Atlanta | 67 | 94 | .416 | 40.5 |
| Houston | 64 | 97 | .398 | 43.5 |

## 1976 American League East

| Team | W | L | Pct | GB |
|---|---|---|---|---|
| New York | 97 | 62 | .610 | -- |
| Baltimore | 88 | 74 | .543 | 10.5 |
| Boston | 83 | 79 | .512 | 15.5 |
| Cleveland | 81 | 78 | .509 | 16.0 |
| Detroit | 74 | 87 | .460 | 24.0 |
| Milwaukee | 66 | 95 | .410 | 32.0 |

## 1976 American League West

| Team | W | L | Pct | GB |
|---|---|---|---|---|
| Kansas City | 90 | 72 | .556 | -- |
| Oakland | 87 | 74 | .540 | 2.5 |
| Minnesota | 85 | 77 | .525 | 5.0 |
| California | 76 | 86 | .469 | 14.0 |
| Texas | 76 | 86 | .469 | 14.0 |
| Chicago | 64 | 97 | .398 | 25.5 |

# FINAL STANDINGS

## 1976 National League East

| Team | W | L | Pct | GB |
|------|---|---|-----|-----|
| Philadelphia | 101 | 61 | .623 | -- |
| Pittsburgh | 92 | 70 | .568 | 9.0 |
| New York | 86 | 76 | .531 | 15.0 |
| Chicago | 75 | 87 | .463 | 26.0 |
| St. Louis | 72 | 90 | .444 | 29.0 |
| Montreal | 55 | 107 | .340 | 46.0 |

## 1976 National League West

| Team | W | L | Pct | GB |
|------|---|---|-----|-----|
| Cincinnati | 102 | 60 | .630 | -- |
| Los Angeles | 92 | 70 | .568 | 10.0 |
| Houston | 80 | 82 | .494 | 22.0 |
| San Francisco | 74 | 88 | .457 | 28.0 |
| San Diego | 73 | 89 | .451 | 29.0 |
| Atlanta | 70 | 92 | .432 | 32.0 |

## 1977 American League East

| Team | W | L | Pct | GB |
|------|---|---|-----|-----|
| New York | 100 | 62 | .617 | -- |
| Baltimore | 97 | 64 | .602 | 2.5 |
| Boston | 97 | 64 | .602 | 2.5 |
| Detroit | 74 | 88 | .457 | 26.0 |
| Cleveland | 71 | 90 | .441 | 28.5 |
| Milwaukee | 67 | 95 | .414 | 33.0 |
| Toronto | 54 | 107 | .335 | 45.5 |

## 1977 American League West

| Team | W | L | Pct | GB |
|------|---|---|-----|-----|
| Kansas City | 102 | 60 | .630 | -- |
| Texas | 94 | 68 | .580 | 8.0 |
| Chicago | 90 | 72 | .556 | 12.0 |
| Minnesota | 84 | 77 | .522 | 17.5 |
| California | 74 | 88 | .457 | 28.0 |
| Seattle | 64 | 98 | .395 | 38.0 |
| Oakland | 63 | 98 | .391 | 38.5 |

## 1977 National League East

| Team | W | L | Pct | GB |
|------|---|---|-----|-----|
| Philadelphia | 101 | 61 | .623 | -- |
| Pittsburgh | 96 | 66 | .593 | 5.0 |
| St. Louis | 83 | 79 | .512 | 18.0 |
| Chicago | 81 | 81 | .500 | 20.0 |
| Montreal | 75 | 87 | .463 | 26.0 |
| New York | 64 | 98 | .395 | 37.0 |

## 1977 National League West

| Team | W | L | Pct | GB |
|------|---|---|-----|-----|
| Los Angeles | 98 | 64 | .605 | -- |
| Cincinnati | 88 | 74 | .543 | 10.0 |
| Houston | 81 | 81 | .500 | 17.0 |
| San Francisco | 75 | 87 | .463 | 23.0 |
| San Diego | 69 | 93 | .426 | 29.0 |
| Atlanta | 61 | 101 | .377 | 37.0 |

## 1978 American League East

| Team | W | L | Pct | GB |
|------|---|---|-----|-----|
| New York | 100 | 63 | .613 | -- |
| Boston | 99 | 64 | .607 | 1.0 |
| Milwaukee | 93 | 69 | .574 | 6.5 |
| Baltimore | 90 | 71 | .559 | 9.0 |
| Detroit | 86 | 76 | .531 | 13.5 |
| Cleveland | 69 | 90 | .434 | 29.0 |
| Toronto | 59 | 102 | .366 | 40.0 |

## 1978 American League West

| Team | W | L | Pct | GB |
|------|---|---|-----|-----|
| Kansas City | 92 | 70 | .568 | -- |
| California | 87 | 75 | .537 | 5.0 |
| Texas | 87 | 75 | .537 | 5.0 |
| Minnesota | 73 | 89 | .451 | 19.0 |
| Chicago | 71 | 90 | .441 | 20.5 |
| Oakland | 69 | 93 | .426 | 23.0 |
| Seattle | 56 | 104 | .350 | 35.0 |

## 1978 National League East

| Team | W | L | Pct | GB |
|------|---|---|-----|-----|
| Philadelphia | 90 | 72 | .556 | -- |
| Pittsburgh | 88 | 73 | .547 | 1.5 |
| Chicago | 79 | 83 | .488 | 11.0 |
| Montreal | 76 | 86 | .469 | 14.0 |
| St. Louis | 69 | 93 | .426 | 21.0 |
| New York | 66 | 96 | .407 | 24.0 |

## 1978 National League West

| Team | W | L | Pct | GB |
|------|---|---|-----|-----|
| Los Angeles | 95 | 67 | .586 | -- |
| Cincinnati | 92 | 69 | .571 | 2.5 |
| San Francisco | 89 | 73 | .549 | 6.0 |
| San Diego | 84 | 78 | .519 | 11.0 |
| Houston | 74 | 88 | .457 | 21.0 |
| Atlanta | 69 | 93 | .426 | 26.0 |

## 1979 American League East

| Team | W | L | Pct | GB |
|------|---|---|-----|-----|
| Baltimore | 102 | 57 | .642 | -- |
| Milwaukee | 95 | 66 | .590 | 8.0 |
| Boston | 91 | 69 | .569 | 11.5 |
| New York | 89 | 71 | .556 | 13.5 |
| Detroit | 85 | 76 | .528 | 18.0 |
| Cleveland | 81 | 80 | .503 | 22.0 |
| Toronto | 53 | 109 | .327 | 50.5 |

## 1979 American League West

| Team | W | L | Pct | GB |
|------|---|---|-----|-----|
| California | 88 | 74 | .543 | -- |
| Kansas City | 85 | 77 | .525 | 3.0 |
| Texas | 83 | 79 | .512 | 5.0 |
| Minnesota | 82 | 80 | .506 | 6.0 |
| Chicago | 73 | 87 | .456 | 14.0 |
| Seattle | 67 | 95 | .414 | 21.0 |
| Oakland | 54 | 108 | .333 | 34.0 |

## 1979 National League East

| Team | W | L | Pct | GB |
|------|---|---|-----|-----|
| Pittsburgh | 98 | 64 | .605 | -- |
| Montreal | 95 | 65 | .594 | 2.0 |
| St. Louis | 86 | 76 | .531 | 12.0 |
| Philadelphia | 84 | 78 | .519 | 14.0 |
| Chicago | 80 | 82 | .494 | 18.0 |
| New York | 63 | 99 | .389 | 35.0 |

## 1979 National League West

| Team | W | L | Pct | GB |
|------|---|---|-----|-----|
| Cincinnati | 90 | 71 | .559 | -- |
| Houston | 89 | 73 | .549 | 1.5 |
| Los Angeles | 79 | 83 | .488 | 11.5 |
| San Francisco | 71 | 91 | .438 | 19.5 |
| San Diego | 68 | 93 | .422 | 22.0 |
| Atlanta | 66 | 94 | .413 | 23.5 |

# FINAL STANDINGS

### 1980 American League East

| Team | W | L | Pct | GB |
|---|---|---|---|---|
| New York | 103 | 59 | .636 | -- |
| Baltimore | 100 | 62 | .617 | 3.0 |
| Milwaukee | 86 | 76 | .531 | 17.0 |
| Boston | 83 | 77 | .519 | 19.0 |
| Detroit | 84 | 78 | .519 | 19.0 |
| Cleveland | 79 | 81 | .494 | 23.0 |
| Toronto | 67 | 95 | .414 | 36.0 |

### 1980 American League West

| Team | W | L | Pct | GB |
|---|---|---|---|---|
| Kansas City | 97 | 65 | .599 | -- |
| Oakland | 83 | 79 | .512 | 14.0 |
| Minnesota | 77 | 84 | .478 | 19.5 |
| Texas | 76 | 85 | .472 | 20.5 |
| Chicago | 70 | 90 | .438 | 26.0 |
| California | 65 | 95 | .406 | 31.0 |
| Seattle | 59 | 103 | .364 | 38.0 |

### 1980 National League East

| Team | W | L | Pct | GB |
|---|---|---|---|---|
| Philadelphia | 91 | 71 | .562 | -- |
| Montreal | 90 | 72 | .556 | 1.0 |
| Pittsburgh | 83 | 79 | .512 | 8.0 |
| St. Louis | 74 | 88 | .457 | 17.0 |
| New York | 67 | 95 | .414 | 24.0 |
| Chicago | 64 | 98 | .395 | 27.0 |

### 1980 National League West

| Team | W | L | Pct | GB |
|---|---|---|---|---|
| Houston | 93 | 70 | .571 | -- |
| Los Angeles | 92 | 71 | .564 | 1.0 |
| Cincinnati | 89 | 73 | .549 | 3.5 |
| Atlanta | 81 | 80 | .503 | 11.0 |
| San Francisco | 75 | 86 | .466 | 17.0 |
| San Diego | 73 | 89 | .451 | 19.5 |

### 1981 American League East

| Team | W | L | Pct | GB |
|---|---|---|---|---|
| Milwaukee | 62 | 47 | .569 | -- |
| Baltimore | 59 | 46 | .562 | 1.0 |
| New York | 59 | 48 | .551 | 2.0 |
| Detroit | 60 | 49 | .550 | 2.0 |
| Boston | 59 | 49 | .546 | 2.5 |
| Cleveland | 52 | 51 | .505 | 7.0 |
| Toronto | 37 | 69 | .349 | 23.5 |

### 1981 American League West

| Team | W | L | Pct | GB |
|---|---|---|---|---|
| Oakland | 64 | 45 | .587 | -- |
| Texas | 57 | 48 | .543 | 5.0 |
| Chicago | 54 | 52 | .509 | 8.5 |
| Kansas City | 50 | 53 | .485 | 11.0 |
| California | 51 | 59 | .464 | 13.5 |
| Seattle | 44 | 65 | .404 | 20.0 |
| Minnesota | 41 | 68 | .376 | 23.0 |

### 1981 National League East

| Team | W | L | Pct | GB |
|---|---|---|---|---|
| St. Louis | 59 | 43 | .578 | -- |
| Montreal | 60 | 48 | .556 | 2.0 |
| Philadelphia | 59 | 48 | .551 | 2.5 |
| Pittsburgh | 46 | 56 | .451 | 13.0 |
| New York | 41 | 62 | .398 | 18.5 |
| Chicago | 38 | 65 | .369 | 21.5 |

### 1981 National League West

| Team | W | L | Pct | GB |
|---|---|---|---|---|
| Cincinnati | 66 | 42 | .611 | -- |
| Los Angeles | 63 | 47 | .573 | 4.0 |
| Houston | 61 | 49 | .555 | 6.0 |
| San Francisco | 56 | 55 | .505 | 11.5 |
| Atlanta | 50 | 56 | .472 | 15.0 |
| San Diego | 41 | 69 | .373 | 26.0 |

### 1982 American League East

| Team | W | L | Pct | GB |
|---|---|---|---|---|
| Milwaukee | 95 | 67 | .586 | -- |
| Baltimore | 94 | 68 | .580 | 1.0 |
| Boston | 89 | 73 | .549 | 6.0 |
| Detroit | 83 | 79 | .512 | 12.0 |
| New York | 79 | 83 | .488 | 16.0 |
| Cleveland | 78 | 84 | .481 | 17.0 |
| Toronto | 78 | 84 | .481 | 17.0 |

### 1982 American League West

| Team | W | L | Pct | GB |
|---|---|---|---|---|
| California | 93 | 69 | .574 | -- |
| Kansas City | 90 | 72 | .556 | 3.0 |
| Chicago | 87 | 75 | .537 | 6.0 |
| Seattle | 76 | 86 | .469 | 17.0 |
| Oakland | 68 | 94 | .420 | 25.0 |
| Texas | 64 | 98 | .395 | 29.0 |
| Minnesota | 60 | 102 | .370 | 33.0 |

### 1982 National League East

| Team | W | L | Pct | GB |
|---|---|---|---|---|
| St. Louis | 92 | 70 | .568 | -- |
| Philadelphia | 89 | 73 | .549 | 3.0 |
| Montreal | 86 | 76 | .531 | 6.0 |
| Pittsburgh | 84 | 78 | .519 | 8.0 |
| Chicago | 73 | 89 | .451 | 19.0 |
| New York | 65 | 97 | .401 | 27.0 |

### 1982 National League West

| Team | W | L | Pct | GB |
|---|---|---|---|---|
| Atlanta | 89 | 73 | .549 | -- |
| Los Angeles | 88 | 74 | .543 | 1.0 |
| San Francisco | 87 | 75 | .537 | 2.0 |
| San Diego | 81 | 81 | .500 | 8.0 |
| Houston | 77 | 85 | .475 | 12.0 |
| Cincinnati | 61 | 101 | .377 | 28.0 |

### 1983 American League East

| Team | W | L | Pct | GB |
|---|---|---|---|---|
| Baltimore | 98 | 64 | .605 | -- |
| Detroit | 92 | 70 | .568 | 6.0 |
| New York | 91 | 71 | .562 | 7.0 |
| Toronto | 89 | 73 | .549 | 9.0 |
| Milwaukee | 87 | 75 | .537 | 11.0 |
| Boston | 78 | 84 | .481 | 20.0 |
| Cleveland | 70 | 92 | .432 | 28.0 |

### 1983 American League West

| Team | W | L | Pct | GB |
|---|---|---|---|---|
| Chicago | 99 | 63 | .611 | -- |
| Kansas City | 79 | 83 | .488 | 20.0 |
| Texas | 77 | 85 | .475 | 22.0 |
| Oakland | 74 | 88 | .457 | 25.0 |
| California | 70 | 92 | .432 | 29.0 |
| Minnesota | 70 | 92 | .432 | 29.0 |
| Seattle | 60 | 102 | .370 | 39.0 |

# FINAL STANDINGS

### 1983 National League East

| Team | W | L | Pct | GB |
|------|---|---|-----|-----|
| Philadelphia | 90 | 72 | .556 | -- |
| Pittsburgh | 84 | 78 | .519 | 6.0 |
| Montreal | 82 | 80 | .506 | 8.0 |
| St. Louis | 79 | 83 | .488 | 11.0 |
| Chicago | 71 | 91 | .438 | 19.0 |
| New York | 68 | 94 | .420 | 22.0 |

### 1983 National League West

| Team | W | L | Pct | GB |
|------|---|---|-----|-----|
| Los Angeles | 91 | 71 | .562 | -- |
| Atlanta | 88 | 74 | .543 | 3.0 |
| Houston | 85 | 77 | .525 | 6.0 |
| San Diego | 81 | 81 | .500 | 10.0 |
| San Francisco | 79 | 83 | .488 | 12.0 |
| Cincinnati | 74 | 88 | .457 | 17.0 |

### 1984 American League East

| Team | W | L | Pct | GB |
|------|---|---|-----|-----|
| Detroit | 104 | 58 | .642 | -- |
| Toronto | 89 | 73 | .549 | 15.0 |
| New York | 87 | 75 | .537 | 17.0 |
| Boston | 86 | 76 | .531 | 18.0 |
| Baltimore | 85 | 77 | .525 | 19.0 |
| Cleveland | 75 | 87 | .463 | 29.0 |
| Milwaukee | 67 | 94 | .416 | 36.5 |

### 1984 American League West

| Team | W | L | Pct | GB |
|------|---|---|-----|-----|
| Kansas City | 84 | 78 | .519 | -- |
| California | 81 | 81 | .500 | 3.0 |
| Minnesota | 81 | 81 | .500 | 3.0 |
| Oakland | 77 | 85 | .475 | 7.0 |
| Chicago | 74 | 88 | .457 | 10.0 |
| Seattle | 74 | 88 | .457 | 10.0 |
| Texas | 69 | 92 | .429 | 14.5 |

### 1984 National League East

| Team | W | L | Pct | GB |
|------|---|---|-----|-----|
| Chicago | 96 | 65 | .596 | -- |
| New York | 90 | 72 | .556 | 6.5 |
| St. Louis | 84 | 78 | .519 | 12.5 |
| Philadelphia | 81 | 81 | .500 | 15.5 |
| Montreal | 78 | 83 | .484 | 18.0 |
| Pittsburgh | 75 | 87 | .463 | 21.5 |

### 1984 National League West

| Team | W | L | Pct | GB |
|------|---|---|-----|-----|
| San Diego | 92 | 70 | .568 | -- |
| Atlanta | 80 | 82 | .494 | 12.0 |
| Houston | 80 | 82 | .494 | 12.0 |
| Los Angeles | 79 | 83 | .488 | 13.0 |
| Cincinnati | 70 | 92 | .432 | 22.0 |
| San Francisco | 66 | 96 | .407 | 26.0 |

### 1985 American League East

| Team | W | L | Pct | GB |
|------|---|---|-----|-----|
| Toronto | 99 | 62 | .615 | -- |
| New York | 97 | 64 | .602 | 2.0 |
| Detroit | 84 | 77 | .522 | 15.0 |
| Baltimore | 83 | 78 | .516 | 16.0 |
| Boston | 81 | 81 | .500 | 18.5 |
| Milwaukee | 71 | 90 | .441 | 28.0 |
| Cleveland | 60 | 102 | .370 | 39.5 |

### 1985 American League West

| Team | W | L | Pct | GB |
|------|---|---|-----|-----|
| Kansas City | 91 | 71 | .562 | -- |
| California | 90 | 72 | .556 | 1.0 |
| Chicago | 85 | 77 | .525 | 6.0 |
| Minnesota | 77 | 85 | .475 | 14.0 |
| Oakland | 77 | 85 | .475 | 14.0 |
| Seattle | 74 | 88 | .457 | 17.0 |
| Texas | 62 | 99 | .385 | 28.5 |

### 1985 National League East

| Team | W | L | Pct | GB |
|------|---|---|-----|-----|
| St. Louis | 101 | 61 | .623 | -- |
| New York | 98 | 64 | .605 | 3.0 |
| Montreal | 84 | 77 | .522 | 16.5 |
| Chicago | 77 | 84 | .478 | 23.5 |
| Philadelphia | 75 | 87 | .463 | 26.0 |
| Pittsburgh | 57 | 104 | .354 | 43.5 |

### 1985 National League West

| Team | W | L | Pct | GB |
|------|---|---|-----|-----|
| Los Angeles | 95 | 67 | .586 | -- |
| Cincinnati | 89 | 72 | .553 | 5.5 |
| Houston | 83 | 79 | .512 | 12.0 |
| San Diego | 83 | 79 | .512 | 12.0 |
| Atlanta | 66 | 96 | .407 | 29.0 |
| San Francisco | 62 | 100 | .383 | 33.0 |

### 1986 American League East

| Team | W | L | Pct | GB |
|------|---|---|-----|-----|
| Boston | 95 | 66 | .590 | -- |
| New York | 90 | 72 | .556 | 5.5 |
| Detroit | 87 | 75 | .537 | 8.5 |
| Toronto | 86 | 76 | .531 | 9.5 |
| Cleveland | 84 | 78 | .519 | 11.5 |
| Milwaukee | 77 | 84 | .478 | 18.0 |
| Baltimore | 73 | 89 | .451 | 22.5 |

### 1986 American League West

| Team | W | L | Pct | GB |
|------|---|---|-----|-----|
| California | 92 | 70 | .568 | -- |
| Texas | 87 | 75 | .537 | 5.0 |
| Kansas City | 76 | 86 | .469 | 16.0 |
| Oakland | 76 | 86 | .469 | 16.0 |
| Chicago | 72 | 90 | .444 | 20.0 |
| Minnesota | 71 | 91 | .438 | 21.0 |
| Seattle | 67 | 95 | .414 | 25.0 |

### 1986 National League East

| Team | W | L | Pct | GB |
|------|---|---|-----|-----|
| New York | 108 | 54 | .667 | -- |
| Philadelphia | 86 | 75 | .534 | 21.5 |
| St. Louis | 79 | 82 | .491 | 28.5 |
| Montreal | 78 | 83 | .484 | 29.5 |
| Chicago | 70 | 90 | .438 | 37.0 |
| Pittsburgh | 64 | 98 | .395 | 44.0 |

### 1986 National League West

| Team | W | L | Pct | GB |
|------|---|---|-----|-----|
| Houston | 96 | 66 | .593 | -- |
| Cincinnati | 86 | 76 | .531 | 10.0 |
| San Francisco | 83 | 79 | .512 | 13.0 |
| San Diego | 74 | 88 | .457 | 22.0 |
| Los Angeles | 73 | 89 | .451 | 23.0 |
| Atlanta | 72 | 89 | .447 | 23.5 |

# FINAL STANDINGS

### 1987 American League East

| Team | W | L | Pct | GB |
|---|---|---|---|---|
| Detroit | 98 | 64 | .605 | -- |
| Toronto | 96 | 66 | .593 | 2.0 |
| Milwaukee | 91 | 71 | .562 | 7.0 |
| New York | 89 | 73 | .549 | 9.0 |
| Boston | 78 | 84 | .481 | 20.0 |
| Baltimore | 67 | 95 | .414 | 31.0 |
| Cleveland | 61 | 101 | .377 | 37.0 |

### 1987 American League West

| Team | W | L | Pct | GB |
|---|---|---|---|---|
| Minnesota | 85 | 77 | .525 | -- |
| Kansas City | 83 | 79 | .512 | 2.0 |
| Oakland | 81 | 81 | .500 | 4.0 |
| Seattle | 78 | 84 | .481 | 7.0 |
| Chicago | 77 | 85 | .475 | 8.0 |
| California | 75 | 87 | .463 | 10.0 |
| Texas | 75 | 87 | .463 | 10.0 |

### 1987 National League East

| Team | W | L | Pct | GB |
|---|---|---|---|---|
| St. Louis | 95 | 67 | .586 | -- |
| New York | 92 | 70 | .568 | 3.0 |
| Montreal | 91 | 71 | .562 | 4.0 |
| Philadelphia | 80 | 82 | .494 | 15.0 |
| Pittsburgh | 80 | 82 | .494 | 15.0 |
| Chicago | 76 | 85 | .472 | 18.5 |

### 1987 National League West

| Team | W | L | Pct | GB |
|---|---|---|---|---|
| San Francisco | 90 | 72 | .556 | -- |
| Cincinnati | 84 | 78 | .519 | 6.0 |
| Houston | 76 | 86 | .469 | 14.0 |
| Los Angeles | 73 | 89 | .451 | 17.0 |
| Atlanta | 69 | 92 | .429 | 20.5 |
| San Diego | 65 | 97 | .401 | 25.0 |

### 1988 American League East

| Team | W | L | Pct | GB |
|---|---|---|---|---|
| Boston | 89 | 73 | .549 | -- |
| Detroit | 88 | 74 | .543 | 1.0 |
| Milwaukee | 87 | 75 | .537 | 2.0 |
| Toronto | 87 | 75 | .537 | 2.0 |
| New York | 85 | 76 | .528 | 3.5 |
| Cleveland | 78 | 84 | .481 | 11.0 |
| Baltimore | 54 | 107 | .335 | 34.5 |

### 1988 American League West

| Team | W | L | Pct | GB |
|---|---|---|---|---|
| Oakland | 104 | 58 | .642 | -- |
| Minnesota | 91 | 71 | .562 | 13.0 |
| Kansas City | 84 | 77 | .522 | 19.5 |
| California | 75 | 87 | .463 | 29.0 |
| Chicago | 71 | 90 | .441 | 32.5 |
| Texas | 70 | 91 | .435 | 33.5 |
| Seattle | 68 | 93 | .422 | 35.5 |

### 1988 National League East

| Team | W | L | Pct | GB |
|---|---|---|---|---|
| New York | 100 | 60 | .625 | -- |
| Pittsburgh | 85 | 75 | .531 | 15.0 |
| Montreal | 81 | 81 | .500 | 20.0 |
| Chicago | 77 | 85 | .475 | 24.0 |
| St. Louis | 76 | 86 | .469 | 25.0 |
| Philadelphia | 65 | 96 | .404 | 35.5 |

### 1988 National League West

| Team | W | L | Pct | GB |
|---|---|---|---|---|
| Los Angeles | 94 | 67 | .584 | -- |
| Cincinnati | 87 | 74 | .540 | 7.0 |
| San Diego | 83 | 78 | .516 | 11.0 |
| San Francisco | 83 | 79 | .512 | 11.5 |
| Houston | 82 | 80 | .506 | 12.5 |
| Atlanta | 54 | 106 | .338 | 39.5 |

### 1989 American League East

| Team | W | L | Pct | GB |
|---|---|---|---|---|
| Toronto | 89 | 73 | .549 | -- |
| Baltimore | 87 | 75 | .537 | 2.0 |
| Boston | 83 | 79 | .512 | 6.0 |
| Milwaukee | 81 | 81 | .500 | 8.0 |
| New York | 74 | 87 | .460 | 14.5 |
| Cleveland | 73 | 89 | .451 | 16.0 |
| Detroit | 59 | 103 | .364 | 30.0 |

### 1989 American League West

| Team | W | L | Pct | GB |
|---|---|---|---|---|
| Oakland | 99 | 63 | .611 | -- |
| Kansas City | 92 | 70 | .568 | 7.0 |
| California | 91 | 71 | .562 | 8.0 |
| Texas | 83 | 79 | .512 | 16.0 |
| Minnesota | 80 | 82 | .494 | 19.0 |
| Seattle | 73 | 89 | .451 | 26.0 |
| Chicago | 69 | 92 | .429 | 29.5 |

### 1989 National League East

| Team | W | L | Pct | GB |
|---|---|---|---|---|
| Chicago | 93 | 69 | .574 | -- |
| New York | 87 | 75 | .537 | 6.0 |
| St. Louis | 86 | 76 | .531 | 7.0 |
| Montreal | 81 | 81 | .500 | 12.0 |
| Pittsburgh | 74 | 88 | .457 | 19.0 |
| Philadelphia | 67 | 95 | .414 | 26.0 |

### 1989 National League West

| Team | W | L | Pct | GB |
|---|---|---|---|---|
| San Francisco | 92 | 70 | .568 | -- |
| San Diego | 89 | 73 | .549 | 3.0 |
| Houston | 86 | 76 | .531 | 6.0 |
| Los Angeles | 77 | 83 | .481 | 14.0 |
| Cincinnati | 75 | 87 | .463 | 17.0 |
| Atlanta | 63 | 97 | .394 | 28.0 |

### 1990 American League East

| Team | W | L | Pct | GB |
|---|---|---|---|---|
| Boston | 88 | 74 | .543 | -- |
| Toronto | 86 | 76 | .531 | 2.0 |
| Detroit | 79 | 83 | .488 | 9.0 |
| Cleveland | 77 | 85 | .475 | 11.0 |
| Baltimore | 76 | 85 | .472 | 11.5 |
| Milwaukee | 74 | 88 | .457 | 14.0 |
| New York | 67 | 95 | .414 | 21.0 |

### 1990 American League West

| Team | W | L | Pct | GB |
|---|---|---|---|---|
| Oakland | 103 | 59 | .636 | -- |
| Chicago | 94 | 68 | .580 | 9.0 |
| Texas | 83 | 79 | .512 | 20.0 |
| California | 80 | 82 | .494 | 23.0 |
| Seattle | 77 | 85 | .475 | 26.0 |
| Kansas City | 75 | 86 | .466 | 27.5 |
| Minnesota | 74 | 88 | .457 | 29.0 |

# FINAL STANDINGS

## 1990 National League East

| Team | W | L | Pct | GB |
|------|---|---|-----|-----|
| Pittsburgh | 95 | 67 | .586 | -- |
| New York | 91 | 71 | .562 | 4.0 |
| Montreal | 85 | 77 | .525 | 10.0 |
| Chicago | 77 | 85 | .475 | 18.0 |
| Philadelphia | 77 | 85 | .475 | 18.0 |
| St. Louis | 70 | 92 | .432 | 25.0 |

## 1990 National League West

| Team | W | L | Pct | GB |
|------|---|---|-----|-----|
| Cincinnati | 91 | 71 | .562 | -- |
| Los Angeles | 86 | 76 | .531 | 5.0 |
| San Francisco | 85 | 77 | .525 | 6.0 |
| Houston | 75 | 87 | .463 | 16.0 |
| San Diego | 75 | 87 | .463 | 16.0 |
| Atlanta | 65 | 97 | .401 | 26.0 |

## 1991 American League East

| Team | W | L | Pct | GB |
|------|---|---|-----|-----|
| Toronto | 91 | 71 | .562 | -- |
| Boston | 84 | 78 | .519 | 7.0 |
| Detroit | 84 | 78 | .519 | 7.0 |
| Milwaukee | 83 | 79 | .512 | 8.0 |
| New York | 71 | 91 | .438 | 20.0 |
| Baltimore | 67 | 95 | .414 | 24.0 |
| Cleveland | 57 | 105 | .352 | 34.0 |

## 1991 American League West

| Team | W | L | Pct | GB |
|------|---|---|-----|-----|
| Minnesota | 95 | 67 | .586 | -- |
| Chicago | 87 | 75 | .537 | 8.0 |
| Texas | 85 | 77 | .525 | 10.0 |
| Oakland | 84 | 78 | .519 | 11.0 |
| Seattle | 83 | 79 | .512 | 12.0 |
| Kansas City | 82 | 80 | .506 | 13.0 |
| California | 81 | 81 | .500 | 14.0 |

## 1991 National League East

| Team | W | L | Pct | GB |
|------|---|---|-----|-----|
| Pittsburgh | 98 | 64 | .605 | -- |
| St. Louis | 84 | 78 | .519 | 14.0 |
| Philadelphia | 78 | 84 | .481 | 20.0 |
| Chicago | 77 | 83 | .481 | 20.0 |
| New York | 77 | 84 | .478 | 20.5 |
| Montreal | 71 | 90 | .441 | 26.5 |

## 1991 National League West

| Team | W | L | Pct | GB |
|------|---|---|-----|-----|
| Atlanta | 94 | 68 | .580 | -- |
| Los Angeles | 93 | 69 | .574 | 1.0 |
| San Diego | 84 | 78 | .519 | 10.0 |
| San Francisco | 75 | 87 | .463 | 19.0 |
| Cincinnati | 74 | 88 | .457 | 20.0 |
| Houston | 65 | 97 | .401 | 29.0 |

## 1992 American League East

| Team | W | L | Pct | GB |
|------|---|---|-----|-----|
| Toronto | 96 | 66 | .593 | -- |
| Milwaukee | 92 | 70 | .568 | 4.0 |
| Baltimore | 89 | 73 | .549 | 7.0 |
| Cleveland | 76 | 86 | .469 | 20.0 |
| New York | 76 | 86 | .469 | 20.0 |
| Detroit | 75 | 87 | .463 | 21.0 |
| Boston | 73 | 89 | .451 | 23.0 |

## 1992 American League West

| Team | W | L | Pct | GB |
|------|---|---|-----|-----|
| Oakland | 96 | 66 | .593 | -- |
| Minnesota | 90 | 72 | .556 | 6.0 |
| Chicago | 86 | 76 | .531 | 10.0 |
| Texas | 77 | 85 | .475 | 19.0 |
| California | 72 | 90 | .444 | 24.0 |
| Kansas City | 72 | 90 | .444 | 24.0 |
| Seattle | 64 | 98 | .395 | 32.0 |

## 1992 National League East

| Team | W | L | Pct | GB |
|------|---|---|-----|-----|
| Pittsburgh | 96 | 66 | .593 | -- |
| Montreal | 87 | 75 | .537 | 9.0 |
| St. Louis | 83 | 79 | .512 | 13.0 |
| Chicago | 78 | 84 | .481 | 18.0 |
| New York | 72 | 90 | .444 | 24.0 |
| Philadelphia | 70 | 92 | .432 | 26.0 |

## 1992 National League West

| Team | W | L | Pct | GB |
|------|---|---|-----|-----|
| Atlanta | 98 | 64 | .605 | -- |
| Cincinnati | 90 | 72 | .556 | 8.0 |
| San Diego | 82 | 80 | .506 | 16.0 |
| Houston | 81 | 81 | .500 | 17.0 |
| San Francisco | 72 | 90 | .444 | 26.0 |
| Los Angeles | 63 | 99 | .389 | 35.0 |

## 1993 American League East

| Team | W | L | Pct | GB |
|------|---|---|-----|-----|
| Toronto | 95 | 67 | .586 | -- |
| New York | 88 | 74 | .543 | 7.0 |
| Baltimore | 85 | 77 | .525 | 10.0 |
| Detroit | 85 | 77 | .525 | 10.0 |
| Boston | 80 | 82 | .494 | 15.0 |
| Cleveland | 76 | 86 | .469 | 19.0 |
| Milwaukee | 69 | 93 | .426 | 26.0 |

## 1993 American League West

| Team | W | L | Pct | GB |
|------|---|---|-----|-----|
| Chicago | 94 | 68 | .580 | -- |
| Texas | 86 | 76 | .531 | 8.0 |
| Kansas City | 84 | 78 | .519 | 10.0 |
| Seattle | 82 | 80 | .506 | 12.0 |
| California | 71 | 91 | .438 | 23.0 |
| Minnesota | 71 | 91 | .438 | 23.0 |
| Oakland | 68 | 94 | .420 | 26.0 |

## 1993 National League East

| Team | W | L | Pct | GB |
|------|---|---|-----|-----|
| Philadelphia | 97 | 65 | .599 | -- |
| Montreal | 94 | 68 | .580 | 3.0 |
| St. Louis | 87 | 75 | .537 | 10.0 |
| Chicago | 84 | 78 | .519 | 13.0 |
| Pittsburgh | 75 | 87 | .463 | 22.0 |
| Florida | 64 | 98 | .395 | 33.0 |
| New York | 59 | 103 | .364 | 38.0 |

## 1993 National League West

| Team | W | L | Pct | GB |
|------|---|---|-----|-----|
| Atlanta | 104 | 58 | .642 | -- |
| San Francisco | 103 | 59 | .636 | 1.0 |
| Houston | 85 | 77 | .525 | 19.0 |
| Los Angeles | 81 | 81 | .500 | 23.0 |
| Cincinnati | 73 | 89 | .451 | 31.0 |
| Colorado | 67 | 95 | .414 | 37.0 |
| San Diego | 61 | 101 | .377 | 43.0 |

# FINAL STANDINGS

## 1994 American League East

| Team | W | L | Pct | GB |
|---|---|---|---|---|
| New York | 70 | 43 | .619 | -- |
| Baltimore | 63 | 49 | .563 | 6.5 |
| Toronto | 55 | 60 | .478 | 16.0 |
| Boston | 54 | 61 | .470 | 17.0 |
| Detroit | 53 | 62 | .461 | 18.0 |

## 1994 American League Central

| Team | W | L | Pct | GB |
|---|---|---|---|---|
| Chicago | 67 | 46 | .593 | -- |
| Cleveland | 66 | 47 | .584 | 1.0 |
| Kansas City | 64 | 51 | .557 | 4.0 |
| Minnesota | 53 | 60 | .469 | 14.0 |
| Milwaukee | 53 | 62 | .461 | 15.0 |

## 1994 American League West

| Team | W | L | Pct | GB |
|---|---|---|---|---|
| Texas | 52 | 62 | .456 | -- |
| Oakland | 51 | 63 | .447 | 1.0 |
| Seattle | 49 | 63 | .438 | 2.0 |
| California | 47 | 68 | .409 | 5.5 |

## 1994 National League East

| Team | W | L | Pct | GB |
|---|---|---|---|---|
| Montreal | 74 | 40 | .649 | -- |
| Atlanta | 68 | 46 | .596 | 6.0 |
| New York | 55 | 58 | .487 | 18.5 |
| Philadelphia | 54 | 61 | .470 | 20.5 |
| Florida | 51 | 64 | .443 | 23.5 |

## 1994 National League Central

| Team | W | L | Pct | GB |
|---|---|---|---|---|
| Cincinnati | 66 | 48 | .579 | -- |
| Houston | 66 | 49 | .574 | 0.5 |
| Pittsburgh | 53 | 61 | .465 | 13.0 |
| St. Louis | 53 | 61 | .465 | 13.0 |
| Chicago | 49 | 64 | .434 | 16.5 |

## 1994 National League West

| Team | W | L | Pct | GB |
|---|---|---|---|---|
| Los Angeles | 58 | 56 | .509 | -- |
| San Francisco | 55 | 60 | .478 | 3.5 |
| Colorado | 53 | 64 | .453 | 6.5 |
| San Diego | 47 | 70 | .402 | 12.5 |

## 1995 American League East

| Team | W | L | Pct | GB |
|---|---|---|---|---|
| Boston | 86 | 58 | .597 | -- |
| New York | 79 | 65 | .549 | 7.0 |
| Baltimore | 71 | 73 | .493 | 15.0 |
| Detroit | 60 | 84 | .417 | 26.0 |
| Toronto | 56 | 88 | .389 | 30.0 |

## 1995 American League Central

| Team | W | L | Pct | GB |
|---|---|---|---|---|
| Cleveland | 100 | 44 | .694 | -- |
| Kansas City | 70 | 74 | .486 | 30.0 |
| Chicago | 68 | 76 | .472 | 32.0 |
| Milwaukee | 65 | 79 | .451 | 35.0 |
| Minnesota | 56 | 88 | .389 | 44.0 |

## 1995 American League West

| Team | W | L | Pct | GB |
|---|---|---|---|---|
| Seattle | 79 | 66 | .545 | -- |
| California | 78 | 67 | .538 | 1.0 |
| Texas | 74 | 70 | .514 | 4.5 |
| Oakland | 67 | 77 | .465 | 11.5 |

## 1995 National League East

| Team | W | L | Pct | GB |
|---|---|---|---|---|
| Atlanta | 90 | 54 | .625 | -- |
| New York | 69 | 75 | .479 | 21.0 |
| Philadelphia | 69 | 75 | .479 | 21.0 |
| Florida | 67 | 76 | .469 | 22.5 |
| Montreal | 66 | 78 | .458 | 24.0 |

## 1995 National League Central

| Team | W | L | Pct | GB |
|---|---|---|---|---|
| Cincinnati | 85 | 59 | .590 | -- |
| Houston | 76 | 68 | .528 | 9.0 |
| Chicago | 73 | 71 | .507 | 12.0 |
| St. Louis | 62 | 81 | .434 | 22.5 |
| Pittsburgh | 58 | 86 | .403 | 27.0 |

## 1995 National League West

| Team | W | L | Pct | GB |
|---|---|---|---|---|
| Los Angeles | 78 | 66 | .542 | -- |
| Colorado | 77 | 67 | .535 | 1.0 |
| San Diego | 70 | 74 | .486 | 8.0 |
| San Francisco | 67 | 77 | .465 | 11.0 |

## 1996 American League East

| Team | W | L | Pct | GB |
|---|---|---|---|---|
| New York | 92 | 70 | .568 | -- |
| Baltimore | 88 | 74 | .543 | 4.0 |
| Boston | 85 | 77 | .525 | 7.0 |
| Toronto | 74 | 88 | .457 | 18.0 |
| Detroit | 53 | 109 | .327 | 39.0 |

## 1996 American League Central

| Team | W | L | Pct | GB |
|---|---|---|---|---|
| Cleveland | 99 | 62 | .615 | -- |
| Chicago | 85 | 77 | .525 | 14.5 |
| Milwaukee | 80 | 82 | .494 | 19.5 |
| Minnesota | 78 | 84 | .481 | 21.5 |
| Kansas City | 75 | 86 | .466 | 24.0 |

## 1996 American League West

| Team | W | L | Pct | GB |
|---|---|---|---|---|
| Texas | 90 | 72 | .556 | -- |
| Seattle | 85 | 76 | .528 | 4.5 |
| Oakland | 78 | 84 | .481 | 12.0 |
| California | 70 | 91 | .435 | 19.5 |

## 1996 National League East

| Team | W | L | Pct | GB |
|---|---|---|---|---|
| Atlanta | 96 | 66 | .593 | -- |
| Montreal | 88 | 74 | .543 | 8.0 |
| Florida | 80 | 82 | .494 | 16.0 |
| New York | 71 | 91 | .438 | 25.0 |
| Philadelphia | 67 | 95 | .414 | 29.0 |

# FINAL STANDINGS

## 1996 National League Central

| Team | W | L | Pct | GB |
|---|---|---|---|---|
| St. Louis | 88 | 74 | .543 | -- |
| Houston | 82 | 80 | .506 | 6.0 |
| Cincinnati | 81 | 81 | .500 | 7.0 |
| Chicago | 76 | 86 | .469 | 12.0 |
| Pittsburgh | 73 | 89 | .451 | 15.0 |

## 1996 National League West

| Team | W | L | Pct | GB |
|---|---|---|---|---|
| San Diego | 91 | 71 | .562 | -- |
| Los Angeles | 90 | 72 | .556 | 1.0 |
| Colorado | 83 | 79 | .512 | 8.0 |
| San Francisco | 68 | 94 | .420 | 23.0 |

## 1997 American League East

| Team | W | L | Pct | GB |
|---|---|---|---|---|
| Baltimore | 98 | 64 | .605 | -- |
| New York | 96 | 66 | .593 | 2.0 |
| Detroit | 79 | 83 | .488 | 19.0 |
| Boston | 78 | 84 | .481 | 20.0 |
| Toronto | 76 | 86 | .469 | 22.0 |

## 1997 American League Central

| Team | W | L | Pct | GB |
|---|---|---|---|---|
| Cleveland | 86 | 75 | .534 | -- |
| Chicago | 80 | 81 | .497 | 6.0 |
| Milwaukee | 78 | 83 | .484 | 8.0 |
| Minnesota | 68 | 94 | .420 | 18.5 |
| Kansas City | 67 | 94 | .416 | 19.0 |

## 1997 American League West

| Team | W | L | Pct | GB |
|---|---|---|---|---|
| Seattle | 90 | 72 | .556 | -- |
| Anaheim | 84 | 78 | .519 | 6.0 |
| Texas | 77 | 85 | .475 | 13.0 |
| Oakland | 65 | 97 | .401 | 25.0 |

## 1997 National League East

| Team | W | L | Pct | GB |
|---|---|---|---|---|
| Atlanta | 101 | 61 | .623 | -- |
| Florida | 92 | 70 | .568 | 9.0 |
| New York | 88 | 74 | .543 | 13.0 |
| Montreal | 78 | 84 | .481 | 23.0 |
| Philadelphia | 68 | 94 | .420 | 33.0 |

## 1997 National League Central

| Team | W | L | Pct | GB |
|---|---|---|---|---|
| Houston | 84 | 78 | .519 | -- |
| Pittsburgh | 79 | 83 | .488 | 5.0 |
| Cincinnati | 76 | 86 | .469 | 8.0 |
| St. Louis | 73 | 89 | .451 | 11.0 |
| Chicago | 68 | 94 | .420 | 16.0 |

## 1997 National League West

| Team | W | L | Pct | GB |
|---|---|---|---|---|
| San Francisco | 90 | 72 | .556 | -- |
| Los Angeles | 88 | 74 | .543 | 2.0 |
| Colorado | 83 | 79 | .512 | 7.0 |
| San Diego | 76 | 86 | .469 | 14.0 |

## 1998 American League East

| Team | W | L | Pct | GB |
|---|---|---|---|---|
| New York | 114 | 48 | .704 | -- |
| Boston | 92 | 70 | .568 | 22.0 |
| Toronto | 88 | 74 | .543 | 26.0 |
| Baltimore | 79 | 83 | .488 | 35.0 |
| Tampa Bay | 63 | 99 | .389 | 51.0 |

## 1998 American League Central

| Team | W | L | Pct | GB |
|---|---|---|---|---|
| Cleveland | 89 | 73 | .549 | -- |
| Chicago | 80 | 82 | .494 | 9.0 |
| Kansas City | 72 | 89 | .447 | 16.5 |
| Minnesota | 70 | 92 | .432 | 19.0 |
| Detroit | 65 | 97 | .401 | 24.0 |

## 1998 American League West

| Team | W | L | Pct | GB |
|---|---|---|---|---|
| Texas | 88 | 74 | .543 | -- |
| Anaheim | 85 | 77 | .525 | 3.0 |
| Seattle | 76 | 85 | .472 | 11.5 |
| Oakland | 74 | 88 | .457 | 14.0 |

## 1998 National League East

| Team | W | L | Pct | GB |
|---|---|---|---|---|
| Atlanta | 106 | 56 | .654 | -- |
| New York | 88 | 74 | .543 | 18.0 |
| Philadelphia | 75 | 87 | .463 | 31.0 |
| Montreal | 65 | 97 | .401 | 41.0 |
| Florida | 54 | 108 | .333 | 52.0 |

## 1998 National League Central

| Team | W | L | Pct | GB |
|---|---|---|---|---|
| Houston | 102 | 60 | .630 | -- |
| Chicago | 90 | 73 | .552 | 12.5 |
| St. Louis | 83 | 79 | .512 | 19.0 |
| Cincinnati | 77 | 85 | .475 | 25.0 |
| Milwaukee | 74 | 88 | .457 | 28.0 |
| Pittsburgh | 69 | 93 | .426 | 33.0 |

## 1998 National League West

| Team | W | L | Pct | GB |
|---|---|---|---|---|
| San Diego | 98 | 64 | .605 | -- |
| San Francisco | 89 | 74 | .546 | 9.5 |
| Los Angeles | 83 | 79 | .512 | 15.0 |
| Colorado | 77 | 85 | .475 | 21.0 |
| Arizona | 65 | 97 | .401 | 33.0 |

## 1999 American League East

| Team | W | L | Pct | GB |
|---|---|---|---|---|
| New York | 98 | 64 | .605 | -- |
| Boston | 94 | 68 | .580 | 4.0 |
| Toronto | 84 | 78 | .519 | 14.0 |
| Baltimore | 78 | 84 | .481 | 20.0 |
| Tampa Bay | 69 | 93 | .426 | 29.0 |

## 1999 American League Central

| Team | W | L | Pct | GB |
|---|---|---|---|---|
| Cleveland | 97 | 65 | .599 | -- |
| Chicago | 75 | 86 | .466 | 21.5 |
| Detroit | 69 | 92 | .429 | 27.5 |
| Kansas City | 64 | 97 | .398 | 32.5 |
| Minnesota | 63 | 97 | .394 | 33.0 |

# FINAL STANDINGS

## 1999 American League West

| Team | W | L | Pct | GB |
|------|---|---|-----|-----|
| Texas | 95 | 67 | .586 | -- |
| Oakland | 87 | 75 | .537 | 8.0 |
| Seattle | 79 | 83 | .488 | 16.0 |
| Anaheim | 70 | 92 | .432 | 25.0 |

## 1999 National League East

| Team | W | L | Pct | GB |
|------|---|---|-----|-----|
| Atlanta | 103 | 59 | .636 | -- |
| New York | 97 | 66 | .595 | 6.5 |
| Philadelphia | 77 | 85 | .475 | 26.0 |
| Montreal | 68 | 94 | .420 | 35.0 |
| Florida | 64 | 98 | .395 | 39.0 |

## 1999 National League Central

| Team | W | L | Pct | GB |
|------|---|---|-----|-----|
| Houston | 97 | 65 | .599 | -- |
| Cincinnati | 96 | 67 | .589 | 1.5 |
| Pittsburgh | 78 | 83 | .484 | 18.5 |
| St. Louis | 75 | 86 | .466 | 21.5 |
| Milwaukee | 74 | 87 | .460 | 22.5 |
| Chicago | 67 | 95 | .414 | 30.0 |

## 1999 National League West

| Team | W | L | Pct | GB |
|------|---|---|-----|-----|
| Arizona | 100 | 62 | .617 | -- |
| San Francisco | 86 | 76 | .531 | 14.0 |
| Los Angeles | 77 | 85 | .475 | 23.0 |
| San Diego | 74 | 88 | .457 | 26.0 |
| Colorado | 72 | 90 | .444 | 28.0 |

## 2000 American League East

| Team | W | L | Pct. | GB |
|------|---|---|-----|-----|
| New York | 87 | 74 | .540 | - |
| Boston | 85 | 77 | .525 | 2.5 |
| Toronto | 83 | 79 | .512 | 4.5 |
| Baltimore | 74 | 88 | .457 | 13.5 |
| Tampa Bay | 69 | 92 | .429 | 18 |

## 2000 American League Central

| Team | W | L | Pct. | GB |
|------|---|---|-----|-----|
| Chicago | 95 | 67 | .586 | - |
| Cleveland | 90 | 72 | .556 | 5 |
| Detroit | 79 | 83 | .488 | 16 |
| Kansas City | 77 | 85 | .475 | 18 |
| Minnesota | 69 | 93 | .426 | 26 |

## 2000 American League West

| Team | W | L | Pct. | GB |
|------|---|---|-----|-----|
| Oakland | 91 | 70 | .565 | - |
| Seattle | 91 | 71 | .562 | 0.5 |
| Anaheim | 82 | 80 | .506 | 9.5 |
| Texas | 71 | 91 | .438 | 20.5 |

## 2000 National League East

| Team | W | L | Pct. | GB |
|------|---|---|-----|-----|
| Atlanta | 95 | 67 | .586 | - |
| New York | 94 | 68 | .580 | 1.0 |
| Florida | 79 | 82 | .491 | 15.5 |
| Montreal | 67 | 95 | .414 | 28.0 |
| Philadelphia | 65 | 97 | .401 | 30.0 |

## 2000 National League Central

| Team | W | L | Pct. | GB |
|------|---|---|-----|-----|
| St. Louis | 95 | 67 | .586 | - |
| Cincinnati | 85 | 77 | .525 | 10.0 |
| Milwaukee | 73 | 89 | .451 | 22.0 |
| Houston | 72 | 90 | .444 | 23.0 |
| Pittsburgh | 69 | 93 | .426 | 26.0 |
| Chicago | 65 | 97 | .401 | 30.0 |

## 2000 National League West

| Team | W | L | Pct. | GB |
|------|---|---|-----|-----|
| San Francisco | 97 | 65 | .599 | - |
| Los Angeles | 86 | 76 | .531 | 11.0 |
| Arizona | 85 | 77 | .525 | 12.0 |
| Colorado | 82 | 80 | .506 | 15.0 |
| San Diego | 76 | 86 | .469 | 21.0 |

## 2001 American League East

| Team | W | L | Pct. | GB |
|------|---|---|-----|-----|
| New York | 95 | 65 | .594 | -- |
| Boston | 82 | 79 | .509 | 13.5 |
| Toronto | 80 | 82 | .494 | 16.0 |
| Baltimore | 63 | 98 | .391 | 32.5 |
| Tampa Bay | 62 | 100 | .383 | 34.0 |

## 2001 American League Central

| Team | W | L | Pct. | GB |
|------|---|---|-----|-----|
| Cleveland | 91 | 71 | .562 | -- |
| Minnesota | 85 | 77 | .525 | 6.0 |
| Chicago | 83 | 79 | .512 | 8.0 |
| Detroit | 66 | 96 | .407 | 25.0 |
| Kansas City | 65 | 97 | .401 | 26.0 |

## 2001 American League West

| Team | W | L | Pct. | GB |
|------|---|---|-----|-----|
| Seattle | 116 | 46 | .716 | -- |
| Oakland | 102 | 60 | .630 | 14.0 |
| Anaheim | 75 | 87 | .463 | 41.0 |
| Texas | 73 | 89 | .451 | 43.0 |

## 2001 National League East

| Team | W | L | Pct. | GB |
|------|---|---|-----|-----|
| Atlanta | 88 | 74 | .543 | -- |
| Philadelphia | 86 | 76 | .531 | 2.0 |
| New York | 82 | 80 | .506 | 6.0 |
| Florida | 76 | 86 | .469 | 12.0 |
| Montreal | 68 | 94 | .420 | 20.0 |

## 2001 National League Central

| Team | W | L | Pct. | GB |
|------|---|---|-----|-----|
| Houston | 93 | 69 | .574 | -- |
| St. Louis | 93 | 69 | .574 | 0.0 |
| Chicago | 88 | 74 | .543 | 5.0 |
| Milwaukee | 68 | 94 | .420 | 25.0 |
| Cincinnati | 66 | 96 | .407 | 27.0 |
| Pittsburgh | 62 | 100 | .383 | 31.0 |

## 2001 National League West

| Team | W | L | Pct. | GB |
|------|---|---|-----|-----|
| Arizona | 92 | 70 | .568 | -- |
| San Francisco | 90 | 72 | .556 | 2.0 |
| Los Angeles | 86 | 76 | .531 | 6.0 |
| San Diego | 79 | 83 | .488 | 13.0 |
| Colorado | 73 | 89 | .451 | 19.0 |

# ALL STAR GAMES

| Year (Gm) | Winner | Score | Loser | Venue |
|---|---|---|---|---|
| 1933 | American | 4–2 | National | Chicago |
| 1934 | American | 9–7 | National | New York |
| 1935 | American | 4–1 | National | Cleveland |
| 1936 | National | 4–3 | American | Boston |
| 1937 | American | 8–3 | National | Washington |
| 1938 | National | 4–1 | American | Cincinnati |
| 1939 | American | 3–1 | National | New York |
| 1940 | National | 4–0 | American | St. Louis |
| 1941 | American | 7–5 | National | Detroit |
| 1942 | American | 3–1 | National | New York |
| 1943 | American | 5–3 | National | Philadelphia |
| 1944 | National | 7–1 | American | Pittsburgh |
| 1946 | American | 12–0 | National | Boston |
| 1947 | American | 2–1 | National | Chicago |
| 1948 | American | 5–2 | National | St. Louis |
| 1949 | American | 11–7 | National | Brooklyn |
| 1950 | National | 4–3 | American | Chicago |
| 1951 | National | 8–3 | American | Detroit |
| 1952 | National | 3–2 | American | Philadelphia |
| 1953 | National | 5–1 | American | Cincinnati |
| 1954 | American | 11–9 | National | Cleveland |
| 1955 | National | 6–5 | American | Milwaukee |
| 1956 | National | 7–3 | American | Washington |
| 1957 | American | 6–5 | National | St. Louis |
| 1958 | American | 4–3 | National | Baltimore |
| 1959 (1) | National | 5–4 | American | Pittsburgh |
| 1959 (2) | American | 5–3 | National | Los Angeles |
| 1960 (1) | National | 5–3 | American | Kansas City |
| 1960 (2) | National | 6–0 | American | New York |
| 1961 (1) | National | 5–4 | American | San Francisco |
| 1961 (2) | National | 1–1 | American | Boston |
| 1962 (1) | National | 3–1 | American | Washington |
| 1962 (2) | American | 9–4 | National | Chicago |
| 1963 | National | 5–3 | American | Cleveland |
| 1964 | National | 7–4 | American | New York |
| 1965 | National | 6–5 | American | Minnesota |

# ALL STAR GAMES

| Year (Gm) | Winner | Score | Loser | Venue |
|---|---|---|---|---|
| 1966 | National | 2–1 | American | St. Louis |
| 1967 | National | 2–1 | American | California |
| 1968 | National | 1–0 | American | Houston |
| 1969 | National | 9–3 | American | Washington |
| 1970 | National | 5–4 | American | Cincinnati |
| 1971 | American | 6–4 | National | Detroit |
| 1972 | National | 4–3 | American | Atlanta |
| 1973 | National | 7–1 | American | Kansas City |
| 1974 | National | 7–2 | American | Pittsburgh |
| 1975 | National | 6–3 | American | Milwaukee |
| 1976 | National | 7–1 | American | Philadelphia |
| 1977 | National | 7–5 | American | New York |
| 1978 | National | 7–3 | American | San Diego |
| 1979 | National | 7–6 | American | Seattle |
| 1980 | National | 4–2 | American | Los Angeles |
| 1981 | National | 5–4 | American | Cleveland |
| 1982 | National | 4–1 | American | Montreal |
| 1983 | American | 13–3 | National | Chicago |
| 1984 | National | 3–1 | American | San Francisco |
| 1985 | National | 6–1 | American | Minnesota |
| 1986 | American | 3–2 | National | Houston |
| 1987 | National | 2–0 | American | Oakland |
| 1988 | American | 2–1 | National | Cincinnati |
| 1989 | American | 5–3 | National | California |
| 1990 | American | 2–0 | National | Chicago |
| 1991 | American | 4–2 | National | Toronto |
| 1992 | American | 13–6 | National | San Diego |
| 1993 | American | 9–3 | National | Baltimore |
| 1994 | National | 8–7 | American | Pittsburgh |
| 1995 | National | 3–2 | American | Texas |
| 1996 | National | 6–0 | American | Philadelphia |
| 1997 | American | 3–1 | National | Cleveland |
| 1998 | American | 13–8 | National | Colorado |
| 1999 | American | 4–1 | National | Boston |
| 2000 | American | 6–3 | National | Atlanta |
| 2001 | American | 4–1 | National | Seattle |

# POST SEASON RESULTS

| Year | Series | Winner | Score | Loser |
|------|--------|--------|-------|-------|
| 1903 | World Series | Boston(AL) | 5–3 | Pittsburgh(NL) |
| 1905 | World Series | New York(NL) | 4–1 | Philadelphia(AL) |
| 1906 | World Series | Chicago(AL) | 4–2 | Chicago(NL) |
| 1907 | World Series | Chicago(NL) | 4–0 | Detroit (AL) |
| 1908 | World Series | Chicago(NL) | 4–1 | Detroit (AL) |
| 1909 | World Series | Pittsburgh(NL) | 4–3 | Detroit(AL) |
| 1910 | World Series | Philadelphia(AL) | 4–1 | Chicago(NL) |
| 1911 | World Series | Philadelphia (AL) | 4–2 | New York(NL) |
| 1912 | World Series | Boston(AL) | 4–3 | New York(NL) |
| 1913 | World Series | Philadelphia(AL) | 4–1 | New York(NL) |
| 1914 | World Series | Boston(NL) | 4–0 | Philadelphia(AL) |
| 1915 | World Series | Boston(AL) | 4–1 | Philadelphia(NL) |
| 1916 | World Series | Boston(AL) | 4–1 | Brooklyn(NL) |
| 1917 | World Series | Chicago(AL) | 4–2 | New York(NL) |
| 1918 | World Series | Boston(AL) | 4–2 | Chicago(NL) |
| 1919 | World Series | Cincinnati(NL) | 5–3 | Chicago(AL) |
| 1920 | World Series | Cleveland(AL) | 5–2 | Brooklyn(NL) |
| 1921 | World Series | New York(NL) | 5–3 | New York(AL) |
| 1922 | World Series | New York(NL) | 4–0 | New York(AL) |
| 1923 | World Series | New York(AL) | 4–2 | New York(NL) |
| 1924 | World Series | Washington (AL) | 4–3 | New York(NL) |
| 1925 | World Series | Pittsburgh(NL) | 4–3 | Washington(AL) |
| 1926 | World Series | St. Louis(NL) | 4–3 | New York(AL) |
| 1927 | World Series | New York(AL) | 4–0 | Pittsburgh(NL) |
| 1928 | World Series | New York(AL) | 4–0 | St. Louis(NL) |
| 1929 | World Series | Philadelphia(AL) | 4–1 | Chicago(NL) |
| 1930 | World Series | Philadelphia(AL) | 4–2 | St. Louis(NL) |
| 1931 | World Series | St. Louis(NL) | 4–3 | Philadelphia(AL) |
| 1932 | World Series | New York(AL) | 4–0 | Chicago(NL) |
| 1933 | World Series | New York(NL) | 4–1 | Washington(AL) |

# POST SEASON RESULTS

| Year | Series | Winner | Score | Loser |
|------|--------|--------|-------|-------|
| 1934 | World Series | St. Louis(NL) | 4–3 | Detroit(AL) |
| 1935 | World Series | Detroit(AL) | 4–2 | Chicago(NL) |
| 1936 | World Series | New York(AL) | 4–2 | New York(NL) |
| 1937 | World Series | New York(AL) | 4–1 | New York(NL) |
| 1938 | World Series | New York (AL) | 4–0 | Chicago(NL) |
| 1939 | World Series | New York(AL) | 4–0 | Cincinnati(NL) |
| 1940 | World Series | Cincinnati(NL) | 4–3 | Detroit(AL) |
| 1941 | World Series | New York(AL) | 4–1 | Brooklyn(NL) |
| 1942 | World Series | St. Louis(NL) | 4–1 | New York(AL) |
| 1943 | World Series | New York(AL) | 4–1 | St. Louis(NL) |
| 1944 | World Series | St. Louis(NL) | 4–2 | St. Louis(AL) |
| 1945 | World Series | Detroit(AL) | 4–3 | Chicago(NL) |
| 1946 | World Series | St. Louis(NL) | 4–3 | Boston(AL) |
| 1947 | World Series | New York(AL) | 4–3 | Brooklyn(NL) |
| 1948 | World Series | Cleveland(AL) | 4–2 | Boston(NL) |
| 1949 | World Series | New York(AL) | 4–1 | Brooklyn(NL) |
| 1950 | World Series | New York(AL) | 4–0 | Philadelphia(NL) |
| 1951 | World Series | New York(AL) | 4–2 | New York(NL) |
| 1952 | World Series | New York(AL) | 4–3 | Brooklyn(NL) |
| 1953 | World Series | New York(AL) | 4–2 | Brooklyn(NL) |
| 1954 | World Series | New York(NL) | 4–0 | Cleveland(AL) |
| 1955 | World Series | Brooklyn(NL) | 4–3 | New York(AL) |
| 1956 | World Series | New York(AL) | 4–3 | Brooklyn(NL) |
| 1957 | World Series | Milwaukee(NL) | 4–3 | New York(AL) |
| 1958 | World Series | New York(AL) | 4–3 | Milwaukee(NL) |
| 1959 | World Series | Los Angeles(NL) | 4–2 | Chicago(AL) |
| 1960 | World Series | Pittsburgh(NL) | 4–3 | New York(AL) |
| 1961 | World Series | New York(AL) | 4–1 | Cincinnati(NL) |
| 1962 | World Series | New York(AL) | 4–3 | San Francisco(NL) |
| 1963 | World Series | Los Angeles(NL) | 4–0 | New York(AL) |

# POST SEASON RESULTS

| Year | Series | Winner | Score | Loser |
|------|--------|--------|-------|-------|
| 1964 | World Series | St. Louis(NL) | 4–3 | New York(AL) |
| 1965 | World Series | Los Angeles(NL) | 4–3 | Minnesota (AL) |
| 1966 | World Series | Baltimore(AL) | 4–0 | Los Angeles(NL) |
| 1967 | World Series | St. Louis(NL) | 4–3 | Boston(AL) |
| 1968 | World Series | Detroit(AL) | 4–3 | St. Louis(NL) |
| 1969 | ALCS | Baltimore | 3–0 | Minnesota |
| 1969 | NLCS | New York | 3–0 | Atlanta |
| 1969 | World Series | New York(NL) | 4–1 | Baltimore(AL) |
| 1970 | ALCS | Baltimore | 3–0 | Minnesota |
| 1970 | NLCS | Cincinnati | 3–0 | Pittsburgh |
| 1970 | World Series | Baltimore(AL) | 4–1 | Cincinnati(NL) |
| 1971 | ALCS | Baltimore | 3–0 | Oakland |
| 1971 | NLCS | Pittsburgh | 3–1 | San Francisco |
| 1971 | World Series | Pittsburgh(NL) | 4–3 | Baltimore(AL) |
| 1972 | ALCS | Oakland | 3–2 | Detroit |
| 1972 | NLCS | Cincinnati | 3–2 | Pittsburgh |
| 1972 | World Series | Oakland(AL) | 4–3 | Cincinnati(NL) |
| 1973 | ALCS | Oakland | 3–2 | Baltimore |
| 1973 | NLCS | New York | 3–2 | Cincinnati |
| 1973 | World Series | Oakland(AL) | 4–3 | New York(NL) |
| 1974 | ALCS | Oakland | 3–1 | Baltimore |
| 1974 | NLCS | Los Angeles | 3–1 | Pittsburgh |
| 1974 | World Series | Oakland(AL) | 4–1 | Los Angeles(NL) |
| 1975 | ALCS | Boston | 3–0 | Oakland |
| 1975 | NLCS | Cincinnati | 3–0 | Pittsburgh |
| 1975 | World Series | Cincinnati(NL) | 4–3 | Boston(AL) |
| 1976 | ALCS | New York | 3–2 | Kansas City |
| 1976 | NLCS | Cincinnati | 3–0 | Philadelphia |
| 1976 | World Series | Cincinnati(NL) | 4–0 | New York(AL) |
| 1977 | ALCS | New York | 3–2 | Kansas City |
| 1977 | NLCS | Los Angeles | 3–1 | Philadelphia |
| 1977 | World Series | New York(AL) | 4–2 | Los Angeles(NL) |
| 1978 | ALCS | New York | 3–1 | Kansas City |
| 1978 | NLCS | Los Angeles | 3–1 | Philadelphia |
| 1978 | World Series | New York(AL) | 4–2 | Los Angeles(NL) |

# POST SEASON RESULTS

| Year | Series | Winner | Score | Loser |
|------|--------|--------|-------|-------|
| 1979 | ALCS | Baltimore | 3–1 | California |
| 1979 | NLCS | Pittsburgh | 3–0 | Cincinnati |
| 1979 | World Series | Pittsburgh(NL) | 4–3 | Baltimore(AL) |
| 1980 | ALCS | Kansas City | 3–0 | New York |
| 1980 | NLCS | Philadelphia | 3–2 | Houston |
| 1980 | World Series | Philadelphia(NL) | 4–2 | Kansas City(AL) |
| 1981 | AL Division | New York | 3–2 | Milwaukee |
| 1981 | AL Division | Oakland | 3–0 | Kansas City |
| 1981 | NL Division | Montreal | 3–2 | Philadelphia |
| 1981 | NL Division | Los Angeles | 3–2 | Houston |
| 1981 | ALCS | New York | 3–0 | Oakland |
| 1981 | NLCS | Los Angeles | 3–2 | Montreal |
| 1981 | World Series | Los Angeles(NL) | 4–2 | New York(AL) |
| 1982 | ALCS | Milwaukee | 3–2 | California |
| 1982 | NLCS | St. Louis | 3–0 | Atlanta |
| 1982 | World Series | St. Louis(NL) | 4–3 | Milwaukee(AL) |
| 1983 | ALCS | Baltimore | 3–1 | Chicago |
| 1983 | NLCS | Philadelphia | 3–1 | Los Angeles |
| 1983 | World Series | Baltimore(AL) | 4–1 | Philadelphia(NL) |
| 1984 | ALCS | Detroit | 3–0 | Kansas City |
| 1984 | NLCS | San Diego | 3–2 | Chicago |
| 1984 | World Series | Detroit(AL) | 4–1 | San Diego(NL) |
| 1985 | ALCS | Kansas City | 4–3 | Toronto |
| 1985 | NLCS | St. Louis | 4–2 | Los Angeles |
| 1985 | World Series | Kansas City(AL) | 4–3 | St. Louis(NL) |
| 1986 | ALCS | Boston | 4–3 | California |
| 1986 | NLCS | New York | 4–2 | Houston |
| 1986 | World Series | New York(NL) | 4–3 | Boston(AL) |
| 1987 | ALCS | Minnesota | 4–1 | Detroit |
| 1987 | NLCS | St. Louis | 4–3 | San Francisco |
| 1987 | World Series | Minnesota(AL) | 4–3 | St. Louis(NL) |
| 1988 | ALCS | Oakland | 4–0 | Boston |
| 1988 | NLCS | Los Angeles | 4–3 | New York |
| 1988 | World Series | Los Angeles(NL) | 4–1 | Oakland(AL) |

# POST SEASON RESULTS

| Year | Series | Winner | Score | Loser |
|------|--------|--------|-------|-------|
| 1989 | ALCS | Oakland | 4–1 | Toronto |
| 1989 | NLCS | San Francisco | 4–1 | Chicago |
| 1989 | World Series | Oakland(AL) | 4–0 | San Francisco(NL) |
| 1990 | ALCS | Oakland | 4–0 | Boston |
| 1990 | NLCS | Cincinnati | 4–2 | Pittsburgh |
| 1990 | World Series | Cincinnati(NL) | 4–0 | Oakland(AL) |
| 1991 | ALCS | Minnesota | 4–1 | Toronto |
| 1991 | NLCS | Atlanta | 4–3 | Pittsburgh |
| 1991 | World Series | Minnesota(AL) | 4–3 | Atlanta(NL) |
| 1992 | ALCS | Toronto | 4–2 | Oakland |
| 1992 | NLCS | Atlanta | 4–3 | Pittsburgh |
| 1992 | World Series | Toronto(AL) | 4–2 | Atlanta(NL) |
| 1993 | ALCS | Toronto | 4–2 | Chicago |
| 1993 | NLCS | Philadelphia | 4–2 | Atlanta |
| 1993 | World Series | Toronto(AL) | 4–2 | Philadelphia(NL) |
| 1994 | *Playoffs canceled* | | | |
| 1995 | AL Division | Cleveland | 3–0 | Boston |
| 1995 | AL Division | Seattle | 3–2 | New York |
| 1995 | NL Division | Atlanta | 3–1 | Colorado |
| 1995 | NL Division | Cincinnati | 3–0 | Los Angeles |
| 1995 | ALCS | Cleveland | 4–2 | Seattle |
| 1995 | NLCS | Atlanta | 4–0 | Cincinnati |
| 1995 | World Series | Atlanta(NL) | 4–2 | Cleveland(AL) |
| 1996 | AL Division | Baltimore | 3–1 | Cleveland |
| 1996 | AL Division | New York | 3–1 | Texas |
| 1996 | NL Division | Atlanta | 3–0 | Los Angeles |
| 1996 | NL Division | St. Louis | 3–0 | San Diego |
| 1996 | ALCS | New York | 4–1 | Baltimore |
| 1996 | NLCS | Atlanta | 4–3 | St. Louis |
| 1996 | World Series | New York(AL) | 4–2 | Atlanta (NL) |
| 1997 | AL Division | Baltimore | 3–1 | Seattle |
| 1997 | AL Division | Cleveland | 3–2 | New York |
| 1997 | NL Division | Atlanta | 3–0 | Houston |
| 1997 | NL Division | Florida | 3–0 | San Francisco |
| 1997 | ALCS | Cleveland | 4–2 | Baltimore |
| 1997 | NLCS | Florida | 4–2 | Atlanta |
| 1997 | World Series | Florida(NL) | 4–3 | Cleveland(AL) |

# POST SEASON RESULTS

| Year | Series | Winner | Score | Loser |
|------|--------|--------|-------|-------|
| 1998 | AL Division | Cleveland | 3–1 | Boston |
| 1998 | AL Division | New York | 3–0 | Texas |
| 1998 | NL Division | Atlanta | 3–0 | Chicago |
| 1998 | NL Division | San Diego | 3–1 | Houston |
| 1998 | ALCS | New York | 4–2 | Cleveland |
| 1998 | NLCS | San Diego | 4–2 | Atlanta |
| 1998 | World Series | New York(AL) | 4–0 | San Diego(NL) |
| 1999 | AL Division | Boston | 3–2 | Cleveland |
| 1999 | AL Division | New York | 3–0 | Texas |
| 1999 | NL Division | Atlanta | 3–1 | Houston |
| 1999 | NL Division | New York | 3–1 | Arizona |
| 1999 | ALCS | New York | 4–1 | Boston |
| 1999 | NLCS | Atlanta | 4–2 | New York |
| 1999 | World Series | New York (AL) | 4–0 | Atlanta(NL) |
| 2000 | AL Division | Seattle | 3–0 | Chicago |
| 2000 | AL Division | New York | 3–2 | Oakland |
| 2000 | NL Division | St. Louis | 3–0 | Atlanta |
| 2000 | NL Division | New York | 3–1 | San Francisco |
| 2000 | ALCS | New York | 4–2 | Seattle |
| 2000 | NLCS | New York | 4–1 | St. Louis |
| 2000 | World Series | New York(AL) | 4–1 | New York(NL) |
| 2001 | AL Division | Seattle | 3–2 | Cleveland |
| 2001 | AL Division | New York | 3–2 | Oakland |
| 2001 | NL Division | Atlanta | 3–0 | Houston |
| 2001 | NL Division | Arizona | 3–2 | St. Louis |
| 2001 | ALCS | New York | 4–1 | Seattle |
| 2001 | NLCS | Arizona | 4–1 | Atlanta |
| 2001 | World Series | Arizona | 4–3 | New York(AL) |

# MOST VALUABLE PLAYER

*(Committee Selection, 1911-1914, 1922-1929; Baseball Writers, 1931-1999)*

| Year | American League | National League |
|------|-----------------|-----------------|
| 1911 | Ty Cobb, Det. | Wildfire Schulte, ChC. |
| 1912 | Tris Speaker, Bos. | Larry Doyle, NYG. |
| 1913 | Walter Johnson, Was. | Jake Daubert, Bro. |
| 1914 | Eddie Collins, Phi. | Johnny Evers, Bos. |
| 1921 | (No Awards) | (No Awards) |
| 1922 | George Sisler, StL. | (No Awards) |
| 1923 | Babe Ruth, NYY. | (No Awards) |
| 1924 | Walter Johnson, Was. | Dazzy Vance, Bro. |
| 1925 | Roger Peckinpaugh, Was. | Rogers Hornsby, StL. |
| 1926 | George Burns, Cle. | Bob O'Farrell, StL. |
| 1927 | Lou Gehrig, NYY. | Paul Waner, Pit. |
| 1928 | Mickey Cochrane, Phi. | Jim Bottomley, StL. |
| 1929 | (No Awards) | Rogers Hornsby, ChC. |
| 1930 | (No Awards) | (No Awards) |
| 1931 | Lefty Grove, Phi. | Frankie Frisch, StL. |
| 1932 | Jimmie Foxx, Phi. | Chuck Klein, Phi. |
| 1933 | Jimmie Foxx, Phi. | Carl Hubbell, NYG. |
| 1934 | Mickey Cochrane, Det. | Dizzy Dean, StL. |
| 1935 | Hank Greenberg, Det. | Gabby Hartnett, ChC. |
| 1936 | Lou Gehrig, NYY. | Carl Hubbell, NYG. |
| 1937 | Charlie Gehringer, Det. | Joe Medwick, StL. |

# MOST VALUABLE PLAYER

| Year | American League | National League |
|------|-----------------|-----------------|
| 1938 | Jimmie Foxx, Bos. | Ernie Lombardi, Cin. |
| 1939 | Joe DiMaggio, NYY. | Bucky Walters, Cin. |
| 1940 | Hank Greenberg, Det. | Frank McCormick, Cin. |
| 1941 | Joe DiMaggio, NYY. | Dolph Camilli, Bro. |
| 1942 | Joe Gordon, NYY. | Mort Cooper, StL. |
| 1943 | Spud Chandler, NYY. | Stan Musial, StL. |
| 1944 | Hal Newhouser, Det. | Marty Marion, StL. |
| 1945 | Hal Newhouser, Det. | Phil Cavarretta, ChC. |
| 1946 | Ted Williams, Bos. | Stan Musial, StL. |
| 1947 | Joe DiMaggio, NYY. | Bob Elliott, Bos. |
| 1948 | Lou Boudreau, Cle. | Stan Musial, StL. |
| 1949 | Ted Williams, Bos. | Jackie Robinson, Bro. |
| 1950 | Phil Rizzuto, NYY. | Jim Konstanty, Phi. |
| 1951 | Yogi Berra, NYY. | Roy Campanella, Bro. |
| 1952 | Bobby Shantz, Phi. | Hank Sauer, ChC. |
| 1953 | Al Rosen, Cle. | Roy Campanella, Bro. |
| 1954 | Yogi Berra, NYY. | Willie Mays, NYG. |
| 1955 | Yogi Berra, NYY. | Roy Campanella, Bro. |
| 1956 | Mickey Mantle, NYY. | Don Newcombe, Bro. |
| 1957 | Mickey Mantle, NYY. | Hank Aaron, Mil. |
| 1958 | Jackie Jensen, Bos. | Ernie Banks, ChC. |
| 1959 | Nellie Fox, CWS. | Ernie Banks, ChC. |

# MOST VALUABLE PLAYER

| Year | American League | National League | |
|------|-----------------|-----------------|---|
| 1960 | Roger Maris, NYY. | Dick Groat, Pit. | |
| 1961 | Roger Maris, NYY. | Frank Robinson, Cin. | |
| 1962 | Mickey Mantle, NYY. | Maury Wills, LA. | |
| 1963 | Elston Howard, NYY. | Sandy Koufax, LA. | |
| 1964 | Brooks Robinson, Bal. | Ken Boyer, StL. | |
| 1965 | Zoilo Versalles, Min. | Willie Mays, SF. | |
| 1966 | Frank Robinson, Bal. | Roberto Clemente, Pit. | |
| 1967 | Carl Yastrzemski, Bos. | Orlando Cepeda, StL. | |
| 1968 | Denny McLain, Det. | Bob Gibson, StL. | |
| 1969 | Harmon Killebrew, Min. | Willie McCovey, SF. | |
| 1970 | Boog Powell, Bal. | Johnny Bench, Cin. | |
| 1971 | Vida Blue, Oak. | Joe Torre, StL. | |
| 1972 | Dick Allen, CWS. | Johnny Bench, Cin. | |
| 1973 | Reggie Jackson, Oak. | Pete Rose, Cin. | |
| 1974 | Jeff Burroughs, Tex. | Steve Garvey, LA. | |
| 1975 | Fred Lynn, Bos. | Joe Morgan, Cin. | |
| 1976 | Thurman Munson, NYY. | Joe Morgan, Cin. | |
| 1977 | Rod Carew, Min. | George Foster, Cin. | |
| 1978 | Jim Rice, Bos. | Dave Parker, Pit. | |
| 1979 | Don Baylor, Cal. | Willie Stargell, Pit.  }<br>Keith Hernandez, StL.  } | }shared |
| 1980 | George Brett, KC. | Mike Schmidt, Phi. | |

# MOST VALUABLE PLAYER

| Year | American League | National League |
|------|-----------------|-----------------|
| 1981 | Rollie Fingers, Mil. | Mike Schmidt, Phi. |
| 1982 | Robin Yount, Mil. | Dale Murphy, Atl. |
| 1983 | Cal Ripken Jr., Bal. | Dale Murphy, Atl. |
| 1984 | Willie Hernandez, Det. | Ryne Sandberg, ChC. |
| 1985 | Don Mattingly, NYY. | Willie McGee, StL. |
| 1986 | Roger Clemens, Bos. | Mike Schmidt, Phi. |
| 1987 | George Bell, Tor. | Andre Dawson, ChC. |
| 1988 | Jose Canseco, Oak. | Kirk Gibson, LA. |
| 1989 | Robin Yount, Mil. | Kevin Mitchell, SF. |
| 1990 | Rickey Henderson, Oak. | Barry Bonds, Pit. |
| 1991 | Cal Ripken Jr., Bal. | Terry Pendleton, Atl. |
| 1992 | Dennis Eckersley, Oak. | Barry Bonds, Pit. |
| 1993 | Frank Thomas, CWS. | Barry Bonds, SF. |
| 1994 | Frank Thomas, CWS. | Jeff Bagwell, Hou. |
| 1995 | Mo Vaughn, Bos. | Barry Larkin, Cin. |
| 1996 | Juan Gonzalez, Tex. | Ken Caminiti, SD. |
| 1997 | Ken Griffey Jr., Sea. | Larry Walker, Col. |
| 1998 | Juan Gonzalez, Tex. | Sammy Sosa, ChC. |
| 1999 | Ivan Rodriguez, Tex. | Chipper Jones, Atl. |
| 2000 | Jason Giambi, Oak. | Jeff Kent, SF. |
| 2001 | Ichiro Suzuki, Sea. | Barry Bonds, SF. |

# CY YOUNG AWARD

The Cy Young Award is made annually to the best pitcher in the each League. It commemorates Cy Young, the turn of the 20th century pitcher who won 511 games in his career.

Prior to 1967, there was only won Cy Young Award winner each year. In the 11 seasons it was awarded to only one pitcher, the National League had seven winners, the American only four, one fewer than the Dodgers managed alone.

## Combined Selection (Both Leagues)

| Year | Winner | Team (League) |
|------|--------|---------------|
| 1956 | Don Newcombe | Brooklyn Dodgers (N) |
| 1957 | Warren Spahn | Milwaukee Braves (N) |
| 1958 | Bob Turley | New York Yankees (A) |
| 1959 | Early Wynn | Chicago White Sox (A) |
| 1960 | Vern Law | Pittsburgh Pirates (N) |
| 1961 | Whitey Ford | New York Yankees (A) |
| 1962 | Don Drysdale | Los Angeles Dodgers (N) |
| 1963 | Sandy Koufax | Los Angeles Dodgers (N) |
| 1964 | Dean Chance | Los Angeles Angels (A) |
| 1965 | Sandy Koufax | Los Angeles Dodgers (N) |
| 1966 | Sandy Koufax | Los Angeles Dodgers (N) |

| Year | American League | National League |
|------|-----------------|-----------------|
| 1967 | Jim Lonborg, Bos. | Mike McCormick, SF |
| 1968 | Denny McLain, Det. | Bob Gibson, StL. |
| 1969 | Mike Cuellar, Bal. } *shared.*<br>Denny McLain, Det. } | Tom Seaver, NYM. |
| 1970 | Jim Perry, Min. | Bob Gibson, StL. |
| 1971 | Vida Blue, Oak. | Fergie Jenkins, ChC. |
| 1972 | Gaylord Perry, Cle. | Steve Carlton, Phi. |
| 1973 | Jim Palmer, Bal. | Tom Seaver, NYM. |
| 1974 | Catfish Hunter, Oak. | Mike Marshall, LA. |
| 1975 | Jim Palmer, Bal. | Tom Seaver, NYM. |
| 1976 | Jim Palmer, Bal. | Randy Jones, SD. |

# CY YOUNG AWARD

| Year | American League | National League |
|------|-----------------|-----------------|
| 1977 | Sparky Lyle, NYY. | Steve Carlton, Phi. |
| 1978 | Ron Guidry, NYY. | Gaylord Perry, SD. |
| 1979 | Mike Flanagan, Bal. | Bruce Sutter, ChC. |
| 1980 | Steve Stone, Bal. | Steve Carlton, Phi. |
| 1981 | Rollie Fingers, Mil. | Fernando Valenzuela, LA. |
| 1982 | Pete Vuckovich, Mil. | Steve Carlton, Phi. |
| 1983 | LaMarr Hoyt, CWS. | John Denny, Phi. |
| 1984 | Willie Hernandez, Det. | Rick Sutcliffe, ChC. |
| 1985 | Bret Saberhagen, KC. | Dwight Gooden, NYM. |
| 1986 | Roger Clemens, Bos. | Mike Scott, Hou. |
| 1987 | Roger Clemens, Bos. | Steve Bedrosian, Phi. |
| 1988 | Frank Viola, Min. | Orel Hershiser, LA. |
| 1989 | Bret Saberhagen, KC. | Mark Davis, SD. |
| 1990 | Bob Welch, Oak. | Doug Drabek, Pit. |
| 1991 | Roger Clemens, Bos. | Tom Glavine, Atl. |
| 1992 | Dennis Eckersley, Oak. | Greg Maddux, ChC. |
| 1993 | Jack McDowell, CWS. | Greg Maddux, Atl. |
| 1994 | David Cone, KC. | Greg Maddux, Atl. |
| 1995 | Randy Johnson, Sea. | Greg Maddux, Atl. |
| 1996 | Pat Hentgen, Tor. | John Smoltz, Atl. |
| 1997 | Roger Clemens, Tor. | Pedro Martinez, Mon. |
| 1998 | Roger Clemens, Tor. | Tom Glavine, Atl. |
| 1999 | Pedro Martinez, Bos. | Randy Johnson, Ari. |
| 2000 | Pedro Martinez, Bos. | Randy Johnson, Ari. |
| 2001 | Roger Clemens, NYY | Randy Johnson, Ari. |

# ROOKIE OF THE YEAR

The present definition of a rookie is a player who has neither recorded 130 at-bats or pitched 50 innings in any season, nor spent more than 45 days on a 25-man Major League roster prior to August 31

## Combined Selection (Both Leagues)

1947    Jackie Robinson, Brooklyn Dodgers (N)

1948    Al Dark, Boston Braves (N).

| Year | American League | National League |
|------|-----------------|-----------------|
| 1949 | Roy Sievers, StL. | Don Newcombe, Bro. |
| 1950 | Walt Dropo, Bos. | Sam Jethroe, Bos. |
| 1951 | Gil McDougald, NYY. | Willie Mays, NYG. |
| 1952 | Harry Byrd, Phi. | Joe Black, Bro. |
| 1953 | Harvey Kuenn, Det. | Jim Gilliam, Bro. |
| 1954 | Bob Grim, NYY. | Wally Moon, StL. |
| 1955 | Herb Score, Cle. | Bill Virdon, StL. |
| 1956 | Luis Aparicio, CWS. | Frank Robinson, Cin. |
| 1957 | Tony Kubek, NYY. | Jack Sanford, Phi. |
| 1958 | Albie Pearson, Was. | Orlando Cepeda, SF. |
| 1959 | Bob Allison, Was. | Willie McCovey, SF. |
| 1960 | Ron Hansen, Bal. | Frank Howard, LA. |
| 1961 | Don Schwall, Bos. | Billy Williams, ChC. |
| 1962 | Tom Tresh, NYY. | Ken Hubbs, ChC. |
| 1963 | Gary Peters, CWS. | Pete Rose, Cin. |
| 1964 | Tony Oliva, Min. | Dick Allen, Phi. |
| 1965 | Curt Blefary, Bal. | Jim Lefebvre, LA. |
| 1966 | Tommie Agee, CWS. | Tommy Helms, Cin. |
| 1967 | Rod Carew, Min. | Tom Seaver, NYM. |
| 1968 | Stan Bahnsen, NYY. | Johnny Bench, Cin. |
| 1969 | Lou Piniella, KC. | Ted Sizemore, LA. |
| 1970 | Thurman Munson, NYY. | Carl Morton, Mon. |
| 1971 | Chris Chambliss, Cle. | Earl Williams, Atl. |
| 1972 | Carlton Fisk, Bos. | Jon Matlack, NYM. |
| 1973 | Al Bumbry, Bal. | Gary Matthews, SF. |

# ROOKIE OF THE YEAR

| Year | American League | National League |
|------|-----------------|-----------------|
| 1974 | Mike Hargrove, Tex. | Bake McBride, StL. |
| 1975 | Fred Lynn, Bos. | John Montefusco, SF. |
| 1976 | Mark Fidrych, Det. | Butch Metzger, SD. } shared<br>Pat Zachry, Cin. |
| 1977 | Eddie Murray, Bal. | Andre Dawson, Mon. |
| 1978 | Lou Whitaker, Det. | Bob Horner, Atl. |
| 1979 | John Castino, Min. } shared<br>Alfredo Griffin, Tor. | Rick Sutcliffe, LA. |
| 1980 | Joe Charboneau, Cle. | Steve Howe, LA. |
| 1981 | Dave Righetti, NYY. | Fernando Valenzuela, LA. |
| 1982 | Cal Ripken Jr., Bal. | Steve Sax, LA. |
| 1983 | Ron Kittle, CWS. | Darryl Strawberry, NYM. |
| 1984 | Alvin Davis, Sea. | Dwight Gooden, NYM. |
| 1985 | Ozzie Guillen, CWS. | Vince Coleman, StL. |
| 1986 | Jose Canseco, Oak. | Todd Worrell, StL. |
| 1987 | Mark McGwire, Oak. | Benito Santiago, SD. |
| 1988 | Walt Weiss, Oak. | Chris Sabo, Cin. |
| 1989 | Gregg Olson, Bal. | Jerome Walton, ChC. |
| 1990 | Sandy Alomar Jr., Cle. | David Justice, Atl. |
| 1991 | Chuck Knoblauch, Min. | Jeff Bagwell, Hou. |
| 1992 | Pat Listach, Mil. | Eric Karros, LA. |
| 1993 | Tim Salmon, Cal. | Mike Piazza, LA. |
| 1994 | Bob Hamelin, KC. | Raul Mondesi, LA. |
| 1995 | Marty Cordova, Min. | Hideo Nomo, LA. |
| 1996 | Derek Jeter, NYY. | Todd Hollandsworth, LA. |
| 1997 | Nomar Garciaparra, Bos. | Scott Rolen, Phi. |
| 1998 | Ben Grieve, Oak. | Kerry Wood, ChC. |
| 1999 | Carlos Beltran, KC. | Scott Williamson, Cin. |
| 2000 | Kazuhiro Sasaki, Sea. | Rafael Furcal, Atl. |
| 2001 | Ichiro Suzuki, Sea. | Albert Pujols, StL. |

# ABOUT STATS INC.

*STATS, Inc.* is the nation's leading sports information and statistical analysis company, providing detailed sports services for a wide array of commercial clients. In January 2000, STATS was purchased by News Digital Media, the digital division of News Corporation. News Digital Media engages in three primary activities: operating FOXNews.com, FOXSports.com, FOXMarketwire.com and FOX.com; developing related interactive services; and directing investment activities and strategy for News Corporation, as they relate to digital media.

As one of the fastest growing companies in sports, STATS provides the most up-to-the-minute sports information to professional teams, print and broadcast media, software developers and interactive service providers around the country. STATS was recently recognized as "One of Chicago's 100 most influential technology players" by Crain's Chicago Business and has been one of 16 finalists for KPMG/Peat Marwick's Illinois High Tech Award for three consecutive years. Some of our major clients are Fox Sports, the Associated Press, America Online, The Sporting News, ESPN, Electronic Arts, MSNBC, SONY and Topps. Much of the information we provide is available to the public via STATS On-Line. With a computer and a modem, you can follow action in the four major professional sports, as well as NCAA football and basketball and other professional and college sports as it happens! STATS Publishing, a division of STATS, Inc., produces 12 annual books, including the Major League Handbook, The Scouting Notebook, the Pro Football Handbook, the Pro Basketball Handbook and the Hockey Handbook. In 1998, we introduced two baseball encyclopedias, the All-Time Major League Handbook and the All-Time Baseball Sourcebook. Together they combine for more than 5,000 pages of baseball history. Also available is From Abba Dabba to Zorro: The World of Baseball Nicknames, a wacky look at monikers and their origins. A new football title was launched in 1999, the Pro Football Scoreboard. These publications deliver STATS' expertise to fans, scouts, general managers and media around the country.

In addition, STATS offers the most innovative--and fun--fantasy sports games around, from Bill James Fantasy Baseball and Bill James Classic Baseball to STATS Fantasy Football and our newest game, Diamond Legends Internet Baseball. Check out our immensely popular Fantasy Portfolios and our great new web-based product, STATS Fantasy Advantage.

Information technology has grown by leaps and bounds in the last decade, and STATS will continue to be at the forefront as both a vendor and supplier of the most up-to-date, in-depth sports information available. For those of you on the information superhighway, you always can catch STATS in our area on America Online or at our Internet site.

For more information on our products or on joining our reporter network, contact us on: **America Online** -- Keyword: STATS **Internet** -- www.stats.com **Toll-Free in the USA at** 1-800-63-STATS (1-800-637-8287) **Outside the USA at** 1-847-470-8798

Or write to:
**STATS, Inc.**
8130 Lehigh Ave.
Morton Grove,
IL 60053

# MAJOR LEAGUE CONTACTS

## OFFICE OF THE COMMISSIONER
245 Park Ave, 31st Floor
New York, NY 10160
(212) 931 7800

## AMERICAN LEAGUE
American
League Office
245 Park Ave
28th Floor
New York, NY 10167
(212) 931 7600

## American League East

**Baltimore Orioles**
Oriole Park
at Camden Yards
333 West Camden Street
Baltimore, MD 21201
(410) 685 9800
www.orioles.mlb.com

**Boston Red Sox**
Fenway Park
4 Yawkey Way
Boston, MA 02215
(617) 267 9440
www.redsox.mlb.com

**New York Yankees**
Yankee Stadium
Bronx, NY 10451
(718) 293 4300
www.yankees.mlb.com

**Tampa Bay Devil Rays**
Tropicana Field
One Tropicana Drive
St Petersburg, FL 33705
(727) 825 3137
www.devilray.mlb.com

**Toronto Blue Jays**
SkyDome
One Blue Jays Way
Suite 3200, Toronto
Ontario M5V 1J1
(416) 341 1000
www.bluejays.mlb.com

## American League Central

**Chicago White Sox**
Comiskey Park
333 West 35th Street
Chicago, IL 60616
(312) 674 1000
www.chisox.mlb.com

**Cleveland Indians**
Jacobs Field
2401 Ontario Drive
Cleveland, OH 44115
(216) 420 4200
www.indians.mlb.com

**Detroit Tigers**
Comerica Park
2100 Woodward Avenue
Detroit,MI 48201
(313) 962 4000
www.tigers.mlb.com

**Kansas City Royals**
Kaufman Stadium
PO Box 419969
Kansas City, MO 64141
(816) 921 8000
www.royals.mlb.com

**Minnesota Twins**
Hubert H. Humphrey
Metrodome
34 Kirby Puckett Place
Minneapolis, MN 55415
(612) 375 1366
www.twins.mlb.com

## American League West

**Anaheim Angels**
Edison Field, PO Box 2000
Anaheim, CA 92803
(714) 940 2000
www.angels.mlb.com

**Oakland Athletics**
Network Assoc. Coliseum
7677 Oakport
Oakland, CA 94621
(510) 638 4900
www.athletics.mlb.com

**Seattle Mariners**
Safeco Field, PO Box 4100
Seattle, WA 98104
(206) 346 4000
www.mariners.mlb.com

**Texas Rangers**
The Ballpark at Arlington
1000 Ballpark Way
Arlington, TX 76011
(817) 273 5222
www.rangers.mlb.com

# MAJOR LEAGUE CONTACTS

## NATIONAL LEAGUE

National
League Office
245 Park Avenue
28th Floor
New York, NY 10022
(212) 931 7700

## National League East

**Atlanta Braves**
Turner Field, PO Box 4063
Atlanta, GA 30302
(404) 522 7630
www.braves.mlb.com

**Florida Marlins**
Pro Player Stadium
2267 NW 199th Street
Miami, FL 33056
(305) 626 7400
www.marlins.mlb.com

**Montreal Expos**
Olympic Stadium
PO Box 500, Station M
Montreal, Quebec H1V 3P2
(514) 253 34334
www.expos.mlb.com

**New York Mets**
Shea Stadium
123–01 Roosevelt Avenue
Flushing, NY 11368
(718) 507 6387
www.mets.mlb.com

**Philadelphia Phillies**
Veterans Stadium
PO Box 7575
Phildadelphia, PA 19101
(215) 463 6000
www.phillies.mlb.com

## National League Central

**Chicago Cubs**
Wrigley Field
1060 West Addison Street
Chicago, IL 60613
(773) 404 2827
www.cubs.mlb.com

**Cincinnati Reds**
Cinergy Field
100 Cinergy Field
Cincinnati, OH 45202
(513) 421 4510
www.reds.mlb.com

**Houston Astros**
Enron Field
501 Crawford Street
Houston, TX 77002
(713) 799-9500
www.astros.mlb.com

**Milwaukee Brewers**
Miller Park
One Brewers Way
Milwaukee, WI 53214
(414) 933 4114
www.brewers.mlb.com

**Pittsburgh Pirates**
PNC Park
115 Federal Street
Pittsburgh, PA 15212
(412) 323 5000
www.pirates.mlb.com

**St. Louis Cardinals**
Busch Stadium
250 Stadium Plaza
St. Louis, MO 63102
(314) 421 3060
www.cardinals.mlb.com

## National League West

**Arizona Diamondbacks**
Bank One Ballpark
PO Box 2095
Phoenix, AZ 85001
(602) 462 6500
www.diamondbacks.mlb.com

**Colorado Rockies**
Coors Field
2001 Blake Street
Denver, CO 80205
(303) 292 0200
www.rockies.mlb.com

**Los Angeles Dodgers**
Dodger Stadium
1000 Elysian Park Avenue
Los Angeles, CA 90012
(323) 224 1500
www.dodgers.mlb.com

**San Diego Padres**
Qualcomm Stadium
PO Box 122000
San Diego, CA 92112
(619) 881 6500
www.padres.mlb.com

**San Francisco Giants**
Pac Bell Park
24 Willie Mays Plaza
San Francisco, CA 94107
(415) 468-3700
www.giants.mlb.com

# OTHER USEFUL WEBSITES

Below is a list of other websites that contain a wide variety of baseball information, from stats to team information, from historical profiles to up-to-date scores.

### www.cnnsi.com

Online version of Sports Illustrated magazine and information courtsey of CNN/SI partnership. Huge database of statistical information as well as up to the minute news.

### www.baseballhalloffame.org

The official website of Cooperstown's most famous landmark. Includes profiles of all inductees and contains an online shop.

### www.sportingnews.com

Contains an expansive collection of archive material and current scores and information from the Sporting News team.

### www.majorleaguebaseball.com

The official website of Major League Baseball containing a wealth of information.

### www.stats.com

Stats inc.'s website. A stats fan's dream!

### www.totalbaseball.com

The online baseball encyclopedia

### www.cbs.sportsline.com

Tons of baseball on this site from the media giant, CBS.

### www.blackbaseball.com

### www.negroleaguebaseball.com

Two great sites dedicated to the Negro Leagues and the men who played in them. Includes player and team profiles and online stores.

### www.fastball.com

One of the very best sites containing nothing but 100% baseball. Information on all 30 major league clubs.

## Statistical

**Batting Average:** Hits ÷ at bats.
**On Base Percentage:** (Hits + walks + hit by pitch) ÷ (At bats + walks + hit by pitch + sacrifice flies)
**Total Bases:** singles + doubles (2 bases) + triples (3 bases) + home runs (4 bases)
**Slugging Percentage:** (Total bases) ÷(at bats)
**Earned Run Average (ERA):** (Earned runs x 9) ÷ innings pitched
**Winning Percentage:** (wins) ÷ (wins + losses)

## Common terms and phrases

**Ace:** Team's best starting pitcher.
**Alley:** The section of the outfield between the outfielders. Also "gap."
**Around the horn:** Double play, from third base to second to first.
**At bat:** A charged time at the plate for a batter. There is no at bat if he hits a sacrifice, receives a base on balls (walk) or is hit by the pitch.
**Backdoor slider:** Pitch that appears to be out of the strike zone, but then breaks back over the plate.
**Bag:** A base.
**Balk:** Illegal pitch or motion by a pitcher, normally trying to pick-off a baserunner or catch the batter unprepared. Can only happen with runners on base.
**Baltimore chop:** Ground ball that hits in front of home plate (or off of it) and takes a large hop over the infielder's head.
**Bandbox:** Small ballpark that favors hitters.
**Bang-bang play:** Play in which the baserunner hits the bag a split-second before the ball arrives or vice versa.
**Base on balls:** Walk
**Basket catch:** When a fielder catches a ball with his glove near belt level, palm up.
**Bronx cheer:** When the crowd boos.
**Brushback:** Pitch that nearly hits a batter.
**Bush:** Also "bush league." An amateur play or behavior.
**Can of corn:** Easy catch by a fielder.

**Caught looking:** When a batter is called out on strikes.
**Cellar/Basement:** Last place
**Cheese:** Refers to a good fastball.
**Chin music:** A pitch that is high and inside.
**Circus catch:** An outstanding catch by a fielder.
**Closer:** A team's relief pitcher who finishes the game.
**Cutter:** Cut fastball (one with a late break to it).
**Cycle:** When a batter hits a single, double, triple and home run in any order in the same game.
**Dinger:** Home run.
**Dish:** Home plate.
**Fireman:** Team's closer or late-inning relief pitcher.
**Fungo:** Ball hit to a fielder during practice, usually by a coach. A "**Fungo bat**," is longer and thinner than a normal bat.
**Gopher ball:** A pitch hit for a home run, as in "go for."
**Heat/heater:** A good fastball
**High and tight:** Pitch high in the strike zone and inside.
**Hill:** Pitcher's mound.
**Homer:** A home run. Other terms include: blast, dong, four-bagger, four-base knock, moon shot, tape-measure blast.
**Hot corner:** Third base.
**In the hole:** (a) Batter after the on-deck hitter. (b) Pitcher or hitter behind in the count.
**Jam:** (a) A pitch near the batter's hands jams him. (b) A pitcher in trouble is said to be "in a jam."
**Leather:** (a) Glove. (b) Good defensive play, "He flashed some leather on that play."
**Meatball:** Easy pitch to hit, usually down the middle of the plate.
**Mendoza line:** A batting average of around .200.
**Moon shot:** Very long, high home run.
**Nail down:** As in "nail down a victory." Refers to a relief pitcher finishing off the game.
**On the button/on the screws:** When a batter hits the ball hard.
**Painting the black:** When a pitcher throws the ball over the edge of the plate.
**Pea:** Ball traveling at high speed, either batted or thrown.
**Pepper:** Pre-game exercise for batters and infielders, involving

constant hitting and throwing at close range. (Some ballparks ban pepper games because wild pitches could land in the stands and injure fans.)
**Pick:** Good defensive play by an infielder on a ground ball. Also a shortened version of "pick-off."
**Pick-off:** Pitcher's throw to a base trying to catch a runner who is too far off the base, maybe about to steal. It is not a pitch.
**Pickle:** A rundown.
**Punchout:** A strikeout.
**Rhubarb:** A fight or scuffle.
**Ribbie:** Another way of saying RBI. Also "ribeye."
**Rope:** A hard line drive hit by a batter. Also "frozen rope."
**Rubber game:** Deciding game of a series.
**Run-down:** When a baserunner gets caught between bases by the fielders. See Pick-off.
**Ruthian:** With great power.
**Seeing-eye single:** A soft ground ball that finds its way between infielders for a base hit. Also called a **gapper** or **tweener**.
**Set-up man:** Relief pitcher who comes on in the 7th or 8th inning.
**Shoestring catch:** Stunning catch made just above the ground.
**Southpaw:** Left-handed pitcher.
**Sweet spot:** The part of the bat just a few inches from the barrel.
**Table setter:** Batter whose job is to get on base for other hitters to drive him in. Usually a leadoff or No. 2 hitter.
**Tape-measure blast:** An extremely long home run.
**Tater:** A home run.
**Texas Leaguer:** Bloop hit that drops between an infielder and outfielder.
**Tools of ignorance:** Catcher's equipment.
**Touch 'em all:** Hitting a home run (touching all the bases).
**Twin killing:** A double play.
**Uncle Charlie:** Curve ball.
**Up and in:** See high and tight.
**Utility player:** A player who fills in at many positions.
**Wheelhouse:** A hitter's power zone. Usually a pitch waist-high and over the heart of the plate.
**Wheels:** A ballplayer's legs.
**Whiff:** Strikeout.
**Yakker:** Curve ball.

# THE AUTHORS

**LUKE FRIEND**

Luke Friend is a freelance writer and editor who has contributed to a diverse range of publications from *Golf World* to *Total Film* as well as the baseball titles *Subway 2000* and *The Chronicle of Baseball*.

**DON ZMINDA**

Don Zminda is Vice President of Publishing Products for STATS, Inc. and a nationally-known expert on sports statistics.
   He is co-editor of the annual *STATS Scouting Notebook* and co-author of *From Abba Dabba to Zorro: the World of Baseball Nickname*.